## Forthcoming Books in the Dove on Fundraising Series:

Conducting a Successful Major Gifts and Planned Giving Program

## Books Currently Available in the Dove on Fundraising Series:

Conducting a Successful Capital Campaign, 2nd Edition
Conducting a Successful Fundraising Program
Conducting a Successful Annual Giving Program
Conducting a Successful Development Services Program

## Other Nonprofit Resources from Jossey-Bass:

CPR for Nonprofits, *Alvin Reiss*
The Five Strategies for Fundraising Success, *Mal Warwick*
Team-Based Fundraising Step by Step, *Mim Carlson and Cheryl Clarke*
Listening to Your Donors, *Bruce Campbell*
The Insider's Guide to Grantmaking, *Joel J. Orosz*
How Foundations Work, *Dennis P. McIlnay*
Winning Grants Step By Step, *Mim Carlson*
The Fundraising Planner: A Working Model for Raising the Dollars You Need, *Terry and Doug Schaff*
The Jossey-Bass Guide to Strategic Communications for Nonprofits, *Kathleen Bonk, Henry Griggs, Emily Tynes*
Marketing Nonprofit Programs and Services, *Douglas B Herron*
Transforming Fundraising: A Practical Guide to Evaluating and Strengthening Fundraising to Grow with Change, *Judith Nichols*
Achieving Excellence in Fund Raising, *Henry A. Rosso and Associates*
The Grantwriter's Start-Up Kit, *Creed C. Black, Tom Ezell, Rhonda Ritchie*
Secrets of Successful Grantsmanship, *Susan L. Golden*

# CONDUCTING A SUCCESSFUL
# DEVELOPMENT SERVICES PROGRAM

**The Dove on Fundraising Series** is a library of premier resource guides that combine practical instruction with real-world examples. In response to the ever-changing challenges nonprofits face, Kent E. Dove, the Indiana University Foundation, and Jossey-Bass have come together to develop and advance professional standards for fundraisers everywhere. Built on the successful fundraising model developed by veteran fundraiser and series editor Kent Dove, these publications provide a flexible campaign-based approach that recognizes fundraising as both a science and an art.

Clustered around the comprehensive *Conducting a Successful Fundraising Program,* each publication examines a key aspect of fundraising, and all authors bring years of experience and knowledge to their topics. Together, these guides present an integrated framework validated by research and practical results. **The Dove on Fundraising Series** seeks to provide nonprofit leaders, fundraisers, consultants, and students with not only time-tested principles, but also successful examples, strategies, and publications that readers can use to shape their own development programs.

# CONDUCTING A SUCCESSFUL DEVELOPMENT SERVICES PROGRAM

## A Comprehensive Guide and Resource

Kent E. Dove
Vicky L. Martin
Kathy K. Wilson
Mary M. Bonk
Sarah C. Beggs

JOSSEY-BASS
A Wiley Company
www.josseybass.com

Published by

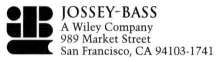

**JOSSEY-BASS**
A Wiley Company
989 Market Street
San Francisco, CA 94103-1741

www.josseybass.com

Jossey-Bass books and products are available through most bookstores. To contact Jossey-Bass directly, call (888) 378-2537, fax to (800) 605-2665, or visit our website at www.josseybass.com.

Substantial discounts on bulk quantities of Jossey-Bass books are available to corporations, professional associations, and other organizations. For details and discount information, contact the special sales department at Jossey-Bass.

We at Jossey-Bass strive to use the most environmentally sensitive paper stocks available to us. Our publications are printed on acid-free recycled stock whenever possible, and our paper always meets or exceeds minimum GPO and EPA requirements.

**Library of Congress Cataloging-in-Publication Data**

Conducting a successful development services program : a
comprehensive guide and resource / Kent E. Dove . . . [et al.].—
1st ed.
     p. cm.
Includes bibliographical references and index.
    ISBN 0-7879-5624-4 (alk. paper)
  1. Fund raising. 2. Nonprofit organizations. I. Dove, Kent E., date.
   HV41.2 .C66 2001
   658.15'224—dc21

2001006208

*HB Printing*  10 9 8 7 6 5 4 3 2 1          FIRST EDITION

# CONTENTS

**PART ONE: PLANNING AND IMPLEMENTING
YOUR DEVELOPMENT SERVICES PROGRAM   7**

---

**PART TWO: THE DEVELOPMENT SERVICES RESOURCE GUIDE   179**

This book is dedicated to our Indiana University Foundation colleagues and associates who work behind the scenes without notice and with little recognition.
Too, it is dedicated to Grant D. Wilson, the special son of our colleagues Doug and Kathy Wilson.

—Kent E. Dove

It is with deep gratitude that I dedicate the research segment of this book to the staff of the Research Management and Information Services Department of the Indiana University Foundation.
The depth of their knowledge and expertise and their professionalism and dedication to the field of prospect research are reflected throughout Chapters Three and Four.
Too, I include a very special dedication to Jill, the beloved daughter of our dear friend and colleague, Marilyn Behrman.

—Vicky L. Martin

I dedicate this book to the best philanthropic educators I've experienced: Curtis R. Simic, Kent E. Dove, Robert L. Payton, Eugene R. Tempel, Timothy L. Seiler, and Anita Rook.
Special thanks also go to Doug, Hilary, David, Haley, Grant, my parents, and other family members who daily teach me about life and its priorities.

—Kathy K. Wilson

To my husband, Curtis, and our children, Alex and Nicki, for their love and support.

—Mary M. Bonk

Heartfelt thanks to my wonderful husband, Bill, and our children, Betsy and Thomas; to Kent Dove for providing this opportunity and many others; and to my family, friends, and colleagues.

—Sarah C. Beggs

# PREFACE

This is the fourth in a five-book foundational series on fundraising. It addresses the most elusive of topics the series examines: development services. It isn't possible to say, once and for all, what development services is; the area is still in the process of defining itself. However, this book attempts to establish a standard definition that will carry nonprofits into the future.

The discrete functions that are collectively called development services used to be *complementary to* fundraising. Although that's still true, these functions are now *companions with* fundraising as well. They no longer linger in the shadows; these behind-the-scenes professionals provide vital support for the fundraisers who occupy the public stage. This text is written to recognize, honor, and establish the prominence and central importance of these functions and to give those who perform them due recognition.

Although I have spent a lifetime on the public stage of fundraising, I have never performed development service work myself. However, I have long been a proponent of and advocate for not only maintaining high-quality development services but elevating them to their proper stature and professional place within the nonprofit framework. So I am extremely pleased to introduce two colleagues who are truly leaders in this field and who generously joined me in the writing of this book; they also participated in the preparation of text for other books in this series.

Kathy K. Wilson and Vicky L. Martin are to development services what Carolyn P. Madvig and Jeffrey A. Lindauer are to annual giving and special gift programs. They are complementary, inseparable colleagues. Kathy was a pioneer and is a leader in the area of prospect research. She was an early president of the Association of Professional Researchers for Advancement (APRA), so there are few in the field who don't know her name. She brought Vicky to the Indiana University (IU) Foundation in the early 1990s, initially to do research for a capital campaign for one of IU's large academic units—one I was serving as a consultant to. This happy professional union lasted for nearly a decade and ended only recently when Kathy left full-time employment to spend more time with her family. Vicky and I remain to carry on, but it isn't the same without Kathy.

What made Kathy and Vicky such a great team? It was their energy, dedication, skill, experience, expertise, love of task, ability with people, service orientation, and personal character. The last two traits are especially noteworthy. These two women define service. Their sincere desire to serve fundraisers on eight campuses and in over thirty separate fundraising programs at IU (this is a fairly big place) sets the standard for the entire field. And not only were they dedicated to service but they expected the service to be of high quality. Completed staff work in development services under their direction meant just that—no gaps, no holes, no sloppiness. And both are deeply religious. This is especially important in research because of the constant ethical concerns and potential conflicts of interest that arise. Nowhere in the fundraising process is it more important to have moral, ethical people than in research. At IU we enjoy the peace of mind that Kathy's and Vicky's presence brings. They can be paid no higher compliment.

The IU Foundation is fortunate to have an exceptional group that handles gift administration in very precise ways. Mary M. Bonk, who assisted with this section of the book, headed the gift administration operation for a time. She is a certified public accountant (CPA) and has been involved in many aspects of accounting over the past twenty years, including public, health care, and nonprofit accounting. Over the past seven years, she has been involved in gift administration at the IU Foundation.

Mary has been director of account services and executive director of administration; she is currently the executive director of alumni and foundation information systems. As executive director of administration, she was responsible for overseeing more than twenty staff in the areas of gift administration, account administration, and accounts payable. Mary is an active member in the American Women's Society of CPAs and the Institute of Management Accountants.

She is also the mother of two and is active with her son's traveling soccer and cross-country teams; she volunteers with her daughter's Girl Scout troop.

Sarah C. Beggs assisted in the writing of the chapter on donor relations. Recently a new mother for the second time, Sarah is very special to all of us here. Look in any dictionary for a definition of *all-American girl,* and Sarah's image will appear. She is an exceptional young woman, still a part of the twenty-something generation but already one of our most valued colleagues. Even as an undergraduate at IU, she stood out. As one of the most active women on campus, she was president of both her social sorority and the IU Student Foundation, one of America's largest and best-known student programs. She swears she even went to class. The only thing it appears she didn't do was sleep. After graduation, Kathy hired Sarah to work in research. In 1997 I asked her to become my assistant, and in 1998 I asked her to give leadership to our donor relations and stewardship program. In 2000, following the birth of her second child, she returned to my office to work on special projects on a part-time basis so she could spend more time with her family. Her new job description, she tells me with a smile, is "other duties as assigned." In fact, it's "only important duties requiring special handling."

## Audience

*Conducting a Successful Development Services Program* is written for two primary audiences. It is intended to serve as a constant companion to those who work actively behind the scenes in service to the more than 730,000 registered nonprofit organizations in the United States, for the countless others that are not registered, and for our friends and colleagues outside the United States who engage in these activities, too, wherever they might be. Administrators, fundraisers, staff, board members, and volunteers can benefit from this book.

The second intended audience is students. The book is written to serve as a textbook. One of the aims of this book and its companion pieces now being produced as part of this Jossey-Bass series is to encourage the teaching of the subject of fundraising in educational settings across the country.

## Overview of the Contents

Development services envelop the fundraising process. The range of services covers everything from discovering potential prospects to stewarding gifts and donors. There is a logical progression to all this, and the book follows that progression in Part One.

Chapters One and Two have two primary foci. The first is to introduce the technologies that serve development. Virtually every modern development effort is built on a technology base. The second is to describe how these technologies are helpful. Chapter One focuses on information systems—the bedrock on which development services rely. Chapter Two briefly explores other useful technologies and concludes with an assessment of the advantages and disadvantages technologies create for fundraising.

Chapters Three and Four focus on prospect research. Chapter Three discusses creating and managing a research function, and Chapter Four is a guide to the techniques used in research, the resources available to support researchers, and the way researchers do their jobs.

Managing prospects systematically is the topic of Chapter Five. A model program outline is presented; the strategies of cultivation and solicitation are reviewed; and a way of measuring staff performance and productivity is introduced.

Stewarding the gift is the topic of Chapter Six. Mary Bonk walks the reader through an overview of the governing bodies that affect nonprofits and creates a clear trail for documenting, handling and processing, and assuring accountability for every gift.

Chapter Seven discusses stewarding the donor. Sarah Beggs covers acknowledging and recognizing donors, showing appreciation and saying thank-you, and reporting to donors.

The text concludes at the end of Chapter Seven, but the book does not end there. Part Two contains a large resource section. One of the aims of this book is to provide a visual aid to support each of the major points addressed in the text. This is a feature common to the books in this series. It is important not only to tell readers how to do things but to show them how. Too often, busy people do not have time to begin a task with only a blank piece of paper for guidance. They would like something to look at, something they can quickly and easily adopt or adapt. Our goal is to give readers the guidance they need. We hope we have achieved it.

*Bloomington, Indiana*                                                              Kent E. Dove
*September 2001*

# ACKNOWLEDGMENTS

Neither this book nor the others in this series were compiled and written by one person alone. It was a large team effort. Space does not permit the mentioning of everyone who assisted, but some people must be mentioned by name.

The board of directors of the Indiana University Foundation and Curtis R. Simic, its president, deserve special mention. The board approved this enterprise with the full understanding that it would take time, energy, effort, and resources from very busy people who are responsible for conducting a $100-million-a-year program on a daily basis. The board feels the project is worthwhile for what it promises to share with the larger nonprofit community, and there is a commitment on the part of everyone at IU to encourage best practices in fundraising whenever possible. Without board permission, we could not have done this. We thank the board members for their support.

This text, like all the books in the series, is resource-rich. At the risk of offending some whose names are not cited here, I want to mention a few of the people who were especially helpful as we gathered the many exhibits and resources that fill the following pages: Kristin V. Rehder; Peg Stice; L. Clark Wilson, University of British Columbia; Jayne E. Irvin, Debbie Meyers, and Paul Robell, University of Florida; Rod Kirsch, Penn State University; Jim Smith, United Way of Central Indiana; David Lawson, Prospect Information Network; Jay Frost, Thomson Financial; Christina Pulawski, Northwestern University; Sarah McGinley, Wright State University; Karen Stitsworth, Purdue University; Susan Lyons, Bloomington

(Indiana) Hospital Foundation; Julie Dailey, Tulip Trace Council of Girl Scouts, Inc.; and the Association of Professional Researchers for Advancement.

As always, there is the editorial team for the Nonprofit and Public Management Series at Jossey-Bass to thank: Johanna Vondeling, associate editor, and Ocean Howell, assistant editor. And Xenia Lisanevich is the production editor. She is my hero. What she does in production to the manuscripts we give her is pure magic.

Very special mention also has to be made of my assistant, Trisha Moutardier, who spent countless hours working and reworking the manuscript until we both exhaustedly agreed it met with our approval.

Thanks to everyone for their support, encouragement, and understanding. We will be back soon with another book in this series. The next one is already in process.

—K.E.D.

# THE AUTHORS

KENT E. DOVE is the author of *Conducting a Successful Capital Campaign* (2nd ed., Jossey-Bass, 2000), which has been proclaimed the leading guide to planning and implementing a capital campaign. He also wrote *Conducting a Successful Fundraising Program: A Comprehensive Guide and Resource* (Jossey-Bass, 2001) and *Conducting a Successful Annual Giving Program,* which he coauthored with Carolyn P. Madvig and Jeffrey A. Lindauer (Jossey-Bass, 2001).

Dove's interest in the area of development services dates to 1978, when he first spoke publicly on the subject at a district conference in Atlanta. He chaired the first two conferences ever sponsored by the Council for Advancement and Support of Education (CASE) that were devoted to prospect research; one was held in San Antonio in November 1980, the other in Boston in April 1981. He was one of the first to write about and advocate for elevating development services to the same stature in the development office as that enjoyed by the annual giving program, major gifts program, planned giving program, and development publications.

Dove's career began shortly after his graduation from Indiana University when he joined the Indiana University (IU) Foundation staff as a publications writer for the university's 150th birthday campaign. He also directed annual giving programs for several of the university's professional schools. Over the next decade he moved to progressively more responsible positions—director of annual giving, assistant director of development, director of development—leading to his appointment as vice president of development at thirty-four years of age, making him the youngest chief advancement officer at a major U.S. university. He coordinated the offices of development, alumni relations, public relations, and government relations. Six years later he was counsel to and resident director of the then-largest capital campaign for a public university in America while also serving as a consultant to the largest campaign ever undertaken in Canada to that time.

Dove is considered the preeminent fundraising practitioner working in America today, and his career spans five decades. He currently serves as vice president for development at the IU Foundation, where he returned in 1993 to serve as executive director of capital campaigns to manage a six-year, $350-million endowment campaign for Indiana University Bloomington, the largest campaign ever undertaken by the university. The campaign surpassed its goal in the summer of 1999, having raised $373 million more than a year ahead of schedule, and concluded on December 31, 2000, with $504 million raised. He was named vice president for development in 1997, and in 1999 CASE recognized the IU Foundation with its highest award of excellence for overall fundraising performance for the period 1993–1998. It won the same award again in 2000 for the period 1994–1999.

Dove previously held various educational fundraising management positions at Rice University, the University of California-Berkeley, Drake University, the University of Alabama, Northwestern University, the University of Tennessee Center for the Health Sciences, and West Virginia University.

From June 1989 to December 1993 he operated Kent E. Dove & Associates, a small firm designed and organized to offer highly personal, specialized attention to a select client base. His areas of interest are assessment of institutional development programs, institutional planning, market surveys, management and supervision of capital campaigns, staff and board training, and management of nonprofit organizations.

Dove has served three terms on CASE's educational fundraising committee and one term on the board of directors of the National Society of Fund-Raising Executives, now the Association of Fundraising Professionals (AFP). In 1986 he received the CASE Steuben Glass Apple Award for Outstanding Teaching.

VICKY L. MARTIN is director of research management and information services at the IU Foundation. She is also an active member of the Indiana chapter of the Association of Professional Researchers for Advancement (APRA) and currently sits on the board of the Indiana chapter, serving as chair of the mentor program. In that capacity Martin organizes the beginners' workshops, a popular event among new researchers to the field.

She is one of the most sought-after presenters and lecturers in the field of research and teaches in both the schools of Health, Physical Education, and Recreation and Public and Environmental Affairs at IU.

KATHY K. WILSON received her B.S. degree in management from Indiana Wesleyan University in 1989. She started her fundraising career in research in 1987. In March 2001 she left her position as director of the Office of Development Services at the IU Foundation to join her husband, who also retired from the IU Foundation, in spending more time with their son, who has special needs.

Her responsibilities included managing the office of prospect management, research management and information services, development reports, special events, and donor relations and stewardship for all IU campuses.

Wilson cofounded and was the first president of APRA-Indiana. She was also involved with APRA at the national level and served as its president in 1992. She was regularly invited to be a guest classroom presenter at IU, spoke at APRA and CASE conferences, and regularly consulted with other colleges, universities, and other nonprofit organizations.

MARY M. BONK is executive director of information technology services at the IU Foundation. She received her B.S. degree from the University of Wisconsin-Whitewater in 1981 with a major in business administration and accounting. Prior to joining the IU Foundation in February 1993, she spent more than a decade working in public accounting and health care accounting for employers in both Wisconsin and West Virginia and was granted her certified public accountant license in Wisconsin in 1985. While at the IU Foundation, she moved steadily to increasingly more responsible positions, beginning as director of account services and then adding operations to her portfolio before becoming executive director of administration in 1995 and being promoted to her current position in 2000.

SARAH C. BEGGS is coordinator of special projects in the office of the vice president for development at IU Foundation. She received her B.A. degree in speech communication from Indiana University in 1995 and joined the IU Foundation as a research associate upon her graduation. In February of 1997 she was named executive assistant to the executive director of capital campaigns and in October of 1998 was promoted to director of donor relations and stewardship. She has held her current position since October 2000.

# INTRODUCTION

All nonprofit organizations exist on the premise that there is a need and the organization will address that need. To accomplish its aims, the nonprofit must not only identify the need, or problem, but propose a solution. The solution inevitably involves money. Nonprofits satisfy this need for funding in a variety of ways, including by applying for and receiving contracts and grants, receiving fees for services, and fundraising in the private sector.

The term *development* (or *advancement* may be used in the education sector) is often considered a synonym, or even a euphemism, for *fundraising*. And certainly no development program can succeed without an effective fundraising operation to provide necessary resources. But development in the broadest sense includes much more than fundraising per se. And the nonprofits that enjoy the greatest success in fundraising are those that understand the concept of development and know how to translate it into an effective institutional effort.

Certain prerequisites point to success in a development effort. First on the list is this: *A commitment of time and support is needed from all key participants,* including the governing board, the chief executive officer, prospective major donors, key volunteer leaders, the professional fundraising staff, and the entire institutional family. Teamwork is required. A total effort by the total team—one that is fully integrated and completely understood and appreciated by all—is optimal (see Figure I.1).

### FIGURE I.1. THE MODERN DEVELOPMENT PARADIGM.

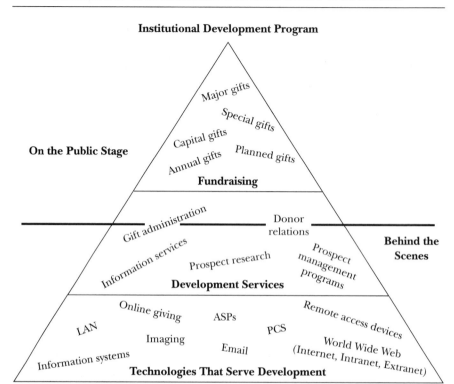

## The Development Services Cycle

Although the roots of development services go deep, the concepts and functions described today as development services have fully emerged only in the past quarter century. Why has the need for these services emerged, and why is so much importance now placed on them? There are three primary reasons: (1) increased fundraising competition, (2) growth in professional specialization, and (3) a growing body of rules and regulations requiring continuing attention. Today more than 730,000 nonprofits are registered with the IRS, and the INDEPENDENT SECTOR estimates that there are more than 1.5 million nonprofits in the United States. Thus it is mandatory that frontline fundraisers spend as much time as possible working directly with prospects and donors and as little time as possible doing the tasks—important as they are—that can be undertaken by other professional and support personnel.

A quarter of a century ago, many fundraisers were generalists. They did their own research (if any was done), wrote their own proposals, maintained their own manual prospect management systems, provided stewardship, and did a variety of other tasks as well. Today's trend is toward specialization. Modern development programs are designed to attract annual gifts, special gifts, major gifts, planned gifts, and, periodically, capital gifts. The fundraising specialists who work in each of their areas are often complemented by researchers, gift administration specialists, information officers, and donor relations specialists. This age of specialization has given distinctive form and growing importance to the services that support fundraising. Along with specialization has come a growing body of rules, regulations, guidelines, and standards—and a growing number of governing bodies to enforce and oversee them. The need for enforcement has spawned the need for an additional layer of trained, knowledgeable personnel to ensure institutional compliance not only with the rules but with the donor's intent.

Functions appropriately defined as development services share three characteristics:

1. They provide the necessary trappings of fundraising that detract time, energy, and effort from the actual practice of fundraising, thereby directly assisting, strengthening, and enhancing the fundraising process.
2. They occur primarily behind the scenes.
3. Some occur in places other than the development office, primarily the business office.

The idea is to make these interactions as seamless as possible. After all, development services are about supporting the institutional fund development effort more than they are about who does what or how things get done or who gets credit.

The five discrete functions that meet these criteria are as follows:

- Information services
- Prospect research
- Prospect management
- Gift administration
- Donor relations

These discrete functions are interrelated and connected by the common bond that links them all—the gift and its donor (see Figure I.2). They ensure the transformation of fundraising into an institutional activity and are the essence of a total development experience. This set of support services is what transforms a fundraising effort into a development program.

**FIGURE I.2. DEVELOPMENT SERVICES CYCLE.**

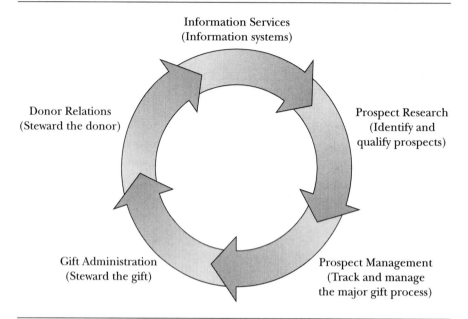

Information Services
(Information systems)

Prospect Research
(Identify and
qualify prospects)

Donor Relations
(Steward the donor)

Gift Administration
(Steward the gift)

Prospect Management
(Track and manage
the major gift process)

## Making the Pieces Fit

In its most basic form, a fundraising program needs three things: (1) a case for support, (2) prospects to support it, and (3) a method to connect the two. A gift cannot be made without a prospect to give it. Therefore a fundraising program is predicated on the fact that a nonprofit organization has a list, or pool, of prospective donors or prospects.

The term *prospect* is used throughout this book to describe in general, familiar terms anyone who has the financial ability to give, as well as an interest, demonstrated or anticipated, in making a contribution. A *prospect pool* is the number of names to be included in a specific (segmented) appeal or approach. For a general appeal, the *donor pool* equals the number of names in the organization's database.

Creating, maintaining, and using this database, the most basic of all fundraising tools, is where the effort to raise funds begins and is the responsibility of those who provide information services. To differentiate the names in the database as to areas of interest and levels of giving capacity is the responsibility of prospect research.

Once research is done, the more important prospects—the affluent and influential, those with previous giving histories, and those with progressively more significant giving levels—require closer attention to ensure a systematic approach to cultivation and solicitation. *Prospect management systems* are designed to accomplish this.

The hoped-for outcome of a properly managed solicitation is a gift. The happy event of receiving the gift creates a need to properly receive, receipt, and administer it—the foundations of gift administration. The next step in the progression is to express thanks and give recognition to the donor. This is called donor relations and is often referred to as stewardship. Stewardship is a wider concept, however; stewardship is an ongoing process. It is designed not only to recognize past support but to be part of the cultivation program that leads to the donor's next gift. The frames of reference for stewardship are both the past (what has already been done) and the future (what might still be done), but its setting is the present (what can be done now to achieve the bookend goals of thanking for the past and cultivating for the future simultaneously). Stewardship involves both taking good care of the donor and taking good care of the gift (see Figure I.3).

This text follows the path of the donor and his or her gift from the time the donor's name is surfaced through an entire cycle of support activities or development services designed to make giving a satisfying experience and to bring the

## FIGURE I.3. DESIGNING A STEWARDSHIP MODEL.

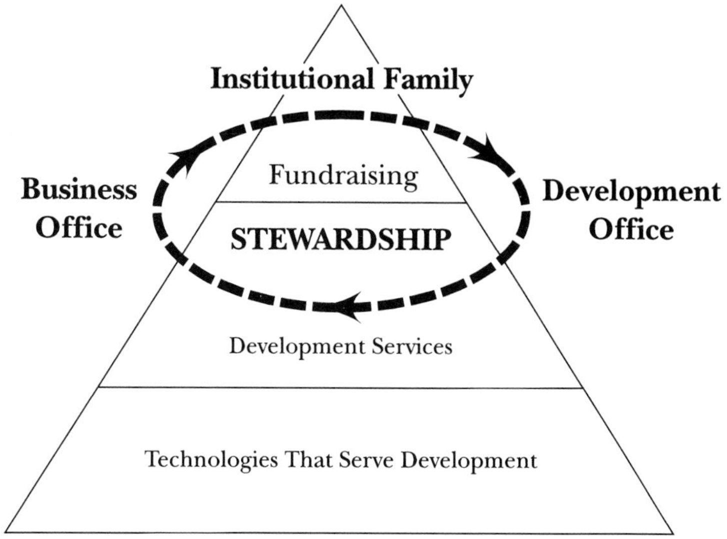

donor back again in the future. This progression is driven from the same base in virtually every nonprofit today: technology. Technologies that serve development are the foundation on which successful, modern development programs are built. No discussion of development services or fundraising or an institutional development program can proceed until the foundation that technology provides is laid.

Providing this series of services is an institutional responsibility. These subterranean pathways cross back and forth between the administrative suite, the development office, and the business function. After all, development services are about supporting the institution's development effort more than they are about who performs the services or how they do it.

# PART ONE

# PLANNING AND IMPLEMENTING YOUR DEVELOPMENT SERVICES PROGRAM

# TABLES, FIGURES, AND EXHIBITS IN PART ONE

## Tables

## Figures

# Exhibits

# CHAPTER ONE

# SELECTING AND BUILDING YOUR DONOR DATABASE

In the modern development program, virtually all development services rest on a technology base. But technology is like fundraising literature: it will not, in and of itself, raise money. Without technology, however, it is difficult if not impossible to raise money effectively, efficiently, and economically. Only the smallest nonprofits can succeed using manual systems.

Several technologies serve development and the discrete support services that underpin it; we introduce these here and in Chapter Two. In this chapter, we focus on (1) the selection and installation of an information system, (2) the considerations to be weighed in choosing it, and (3) the steps to be taken to implement it. The chapter concludes by describing the core functions that the system must support.

## Selecting an Information System

One of the most important parts of an effective fundraising organization is the information system that supports it. The term *information system,* broadly defined in the present day, refers to the electronic data management systems (hardware and software) that enable electronic business processes such as data warehousing, research, analysis, communication, and e-commerce to take place. Information systems can be as small-scale as a pocket organizer or may be grandiose in scale, restricted only by the resources and creativity of the user. In an ideal world, the information system should be as transparent to the fundraising process as the telephone; that is, it should be readily available and easy to use. And it should contain needed information.

A good information system provides a nonprofit with the ability to easily and quickly access the information it needs to serve the organization and its donors. For the large majority of small and midsize nonprofits, it isn't necessary to have individuals on staff who are well trained in system selection, installation, and maintenance. Using off-the-shelf software or having staff who are trained in basic programming (sometimes with assistance from a vendor or in consultation with peers) will usually satisfy this type of nonprofit's needs. A few fundraisers are deeply into technology and give leadership to the effort to use it well, but most technology use is managed by someone other than the frontline fundraisers.

Researchers, because they rely so heavily on the Internet, often become the focal point for technology in smaller nonprofits. This added responsibility enhances their place in the nonprofit and brings them closer to the center of the fundraising effort. Support staff, particularly those with an interest in technology, occasionally become technology specialists for nonprofits, thereby adding value to their positions. But no matter who is responsible, maintenance of the technology environment is essential.

For many midsize and most large nonprofits, the needs are more involved. Information services are becoming an organizational priority on a line with the chief development officer, the chief financial officer, and the chief service or program officer. The chief information officer, reporting directly to the chief executive officer, is already a growing fact of life. Many educational institutions, most larger hospitals and medical centers, and nonprofit organizations in all sectors with multiple office sites and operations have already created this position. They will not be alone in doing so; they are simply leading the way.

For small nonprofits, information system needs may be met by emerging online systems that are available through application software providers (ASPs; see Chapter Two), but the dot-com environment remains mercurial. You may be well advised to move cautiously into this area, at least until the initial shake-out is complete and the survivors are stable. This is not yet the case. A safer option is to purchase off-the-shelf software that runs on a personal computer. Access (the database component of Microsoft Windows 2000) is a reliable product. In programs with four or more users and twenty-five hundred or more names in the database, Blackbaud's Raiser's Edge and the JSI Millennium system are popular products. In settings with twenty or more users and correspondingly larger databases, organizations often explore the possibility of developing more individually distinctive information systems and purchasing software applications from established vendors. In this size range, three well-known names are Datatel's Benefactor and Colleague systems and the Iowa and SunGard BSR's Advance systems.

## Weighing the Requirements of an Effective System

Two fundamental requirements for establishing an efficient and effective system are (1) selecting the right system for your environment and (2) selecting the right people to install and support that system. The 80-20 rule is an important consideration in selecting the right computer system. This rule states that 80 percent of users just want access to data (and want it now); they need to be able to see the data and to quickly and easily produce reports that support them. Only 20 percent will actually use the detailed functionality of any system. Following the 80-20 rule is fundamental in choosing the right system. Failure to do so will have two consequences: (1) the system will contain primarily those features that support its most sophisticated users (the 20 percent), and (2) your organization's systems staff will have the expensive task of building in the features that will support the remaining 80 percent of the users.

The selection of a development information system starts by putting a team together that is likely to make a good choice. This team should strike a balance between the 20 percent of users who *enter* data and the 80 percent who *use* the data. Selection team members should include representatives of the following groups:

- Frontline development officers
- Development administrators
- Research analysts
- Data and gift processors
- Technical support staff
- High-level directors
- Support staff (those who actually use the information system in the course of doing their daily work)

All these people should have a good understanding of the detailed processes in their functional areas.

## Selecting an Effective Leader

In the information system selection process, leadership is critical. The keys to selecting the right leader are *accountability* and *involvement*. The leader is accountable because the success of the organization depends on selecting the right system. And the leader should be heavily involved at every step of the selection process. A leader who simply shows up for project meetings and does not understand the system's details cannot be effective. The leader should not be from the organization's technology department, however. It is best if the leader is from the development office or the executive office. The organization's development function should take ownership of the selection process—but with the technology function serving as a strong partner. The selection of a system that really impresses the development office but is impossible to support or enhance will lead to failure just as quickly as the selection of a system that uses "fresh" technology but does not satisfy development's needs.

## Defining Functional Requirements

Defining the system's functional requirements—what the system needs to do—is an important step. The requirements must include a definition of the organization's core processes—the essential functions that the organization requires in order to conduct its business. The only thing more important than carefully defining requirements is making sure the system has flexibility in terms of its software and your environment. It is often easier to change a process or a report than it is to change a system. Rarely will you find a new system that can produce, in the same format, every report that you now use. The focus should be on the marriage between functional needs and the system's capabilities. If that focus is achieved, the system should be flexible enough to enhance its functionality as changes occur in the organizational environment.

We are in the midst of an explosion of new technologies, with new products coming to market literally every week. In their eagerness and excitement, some vendors make exaggerated claims, impossible promises, and empty guarantees. Guard against vendors like these, and make intelligent decisions that address your current and future needs. But how do you do this in a marketplace that sometimes seems like quicksand? William V. West (1999) says three techniques work very well:

1. *Attend meetings of a user group.* (If your vendor does not sponsor a user group, you are working with the wrong vendor.) Attend the sessions that deal with the technical and functional aspects of the information system being considered. Talk to individuals from institutions that are equivalent to yours in size. This step is vital because some of the systems now on the market work beautifully in small institutions but fail in larger ones, and vice versa. Assess the types of staff people making presentations at user meetings. Ask yourself what type of staff you have and what type you can afford. Talk with users from development, information systems, accounting, and other departments. Take the opportunity to get the total picture and identify potential weaknesses.

2. *Meet with current users of the information system being considered.* Go to these customers' sites. Make sure that you have adequate travel funds in the selection project's budget to do this because buying a few $300 plane tickets now could save hundreds or thousands of dollars later. A site visit provides a chance to see the information system in action, talk to its users and support staff, learn about the customer's conversion or installation process (never visit a site that has not yet gone live), and assess the customer's satisfaction. It is best to make such a visit without the vendor. Most customers are willing to be open but not when the vendor is there. Do not allow the vendor to select the customers to be visited, and make sure that those visited are selected from a full list of the vendor's current customers. Be sure to bring along representatives from each of the major functional areas that will be using the system.

3. *Test the system by installing it at your site.* A true pilot installation (*true* meaning that you are not committed to buying the system) will quickly tell you how easy or hard the system will be to support and use. Pilot tests are not cheap; they take system resources and time. But if you think you are ready to make a selection, a pilot test will either confirm your decision or warn you of impending danger. It will also identify any phantom functionality that may have appeared in the vendor's demo. Buy a small server, install the system, configure it for your environment, import some real data, and install the system on the desks of your major functional departments. Then try to use it—*really* use it. This will not be an easy phase, and it will make demands on the participants. If this approach seems expensive, remember that nothing is more costly than regret.

## Evaluating Systems

The information system selected should be easy to support, especially if yours is a small organization with limited resources. The tools used to develop the system should be standard and widely available. Selecting a system built with the vendor's proprietary tools puts an organization in the position of being dependent on its vendor for support, and this arrangement can make the system's future growth and enhancement difficult. Moreover, recruiting and training staff will be much easier if your system's architecture is a common or popular one. If the vendor is the only source of contract support, this is a good sign of a "closed" system architecture. That system should be avoided. A system developed with a common programming language known as report programming generator (RPG) or with PowerBuilder (Powersoft's tool for access to databases) can be integrated with a wide variety of other systems and platforms, whereas a system developed with a custom-made, computer-aided software engineering (CASE) tool or programming language cannot be easily integrated with other systems without significant assistance from the vendor.

The system's database and its operating system should also have an "open" architecture. A system developed on any of the top databases (Oracle, Sybase, DB2, DB/400, Microsoft SQL Server) is much more likely to grow with your needs than is a system developed on a proprietary database that you've never heard of. The operating system selected will also have a significant impact on long-term costs. A system that runs on Unix or OS/400 may offer more flexibility but will also require more expensive hardware than a system running on Windows NT.

Also consider the direction the vendor's software company is going in. The system has to grow with your organization and keep pace with changes in the technology sector. If a system is currently running on technology built in the 1980s, its vendor may be unwilling to invest in and grow the software that will meet future needs. A vendor who claims to be enhancing a system with new technology should be put on hold until the enhancement has been completed; otherwise, an organization could make an unwitting investment in "vaporware." For example, information system vendors who are aligned with emerging trends should have already developed browser technology, a tool to explore the Internet. Much of a development officer's job is conducted outside the office, and access to the World Wide Web makes up-to-date information quickly available. Browser technology also significantly reduces the load that software puts on a personal computer (PC) and therefore may reduce the cost of the computer's support.

## Installing the Information System

Installation of the information system is an ongoing process for two reasons. First, the needs of the development staff are constantly changing as the organization moves from one fundraising effort to the next, and the installation process has to account for the enhancements that will be requested. And second, because the installation of a new system is a major distraction from building anything else, there is certain to be a backlog of priority projects waiting after the system is installed. So don't imagine that you will be able to hire temporary staff just for the installation and then let them go. The keys to successful installation are discussed next, in order of their importance.

### Leadership

From the most senior executive of the entire organization to the heads of each functional area, your leadership must be solid if the project is to be successful.

## Time

Your best friend is time—the time to do it right. Deadlines are important in maintaining a sense of urgency about the project, but unrealistic time lines will damage the project. It is better to say that the project will take three years and then finish it a year early than to say it will take one year and finish it a year late. Do the math. In both instances, the project takes two years.

## Funding

Installing a new information system is expensive, no matter how good your staff is. The budget manager needs to be accountable at each stage of the project and must continue to demonstrate progress—real progress, not status reports and time lines. It is vital to know that you are getting the most for each dollar.

## Involvement

Nobody gets to sit on the sidelines and throw rocks at the project. For the capabilities of the information system to be integrated with the processes in each functional area, the staff and managers of each area have to be involved. They should be involved in the definition of the processes, the data, and the interactions with other departments. This is the area where you are most likely to encounter resistance to change, but strong leadership and executive sponsorship can stifle it. Keep others involved, responsible, and accountable. Make it their project, too.

## Communication and Management of Expectations

Constant, consistent, positive, and honest communication has to be the rule. The installation of the information system should not occur in the dark; communicate expectations clearly in the beginning. *Do not* let staff, employees, or executives believe that the system will be a panacea. *Do* tell them all the reasons why they should be excited, but prepare them for the work associated with the changes they will encounter.

## Expertise of the Technical Team

Select an information system you can support. If that is impossible, get your technical staff into training. Make sure that the stars on staff know how to make the information system work. Beware of simply hiring someone who has experience in the technical environment of the new information system. Doing that may get a system up and running faster, but it could hurt in the long run because it takes time to learn and understand a development environment.

Make sure to recognize the value of the institutional knowledge in your existing staff. Contract with outside experts to coach, mentor, and guide you through the installation process, but do not hire contractors to install the new system. Contractors will not understand your environment; in the long run, turning installation over to contractors will not help your staff support the information system. It is better to contract for education than to contract for labor. Bring in experts from other sites to check your project's quality and provide a reality check for your decisions. Your consulting support should ensure that you are asking the right questions, making the right decisions, and learning along the way.

## Pilot Testing

Nothing provides a better reality check than a good pilot test. Make it a real one. Be sure there is ample time to conduct the test and evaluate the results before full installation of the system begins. Use real data, process parallel transactions, and then compare the results of these transactions. Most of all, build some reports that simulate your current ones.

## Education and Training

Invest time and money in training. If people lack skill and knowledge, they will either ignore the system or use it incorrectly. It is essential that key users and technical staff understand the functionality of the information system. Conduct basic training courses after the system goes live, and conduct refresher training frequently and repeatedly until the users stop attending.

## Reports

No functionality is more important than the system's ability to build and produce reports (see Table 1.1). The information system should offer report capabilities to users at all levels of experience as well as to the system's programmers; any system that requires experienced programmers for the production of simple reports should send you running for the hills. As soon as the system goes live—not after—have several standard reports ready to launch (for example, weekly giving activity, a month-by-month comparison of the current year with the previous year, donor profiles, completed pledges, campaign tracking, account balances). These reports will satisfy most users while additional reports are being developed. Nonprofits should also create the various printed forms and computer programs needed to record, retain, retrieve, and reproduce the information associated with the wide variety of fundraising tasks.

## TABLE 1.1. TYPICAL MENU OF STANDARD REPORTS.

| Name of Report | Description | Frequency |
| --- | --- | --- |
| Comparison report | Compares fundraising totals and numbers of donors for the current year and the previous year | Monthly |
| Pledge reports | Three separate reports: (1) pledges with payments currently due and 30–90 days past due and will receive a pledge reminder; (2) pledges that are 120–150 days past due; (3) pledges that are 180 days past due | Monthly |
| Completed pledges report | List of all completed pledges | Weekly |
| Productivity report | Three separate reports: (1) comparison of gifts in month just completed to same month in previous year; (2) comparison of year-to-date gifts to same period in previous year; (3) comparison of total gifts in past three fiscal years | Monthly |
| Giving analysis | Provides statistics for numbers of donors and total contributions in various giving levels during the past year | Annually |
| Five-year giving trends | Comparison of numbers of donors and total contributions by source of gifts | Annually |
| Capital campaign reports | Status report, progress report, gift table report (see Resource 1) | Monthly |

Two types of basic reports for which the professional staff is responsible are (1) financial reports (see Exhibit 1.1 and Resource 1) and (2) reports on people (volunteers and prospects; see Exhibit 1.2). The business office will usually be responsible for either producing the reports or supplying the data needed to produce them (see Exhibits 1.3 and 1.4).

The number and sophistication of the financial reports will vary according to the size and complexity of the fundraising program. A typical menu of basic periodic financial reports to support the fundraising program might include the reports described in Table 1.1.

## Standards and Procedures

As a corollary to this, it is important to "clean up" the database before conversion so that bad data are not converted. Nothing in a system is harder to fix than bad data, so standards and procedures must be defined before the system is installed. These standards are essential to converting and importing historical data and will be vital if your data entry operations are decentralized.

## EXHIBIT 1.1. CAMPAIGN PROGRESS REPORT FORM.

*Week ending* _____

| | |
|---|---|
| I. Campaign goal | $ |
| II. New gifts and pledges | |
| III. Total previous gifts and pledges | |
| Grand total gifts and pledges | |
| IV. Amount needed to reach goal | |
| V. Recent campaign activities | |
| VI. Appointments scheduled | |

| Donor Category | Campaign Goal | Received to Date | Balance Needed |
|---|---|---|---|
| Board | $ | $ | $ |
| Individuals | | | |
| Corporations | | | |
| Foundations | | | |
| Other | | | |
| TOTALS | | | |

The following are standards and procedures one would adopt when doing a database cleanup before a conversation:

- Do a complete review of current architecture (process and data stored).
- Document what's working.
- Document what's not working.
- Review data standards for how data are entered and what fields are used for what. (Data definitions can evolve over time, so a single field could contain data that have been defined four different ways over a span of ten years. If you are using a "current" definition, you may get unexpected results when the data are converted.)
- Determine whether certain data fields can be combined or split apart. (Are data elements a one-to-one conversion?)
- Understand and document new architecture.
  Document data fields.
  Document what fields from the old system were combined with the new system.
  Note whether current data standards still apply.

# EXHIBIT 1.2. PROSPECT STATUS SUMMARY REPORT FORM.

| Major Prospects | Researched | Prospect | Assigned to Staff | Possible Volunteer(s) | Assigned to Volunteer | Meeting Held | Letter and/or Proposal Submitted | Gift/Pledge Made; Seek More | Refused; Try Again | Gift/Pledge Made Adequate | Firm Refusal | Comments |
|---|---|---|---|---|---|---|---|---|---|---|---|---|
| | | | | | | | | | | | | |
| | | | | | | | | | | | | |
| | | | | | | | | | | | | |
| | | | | | | | | | | | | |
| | | | | | | | | | | | | |
| | | | | | | | | | | | | |
| | | | | | | | | | | | | |
| | | | | | | | | | | | | |
| | | | | | | | | | | | | |
| | | | | | | | | | | | | |
| | | | | | | | | | | | | |
| | | | | | | | | | | | | |
| | | | | | | | | | | | | |
| | | | | | | | | | | | | |
| | | | | | | | | | | | | |
| | | | | | | | | | | | | |
| | | | | | | | | | | | | |
| | | | | | | | | | | | | |

# EXHIBIT 1.3. ANNUAL CAMPAIGN BUDGET REPORT FORM.

### For the month of

| Current Month Actual | Current Month Budget | Percent Variance | Prior Year Actual | Percent Variance | Line No. | Description | Year-to-Date Actual | Year-to-Date Budget | Percent Variance | Annual Budget | Amount Remaining | Prior Year Actual | Percent Variance |
|---|---|---|---|---|---|---|---|---|---|---|---|---|---|
| | | | | | 1 | Salaries | | | | | | | |
| | | | | | 2 | Overtime wages | | | | | | | |
| | | | | | 3 | Fringe benefits | | | | | | | |
| | | | | | 4 | Less: Allowance for attrition | | | | | | | |
| | | | | | 5 | Total personnel | | | | | | | |
| | | | | | 6 | Training and recruiting | | | | | | | |
| | | | | | 7 | Travel | | | | | | | |
| | | | | | 8 | Representation | | | | | | | |
| | | | | | 9 | Supplies | | | | | | | |
| | | | | | 10 | Printing | | | | | | | |
| | | | | | 11 | Postage and shipping | | | | | | | |
| | | | | | 12 | Telephone | | | | | | | |
| | | | | | 13 | Copier maintenance and supplies | | | | | | | |
| | | | | | 14 | Building repair and maintenance | | | | | | | |
| | | | | | 15 | Vehicle repair and maintenance | | | | | | | |
| | | | | | 16 | Computer repair and maintenance | | | | | | | |
| | | | | | 17 | Other equipment and furnishings | | | | | | | |
| | | | | | 18 | Legal fees | | | | | | | |
| | | | | | 19 | Professional and other fees | | | | | | | |
| | | | | | 20 | Insurance | | | | | | | |
| | | | | | 21 | Miscellaneous | | | | | | | |
| | | | | | 22 | Total program | | | | | | | |
| | | | | | 23 | Capital expenditures | | | | | | | |
| | | | | | 24 | Total expenditures | | | | | | | |

# EXHIBIT 1.4. MULTIYEAR CAMPAIGN BUDGET REPORT FORM.

Expenses to date as of 8/31/98

| Line No. | Description | FY '96 Actual | FY '97 Actual | FY '98 Actual | To-Date Actual 8/31/98 | '99 Budget | '00 Budget | '01 Budget | To-Date Budget | Total Budget | Amount Remaining | Percent Variance |
|---|---|---|---|---|---|---|---|---|---|---|---|---|
| 1 | Salaries (net of allowance) | | | | | | | | | | | |
| 2 | Overtime Wages | | | | | | | | | | | |
| 3 | Fringe Benefits | | | | | | | | | | | |
| 4 | Total Personnel | | | | | | | | | | | |
| 5 | Training & Recruiting | | | | | | | | | | | |
| 6 | Travel | | | | | | | | | | | |
| 7 | Representation | | | | | | | | | | | |
| 8 | Supplies | | | | | | | | | | | |
| 9 | Printing | | | | | | | | | | | |
| 10 | Postage & Shipping | | | | | | | | | | | |
| 11 | Telephone | | | | | | | | | | | |
| 12 | Copier Maintenance & Supplies | | | | | | | | | | | |
| 13 | Building Repair & Maintenance | | | | | | | | | | | |
| 14 | Vehicle Repair & Maintenance | | | | | | | | | | | |
| 15 | Computer Repair & Maintenance | | | | | | | | | | | |
| 16 | Other Equipment & Furnishings | | | | | | | | | | | |
| 17 | Legal Fees | | | | | | | | | | | |
| 18 | Professional and Other Fees | | | | | | | | | | | |
| 19 | Insurance | | | | | | | | | | | |
| 20 | Miscellaneous | | | | | | | | | | | |
| 21 | Total Program | | | | | | | | | | | |
| 22 | Capital Expenditures | | | | | | | | | | | |
| 23 | Total Expenditures | | | | | | | | | | | |

- Set priorities.

  Set a date to freeze the current system from any changes.

  Determine what should come first in the conversion process in order to minimize work.

  Determine whether you will run parallel systems.

- Develop a written plan for converting data; be sure the conversion will occur with minimum risk to the organization.

  What data will be moved programmatically?

  What data will have to be entered manually?

  Who will review data that are rejected in the move?

  How will rejected data elements be handled?

  What controls will be put in place to prevent duplicate converted records?

- Develop a plan to balance and verify the data that were converted to ensure data integrity.

## Coding Structure

Just as important to define are *access to data* and *confidentiality of information policies.* The coding structure used throughout your information system should be defined by people who understand both the business of the institution and its data (see Resource 2). At this stage, it is also crucial to have someone on hand who is an expert in the particular information system that has been installed. Therefore the team defining the coding structure should include a representative from the vendor's company who knows the system inside and out—that is, who understands how information is processed on the screens and how data are processed by the programs. Failure to define the codes correctly may prevent entire modules of the system from functioning in response to your needs. This expert must also have experience using the system's software in an environment comparable to yours because the coding scheme used by a small institution may be significantly different from that used by a large one.

## Support of Core Processes

With every new decision ask yourself, "Does this feature support a core process?" Many bells and whistles can be included in a development information system, and many among the sophisticated 20 percent of users believe they "gotta have it." The 20 percent will have a knack for quibbling and distracting the project from its purpose, and this is why strong, knowledgeable leadership is so important. An essential part of the leader's role is to ensure that the functions installed are those that support the institution's core processes. A new system often requires a fundamental change in mind-set, especially if you are making the change from an existing system. Saying "We've always done it this way" could cripple your project. Your focus should always be the marriage of your functional needs with the capabilities of the system.

## Setting Clear Priorities for the Information System

One of the key success factors in an efficient and effective information system operation is the setting of clear priorities. These priorities must be set through a balance of the needs of the system's users and the needs of the infrastructure. The information system staff is responsible for defining and communicating the needs of the infrastructure; in order for the needs of users to be defined, however, organizational leaders must be involved. Organizational environments can be hotly political at times, and there is always a slate of high-priority projects under way. It should not be the responsibility of the information system department to determine which projects will receive its attention; saying no is not a successful position to be in. Assigning an information system director the job of saying no can quickly alienate the director and produce animosity between the departments that get top priority and those that do not. Cross-functional representation ensures that every priority is set with the best interests of the organization in mind and that all departments will understand why. Moreover, there are never enough information system resources to implement every project, solve every emergency, or design every good idea introduced by users. Therefore an empowered team of organizational leaders must be responsible for setting priorities.

The forum and process for establishing priorities can be very simple. It starts with a request form (see Exhibit 1.5)—a simple form that states the nature of the project, records who has requested it, says how it will benefit the organization, and provides a place where a programmer can make an assessment and estimate the time needed for the project. All requests should be logged in a database or spreadsheet so that a report of new requests can be produced (see Resource 3). The team of organizational leaders should gather regularly to go over the new requests, review the status of current projects, and set priorities for the new requests.

This process has two clear benefits for both the information system staff and the development staff. First, the programmers are given clear priorities; they know what to work on first and can complete projects in order. Second, this process ensures that limited programming resources are focused on the areas of most benefit to the organization as a whole. The needs of the infrastructure may or may not be discussed by way of this forum. These include upgrades to network and server equipment that will be transparent to the users. Staff and executives alike

## EXHIBIT 1.5. INFORMATION SYSTEMS TASK REQUEST FORM.

REQUESTER INFORMATION

Task Title _____

Submitted By _____     Date Submitted _____

                 _____     Phone _____

Received By _____     Date Received _____

---

TYPE OF REQUEST

___ Special Report    ___ Records Load/Modification    ___ Workflow/Office Automation
___ Database          ___ Web Page                    ___ Other _____

Describe the request
_____
_____
_____
_____
_____

---

REQUEST ASSESSMENT

Information Systems Representative _____

Assessment of work required (estimated hours and cost)
_____
_____

---

DISPOSITION: The following is the result of the review of this request:

Priority: _____       Staff Assigned: _____

___ Emergency Response    ___ Projects: On Hold
___ Priority Project         ___ Maintenance: On Hold
___ Maintenance Task      ___ Reviewed: Not Assigned
_____
_____

Please send all requests to: _____

---

will turn to these forms as a way to communicate their needs. Accountability and reaction to their requests will lend future support and understanding to any technical difficulties that occur. These needs must be factored into the discussion if a shared pool of staff is required for both project types and will have to be coordinated with upcoming projects, of course. But often the priorities for the infrastructure projects are defined or required by changes in the technology industry; solid leadership in the information system function can ensure that the needs of the infrastructure are well orchestrated with other priorities.

# Updating and Maintaining a Technical Environment

Updating and maintaining a technical environment is a strategic imperative of any development program. It costs less to maintain a position ahead of the advancement curve than it does to regain a position once it has been lost. As newer technologies have emerged and faster computers have been developed, the cost of maintaining a positive position in technology has been coming down. In the early 1990s, PCs had to be upgraded or replaced every three years in order to run current software. This meant that 30 percent of an organization's computers had to be replaced every year. In 1998, a PC with the best-valued processor and a fifteen-inch monitor cost between $2,000 and $2,500. A year later, a PC with twice the power and a seventeen-inch screen cost between $1,200 and $1,800. The newer PCs can last four to five years and even after five years will house enough power to satisfy low-end, occasional users. This means that now only 20 to 25 percent of your equipment needs to be upgraded every year. The price for powerful PCs will continue to drop.

## Maintaining Data

Maintenance of the data in a development system can be a complex, time-consuming task. Key factors that affect how complex this task will be include the following:

• *The number of prospects and donors in the database.* Complexity increases as the number of records increases. A staff of two or three may be effective in maintaining a database of 25,000 constituents but cannot maintain a database of 250,000 with the same degree of efficiency. Likewise, a large organization may have 250,000 constituents but may not be able to afford to hire twenty people for its records department. Therefore you must determine the database priorities, the technologies and techniques to be used, and the acceptance costs to maintain data.

- *The number of gift and accounting transactions completed each year.* The more transactions in a system and the more added each year, the more efficient data maintenance processes need to be, especially if there are many years of historical data in the system. Maintaining accuracy in the files that contain the giving history and in all the subtotal files requires strict standards for processing. The need for accuracy and for the ability to subdivide these data will increase as the number of transactions increases.

- *The number of fields important to the organization.* Maintaining only donors' home addresses makes for a simple data maintenance process, no matter how many records you have. If the primary focus is on home mailings, staff can focus on strategies that enable this level of data maintenance. But if telephone numbers and information about prospects' employment, activities, and affiliations are also required, the complexity of the data maintenance process increases. In sophisticated organizations—those with programs for annual giving, special giving, major gifts, planned and deferred giving, capital campaigns, donor relations, and prospect management—it is not uncommon to maintain more than one hundred data elements for each record.

- *Accuracy requirements.* Accuracy in constituents' records is often measured by addressability, and addressability is a moving target; more than 20 percent of the population may move in any given year. The costs and efficiency of record maintenance will be closely tied to the need for accuracy. For example, although average addressability in the United States is around 80 percent, which means that 20 percent of the addresses in organizations' databases are not valid, one leading U.S. university's addressability exceeds 92 percent. This figure relates to the strategic importance of valid addresses to that institution, given its large size and its decentralized structure. But that kind of accuracy comes at a price: $250,000 per year.

## Upgrading the System

The updating and upgrading of your primary applications and your operating systems will need to be justified and handled with due diligence. Software vendors commonly try to force an organization to upgrade, but the value added to the system does not always justify the cost of the upgrade. Moreover, a software upgrade can shorten the life of hardware. To protect your investment, control staffing, support costs, and ensure that priorities are focused on the projects that offer the most value to the organization, do not upgrade software unless there is a real need to do so. Any plans for a software upgrade should justify the expense and guarantee that the upgrade will not make current hardware obsolete. This is not an issue, of course, if the current computer hardware has already outlived its usefulness.

Business managers should be involved in the planning process for a software upgrade to ensure their understanding of the added functionality and the changes to existing systems. Technical professionals should not be expected to make an upgrade decision alone. The key success factors for an upgrade are similar to those for selecting a new system. The involvement of everyone is essential to making sure the decision that gets made is the right one for the organization.

Enough money to maintain a technical environment needs to be in the baseline of the capital budget; it should not be an add-on. Technology is a strategic tool. Those who use it well gain an advantage over those who do not. The effective use of technology provides the ability to reduce business costs, improve the efficiency of all processes, and increase fundraising. It is difficult to prove that adding technology increases success, but it is often very easy to spot cases in which poor technology or failed technology projects have seriously hampered the success of a development program, so the baseline budget should include the funds required to maintain your position.

The budget for a new technology project should be independent of the operational budget. The funds for new technology should be justified and requested separately on the basis of the value that the technology can add to the organization. The technology-related expenditures and returns should also be tracked separately so that the progress, success, or failure of the project can be monitored. This procedure ensures that the project's performance will not have an impact, positive or negative, on the operational budget—a precaution that is most important when a new technology project runs over budget.

## Organizing the Records Department

There are many options for organizing the records department. Put records staff in the department where it will receive the most support, regardless of that department's primary function. This may mean putting the department in the research area, in the alumni association (if yours is an educational institution), in accounting, in another development office, in the information technology area, or somewhere else. Most important is that the records staff receive the tools, guidance, and direction they need and that they are not expected to carry out duties in addition to maintaining records. Record maintenance is hard, tedious work, and if staff must choose among competing priorities, record maintenance will always be the first to go.

Several techniques and technologies can improve the process of maintaining records; what works at a given organization may very well depend on a number of external factors. In a large, complex environment, take advantage of its large core of development officers to gather new data from a wide variety of sources such as events, meetings, telemarketing, and Web pages.

It is best not to decentralize data entry; centralized control of data entry standards is important for the long-term integrity of the data. One key to ensuring integrity is to have a single individual responsible and accountable for that task. This individual should be in charge of all code definitions and oversee the data entry process. It is vital that this individual understand the objectives of the organization and become an integral contributor to its business functions.

With strong, well-defined, documented data standards, you can make it possible for all users to contribute to the accuracy of information. If you do not already have that ability, consider adding a function to your system that allows every user to send updates to the records department directly through the system. Updates are made by the records department, but every user contributes to the update process. Decentralization of access to record maintenance is one of the key success factors in many large, complex organizations.

The future offers the use of e-mail and the World Wide Web as outstanding mechanisms for further decentralizing the collection of data from constituents. An organization-sponsored e-mail address gives constituents an affinity mechanism and provides a means of making contacts electronically, thereby saving postage throughout many career transitions. The Web also offers the ability to post an on-line form that enables constituents to update their own information as often as necessary. Many times an electronic form can be downloaded into your database system; no data reentry is necessary. Very efficient! (See Exhibit 1.6.) This electronic form should send the updated data to the records staff, who will enter or upload them into the system. A form like this one is easy to create and very cost-effective; both services should be advertised on every publication and mailing sent out.

Postage is an expensive part of record maintenance and development. Coordinating mailing efforts can save expenses and increase the ability to update constituents' information. For example, when mailing a gift receipt to a donor, check to see if the phone number and employment data are complete. If not, include a mini-survey form in the receipt envelope. In addition, pay for the returned postage on at least one major mailing a year. When you mail a receipt, solicitation, magazine, or invitation, make sure that you get the item returned with any address correction information from the U.S. Postal Service. If employment data and telephone numbers are important, then send out a survey form for every address update made. The logic here goes this way: "We noticed that your address changed. Has anything else?"

Address information is available through several third-party sources that work with the U.S. Postal Service. Many nonprofits use these services to update addresses on a quarterly basis, more or less. This approach can save money in data

## EXHIBIT 1.6. ON-LINE ALUMNI RECORD UPDATE AND CLASS NOTE FORM.

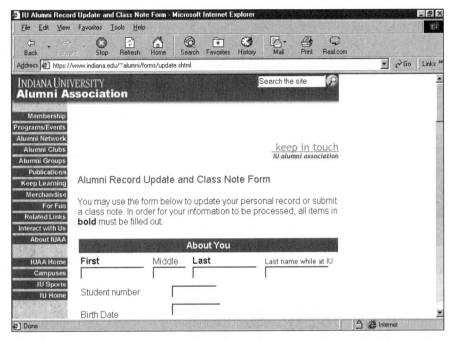

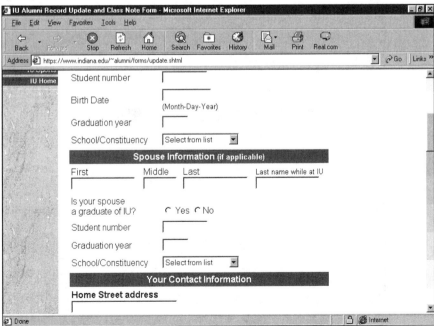

## EXHIBIT 1.6.  ON-LINE ALUMNI RECORD UPDATE AND CLASS NOTE FORM, Cont'd.

```
IU Alumni Record Update and Class Note Form - Microsoft Internet Explorer        _ 8 X
 File   Edit   View   Favorites   Tools   Help
  Back      Forward    Stop   Refresh   Home    Search  Favorites  History    Mail    Print   Real.com
 Address  https://www.indiana.edu/~alumni/forms/update.shtml                    Go    Links »
```

**Home Street address**

Additional address info

**City**                    State/Province        **Zipcode/Mailcode**

Country
Select from list

If your country is not listed above, please type it in here

Home phone
          (xxx)xxx-xxxx
Fax
          (xxx)xxx-xxxx
E-mail address

**Business Information**

```
 Done                                                         Internet
```

```
IU Alumni Record Update and Class Note Form - Microsoft Internet Explorer        _ 8 X
 File   Edit   View   Favorites   Tools   Help
  Back      Forward    Stop   Refresh   Home    Search  Favorites  History    Mail    Print   Real.com
 Address  https://www.indiana.edu/~alumni/forms/update.shtml                    Go    Links »
```

(xxx)xxx-xxxx

E-mail address

**Business Information**

Occupation

Employer (name of company or organization)

Street address

Street address

City                    State/Province        Zipcode/Mailcode

Country
Select from list

If your country is not listed above, please type it in here

```
 Done                                                         Internet
```

## EXHIBIT 1.6. ON-LINE ALUMNI RECORD
## UPDATE AND CLASS NOTE FORM, Cont'd.

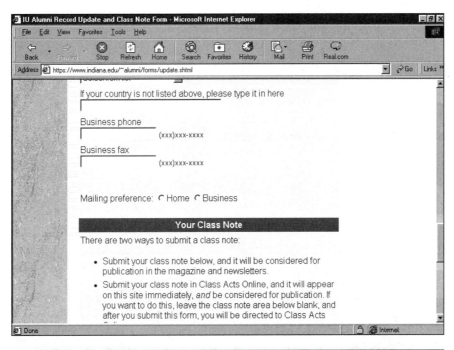

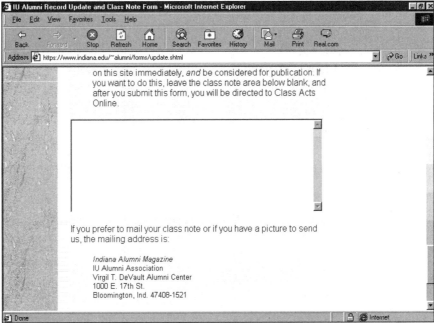

## EXHIBIT 1.6. ON-LINE ALUMNI RECORD
## UPDATE AND CLASS NOTE FORM, Cont'd.

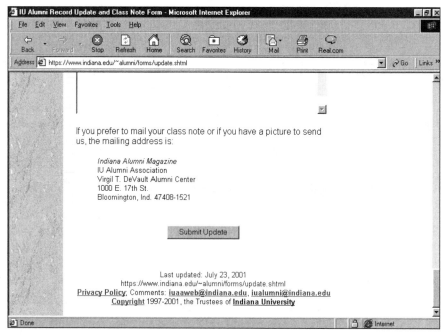

*Source:* Indiana University Alumni Association. Reprinted with permission.

entry personnel, but it sacrifices some accuracy. Cost versus accuracy is the decision that needs to be made here.

The use of an information system and the services it can provide when properly developed is the most basic use of technology to serve development, but other technologies can serve development, too. In Chapter Two the discussion broadens to include them.

# CHOOSING TECHNOLOGIES TO SUPPORT COMMUNICATION

The use of technology to support a nonprofit's information system in the twenty-first century is virtually a given. Some technologies, like PCs, are time-tested; others, like on-line giving and wireless communication, are emerging.

Before beginning a discussion of how technology can support development services, some definitions are in order. The meaning of the terms *Internet* and *Web site* is no doubt obvious to most readers, but *intranet* and *extranet* may not be as familiar. An *intranet* is like a mini-Internet; that is, instead of being accessible to anyone with an Internet connection, it is used only by the personnel in a single office or organization. An *extranet* is used by those outside the immediate environment, for example, by external development units, alumni relations or business offices, and banking and investment partners. Note that an Internet connection is basic. All the services described here depend on having that connection. Fortunately, most large organizations and universities are already wired for Internet access.

Having an Internet Web site as your primary window to the world will enable you to increase giving; this site presents your image and enables you to interact with prospects and donors. Intranet and extranet connections will provide long-term productivity enhancements, facilitate communications, and realize cost reductions—an effort that benefits internal customers and staff. Whether all three functions are needed is determined by the size of the organization, the complexity of the services offered, and the short-term and long-term strategic plans. However, every organization needs an Internet site. Smaller ones (fewer than fifty employees) may not need both an intranet and extranet, but one or the other would be essential to a large organization with development and administrative personnel spread across a multisite institution where communications and effective business operations are essential.

## New Technologies for Fundraising

This chapter examines the truly helpful technologies that all development organizations should review, including local area networks (LANs), e-mail, on-line giving, automated telemarketing, portable computing, imaging, and outsourcing to ASPs.

Following a description of each of these tools is a full discussion of how to develop Web sites. Web site development is quite possibly the technology that will come to rival the information system as the most dominant, pervasive, and powerful use of technology in development programs.

### LANs

LANs are groups of computers connected by cables; that is, they are networked. Once a LAN connection has been made, many other tools become available, and everyone in the development office then has access to a wide array of development services. Networks are especially useful when several users must share resources such as data or printers.

### E-Mail

A staff constantly on the move, on the road, and in meetings can find e-mail extremely useful. It is an excellent tool for receiving and responding to messages. The disadvantage of e-mail, relative to the telephone, is that you cannot use it to have a real conversation. And because a text message contains no audible emotional cues, messages can be misinterpreted. The advantages of e-mail over the telephone are that you can read and respond at your convenience (you are not interrupted), you do not have to take written notes, and you can easily keep a log of correspondence. If you are asked which medium to choose, the telephone or e-mail, your answer should be both. An e-mail program usually offers other tools, including an officewide calendar, an officewide address book, and a tool for contact management, that make life in the office easier.

If yours is a small development office, you can piggyback your e-mail on someone else's system—your organization's, for example. Supporting an e-mail system is expensive; do not install your own unless your office is large enough to afford support staff or you absolutely have no other choice. The advantage of using an organization-wide system is that you can share an address book and calendar with colleagues and associates.

If tying your e-mail to your organization's service is not an option, you may find an Internet service provider (ISP) in your area that provides e-mail service. And ISPs can now offer on-line giving capabilities. These need to be examined carefully, particularly with regard to confidentiality issues.

## On-Line Giving

The number of individuals with access to the Internet continues to grow at an amazing pace. With more and more organizations capturing e-mail addresses, this medium offers nonprofits an opportunity to produce direct mail without additional printing and postage costs.

Although soliciting by e-mail and on-line giving are still in their infancy, they are viable options for many. However, the basic development principles remain the same, whether or not these technologies are used: (1) there is still a need for a strong case for support; (2) the organization's message must be clear; and (3) there must be a way for the prospect to make a gift easily. The solicitation may simply include a telephone number to call to make a gift or an address to which payment can be sent.

The more sophisticated solicitations contain an embedded link that, when clicked, not only directs the prospect to the appropriate on-line giving form but populates the form with the prospect's name, address, identification number, and other necessary items to complete the transaction. At that point, the prospect can enter a credit card and complete the transaction. If the prospect does not feel comfortable doing that, he or she can print and mail the form with a check.

On-line giving will continue to grow and develop rapidly. Concerns over security issues such as storage of credit card numbers for billing purposes must be addressed at length by the nonprofit sector. Currently, many organizations are offering "on-line giving" that is nothing more than a form to be filled out on the Web and simply mailed in with a check or credit card. This type of giving helps circumvent many security issues. For those interested in electronic processing, a secure server, encrypted e-mail, a third-party processor, and other security functions are mandatory. In some cases, outside vendors may offer solutions to these issues; in others, the organization may wish to invest in a secure server, along with applicable software, and enter into agreements with banks and other companies to facilitate secure on-line giving.

## Automated Telemarketing

Automated telemarketing systems offer another kind of helpful technology. These systems come in all shapes and sizes, with prices ranging from $15,000 to more than $200,000. The cost depends on the system selected, the functionality it provides, and the size of your institution (that is, the number of callers). An automated telemarketing system, implemented correctly, can pay off handsomely. For example, the IU Foundation's installation of a telemarketing system (EIS's Centenium) cost nearly $400,000 for all the software, hardware, and installation services but paid for itself in one year through the increased donations and lower staff costs that the system made possible. Complete installation took only twelve weeks—four to get the system live and eight to get it fully integrated with the development system. Note that this telemarketing system took nearly one year to "select." Careful planning during the selection process made the short installation time possible.

An automated telemarketing system provides a wide range of functions. Those you require will depend on the current sophistication and philosophy of your calling program. Smaller systems offer convenient data entry screens that allow you to load donors' data from your development information system and update this information during a telephone call. More advanced systems offer programming capabilities that enable you to "script" your calling programs and respond to the multitude of prospects' responses. These advanced systems also suggest approaches to making calls, and they track the results of each call.

An even more sophisticated system can be integrated with a telephone system and makes calls by reading telephone numbers from donor data. This feature, used correctly, can save enormous amounts of time by eliminating many no-answers, busy signals, answering-machine responses, and wrong numbers, thus allowing callers to spend the vast majority of their time talking to prospects instead of pushing buttons.

Like most technology projects, installation of an automated telemarketing system is a "process" project, not just a systems project. Its full benefits will be realized only if the telemarketing system is integrated with an organization's development information system at the front end, integrated with it at the back end, and able to provide its own statistical reports. These three features will ensure that minimal staff time is spent supporting the system; the majority of staff time will be spent using it.

At the front end, the automated telemarketing system should accept data from your development information system and allow you to pare it down and group it into calling programs. It should allow you to store data from your development information system and allow the caller to update any and all data elements while still on the telephone. At the back end, after the calling program is completed each night, pledges, gifts, and data should be uploaded back into your development information system and posted with the daily gift batches. (Transactions received from the automated telemarketing system should be coded in the system in some distinctive way for later tracking purposes.) All updates to addresses, employment data, and other information should be reported to the records department for entry into the development information system. Whether entry of these data should be direct, automatically uploaded, or manual will depend on the quality of your calling staff, their understanding of data, and the priority of data in their jobs; not uploading them automatically will protect the integrity of the data and maintain high data standards. Finally, after the total calling program is complete, the system should produce the pledge acknowledgments to be mailed to the donors, as well as all statistical reports that will be needed in tracking the effectiveness of the program and each caller.

## Portable Computing

Laptop computers have continued to drop in price while increasing in quality and power. A full-powered laptop with a user-friendly monitor costs the same as desktop computers did three years ago and provides five times the power. A laptop with a docking station that allows it to be connected to your network and has a full-size keyboard and screen provides all the services of a desktop computer but offers the advantage of portability. After work or as you head off on a trip, you can detach your laptop from your docking station and take it along. This means that you can take your tools and information—essentially your whole office—with you.

A laptop becomes a mobile office once you have remote access to your servers and to the Internet. Remote access can be provided in three ways: (1) through an organizational dial-up (another reason to connect your office with your organization's network), (2) through an ISP, or (3) through your own modem pool, which is a bank of dedicated telephone lines for use in dialing in to the office. These options are listed in increasing order of cost. Supporting your own remote access server (RAS) is much more expensive than piggybacking on your organization's server; the larger an organization, however, the easier it is to support a RAS. Having a RAS provides dedicated lines and the ability to connect toll-free, which can save significant long-distance charges while simplifying the dial-in process.

Palmtop devices are providing increasing power and functionality in a small package. Many staff on the move prefer a palmtop to a laptop. A palmtop device cannot serve as a fully mobile office, but it will provide many of the essentials such as e-mail, an appointment calendar, a contact list, expense reporting, and other features helpful to the traveling development officer. The price of a palmtop is one-tenth that of a laptop. For an office on a small budget, palmtops and a link to the Internet could provide a cost-effective, functional package.

Another helpful software product is the system for geographical mapping and location finding. Such a system allows you to import a name and an address from your development database. It then plots the location of the address on an interactive map and shows you how to drive to the location. The more advanced systems can work in your car and be integrated with a global positioning system (GPS) that tracks your current location and plots current position with respect to destination.

## Imaging

Growing mountains of paper plague many nonprofit organizations, and imaging is one way to reduce the volume and amount of paper in an office. Imaging is the use of technology to capture printed documents electronically—an electronic filing system. Images can be efficiently routed, copied, or sorted.

Some of the initial objectives of an imaging system include

- Reducing the amount of storage required for paper files
- Providing a safe backup for original documents
- Providing instant access to documentation
- Reducing redundancy and multiple copies
- Increasing efficiency within business operations

How does imaging work? First, documents are scanned or copied into the system where they are stored on an optical disk. These images can then be viewed on a computer screen and reprinted, faxed, or sent. Some of the basic categories for applications that are used in development include

- *Prospect research files:* donor profiles and biographies, contact reports, news clippings
- *Planned giving:* all legal documents and correspondence
- *Account and gift administration:* all account files, as well as documentation of gifts and memorial gifts (possibly assisting in preparing acknowledgment letters and verifying appropriate signatures and compliance with donor intent)

Imaging is an emerging use of technology, but its use is growing rapidly, and its presence in development environments will be commonplace within this decade.

## ASPs

An ASP is a company that rents its software to customers and delivers it on the Internet as customers use it. ASPs are projected to be one of the fastest-growing technologies of the next several years. According to etapestry.com (the first fund-raising ASP in the United States), the experts say:

- ASP industry revenues will grow a thousandfold, from $7 million in 2001 to $7 billion by 2004 (Cahners In-Stat Group).
- The number of ASP users will grow from twenty thousand to thirty million in the same period.
- Businesses, including nonprofits, can save as much as 50 percent on the cost of an application by renting (Forrester Research).
- The number of ASPs will grow from forty to four hundred in 2001 (Gartner Group).

Today only a handful of ASPs have demonstrated success in on-line software implementation. If these so-called dot-coms prove successful, they may create a major benefit for nonprofit organizations of all types and sizes. ASPs claim to be less expensive and more versatile than competing products. If these claims are supported, smaller nonprofits may benefit the most; ASPs may give them great service at lower cost, thus opening doors to technology that are now closed.

More information about ASPs can be found at two Web sites: www.ASP-News.com and www.ASPIsland.com.

## Outsourcing to ASPs

The emergence of ASPs may help answer another question that is asked more and more today: Should we develop our technology capabilities in-house or outsource them? And how do we make that determination? These are important questions for all nonprofits but are especially critical for smaller nonprofits with small staffs and budgets. Although there is no single, clear answer—the answer may be to do everything in-house, outsource it all, or work some combination of both—the leading questions should be these:

Can outsourcing to ASPs or other vendors provide a critical, needed service at a lower cost or higher quality, or both?

How are quality controls established and performance expectations monitored?

Will the nonprofit's integrity be compromised in any way?

Are you confident of the security assurance, if any security issues are involved?

Will outsourcing provide added value to the nonprofit?

## Using Technology to Develop a Web Presence

The process of developing a Web presence is identical to the process followed to introduce any new campaign, program, or service. Senior management and the fundraising team determine what programs and services an organization will provide. The business manager then determines what details are required to implement the individual programs and may work with publications to produce the marketing materials, brochures, and testimonials that the programs will use.

Meanwhile, members of the technical staff provide systems, tools, and training; they are also programming and integrating applications behind the scenes that support programs such as gift processing, prospect tracking, telemarketing, and other programs that are used to support business processes and interactions with donors. The design for a Web presence works the same way. The plan comes from the top, the details and approach are worked out in the middle, writers and artists develop the "look," and the technical staff build the infrastructure tools, training, and support. Together they produce the results.

The key is to recognize that existing programs have a head start on Web efforts. The Web development staff will be tempted to try to include all the programs within an organization that are already well established—an effort that will overwhelm an organization quickly. You must take a strategic and deliberate approach to developing a Web site. It cannot be done all at once.

## Developing Web Sites

Since the introduction of the Web browser in 1993, the World Wide Web has grown from anonymity to popularity; it is the most popular medium in use today. Businesses, both for-profit and nonprofit, view the Web with a mixture of awe and uncertainty.

Nonprofits are likely to need or want a Web presence. But where to start? There are many approaches to developing a Web site. Some organizations hire a developer or Webmaster and train their own staff to develop the entire site in-house. Others contract with a company to develop their site; some do a little of both. There are advantages to each approach.

Whatever approach you take, move slowly. Recognize your organization's strengths, and build on those as you branch into the Web's world. It is easy to do the basics of the Web. Most new college graduates enter the workforce with basic Web development skills. However, the world of the Web gets complicated quickly.

A conservative and deliberate approach will ensure that each stage achieves at least one objective well, while preparing to achieve the next, usually more complicated, objective.

Senior management, with competent facilitation and education, should provide solid direction and input into the overall strategy and design of the Web site. Begin by preparing your staff to support a site, addressing the five primary components of Web site support: (1) content management, (2) content design and development, (3) programming and integration, (4) system administration, and (5) training and education. Even when using a team approach, each component should be addressed.

## Content Management

Content management needs to be led by someone who fully understands the mission and operation of the organization. The focus of content management is marketing and service. A word of caution: as the Web site grows, the time requirements of content management will grow. This function needs to work from a well-defined set of priorities to ensure that the strategic goals of the site are met. The success of content management will be predicated on the implementation of an effective process that enables current content to be maintained without hampering the development of new content.

Effective content management for Web sites also depends on having a well-established team of content providers—key individuals throughout the organization who represent and provide information for various information categories contained in the Web site. Content providers are responsible for providing information in which they specialize. For instance, a communications expert may provide the news items that appear in the "News and Events" category of the site. The content provider may or may not write the copy; a Web editor or someone skilled in writing for the Web could do so.

*Advantages of the Approach.* This team approach to content management has several advantages. For one, when only one individual is responsible for maintaining and creating fresh content, the amount of time it takes to refresh the content of the site can be extensive and may result in stale information being mixed in with fresh. By appointing different content providers for the site, the content management tasks can be distributed. Another advantage is that when content providers are responsible for their own areas of specialty, the information they provide will always be the most accurate, up-to-date information for the category they represent.

***Tools for Managing Content.*** Various systems, products, and custom solutions are available for managing a site's content. One system involves the establishment of written protocols for content providers. This system may be most effective for a small organization or one just beginning to develop its Web site; the Web budget may be limited, and only one or two people may be able to program. The protocols outline the chain of events and the style guidelines that content providers must follow to write for the Web, as well as to update, refresh, and add new content to their information category.

The content provider uses a template to produce suitable content and provides keywords and a document description for the Web page to be indexed by search engines. The provider may then send the copy to an editor to be proofread; the editor might then send the copy to the Web developer to be coded into the Web site.

Products such as Microsoft's FrontPage, in conjunction with Microsoft's NT Server, can remove the necessity for such lengthy protocols. Content providers can write new content directly into the Web pages because they do not have to know hypertext markup language (HTML) to produce Web pages through FrontPage's interface.

Some organizations develop custom solutions that fit tightly with their own needs—solutions that sometimes involve housing the site content inside a database so that content can be managed and recalled quickly. Custom solutions may also involve the creation of forms that produce Web pages containing specific attributes that fit into the site. In this scenario, too, the content providers can enter new information for their Web page into custom forms without coding the information in HTML. The best solution depends on whether the organization is starting from scratch or redesigning an existing site; other considerations are the skills of the Web developers or programmers and the type of budget they have.

## Content Design and Development

Content design and development are traditionally handled by the publication staff, writers, and graphic artists. If the Web site is not too sophisticated, many individuals in an organization can be trained to be content developers. Basic design and development of Web pages is quickly becoming a common skill, like word processing and desktop publishing. From the publication staff's standpoint, the Web is simply a new medium. Development of Web publications is similar to the development of print-based publications; the constituencies and desired outcomes are the same.

***The Basics of Web Content.*** Donors have certain expectations when they arrive at a Web site. They want to know who, what, and where. Start with a staff directory, a picture of your institution and building (so they can find you later), basic statistics that demonstrate your success, and a feedback mechanism that enables two-way communication. At a minimum, your site should contain these easy-to-find items. From there you can begin introducing your constituents to the programs that support your strategic plans.

Some keys here are to

- Keep it simple and make it interesting.
- Make the basic information easy to find.
- Be sure the strategic information is interesting and interactive (pages of text describing all the forms of giving are good reference but are not likely to entertain site visitors).
- Introduce your goals and success to the visitor in an interactive fashion that keeps them clicking. To visit an active Web site, go to www.iuf.indiana.edu/.

Don't assume that visitors want to be at your site. Give them a reason to stay. Explain to them what you are and why your organization is important, and then produce results.

*Services on the Web.* You must provide service through your Web site. Find out what your constituents need (or want) most and provide it. This is where an educated senior management team, supported by a skilled development team, can really begin to create new ideas and methods to interact with and reach out to constituents. Some fundamental services include the ability of donors to make a gift or pledge, to see their past giving record, or update their address and profile information. Many university-related organizations have found success by providing their alumni and donors an affinity-based e-mail address that looks something like this: YourName@alumni.institution.edu.

On-line, searchable directories of alumni, friends, and business contacts are also a valuable service that can be provided via the Web. New, emerging ideas include assisting with tax and estate planning, education cost projections and savings plans, and the identification and application of scholarships. These services pull constituents into the organization by providing a service they want while introducing important programs like planned giving, endowment funding, and other campaigns.

## Programming and Integrating Content

Implementation of the services described requires a strong programming and support staff. Development of Web sites that interact with your information system in a secure and easy-to-use environment is identical to the implementation of a new application system—telemarketing. It shares the same level of complexity.

Note that these services may require a solid partnership with departments within the institution that have traditionally provided services. The Web has required, like nothing else before it, a greater need for cooperation among departments across an institution.

Programming and integrating Web pages are not trivial matters. Although simple, static, and noninteractive Web pages (read boring) are easy to build, designing a Web site that is truly interactive and enables constituents to donate gifts, update their profile, view their account, and register for events and that provides the myriad of services that can truly make a Web site successful, all within a secure environment, requires a trained programming staff that can work as part of the team with the content developers. Programmers don't typically make good Web designers, but a solid, supportive Web programmer gives content developers more flexibility to be creative and reach the limits of a site's potential.

For organizations that cannot afford to hire an entire Web team with talents ranging from programming interactive forms to creating multimedia content, there are companies that provide interactive, multimedia services on the Web. These can be subscribed to for a yearly fee. An example could be a gift-matching look-up service that is displayed on a Web page that looks like the rest of your Web site. The program and database responsible for looking up a company to determine whether it matches employee gifts actually lie on the Web site of the provider of this service. Yet because the Web page has the same look and offers the same navigation potential as the rest of your site, it is not apparent to your Web site's visitors that they have temporarily left your site.

## System Administration

The system administration functions that are required for fundraising information systems and networks are also required for the Web site. The installation and support of the Web server (the computer that controls the network) is similar in many ways to that of supporting other enterprise (internal) servers; however, some nuances must be learned by each institution's support staff. A solid system administration function should provide content developers the tools and environment needed to be creative. A well-designed system infrastructure will provide a secure and reliable environment that is easy to support and that promotes the sharing and reuse of Web content.

You can also rent Web server space from some ISPs or Web-hosting services on the Internet if you do not have a system administrator or an information technology department. A good Web-hosting service will provide you with the necessary tools for creating all the common elements of today's Web sites, including security and e-commerce tools such as on-line credit card processing.

## Training and Education

Training and education are required for the long-term development of a Web site. Content developers need to be trained to use Web-based tools, just as they use word processors, to develop the information that will be placed on the Web. As their skills improve, continuous training will enable them to reach new heights.

Senior management and the business managers need to be educated on the possibilities of the Web. Increasing their awareness and understanding of the Web will enable them to create new ideas, strategies, and programs that are incorporated into the Web strategy. The Web offers new and exciting ways to interact with prospects and donors. Understanding the potential that the Web offers and preparing a skilled staff to implement your ideas will enable you to take advantage of this forum to maximize the success of your programs. Using the content management strategies discussed earlier may eliminate the need to train staff to code their content for the Web.

And you should begin training other key staff on basic Web development skills so they can contribute to the contents of the Web. The publication staff should begin training to develop on-line publications. From this standpoint, the publication department's constituencies will not change, but the media they use now include the Web. As technology progresses, Web content will become as easy to develop as documents on a word processor.

Training internal staff to develop Web content results in two strategic advantages to any organization: (1) it increases the capacity to develop a Web presence by having more staff with the skills to do so, and (2) it produces a transformation in workers by providing them the ability to be creative, develop new ideas, and interact directly with target markets via the Web site.

# Selecting a Web Developer

One approach to Web development (for organizations that can afford to do so) is to hire a Webmaster, or developer. This person's mission is to provide leadership and ensure that the Web development team works together. The availability of this type of person has grown over the last few years as more and more programmers, graphic artists, instructional designers, and other professionals have developed Web skills. Hiring an expert Webmaster provides an organization the opportunity to inject new and valuable skills into that organization.

A competent Web developer can create solid Web pages while coaching and educating staff about Web development. However, the knowledge and leadership required to develop a Web site must come from within the organization. A new developer will need time to learn about the organization and its fundraising process. With the right organizational structure and attitude, however, this person can become very successful very quickly.

The ideal Web developer possesses a combination of skills not often found in a single individual, which presents a fundamental hiring challenge. If you do find the skills in one person, chances are you can't afford the person. This is why a team approach to Web development is often essential.

A good Web developer must

- Be technically astute enough to work within the Web site, which is, after all, still a technical environment
- Have marketing talent because your Web site will become a major medium through which your organization's image is revealed
- Be aesthetically inclined in order to develop Web pages that are clean and well organized
- Be well organized so that the Web site's appearance, supporting file structure, and the process used to prioritize additions to the site are clear and systematic
- Be a great listener who can collect ideas, knowledge, and facts from the organization and incorporate them into the contents of the Web pages
- Be an effective communicator and project manager who can facilitate groups of staff from different areas of an organization and lead them to the construction of a solution that meets the needs of the donors while satisfying the demands of the internal business processes
- Be able to accept good ideas and understand the needs of the creator of those ideas, then produce a result that not only reflects those ideas but takes them to the next level

Nothing feels better than to work with a Web developer who can take ideas and make them come to life, producing even more than imagined. That's when you know you've hired the right person. But don't expect the developer to support the technical environment used by the Web: the programming, integration, and system administration tasks. Web developers need to be constantly taking the time to develop and enhance their Web skills and learn the intricacies of the related systems environment.

Both the Web and the system environments are quickly maturing and changing. Becoming a competent Web developer in an ever-changing technical environment is not a small endeavor for three primary reasons: (1) the ability to fully understand the supporting systems environment often surpasses the capability of Web developers who emerge from nontechnical backgrounds; (2) programming complex interactions such as on-line forms and reports requires extensive time, which can significantly delay other content-only projects; and (3) as the Web site gains popularity, the onslaught of new projects and maintenance work often prevents the developer from acquiring new skills. Doing so requires time, training, and practice—mostly time. Resolving this dilemma requires that a solid technical support team be in place to provide programming and systems administration support so that the Web developer can focus on developing and enhancing the content without losing time supporting the infrastructure.

# Advantages and Disadvantages of Using Internet Technology

The Fund Raising School (2001) lists the following advantages and disadvantages of using the Internet for fundraising:

*Advantages*

- It is possible to access more people than with other methods.
- The ongoing expense is fairly low. It is a low-cost way to inform, although it may be expensive to get people to the site initially.
- Information going to donors and prospects is easily and quickly updateable.
- Pictures can be included at low cost.
- Dissemination of newsletters to affiliates of a parent organization is easy; there they can print and distribute the publication.
- Although attention is often on crises, awareness of a Web page can help retain donors.
- A Web page displays an organization's ability to be innovative and progressive.
- One-on-one, immediate communications can be made through e-mail.
- Networking, exchanging thoughts and ideas with people whom we might not meet, and contacting experts are easily done by e-mail.
- Information can be disseminated efficiently.
- Hard-to-access or nontraditional audiences can be reached.
- Interactive survey tools are useful. Through infoactive.com, charities can create and edit questionnaires, invite certain audiences to participate, analyze results, and compare themselves with other organizations.
- More personal contact is possible than with direct mail. Follow-up e-mail as a result of a Web page hit can continue and build a relationship.
- It is good for a small staff, providing a tool without much staff time involved.
- Some software companies help nonprofits put public service announcements on-line at no charge (for example, see www.alive.com/nonprofit.html).
- It provides a sense of immediacy.

- The Association of Fundraising Professionals (AFP), formerly the National Society of Fund-Raising Executives (NSFRE), has issued a policy statement that transaction costs associated with Internet fundraising may be considered as fundraising costs, not commission.

*Disadvantages*

- E-commerce that promises funds to charity is not consistent. Money may not be credited to the charity, or there may be a cap on how much is to be donated, or shoppers may fail to follow instructions or be confused by the many sites available.
- Tracking money for charities is difficult, and checks may be slow in coming.
- Some merchants change the charitable source without telling donors.
- Donations may not be tax deductible; this is a complex issue, and the IRS has not yet issued formal guidance. Some e-commerce giving sites have a charity to receive gifts on their behalf, such as the National Philanthropic Trust.
- Fraud is an issue. Under consideration is whether giving sites must comply with the same rules as direct mail and telemarketing companies.
- Donors may be unhappy about the percentage of each gift a philanthropic site takes to cover costs. Letting potential donors know of a site and having them visit it regularly is expensive; costs for advertising and promotion may be prohibitive.
- All legal complexities haven't been worked out. See www.nonprofits.org/library/gov.urs for an explanation of the Uniform Registration Statement project. The National Association of State Charity Officials considers Internet regulation one of its top priorities.
- Pledges made on the Web may be hard to collect unless information such as a driver's license or credit card number is requested.
- There is competition among giving sites.
- Systems may break down unexpectedly.
- Systems for popular causes and sites may become overloaded; a donation page may be rendered inoperable for long periods of time.
- Markets become saturated; it's hard to get noticed.
- Unless the Web site is advertised or linked to some other organization, the public may not be aware of it. This is another "hidden" cost that must be considered.
- Processing credit card donations may be costly and time consuming. Establishing a Web site that can process credit card transactions automatically is complicated and expensive. There are also security concerns regarding access to credit card numbers.
- If a Web page is sponsored, the organization may be subject to an unrelated business income tax (UBIT) because information is perceived as advertising.

- A fee that is not apparent to the donor may be charged for some "transactions" by Web sites offering to receive gifts on behalf of charities.
- Commercial promotions from charity on-line malls could be harmful to the nonprofit because they may not be congruent with the mission.
- Costs of hardware, software, and network connections can limit access to the Internet.
- Technical support may be lacking.
- There may be privacy issues.
- Disorganized Internet information can cause confusion for the average individual.
- Donor loyalty may become an issue, that is, the question of staying power through on-line giving.
- There is an increasing backlash against a digital lifestyle (as described in *USA Today*, Iwata, 2000). Approximately 108 million Americans have no desire to get onto the Internet; 60 percent of consumers have stopped buying the latest high-tech gadgets and devices; 43 percent believe technology is advancing too quickly. A fast-growing number of occasional on-line users reject the Internet.

## The Promise of Technology

The emergence of the Internet as an international communications pathway has opened the door for all institutions, large and small, to enhance information gathering and sharing, both internally and with the general public. Most of the technologies relevant to the development function are now more useful because of the Internet. But at the heart of the matter lies the fundamental reason that most nonprofits view the modern wonders of technology with wide, beaming eyes: the potential it holds for enhancing fundraising. This possibility clearly exists, but the Internet and the Web are not for everyone; neither are they a panacea for anyone.

What Johnston (1999) describes as "cyber-fund-raising" is in its infancy. Changes occur daily. Growing pains abound. And one of the most fundamental questions about the role of technology in fundraising remains a hot topic of discussion. The question, simply put, is this: Are we talking about Internet fundraising or are we using the Internet to assist us in fundraising? Let's answer that question unequivocally. The Internet is a tool, a means to an end. It is not an end unto itself. This understanding is fundamental to any discussion that ensues about the use of technology in fundraising, which remains a human endeavor.

As the world goes more high-tech, fundraising must remain a high-touch enterprise. This news should be comforting to all but especially to those in the nonprofit sector who do not have Internet access or knowledge of its use or the resources to use it—not to mention those who do not even own computers. Today

730,000 nonprofits are registered with the IRS, and the INDEPENDENT SECTOR estimates that there are more than 1.5 million nonprofits all told. These numbers include far more technology "have-nots" than "haves," and they must be encouraged to realize their fundraising potential, too, using time-tested, proven methods available to all.

Consequently, one should remember the following:

- The Internet is a tool only; it is not a panacea. It is a servant, not the master.
- The Internet can enhance fundraising capabilities, but it is not an imperative or a quick fix or the goose that lays golden eggs. No matter how gaudy the paint of technology, it cannot mask cracks in the organizational plaster caused by a weak case or a poorly designed fundraising program.
- The Internet remains basically unproven and should not be used to replace proven fundraising methods. Even when it becomes proven, it should enhance but not replace proven methodologies and techniques.
- Beware of the siren's song praising technology: listen carefully; understand completely; react carefully, even cautiously. That's old advice, but freshly true. As long as the basics of human psychology and sociology remain constant, so too will the basic tenets and techniques of successful fundraising programs.

The consensus among experts and professionals is that the Internet has many excellent uses that support and enhance a fundraising program, but at higher giving levels personal contact is still very important. In many experts' opinion, the Internet is overestimated and excessively promoted as a fundraising tool, and the caution is that time-tested and proven fundraising strategies may be neglected.

# CHAPTER THREE

# ESTABLISHING YOUR RESEARCH INFRASTRUCTURE

This chapter and the next discuss prospect research. The goal of these chapters is to provide a starting point for the beginner and options for enhancing a research program for the more advanced. This chapter addresses establishing and maintaining a research function; Chapter Four deals in detail with the techniques and tools that successful researchers use. The information in these chapters, along with the many resources referenced, will aid in the establishment or enhancement of a research program. It's important to recognize, though, that prospect research is fluid, and the methods of performing good research vary from region to region.

According to Martha Murphy, director of prospect research at Valparaiso University, "Prospect research is an important step in the process of increasing the philanthropic resources of an institution. We seek to identify the shared values between an organization and its prospective donors through the collection, organization, and presentation of significant information for development purposes" (personal communication, April 1996).

This definition of prospect research illustrates clearly how far the field has progressed in the last two decades. Jonathan Lindsey (Taylor, 1999), director of donor information services at Baylor University, describes the advances made in prospect research: "Until the early 1980s, only a few major educational institutions had formal research units in their advancement offices" (p. 4). Not long after that, the information revolution began, and development programs of all types began to recognize the need for a mechanism within their organizations to capture the vast amounts of information that were becoming readily available on their prospects and donors. As the age of information and technology has progressed, the need to find information and the ability to decipher and discern what is truly relevant and valuable in a world filled with too much information have become key issues.

The birth of the information age was precisely the vehicle needed to surface research and researchers and to bring notice and appreciation to their expertise and value to the field of development. Prospect research has now grown from a handful of clerical-level, newspaper-clipping staffers to a profession of choice. Researchers are increasingly being viewed as a valuable part of the overall development team and, in many nonprofits, their positions have been elevated to a new, higher status. Researchers are not just researchers any more; they are development officers working alongside the frontline fundraisers in their organizations.

## Establishing a Research Function

Many nonprofits are just beginning to realize the value of establishing a research function within their organizations. The following information is provided as a general guideline for the establishment of a research function, regardless of the size of the development effort.

### Creating a Budget

It is difficult to recommend a reasonable budget because every research effort is different in size and desired or expected output. In many cases, research will be given a rather small budget initially. It is the responsibility of the researcher to investigate and demonstrate true financial needs. Many times this is only done through trial and error.

*Locating Resources.* Start with a few of the resources that will be most heavily used, whether in the form of books, CD-ROMs, on-line services, or a combination of these. If the budget for resources is small, include the funds necessary to travel to and from libraries and to make the many copies that will be needed when using reference materials in these settings.

While you are trying to establish the resources that would be of most use to a particular research office, be sure to work with the various vendors who offer these products. Many will offer a free trial (typically thirty days, but most will work with you), which is extremely useful when the full benefit of a product to a research office is relatively unknown. Ask for the free trials. Work the product as thoroughly as possible before deciding whether it is worthwhile. If a long-term relationship is already established with a particular vendor, be sure to ask about a customer loyalty discount for the continued use of its products.

***Budgeting for Professional Development.*** Professional development is a key factor in growing personally and professionally within the field and within one's own development culture. Try to budget for at least one conference a year that provides many and varied learning experiences that are of high quality and are pertinent to the needs of the organization or to the researcher; those needs could either be immediate or in the foreseeable future. A major conference costs between $550 and $800, plus airfare and hotel costs, as well as costs for meals not covered in the conference fee.

One item that should be mandatory in any research budget is membership for all researchers in the Association of Professional Researchers for Advancement (APRA), which is "a private, non-profit organization dedicated to promoting educational and professional opportunities in the field of fundraising research. Since its beginnings in 1987, APRA has grown to over 1,700 members and facilitated the formation of over 25 chapters worldwide. APRA has positioned itself as the premier international professional association for philanthropic research."

In addition to offering an annual international conference that is superb for both new and seasoned researchers, APRA offers a variety of services to its members that enhance the professional opportunities for researchers. There are many state and regional chapters of APRA; nearly every prospect researcher in any part of the United States (and some additional countries) can join to enjoy educational and professional opportunities year-round. The cost of an annual membership in APRA in 2001 is $100.

The Council for Advancement and Support of Education (CASE) also presents an annual conference for development researchers that provides excellent programming but focuses primarily on institutions of higher education.

Another option for conferences offering quality educational opportunities in development is the Association of Fundraising Professionals (formerly known as the National Society of Fund-Raising Executives). AFP does not offer a conference strictly dedicated to prospect research; however, the conference offerings are well rounded and provide a balance of information for anyone in the fundraising field.

## Staffing the Office

The size of staff needed to efficiently conduct a research effort varies according to the needs of the institution. Small nonprofits often have a researcher who is also responsible for special events, donor relations, and perhaps even fundraising. This is the norm in today's nonprofit environment. The largest research offices, which are typically found in major universities, have a dedicated research function with several staff members. Regardless of size, job descriptions are an essential tool to define the role an individual will play. Titles can be varied in many ways, but the basic functions of a researcher will be quite similar.

APRA has adopted a set of standards for the field of prospect research, divided into a basic skills set and an advanced skills set (see www.APRAhome.org). Many research offices are incorporating these skills into their in-house job descriptions and even using them in the performance merit review process. Examples of how various research offices around the country are defining their roles can be found in the sample job descriptions found in Resource 4.

It is important that the researcher, regardless of the size of the office, have realistic expectations. For example, a lone researcher in a small nonprofit should not be expected to provide meaningful, detailed analyses on prospects and also do the clerical tasks and data entry for the office. In the same vein, expectations in a large shop need to be reasonable. One researcher for every six to eight fundraisers is fairly manageable, but beyond that the workload can become unrealistic and overwhelming, creating an atmosphere of stress and burnout.

## Equipping the Office

Regardless of the size of the research operation, there are basic necessities. The most important piece of equipment to a researcher is the computer. A high-speed PC with Internet access is the key to being able to manage the data acquired on prospects, as well as to allow for quality on-line searching. This will vary by institution, but any computer running with a Pentium II processor should provide enough speed to adequately perform database operations. Internet speed is determined by the type of connection. A home computer will run off a standard telephone line, and Internet speed will be fairly slow and sluggish, whereas an organization connected via a LAN or wide area network (such as a T1 connection) will provide a significantly improved connection to the Internet. An older computer will not only create a high degree of frustration but will make data acquisition and management next to impossible.

For any research program, the following resources are highly recommended. But keep in mind that this is not an exhaustive list; it is merely a suggestion as to what to begin looking at. Price ranges are noted in order to help those with budget constraints determine how resources might best be spent.

*Books*

> *Marquis Who's Who in America:* A good source of biographical information on individuals; however, information is self-provided so care should be taken to verify data. The "Who's Who" reference for the geographical area in which you operate is also a good one to have on hand. Cost: $270–$575

*Standard and Poor's Register of Corporations and Directors:* Limited information on public and private companies, but helpful professional information on executives and directors. Many times other directorships held can be found here that provide valuable linkage information. Cost: $600–$800

*Industrial directories* (for your area): Provide valuable basic information on many manufacturing companies, including names of general managers and other key employees. There are several publishers of this type of directory and many are published for geographical regions. Cost: $159–$200

*The Foundation Directory:* An excellent, standard tool for any research office. Over 100,000 foundations are listed, along with detailed information on giving guidelines, officers, and so on. Cost: $215

*Directory of Corporate Affiliations:* A good, standard resource. Over 100,000 public, private, and international companies are listed, along with the corporate family structures, which is invaluable. Indexes make for easy searching. Cost: $600+

## CD-ROMs

*Biography and Genealogy Master Index:* Over 13,000,000 references to individuals listed, directing the researcher to publications containing desired biographical information. Cost: $500+

*Marquis Who's Who* (Reed Elservier): The complete collection of *Marquis Who's Who* on CD-ROM. Cost: $1,089

*Prospector's Choice* (Taft): A compilation of private and corporate foundations, along with their giving guidelines, directors and officers, giving areas, and so forth. Searchable by keywords, grant types. Cost: $579

*FC Search* (The Foundation Center): Companion to *The Foundation Directory* with much of the same information. Searchable by keywords, grant types. Cost: $1,195 with updates

*Corporate Affiliations Plus:* Companion to the *Directory of Corporate Affiliations.* Searchable by numerous variables, such as company name, executive name, SIC codes. Cost: $1,820

## Fee-Based On-Line Databases

Dun & Bradstreet (www.dnb.com): Excellent source of corporate information, particularly private companies. Most valuable information found in History and Operations section of Business Information Report, such as key officers, brief biographical information about the key officers, as well as the percentage of the company they own. Cost: varies depending on what is purchased. A full Business Information Report can run around $60 each; the History and Operations section would cost about $16.40. Corporate name lookups and addresses are free, and the company offers numerous other services that are invaluable to research offices. Fees vary depending on the service purchased.

Hoover's (www.hoovers.com): Provides extensive profiles on public and private companies, including officers and in-depth financials, for a fee. However, there is much information available at the Hoover's site for free, including company snapshots and initial public offering (IPO) information. Cost: basic subscription $199.95 annually or $29.95 per month.

Prospect Research Online (PRO by iWave; www.rpbooks.com): iWave operates out of Canada and has spent several years producing a nice product that can be of tremendous value to most research operations. They continually add to the database; everything from public and private company profiles to lists of people within a given profession in a specific geographical region to articles and trends in fundraising and philanthropy can be found. A nice, largely unknown perk available to subscribers is the ability to request information via e-mail if the desired information is not found on the database. The folks at iWave will explore and e-mail back in a relatively short time indicating whether anything could be found and, if so, where on the site to go and obtain it. Cost: $1,995

Dialog (www.dialog.com): Used to be the premier research tool for any research office; however, with the advent of the Internet, much data are becoming available either free or through other venues more cheaply. As a result, Dialog has been undergoing a metamorphosis, having been purchased by Thomson. Dialog is still a viable research tool, offering hundreds of databases to choose from when searching for information, including the *Marquis Who's Who* directories, *The Foundation Directory*, and hundreds of full-text newspapers. Cost: variable, depending on the database selected; database charges are in addition to charges for output, search time, and telecommunicating.

Lexis-Nexis Universe for Development Professionals (www.lexis-nexis.com): Rapidly becoming a database of choice for many research offices. It offers two modules: (1) *People* & *Company* and (2) *People* & *Company* plus *News, Public Records, Demographics* and *Advanced Search*. Module 1 provides news, people, assets, company information, campaign contributions, lawyers directory, physicians directory, major trade journals, liens, and tax exempt organizations. Module 2 provides updated news, magazine articles, newspapers (including obituaries), newsletters, trade journals, transcripts, wire services, the *Chronicle of Philanthropy* and *Chronicle of Higher Education*, public records, civil and criminal filings, judgments and liens, verdicts and settlements, asset valuation (blue book value of cars, trucks, boats, and airplanes), demographics information by ZIP code, state, country, congressional district, and workplace. Cost: Module 1—$8,400; Module 2—$4,000

Collectively, these resources can be rather costly, and many small nonprofits may not be able to afford them. Some may be available through local and university or college libraries. It is important to demonstrate to management the value of having in-house resources rather than spending time away from work at the office to go to various libraries. And, as mentioned earlier, be sure to work with the vendors who offer these resources for free trial subscriptions and discounts.

## Managing the Office

As the field of prospect research grows and prospers, many veteran researchers are being elevated to manager or director status in their departments. This is an exciting change, but along with the elevated position come new challenges and obstacles. Many in this position have spent most of their careers as researchers; they have little experience with administration.

Successful administrators know how to delegate. And one of the first things a researcher-turned-manager must do is learn that skill. How much is delegated depends largely on the size of the program being managed. Small shops may have only one other researcher or a few part-time volunteers helping on an irregular basis. In this situation, the manager will probably be in the position of having to handle the administrative responsibilities of the department, as well as keep up with research projects. The key here is to delegate as much as possible to others in order to be freer to respond to and keep up with administrative responsibilities.

Larger shops have the advantage of more professional research staff. The challenge here is for the manager to distribute most, if not all, of the research work to those staffers—often quite a difficult task. Research-related tasks are typically something the manager really loves to do! The larger the shop, the greater the administrative responsibilities, and most people quickly find out that continuing to work on research projects and keep up with the new managerial role at the same time leads to unnecessary stress and the inability to be an effective manager. Focus needs to shift to managing the staff and the budget, and to marketing the department.

***Keeping Track of the Work Flow.*** In any research effort, small or large, it is important to keep track of what requests come in and what information is sent out. This allows not only monitoring of the workload but benchmarking of accomplishments as well. How this is done is purely a matter of choice. The best method is to keep logs (see Exhibit 3.1).

## EXHIBIT 3.1. TRACKING LOG.

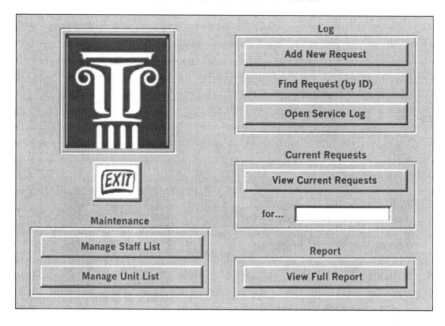

## EXHIBIT 3.1.  TRACKING LOG, Cont'd.

| | |
|---|---|
| Request ID | 2 |
| Date Received | 7/1/99 |
| Due Date | 7/9/99 |
| Unit | IUB - IUF |
| Requestor | Marilyn LaBarr |
| Prospect/Request | |
| Notes | |

| | |
|---|---|
| Type | Specific Request |
| Staff | Jo Huffman |
| Date Completed | 7/7/99 |
| Lead Time | 8 day(s) |
| Completion Time | 6 day(s) |
| Completed | 2 day(s) early |

[Close]

| | |
|---|---|
| Request ID | 3 |
| Date Received | 7/2/99 |
| Due Date | 7/19/99 |
| Unit | IUPUI - Science |
| Requestor | Brenda Bishop |
| Prospect/Request | |
| Notes | |

| | |
|---|---|
| Type | In-Depth |
| Staff | Bonita Hanson |
| Date Completed | 7/12/99 |
| Lead Time | 7 day(s) |
| Completion Time | 0 day(s) |
| Completed | 7 day(s) early |

[Close]

| | |
|---|---|
| Request ID | 4 |
| Date Received | 7/2/99 |
| Due Date | 7/6/99 |
| Unit | IUB - HPER |

| | |
|---|---|
| Type | Specific Request |
| Staff | Jo Huffman |
| Date Completed | 7/6/99 |
| Lead Time | 4 day(s) |

# EXHIBIT 3.1. TRACKING LOG, Cont'd.

Service Log—old

9/18/00

| Request ID | Date Received | Due Date | Unit | Requestor | Prospect | Type | Date Com | Staff |
|---|---|---|---|---|---|---|---|---|
| 1 | 7/1/99 | 7/9/99 | IUB-IUF | | | Specific Request | 7/7/99 | |
| 2 | 7/1/99 | 7/9/99 | IUB-IUF | | | Specific Request | 7/7/99 | |
| 3 | 7/2/99 | 7/19/99 | IUB | | | In-Depth | 7/12/99 | |
| 4 | 7/2/99 | 7/6/99 | IUB | | | Specific Request | 7/6/99 | |
| 5 | 7/5/99 | 7/20/99 | IUB | | | Specific Request | 7/6/99 | |
| 6 | 7/5/99 | 8/1/99 | IUPUI-IUF | | | In-Depth | 7/29/99 | |
| 7 | 7/5/99 | 7/9/99 | IUB-IUF | | | Specific Request | 7/8/99 | |
| 8 | 7/5/99 | 7/9/99 | IUB-IUF | | | Specific Request | 7/8/99 | |
| 9 | 7/5/99 | 7/9/99 | IUB-IUF | | | Specific Request | 7/8/99 | |
| 10 | 7/5/99 | 7/9/99 | IUB-IUF | | | Specific Request | 7/8/99 | |
| 11 | 7/5/99 | 7/30/99 | IUB-IUF | | | Specific Request | 7/8/99 | |
| 12 | 7/5/99 | 7/30/99 | IUB-IUF | | | Specific Request | 7/23/99 | |
| 13 | 7/5/99 | 7/30/99 | IUB-IUF | | | Specific Request | 7/23/99 | |
| 14 | 7/5/99 | 7/30/99 | IUB-IUF | | | Specific Request | 7/23/99 | |
| 15 | 7/5/99 | 7/30/99 | IUB-IUF | | | Specific Request | 7/23/99 | |
| 16 | 7/5/99 | 7/30/99 | IUB-IUF | | | Specific Request | 7/23/99 | |
| 17 | 7/5/99 | 8/31/99 | IUB-IUF | | | Specific Request | 7/23/99 | |
| 18 | 7/5/99 | 12/31/99 | IUB-IUF | | | Specific Request | 12/23/99 | |
| 19 | 7/5/99 | 7/30/99 | IUB-IUF | | | Specific Request | 7/23/99 | |
| 20 | 7/5/99 | 8/31/99 | IUB-IUF | | | Specific Request | 8/30/99 | |
| 21 | 7/5/99 | 7/30/99 | IUB-IUF | | | Specific Request | 7/23/99 | |
| 22 | 7/5/99 | 7/30/99 | IUB-IUF | | | Specific Request | 7/23/99 | |
| 23 | 7/5/99 | 7/30/99 | IUB-IUF | | | Specific Request | 7/23/99 | |
| 24 | 7/6/99 | 7/15/99 | IUPUI-IUF | | | Special Project | 7/23/99 | |
| 25 | 7/7/99 | 7/7/99 | IUB-IUF | | | Specific Request | 7/7/99 | |
| 26 | 7/7/99 | 7/7/99 | IUB-IUF | | | Expanded Brief | 7/7/99 | |
| 27 | 7/8/99 | 7/8/99 | IUB-IUF | | | Specific Request | 7/8/99 | |
| 28 | 7/8/99 | 7/8/99 | IUB-IUF | | | Specific Request | 7/8/99 | |
| 29 | 7/8/99 | 7/30/99 | IUB-IUF | | | Special Project | 7/27/99 | |
| 30 | 7/9/99 | 8/6/99 | IUPUI-IUF | | | In-Depth | 7/27/99 | |
| 31 | 7/9/99 | 8/6/99 | IUPUI-IUF | | | Expanded Brief | 7/29/99 | |
| 32 | 7/12/99 | 7/30/99 | IUB | | | In-Depth | 7/21/99 | |
| 33 | 7/12/99 | 7/23/99 | IUB | | | Expanded Brief | 7/26/99 | |

*Note:* Names of requestors, prospects, and staff have been removed for reasons of confidentiality.

The Research Management and Information Services Department at the IU Foundation has a reactive log that is maintained and monitored by the department's manager; proactive logs are kept by the individual researchers. The information captured in these logs includes

- Date of request
- Due date
- Name of requestor and his or her affiliation
- Nature of request
- Researcher assigned
- Completion date

Benchmarking and status reports are pulled from this captured information and shared with the research staff as well as management. This can easily be managed using a Microsoft Excel or Microsoft Access database, or a similar spreadsheet-type database.

Requests can be accepted by research in any number of ways, but most operations seem to prefer the use of a research request form that aids in capturing some of the data already known by the requestor (see Resource 5). It is important to note here that frequent communication between researchers and requestors is vital, and forms should not become an easy way to communicate needs and avoid face-to-face dialogue about prospects and project needs.

***Keeping Up with Trends and Ever-Changing Resources.*** Another aspect of managing the research shop is keeping up with the trends in philanthropy and research. The information and technology revolutions have caused many and varied changes in the world of philanthropy. With more and more women holding professional, high-paying jobs, more and successful minority businesses, and the newest boom of very young, very rich high-tech professionals emerging today, it is vital that prospect research keep its knowledge of what's going on in the world as current as possible. This requires a very aggressive schedule of reading newspapers, periodicals, trade journals, and so on as part of a busy workload. It is not sufficient to merely respond to requests for research. The researcher must be aware of current events and how they will affect his or her organization. This activity also provides numerous opportunities for researchers to become aware of potential prospects and make suggestions for possible approaches to these proactively identified individuals and corporations. Management must be supportive of this and allow the time necessary to stay current.

It is also critical for researchers to stay abreast of current technology and resources. This is difficult when researchers spend most of their time attending meetings and trying to keep up with administrative tasks and other duties. However, it can be done by developing and maintaining good working relationships with various vendors, by reading the promotional materials that come in the mail, by requesting free trials of new databases, by continuing to monitor PRSPCT-L (see Exhibit 3.2) or other development listservs for new resources mentioned, and by asking the staff and volunteers to keep them informed of new resources they discover that may be worth investigating. It takes a great deal of time to stay on top of all the changes and updates to the many resources research uses every day, but the time spent is well worth it.

## Marketing the Research Department

Because prospect research has evolved into a profession in demand, it is increasingly important that research market its services properly. Frontline fundraisers must be aware that prospect research is there to partner in identifying a prospect and developing information about that prospect, as well as for developing a strategy for moving the prospect forward—the end result being a gift to the institution.

Many fundraisers are fully aware of the value of prospect research and use their research partners to the ultimate degree. However, many are not aware of this valuable service, and their education is the responsibility of the researcher. Researchers must ensure that their services are used in the most professional, ethical manner possible and not viewed as performing clerical functions within the organization.

One key way to promote research is to create strategic partnerships with the frontline fundraisers. Assigning researchers to a fundraiser or a group of fundraisers, or to corresponding geographical areas, is an effective way to foster com-

### EXHIBIT 3.2. PRSPCT-L.

Description: PRSPCT-L (pronounced "prospect el") is an electronic mail list provided as a forum for discussion of prospect research issues. More generally, PRSPCT-L is a collection of individuals' INTERNET e-mail addresses that allows subscribers to instantaneously (well practically) send and receive messages between hundreds of their colleagues. The electronic nature allows discussions to take place in "real time" and thus serves as an important conduit of information in the Prospect Research field. Joseph Boeke (joseph.boeke@marquette.edu) founded the list at the University of California, Irvine, in 1992. From 1995–1999, Bucknell University hosted the list.

Post message: PRSPCT-L@yahoogroups.com
Subscribe:      PRSPCT-L-subscribe@yahoogroups.com
Unsubscribe:  PRSPCT-L-unsubscribe@yahoogroups.com
List owner:     PRSPCT-L-owner@yahoogroups.com

munication and create partnerships. The level of trust and cooperation created in this situation promotes a high level of information sharing and heightens the integrity and quality of the data compiled on a prospect, allowing for a fine-tuned, high-quality, and effective strategy for the continuous lifetime involvement of the prospect. Whatever the structure of the research office, the goal is to create an atmosphere of teamwork between researchers and fundraisers.

The researcher should also be involved in meeting with new development staff to inform them of the services offered by research. If possible, periodic discussions of the role and responsibility of research at full staff meetings can be very beneficial. See examples of orientation procedures from various organizations in Resource 6.

In 1998, APRA published a general statement for its members defining the strategic role of research in the development process, affirming that the role of research is essential at each stage of the development process: identification, verification, cultivation, solicitation, and stewardship (see APRA's "Strategic Role of Research in the Development Process" at www.APRAhome.org).

This statement provides an excellent guideline for moving the profile of the department to a higher level of visibility within the development program of any institution. Individual researchers are also encouraged to strive for a high level of professionalism, not only in the field of prospect research but as development professionals.

## Establishing a Vision, a Mission, Goals, and Procedures

It is advisable to establish the vision, mission, and goals of the research program as it relates to the organization as a whole. A large shop might accomplish this by having a retreat involving the whole staff to work together as a team to develop the long-term vision and ongoing mission of the effort, then determining short- and long-term goals to strive for in order to accomplish the vision and follow the mission. It is also important to share the research vision, mission, and goals with the full development team and senior administrators of the organization. Smaller research shops could strategize with their development team to develop their vision, mission, and goals (see Resource 7 for examples).

It is also critical to have documented procedures. Even though the basic principles of conducting research are fundamentally the same, every nonprofit has its own way of conducting business, developing reports, entering information into the database, and so on. It is vital that written procedures be developed clearly and concisely, not only to maintain continuity and standards but to aid in training new staff. Examples of procedures developed by a couple of research shops are included in Resource 8.

## Ethics in Research

The nature of the work involved in the field of prospect research requires the garnering and analyzing of vast amounts of information. There are different levels of information gathering. Journalists talk with associates and acquaintances of a story subject and research newspaper articles and the like to find the information they need to make their story interesting. Private investigators track down credit histories, telephone records, driving records, and so on to find what their clients want to know. Because the researcher roles are so different, yet are in many ways similar to those of journalists and private investigators, it is vital that the differentiation be clear. This not only protects the integrity of the researcher and the institution but also provides a degree of comfort to donors and prospective donors if they know that the development officers do not intend to intrude into their private matters.

For fundraisers in general, AFP has a Code of Ethical Principles and Standards of Professional Practice that is subscribed to by the fundraising community (see Resource 9).

CASE provides a statement of ethics for advancement professionals in the world of higher education (see Resource 9).

The community of prospect researchers also adheres to ethical guidelines such as those adopted by APRA (see Resource 9). These guidelines generally state:

> Association of Professional Researchers for Advancement (APRA) members shall support and further the individual's fundamental right to privacy and protect the confidential information of their institutions. APRA members are committed to the ethical collection and use of information. Members shall follow all applicable federal, state, and local laws, as well as institutional policies, governing the collection, use, maintenance, and dissemination of information in the pursuit of the missions of their institutions. APRA members shall respect all people and organizations.

It is highly recommended that individual nonprofits, regardless of size, develop an internal ethics policy. The ethics statement issued by APRA is a general, one-size-fits-all policy; however, each nonprofit is different and the expectations of boards, volunteers, donors, management, and fundraisers are different. It is up to individual nonprofits to establish ethical guidelines that generally follow those set out by APRA, CASE, and AFP but are fine-tuned to the needs and expectations of each institution, then communicate those standards. It is also critical for any ethics policy to be reviewed by the nonprofit organization's legal counsel prior to adoption. Legal as well as ethical standards must be addressed.

# CHAPTER FOUR

# CONDUCTING PROSPECT RESEARCH

This chapter is devoted to the serious research practitioner. It contains a detailed look at the techniques and resources available for conducting in-depth research on individuals, foundations, and corporations. Although various sources of information and services are cited throughout the chapter, a more complete directory of vendors can be found in Resource 10.

Prospect research focuses on three broad categories of prospects: individuals, corporations, and foundations. It can be done at the initiative of the researcher (proactive) or at the request of a board member, staff member, key volunteer, or another person appropriately associated with the fundraising program of the nonprofit (reactive). Traditionally, research has been done on domestic prospects. Today, however, there is a growing interest in international prospects, too. The world is becoming a true global village as a result of the Internet and of Americans working and living around the world. More international and multinational companies are being created, and more nonprofit organizations are focusing on international priorities and missions—a movement adding a new dimension to many research operations.

## Proactive Research

With the world of nonprofit fundraising becoming more competitive every day, proactive research has become more important than ever. Proactive research allows an organization to discover prospects and constituents who may have otherwise remained unknown to the institution. Methods for conducting proactive research are many and varied and are discussed in the sections to follow.

## Database Screening

One excellent way of identifying new prospects is to engage a vendor to provide electronic screening of an existing database. Although electronic screening is not new, such services have become more sophisticated with the use of computer-based methods. According to Barth (1998), screening companies often use a combination of tools to provide data. One such tool is geodemographic screening, that is, matching your constituents against the characteristics of their neighborhoods and against models of consumer behavior in order to rate their probable interests, lifestyles, and philanthropic giving trends. Recognized companies that provide geodemographic screening include Grenzebach Glier, Marts & Lundy, and Econometrics.

## Asset Screening

Another tool is asset screening, which compares publicly reported stock holdings and property ownership, as well as private company ownership, to the names in your database. Companies that provide this sort of data include Thomson Financial Wealth Indication (formerly CDA/Investnet), Prospect Identification Network (PIN), and Major Gifts Identification/Consulting (MaGIC), owned by Alexander Haas Martin and Partners.

Lifestyle clustering assigns households to socioeconomic categories. Companies that fall into this category include Experian and Claritas.

A more comprehensive list of companies that provide this type of service, as well as other companies that provide many and varied services to the nonprofit sector, can be found in Resource 10. The information in this resource is selected from the CASE Educational Partners listing and reprinted with permission from CASE. Contact information for these vendors is included for convenience.

Regardless of the type of demographic service you use, the data should enhance, not replace, your own. Because screenings like these often increase staff workloads when they're asked to validate or negate the ratings for particular prospects, it is a good idea, before contracting with a screening vendor, to ask some questions: What is the purpose of our using this service? What do we want to achieve? How will the results be processed? How much data can we process internally?

Once research is completed, the development team (fundraisers, researchers, and others, including key volunteers) should review the results to determine whether all the needed information is there and whether the prospect belongs in the prospect pool. Prospects who do not belong should be deleted from the list early in the review process, and these names should be given to the annual giving program.

## Financial Rating

The next step is an in-house financial rating of the prospects. This rating includes prospects' *potential* to give (what they would give if the institution were their number one philanthropic cause and they wanted to make the biggest gift of their lives) and a *probable* gift size (the gift they could pledge over the next eighteen months, without much solicitation, and that would be payable over the next three to five years).

Once the potential and probable gift sizes have been determined, it is time to evolve a strategy. Look at the nature of the prospect's asset base. Is it liquid? Is it in stock? Define how the institution wants the prospect to give. Are there tax considerations? What are the prospect's possible interests in the institution, and how are those interests tied in to their priorities? Who is the best person to make the first contact, and who is the best to make the solicitation? Determine the next move: whether to get more information, visit the prospect, invite the prospect to attend some function, and so on.

## Peer Screening

Susan Ruderman (2000), vice president of Veritas Information Services, explains that peer screening is a system using volunteers to indicate what information (financial and biographical) they have about prospects.

During any rating and screening session conducted by or with volunteer evaluators, the sole criterion should be what a donor can do, given his or her personal circumstances. Staff members should not participate in this evaluation other than to explain the purpose of the session, keep the session moving, and clarify and answer questions about form and procedure.

Four rating session procedures are commonly used:

1. In *group discussion*, evaluators engage in roundtable discussion until they agree on a rating. A group leader (volunteer, nonstaff) should conduct this session. A professional staff member should be present to record observations but should make no comments that could influence the ratings. This is the best method of evaluation, but its success depends on the group leader's ability to initiate discussion and on the group's willingness to participate openly and forthrightly, as well as on the evaluators' ability to make informed ratings.

2. In *group or individual ratings,* each member of the group is given a rating book and works individually, without discussion, to rate the prospects and offer appropriate written comments. A professional staff member collects the evaluations at the end of the rating session and tabulates the information after the meeting. The major disadvantage here is the lack of exchange of ideas or information within the group. The advantage is that the confidentiality of this method may lead the evaluators to provide higher evaluations, as well as more pointed and more useful comments. The success of this kind of session often depends on getting someone who is well known and well connected to serve as host or hostess and on the ability of the nonprofit to provide lists customized to the raters' interests, circle of peers, acquaintances, and so on.

3. In the *individual* or *one-to-one* approach, a professional staff member meets individually with volunteer evaluators and goes through a prospect list verbally, recording pertinent comments on the evaluation form. The advantage to this process is that the evaluator can feel complete assurance of confidentiality; no one else will hear the comments or know the evaluator's personal feelings about the prospect. The disadvantage is that the validity of the evaluation is limited to the extent of the evaluator's knowledge; there are no second or third opinions. Moreover, the evaluator may not know a number of the prospects well enough to rate them, so it will be necessary to hold additional rating sessions with other evaluators.

4. In the *individual* or *solitary* approach, evaluators are given a list of prospects and rating instructions and left on their own. The evaluation book is either picked up or mailed back by a mutually agreed-on date. This procedure should be used only in special circumstances. Its advantage is that it gives the evaluator time to reflect on and consider the ratings and comments; properly used, this procedure generally leads to very thoughtful, thorough evaluations. Its disadvantage is that individuals often put off doing the evaluations and thereby stall the process.

No matter which procedure is used, the evaluations should be done by knowledgeable individuals. Secondhand and hearsay information is of little or no value; speculation is just that. The best evaluators tend to be bankers, lawyers, investment counselors, financial planners, insurance executives, those who are socially prominent, and those actively involved in philanthropy in communities with organized efforts. Evaluation of individual prospects should continue until an adequate database is established. For each prospect, many institutions acquire at least three valuations, preferably all within a fairly narrow range (say, $10,000, $15,000, and $12,000) before assuming that the prospect's rating has been validated. This entire process must be conducted with an appropriate, even high, level of sensitivity for individual confidentiality. Many times those who make the best raters will find themselves evaluating names that present potential or real conflict of interest. In all such cases, the rater must excuse himself or herself from that particular rating.

Ruderman (2000) observes that "regardless of the type of screening you conduct, remember that data is only data. Nothing replaces the personal contact and relationship with a prospect. Capacity, either real or imagined, is no substitute for inclination, although wealth and its identification are obvious prerequisites for a major gift. Screening may, however, help you decide where best to direct limited cultivation resources" (p. 12).

## Reviewing Periodicals

Reviewing newspapers, magazines, and other print media is a beneficial, albeit time-consuming, method of proactive prospect identification. Using this method usually requires familiarity with the names of existing prospects and close proximity to a computer housing your database; you'll need to look up names as they are found to determine whether they are constituents of the organization.

Some reviewing can occur using Internet Web sites that house newspapers and other periodicals. However, experienced researchers feel that much information is missed using this method. For any who are inclined to review via the Internet, though, a few excellent sites for newspapers and periodicals are

- American Journalism Review News Link (ajr.org)
- Factiva (formerly Dow Jones Interactive; factiva.com)
- Folio: The Magazine for Magazine Management (foliomag.com)
- Gebbie Press (gebbieinc.com)
- MagPortal (magportal.com)
- News Directory: Newspapers and Media (newsdirectory.com)

When deciding which publications to review, a researcher should first evaluate the nonprofit's constituency. Are the constituents primarily local, or are they scattered throughout the country? Are the constituents focused in a particular field or business? Once these determinations are made, the appropriate publications can either be purchased or viewed on-line if they are available in that format.

## Using Push Technology

Push technology is a powerful proactive tool that should be standard to every nonprofit organization. Basically, you choose an Internet site (or several sites) that offers this service and establish the parameters for the kind of information sought (keywords). Registration on these sites may be required, but the service is usually free. Once you have determined the keywords you are interested in (name of your institution, name of an individual or corporation, and so on), the site you are using will "push" information containing your keywords to you either via e-mail or within the site itself. Not all information received will be useful, but many new prospects can be found using this technology with little effort beyond the initial setup. Push technology is also beneficial in staying current with the prospects you are already cultivating. A few excellent sites for push technology are

- newsalert.com
- 10kwizard.com
- freedgar.com
- prnewswire.com
- businesswire.com

## Reactive Research

Reactive research is just what the name implies: reacting to a request for information. Even though proactive research is more fun and many times more rewarding when that special prospect is discovered who had previously gone unnoticed, the reality of most research is responding to requests from development staff for information on known prospects.

### Researching Individuals

The fundamentals for conducting research, as noted by The Fund Raising School (1995), are linkage, ability, and interest, otherwise known as the LAI principle.

*Linkage.* How is the prospect connected to your institution? As a board member, graduate, donor, volunteer, parent, service user, member?

To determine linkage, the first place to look is within the institution itself, checking existing files and records for any contact information and examining the database for a record of giving to the institution. Linkages can also be uncovered through relationships with someone else already associated with the institution, such as a board member, volunteer, professor, and so on.

*Ability.* Does the prospect have the ability to make a financial contribution, or does the person's current life circumstance prohibit that?

There are two schools of thought with regard to estimating the net worth of an individual: for and against. Most institutions do not attempt to estimate an individual's net worth, simply because it is impossible to know all the details of a prospect's assets and liabilities unless the prospect tells you. However, some research offices do try to work out formulas to arrive at a ballpark figure from which to assume gift-giving capacity. The University of Virginia, through much trial and error, has set the following formula for estimating a prospect's net worth and giving capacity (see Resource 11):

Total real estate holdings × 3 = estimated net worth
3 percent of estimated net worth = estimated giving capacity

There are several other methods, depending on the quality and quantity of information you have available, that are widely used:

- 1 to 5 percent of net worth
- 20 × level of consistent annual giving
- 10 × largest annual gift
- 10 percent of annual income (2 percent per year for five years)
- 1–4 percent of stock worth $1–$499,999; 5–9 percent of stock worth $500,000–$999,000; 10 percent of stock worth $1 million or more
- Standard formula: 5 × the total of four annual gifts to charities in the community (including your institution)

Millar (1995) warns that "even with a good estimate, net worth alone doesn't tell you and the fundraiser how much a prospect is able (let alone willing) to give" (p. 40). He also cites several formulas for estimating giving ability by determining a prospect's holdings in a *private* company, using the *Fortune* formula if you know the percentage of a company the prospect owns and an estimate of the company's overall market value. The two-part formula is as follows:

25–50 percent of the value of a prospect's holdings
in a company = his or her net worth in that company.
Where the percentage actually falls in the 25–50 percent range depends
on how much equipment and property the company owns.

1.5–5 percent of net worth in the company = giving ability.
The appropriate percentage depends on the
liquidity of holdings in the company.

These are just a few examples of how net worth and giving capacity may be estimated. There is no hard rule except to use great caution any time a decision is made to make these estimations.

A more common approach to determining giving ability is to simply compile the indications of wealth through the use of various databases and references on a prospect's known *public* assets. A few of the favorite sources for this type of information are

- JobSmart Salary Surveys (jobsmart.org/tools/salary/index.htm)
- Forbes Rich Lists (forbes.com)
- Assessor/Appraisal Sites (iaao.org/1234.htm)
- Yahoo! Home Values (realestate.yahoo.com/realestate/homevalues)
- KnowX—Public Records (knowx.com)
- Plane Owners (landings.com)
- Yacht World (yachtworld.com)
- EDGAR (sec.gov/cgi-bin/srch-edgar)
- InsiderTrader (insidertrader.com)
- 10K Wizard (tenkwizard.com)

*Interest.* Does your institution have programs or activities that would interest the prospect to the point of making a financial contribution or becoming involved as a volunteer?

Finding answers to this question and others is the heart of prospect research. For current donors, interest is obvious. Just look at where their money is going into your institution, where they may be spending time volunteering, and what events they attend. However, prospective donors' interests may not be quite so obvious. If a fundraiser has visited with the prospect, check the files for a contact report that may indicate areas of interest based on the conversation during that visit. Searching the local newspapers and business journals may also shed some light on civic and philanthropic activity in the community. Are there indications that the prospect collects art or rare books or supports museums or youth organizations?

A review of local or similar institutions' annual reports, donor lists, and programs can also shed light on a prospect's activities and interests. Any of these indicators will give a good idea about what pulls at the prospect's heartstrings and purse strings.

## Asking Basic Questions

Next are some important questions to ask yourself as you begin researching an individual:

- *What do you currently know about the prospect?* Once a prospect has been identified, the first step is to answer that question. Check the files and the database and have conversations with the development staff to pull together the information that already exists and to determine where the holes are that need to be filled. It is critical that the accurate recording of contacts is done by the fundraiser, noting observations and other information gleaned from personal visits or conversations with the prospect. The best place for this information is in the donor database or other centralized source. If fundraisers in a given institution are slow to report on their contacts, the researcher should schedule time to sit down and debrief with the fundraiser as soon after the contact with the prospect as possible in order to gather this vital information.

• *What do you need to know about the prospect?* After identifying the gaps in information, it is imperative to determine exactly what information is needed. It is not always necessary to find everything on everybody. Be sure to work closely with the fundraiser requesting the information in order to target the quest for information.

• *Why do you need to know?* It is extremely important in the research process to be aware of the big picture. Often, researchers are omitted from strategic discussions and planning and are only brought in to supply information. However, knowing the big picture will allow the researcher to think more strategically and establish a more targeted search, resulting in information pertinent to the need.

• *When do you need to know?* It is imperative that a realistic, reasonable deadline be assigned to all requests. The workload on most researchers is tremendous, and deadlines aid in prioritization. Be sure to always insist on an actual date; never accept ASAP as a deadline.

• *What are the best resources?* It's very difficult to list the best resources, because whatever provides the information needed at the time is the best resource. However, three of the most frequently used resources are in-house information, community and college libraries, and the Internet:

1. *In-house information: files, database, staff.* Don't start using other resources until you've determined what you already have. Using existing information will many times lead you to the resources you need to take advantage of.
2. *Community and university or college libraries.* Computers, the World Wide Web, online resources, and CD-ROMs are romantic research tools in this day and age, and they do help researchers do their jobs more efficiently. However, they may not be providing the whole picture. One of the best resources a researcher can have is the local library and librarian. It may seem old-fashioned, but libraries continue to house some of the best information you can find, and the staff is highly trained and willing to help you accomplish your goals. For a small research shop with a limited budget, the library will be one of the best resources available.
3. *The Internet.* The World Wide Web provides a wealth of free and fee-based information at just the click of a button. Useful sites are discussed later in this chapter; however, see Resource 12 for Sarah McGinley's take on researching

an individual, assuming that little information is available about him or her, using only free Web sites that offer public records or published information. (Sarah is a research analyst at Wright State University.)

The last question you should ask is this: *When do you stop looking?* With the vast amount of data readily available at the push of a button, it is easy to get caught up in an endless cycle of searching. Sometimes researchers have a difficult time stopping the search, especially if there is not much information about the prospect to be found. The information freeway beckons, teasing with the possibility that if the search continues it will eventually yield that one desperately needed piece of information. This is a dangerous trap to fall into and can easily cause the research effort to become counterproductive. It is critical that levels of research be defined within an institution. On the one hand, a brief profile may be defined as needing only address, telephone, and business information verification, thus eliminating the need for extensive searching through various databases. On the other, a request for an in-depth profile may justify time spent searching through various Web sites and funds expended on fee-based services, especially if the prospect is identified as having major gift potential and the information is needed in order to develop an informed strategy for solicitation. Even then, however, a researcher must establish guidelines and use self-discipline in order not to get caught up in an endless cycle of searching and data gathering.

## Sorting and Analyzing Data

Prospect research has become so much more sophisticated over the years that the role of the researcher is becoming more deeply ingrained in the development process than ever. As a result, it is no longer sufficient to simply compile various facts about the prospect. It has become necessary for a researcher to be strategic in his or her thinking and analyze all the information available on a prospect, developing not only a comprehensive profile but putting forth a recommended strategy for involving the prospect in the life of the organization. Many nonprofits still do not involve their researcher in strategy development, but those who do reap many benefits. In order to have a complete, well-prepared strategy, the information gleaned through the research office (paper knowledge) must be paired with that of the fundraiser (personal knowledge). The types of information that should be contained in a strategy include the following:

- Prospect name
- Business title
- Address

- Telephone
- Strategy type (cultivation, solicitation, stewardship)
- Name of appropriate volunteer or other staff
- Expected solicitation date
- Summary of analysis and objectives (action plan)

## Putting the Profile Together

The format of the profile is not as important as the content. Certain standard information should be included in every profile if available:

Name and nickname

Home address (all addresses if the prospect has multiple residences)

Home telephone (for all residences)

Cellphone number(s)

Fax number(s) (home and business)

Pager number

E-mail address (home and business)

Business title, address, and telephone number

Name of secretary or assistant

Date and place of birth

Education (secondary and higher, along with academic major)

Academic awards and achievements

Employment history

Marital status

Spouse's name

Spouse's education

Spouse's business affiliation

Number, names, and ages of children

Family connection to the institution

Family connections to other institutions

Honors and achievements

Clubs and organizations

Political affiliation

Religious affiliation

Personal interests

Estimated net worth

Estimated giving ability

Net salary

Stock holdings

Directorships

Family foundations

Favorite charities

Gift record

Name of attorney

Name of banker

Names of close friends

A good rule of thumb when preparing a profile is to be sure to attribute all information to its sources and to indicate the resources that were consulted when preparing the profile. Include also the name of the preparer, the date the profile was completed, and the person for whom it was completed. This is beneficial information, especially if there are multiple requests for information on the same prospect (see Resource 13).

When distributing profile information throughout an organization, the originator of a request for research will obviously be a recipient. However, it is important to note that when proactive research is prepared, more than one individual may need to receive the information. Knowledge of the nonprofit's hierarchy is key to a research office's ability to adequately distribute important prospect information.

## Researching Corporations and Foundations

Researchers are involved not only in seeking out and compiling information on individuals but in preparing profiles for corporations and foundations. These entities are rich sources of philanthropy and generally not difficult to research. The difficulty lies in determining the likelihood that a company or foundation will give to a particular nonprofit.

Along with information gleaned from reference tools, additional pieces of information should be searched out in order to get a clear picture of an organization's likelihood of giving. Look at obligations to other nonprofit organizations. More important, study current interests and funding trends closely. In determining how much to ask for, think of the organization as also representing sources of other income. Corporations may have five or six channels of potential funding (corporate foundations, matching gift programs, research and development, marketing, advertising, and the discretionary budget of the executive office).

Research on corporate prospects needs to address four vital questions:

1. How financially healthy is the business?
2. What are its current products, and what are its interests in your institution?
3. What existing relationships could be used for moving the prospect to the next step of cultivation or solicitation?
4. How has the corporation supported your institution in the past, and why would it want to give support again?

From the standpoint of corporate and foundation relations, it is equally important to learn something about company products, research and development, and future marketing plans. An annual report can supply some of this information. Other possible sources are the institution's office of sponsored research (if it has one), which may be aware of research and development interests within the corporation. Philanthropic publications such as *Taft Giving Watch* and *Philanthropic Digest* list corporate contributions, which can be reviewed for trends in grants for research and development. In addition, several databases list the awards of government contracts. Finally, newspapers and journals can provide a glimpse of the future. Articles in such magazines as *Fortune* and *Forbes* may provide a vision of the direction in which the corporate prospect is moving. Local newspapers are an equally valuable resource.

Working with the appropriate in-house staff, the researcher needs to expand on the basic questions about relationships with corporate prospects. If yours is an educational institution, for instance, how many alumni are employed by the corporation? Do any members of your institution's staff serve on the corporation's advisory board or science advisory panel? Does the corporation in any way rely on your institution for services? What about funding history? Has funding come from the corporation or from the corporate foundation? Enlightened corporate self-interest is the basis for these relationships, so it is important to understand these components in planning an approach. Except for a few national corporations and corporate foundations, as well as the local corporate community, this category of prospects has become more specialized in recent years. Most do not give outside the areas where they have plants, programs, or people. Very often quid pro quo considerations (stockholder concerns, for example) determine the granting policies of national corporations.

Corporations tend to lend their financial support in areas where they have plant operations, particularly headquarters. Corporations will also consider support if they have subsidiaries in the service area of an institution. Besides major corporations, other sources for support include local independent businesses, vendors, and businesses that are owned by or that employ people who are affiliated with the institution, whatever their geographical locations. In dealing with any prospect, but especially a corporate or foundation prospect, an institution should never extend its boundaries beyond the circle represented by its volunteer leaders. This is a cardinal rule but one that is often broken.

## Researching Public Companies

Researching public companies has never been easier, thanks to the Internet. Most public companies have their own Web site. Even better, all of the tax forms that public companies are required to file by the Securities and Exchange Commission (SEC) are virtually free and easily accessible through a Web site known as EDGAR (sec.gov/cgi-bin/srch-edgar). The information contained in these SEC documents is invaluable in that it gives a much truer picture of a company's status than the annual reports published by the companies for the general public. The trick, however, is to gain an understanding of the information contained in these documents. In Resource 14, there are critical definitions to note when attempting to sort through the complex myriad of corporate information available (provided by David Lawson, founder and president, Prospect Information Network, personal communication, April 1998). These do not represent all the filings that are available, rather those of most interest to prospect researchers. It is critical to have an understanding of the information available in these filings and how it can be used for prospect research. A comprehensive list of corporate filings required by the SEC and what is contained in them can be found in Resource 15.

It is highly recommended that researchers seek some sort of training to aid in the understanding of financial statements. The wealth of information available on public corporations and individual prospects is invaluable. One good source to turn to in independent study is provided by International Business Machines (IBM). It has published on the Web a "Guide to Understanding Financials" (ibm.com/investor/financialguide). Many of the tools needed to understand complex financial statements can be found in this on-line guide. Other sources of training include consulting with a stockbroker or financial analyst or the business schools of colleges or universities; Dun & Bradstreet periodically offers workshops in understanding financial statements.

Although the information available through the SEC on public companies is rich in detail, it's not the only place where good prospect research can be done. There are many excellent books, CD-ROMs, and on-line resources available to aid in corporate research. A few favorites can be found in Resource 16.

As with conducting research on individuals, at some point a researcher needs to make the decision to stop searching and start analyzing the data and to compile it into a useful report.

The following basic information should be gathered on each corporate prospect:

- Full name and correct address
- Corporate assets
- Type of business
- Names of corporate officers and directors
- Names of officers of any existing corporate foundation
- The corporation's sales volume
- The corporation's previous giving record
- The corporation's decision-making process about charitable giving
- The corporation's gifts to other institutions (more difficult to determine if there is no corporate foundation)
- The corporation's connections with the institution (if yours is an educational institution, names of alumni employed by the corporation; if a hospital, names of past patients the corporation employs; and so forth)
- History of the corporation's dealings with your institution
- The corporation's local subsidiaries and the names of their officers
- Information about the corporate gift committee (names, connections, and kindred interests)

## Researching Foundations

The best foundation prospects for an institution are those nearby or those stating an interest in your geographical area; the likelihood of investment is much greater when the foundation is in the institution's local area, state, or region. A foundation is also more likely to support an institution if its philosophy is similar to that of the institution. It is important that there be a match between the organization's interests and the foundation's. If individuals associated with the foundation are directly or indirectly affiliated with the institution, and especially if they are on the institution's board, the chances are enhanced that it will receive favorable consideration. Any review of foundations requires a systematic study of all sources to locate those foundations that might have matching interests.

Remember to talk to members of the institutional board and others close to the institution to see whether they can help establish links with the foundation. It is extremely important that the effort to secure gifts from foundations be focused on foundations most likely to support the institution. In many instances, the great majority of foundations will not be interested in a particular program, and it makes no sense to pursue those.

Foundations are the easiest of the types of prospects to research in that they usually have specific funding interests that are known or that can be determined easily by potential applicants. For the most part, these interests are dictated by policy and by the foundation's granting history. The information sought about a foundation is basically the same type of information as that sought about a corporation and will include the following elements:

- The full, correct name of the foundation
- The foundation's street address and telephone number, as well as a separate application address, if applicable
- Names of the officers or directors of the foundation and their professional connections
- A brief historical sketch of the foundation (when it was created, by whom, and for what purpose)
- The foundation's current assets
- Amount of the foundation's recent grants by year and individual recipient
- The foundation's decision-making process
- The foundation's pattern of giving (to what kinds of institutions and for what programs, with specific examples)
- Your institution's best contact with the foundation (the person to visit or send a proposal to)
- The foundation's connections with your institution
- History of your institution's contacts with the foundation
- The foundation's giving guidelines and statements of interest published by the foundation
- The foundation's most recent annual report

In addition, it's important to obtain a copy of a recent PF 990 tax form for the foundation, with a listing of income and grants made. Copies of this form are available through the Associates Program of The Foundation Center, a fee-based service through which materials can be requested via e-mail, fax, or the U.S. Postal Service. Recently, many PF 990s have become available via the Guidestar Web site and are free (guidestar.org). PF 990s are also available through the IRS.

In addition to the resources available through The Foundation Center, there exist several other excellent sources of information. Four of the most widely used comprehensive references are

Prospector's Choice, Taft, CD-ROM

*FC Search,* The Foundation Center, CD-ROM

*The Foundation Directory,* The Foundation Center

*Guidestar* (guidestar.org)

These, along with the Associates Program of The Foundation Center, provide information about foundations' financial assets, interests, giving focus, grants to other institutions, and requirements for submitting proposals. One valuable component of these references is their indexing of information according to a foundation's giving interests.

# Project-Oriented Research

Many times researchers are called upon to assist fundraising staff in developing a list of potential donors to a particular project or program. This can be fairly time consuming if not approached correctly. The researcher can simplify the task by having a thorough conversation with the requestor. Information that is necessary in order to provide the best results possible includes

- A copy of the business plan or program description.
- Consensus between requestor and researcher regarding the appropriate keywords for the project. A list of typical keywords is found in Resource 17.
- Amount of funding the requestor is seeking.
- Other funding already obtained (amount and funder).

Once a researcher is equipped with this information, several databases are available that allow for keyword searching for funding opportunities. A few favorite databases are

- Prospector's Choice, published by Taft: A CD-ROM product that gives key financial information on foundations and corporate giving programs, including detailed funder profiles covering nearly ten thousand foundations and corporate giving programs. It provides information on up to fifty grants per profile, as well as total giving figures and helpful directions for making contacts and completing applications. Grant analysis is also provided, as well as each organization's application requirements.
- FC Search—The Foundation Center's database on CD-ROM, published by The Foundation Center: Provides access to The Foundation Center's exclusive

database of foundation and corporate grantmakers, as well as their associated grants. FC Search includes data found in *The Foundation Directory* (Parts 1 and 2), *The Foundation Directory Supplement,* the *Guide to U.S. Foundations, Their Trustees, Officers, and Donors,* the *National Directory of Corporate Giving,* and *The Foundation Grants Index.* FC Search covers every known U.S. grantmaker—over fifty-three thousand foundations and corporate givers, and hundreds of grantmaking charities.

• Sponsored Programs Information Network (SPIN), published by InfoEd International: A database self-described as "the number one worldwide database including government, private, and international funding opportunities. Allows for searches on keywords, sponsors, geographic restrictions, deadline dates, and much more."

• COS Funding Opportunities, published by Community of Science: Self-described as the most comprehensive source of funding information on the Web; COS Funding Opportunities publishes more than fourteen thousand sources of funding. International in terms of both content and audience, it alerts individual researchers and research administrators to available grants from public and private-sector sources around the world, providing them with the timely, relevant, and easy-to-find information they need to secure the funding that is so vital to their work. Updated daily, COS Funding Opportunities offers all users within an Internet domain immediate access to accurate information, freeing them to focus on their primary activity: conducting research. COS Funding Opportunities identifies funding information as it relates to research, collaborative activities, travel, curriculum development, conferences, fellowships, postdoctoral positions, equipment acquisition, and operating or capital expenses. The sources of these awards vary but include federal and regional governments, foundations, professional societies, associations, or corporations.

## International Research

More frequently, many researchers dabble in international research, usually responding to a request for this sort of information when it arises, but have not yet created a focused effort for this market. International research is, obviously, much more difficult to conduct, but it's not impossible. In the global marketplace today, many Americans are living and working in countries around the world. The key is to be familiar with the resources available for international research.

One thing to be aware of is that not all prospects living in other countries are non-U.S. citizens. And the United States is no longer number one in the nonprofit world. Several Western European nations and Israel now have a larger nonprofit sector, measured as a share of total employment. According to Frost (2000), the challenges in accessing this international component are

- International prospects are not necessarily listed in many of the resources commonly used in research, or they are difficult (and time consuming) to find.
- More resources and more time require more investment, both in dollars and institutional focus.
- Prospecting is often cold because asking is less frequent and giving is more sparse.
- Information on people outside the United States is often not public, is public but undisclosed, or is available only in the original language.
- There are no proven means of electronic screening of non-U.S. constituencies.
- Conventional, labor-intensive screenings are still the most commonly used methods of international prospecting.

A viable solution to the problem of international research is to establish a component within the research program that focuses entirely on international prospecting and research. Frost's suggestions for the international research component are

- Making regional assignments (it's critical that international researchers know the customs, currency, and political atmosphere of the country in which they are conducting research)
- Using specially designed methodology
- Contributing to the process
- Seeking counsel
- Setting realistic expectations
- Budgeting for success
- Communicating the effort at large

Further, in conducting international research, similar to research in North America, it is important to determine which information is most important: financial capacity, number of children of college age, where prospects go to school, how "international" they are, what kind of philanthropy, if any, they are involved in. It is also important to be aware of certain financial considerations when rating international prospects: wealth and liquidity, tax implications (deductibility at home and transnational deductibility), and currency exchange rates.

Finally, resources are available to assist in the process of international research. A few favorite sources of international information are

Internet Prospector (Internet-prospector.org)

AJR Newslink (ajr.newslink.org/news.html)

*International Fund Raising for Not-for-Profits: A Country by Country Profile* (Thomas Harris, ed., New York: Wiley, 1999)

Country Studies Pages (lcweb2.loc.gov/frd/cs/cshome.html)

CULTURGRAMS, David M. Kennedy Publications, Brigham Young University, Provo, Utah

In addition to conducting research on the foreign prospect, it is critical for the researcher to prepare a profile of the country in which the prospect lives. Whether a fundraiser is traveling to the country or the prospect is visiting your organization, it is imperative to be aware of the cultural differences that exist and the social protocol that must be extended. Many excellent resources are available that provide this type of information, in addition to those mentioned. A few to make note of are

*Doing Business Internationally: The Resource for Business and Social Etiquette,* Training Management Corporation (available through Amazon.com; ISBN: 1-8823-9016-4)

*Kiss, Bow, or Shake Hands: How to Do Business in Sixty Countries,* Adams Media Corp. (available through Amazon.com; ISBN: 1-5585-0444-3)

Many valuable resources have been shared throughout this chapter, but more are available; some are yet to be discovered. See Resource 18 for the Internet bookmarks used by the IU Foundation research staff—a resource that represents a more comprehensive listing of what's available through the Internet; it is by no means all-inclusive. The key is to explore the Web regularly for new and updated sites that will aid in the research process.

As stated in Chapter Three, prospect research has become a profession of choice for many. The act of seeking and discovering information can be both fun and fulfilling. Prospect research provides fundraisers with tools that are key in the development process as a whole, and deep satisfaction is derived by all involved when the fundraising circle is completed upon the receipt of a gift from a major prospect. As far as research has come in the last quarter century, today's easy access to data made possible by technology has virtually leveled the playing field for most nonprofits, no matter how small or large.

# CHAPTER FIVE

# MANAGING PROSPECTS SYSTEMATICALLY

Obtaining gifts, especially large ones, is a matter of hard work, imagination, and good taste. Although major gifts can occasionally come from unexpected sources, many cultivation contacts by staff and volunteers are usually necessary to bring prospects to the point of significant generosity. Therefore the pursuit of the extraordinary gift should be a well-planned, properly funded, adequately staffed part of every development effort.

This chapter discusses the creation and maintenance of a prospect management program and the proper approach to the cultivation and solicitation of gifts; it concludes with a discussion of how to measure the effectiveness and productivity of a major gifts officer seeking such gifts.

## Goal and Purpose of a Prospect Management Program

Prospect management, as a part of the effort to obtain large gifts, is a systematic approach to identifying and tracking major gift prospects. Prospect management systems almost always focus on a nonprofit's top prospects and donors and are more closely tied to the major and planned gifts programs than to the annual fund. This is for two primary reasons. First, prospects for smaller gifts and annual donors either don't require management yet, or the annual giving program is organized in such a structured fashion that it manages annual donors inherently. Second, managing prospects systematically is labor-intensive. To be cost-effective, the effort needs to focus on the top prospects and donors so that the value of systematic monitoring and management can be measured and its virtues understood.

Prospect management systems, whether they use large and complex databases, straightforward word processing, or manual systems, all rely on and encourage careful planning and follow-through. By recording vital information on major gift candidates and donors, an organization may know at any given time who its best prospects are and what the quality of its own relations with them are.

The goal of a prospect management program should be to maximize support for your organization. The program should effectively manage cultivation, solicitation, and stewardship activities with individuals, corporations, and foundations, as well as other prospects that have been determined to have the interest and capability of making a major gift. According to Baxter (1987), "These top-tier prospects are generally a small percentage of an institution's database, but they account for the greatest proportion of gifts. Whether the threshold for a major gift at an institution is $500 or $50,000, the prospects with the potential to give that or a greater amount are candidates for prospect management."

A well-designed and maintained prospect management program can improve major gift fundraising and help an organization measure the effectiveness of its development efforts. It can provide details about a single prospect, select all prospects with a common trait, or give an overall view of a program's progress.

A management program fulfills its mission in three ways: (1) by creating and maintaining a database that includes major gift prospects, the staff and volunteers assigned to those prospects, documentation of significant contacts and strategic, planned next steps or "moves" with the prospects, and background research information; (2) by regularly reviewing requests for assignment and other issues; and (3) by regularly conducting prospect review sessions to ensure the effective and coordinated management of top-level prospects.

A program functions at its optimum level when development staff members contribute in the following areas of communication and documentation. Development staff are assigned to a prospect; they use a team approach and proactively share strategy plans, activity reports, and information with each other. Development staff document significant contacts and "moves" in the database and share that information with all appropriate staff.

## Setting Up a Program

There are many different ways to set up a prospect management program. Samples of protocols, processes, and reports can be found in Resource 19.

## Hardware and Software Considerations

When planning for a prospect management program, an organization should consider its information needs, the size of its file, and its hardware and software capabilities. If the system is already in place—both computer (hardware) and programs (software)—this will have an effect on the data and the number of records that can be tracked. Ideally, the first two considerations—needs and size—should determine the kind of equipment selected. According to Miller and Strauss in *Improving Fundraising with Technology* (1996), "The chosen system should include networked PCs to allow development officers and researchers to transfer documents between terminals, as well as allow multiple access to the main database" (p. 88).

Some of the more traditional systems are described by Hunsaker (1998): "Organizations have three main options when they select a system: homegrown systems, comprehensive systems, and off-the-shelf modules" (p. 88). According to Hunsaker, the first option is traditionally for smaller shops, which generally are less complex, have limited budgets, and have few or no staff. Working with a PC-based word processor, spreadsheet, and database allows for tracking and maintaining their prospect pools.

The next option is the comprehensive system; several vendors provide these types of systems, which have modules and screens available for volumes of data to be stored, manipulated, and reported. They typically serve larger, more complex organizations. The modules in these systems range from the basic biographical information to major gift prospecting to very sophisticated gift processing, which is becoming more critical due to tightened reporting standards. Most comprehensive systems allow for the information systems staff to build interfaces to other applications to further tailor information to the user's needs.

Finally, a variety of off-the-shelf modules are available. Many larger organizations use these as stand-alone prospect management and tracking systems that can interface with a homegrown or comprehensive system. A few of the benefits of this system are the ability to enter prospect call reports and reminders, track wealth indicators, and document next steps. However, these systems do not always provide enough flexibility to make site-specific implementations.

In some situations, buying a system may not be the best approach to take. Outsourcing to application service providers (ASPs), as discussed in Chapter Two, could be an attractive option for organizations with limited budgets, staff, or technology expertise.

## Questions to Consider

According to Miller and Strauss (1996) in *Improving Fundraising with Technology,* you should select a system that meets your needs today, as well as those needed to support the vision of technology within your organization. Choosing a homegrown system may not allow for this type of growth and subsequent technology needs; a comprehensive or possibly a stand-alone system may be the best tool for prospect management.

Here are some questions you should be asking as you weigh your options:

How large a development staff will you have?

Will your constituency grow modestly (5 percent to 10 percent per year) or are you looking for exponential growth over the next five years?

How many volunteers will you be managing?

How many prospects will you be managing?

When will your next capital campaign begin?

Do you need to be networked to the finance office? The admissions office? The alumni/ae office? The membership department?

Will you need to manage major special events such as gala benefits or class reunions?

Do you need special software for publications design [p. 89]?

## Data Elements to Consider

According to Baxter (1987), the following list of possible data elements is a guide in setting up a prospect management system. Please note that these are suggestions rather than hard-and-fast requirements because each organization has unique characteristics that influence system design.

| Data Element | Comments |
| --- | --- |
| Identification | If possible, should be consistent with master file ID number. |
| Name | Prefix (title), last, first, middle, suffix. |
| Address, telephone | Can allow for home, business, second home, and so on, but must keep in sync with master file. |
| Title | Business or professional position. |
| Salutation | Needed where prospect management system has word processing capabilities. |
| Geographical region | Useful for institutions with constituents spread out over a large area, where location determines staff assignment, and for planning cultivation or solicitation trips and visits. |

| | |
|---|---|
| Source | Indicates type of prospect (alumnus, trustee, parent, corporation, foundation, and so on). |
| Wealth code | For those institutions whose lists have been screened by an outside vendor. |
| Class or degree | For educational institutions. |
| Gift rating | Prospect's capacity to give: usually a range of figures. |
| Interest rating | Prospect's involvement with the institution (readiness for solicitation). |
| Status | Where prospect is in solicitation cycle (cultivation, solicitation, stewardship, and so on). |
| Giving areas | The project, campaign, or type of gift the prospect is targeted for or given clearance for (can be multiple occurrences). |
| Staff | Staff member assigned to manage the prospect. |
| Volunteer | Nonstaff volunteer assigned to prospect. |
| Moves | Contact between institution and prospect, generally a date and brief description of the contact. Systems can be designed to accommodate numerous entries, to record last contact and next move, or to have comment fields that summarize past activity and future plans. |
| Solicitation | Request date, amount, purpose, solicitor (if other than volunteer); response date, amount, purpose. |
| Connections | Other ties to institution: spouse, family, classmates, business associates, and so on. |
| Identifiers | Institutional codes that identify special populations (sometimes called list or select codes). |
| Tickler | Date for staff or volunteer to conduct follow-up. |
| Comments | Free-form text to flag special circumstances or provide additional information. |

Whatever the choice of data elements and the system's configuration might be, fields should be set up to allow for swift and easy information searches.

The prospect management system is an integral part of a comprehensive approach to pursuing the extraordinary gift. It should be designed to ensure that an organization's best prospects are identified, cultivated, and solicited according to a master plan and that all activities are monitored. Used conscientiously, it can be of measurable help to those who have responsibility for the success of major campaigns.

## Deciding Who Will Manage

The program should have approval and ultimate authority with the highest development staff, whether it is the chief executive officer, chief development officer, or top major gifts officer. It is advised that the individuals responsible for the operations of this program work closely with the research and development teams, as well as with their information systems team.

## Determining Clearance Levels

Clearance levels, or stages, can be defined to best suit your organization's needs. At every stage, there needs to be some documented strategy for moving the prospect from level to level. A good strategy plan will contain a long-term goal to be achieved with the prospect, including specific steps to be taken toward that goal. The strategy plan should also be designed to lead to a major gift solicitation and contain an expected solicitation date. In order to keep activity progressing smoothly, there should be time limits for each assignment in the program.

Examples of clearance levels are (1) identification, (2) research, (3) qualification, (4) cultivation, (5) solicitation, (6) stewardship, and (7) donor. These will be discussed in detail in the sections to follow.

*Identification.* Use this level when you suspect someone might be willing to support your organization, but no contact has been made to confirm or deny your suspicion. Included in this category might be prospects who were identified through a screening process (see Chapter Four for screening information). The use of this code might help development officers prioritize their visits, especially if they are in a campaign and need to see several prospects in a short period of time. Another use of this code might be when a volunteer or someone else has suggested a name and you have no prior history with the prospect. A person in the identification stage should be reviewed every six months, with no extensions longer than one year from the assignment date. After a year, the identification code should be moved to research or qualification—or removed altogether.

*Research.* Often after rating or screening sessions or volunteer meetings, more information—research—is needed. This code might be used to set aside prospects when (1) information needs to be clarified or verified, (2) prospects' giving level needs to be ascertained, or (3) their status with others needs to be reviewed. This research can be done either in the research department or in the field by having a fundraiser make a personal call or visit. Research-coded prospects should be reviewed at least yearly.

*Qualification.* Once a prospect has been identified, there is a period of time when visits are made to determine the prospect's interests, capacity to give, and propensity to give, as well as the timing of that person's gifts and those of others who may also have an interest in providing support. If after a visit the individual does not seem to be a prospect, he or she should be removed from the prospect management system; a contact report should be filed that shows why this individual has been removed as a major prospect.

*Cultivation.* Prospects in cultivation should be reviewed at least annually. If no activity has been documented, the prospect should be moved into research or qualification stages or released from the prospect management program.

*Solicitation.* After you have gathered all this information, it is time to solicit the prospect. In your information-gathering stage of cultivation, it is important to determine who the most effective solicitor might be, whether that is the highest development officer or major gifts officer or a volunteer who has been working with this prospect.

Whenever you move into solicitation mode, a new request for assignment should be filed. When a prospect is moved into solicitation, everyone in the development office should be aware of that in order to keep the process moving and to eliminate actions or activities that are at cross-purposes with the impending solicitations. Solicitation status should be assigned for no more than six months before reviewing the validity of this clearance level.

*Stewardship.* You have been successful in getting the gift. Now the true test of development comes with how well the gift is stewarded (see Chapters Six and Seven for a fuller discussion). Again, a stewardship strategy needs to be developed for the most generous donors, as well as for those who are closest to your organization or have the potential to become either. An example of a stewardship strategy plan can be found in Exhibit 5.1.

Prospects in stewardship should be reviewed at least annually. There should be at least one meaningful contact per year for prospects in this stage.

*Donor.* This is another possible level that can be used for regular annual fund donors who need attention but do not necessarily qualify for the attention that major gift prospects receive. However, they need good stewardship and should possibly be moved to the identification stage for development officer prioritization. *Donor* could also stand for those who have completed a gift within a certain time period. This information would be helpful when the development team pulls together invitation lists, has a call from this donor, or related matters occur.

## EXHIBIT 5.1. SAMPLE STEWARDSHIP STRATEGY.

### INDIVIDUAL STRATEGY PLAN©

| | |
|---|---|
| *Prospect Name(s):* | *Rating:* |
| *Title:* | *Capacity to Give:* |
| *Business:* | *Primary Manager:* |
| *Address:* | *Co-managers:* |
| | |
| *Telephone Number:* | *Volunteer:* |
| *Degree(s)/year(s):* | *Prospect for:*     SPEA |

### INDIVIDUAL PLAN

*Summary of Analysis and Objectives:*

Goal: A multi-million dollar gift to SPEA, either individually or through company foundation, endowing minority student and faculty support.

Strategy: Continue to build relationships with both _____ and her spouse, _____ through visits. Invite to campus in fall '00. Most recent visit (7-14-00) led to the couple's first discussion about the possibility of individual and/or corporate gift(s) to the School. More cultivation is needed before solicitation to determine their specific areas of interest, but the initial feeling is in the area of minority support for students and faculty.

*Expected Solicitation Date:*   Spring 2001      Today's Date:   20-Jul-00

7/20/00

# Managing the Program

Many times, especially in larger organizations, several development officers are interested in the same prospect for different reasons. In order to maximize the organization's potential with this prospect, a primary manager should be assigned.

## Role of a Primary Manager

The manager's role can be defined as (1) encouraging complete and timely communication and acting as a central source of information among coassigned staff working with the same prospect; (2) coordinating activity among coassigned staff (for example, to avoid two people calling on the prospect in the same week); (3) collaborating with coassigned staff to develop a strategy that would culminate in a maximum gift from the prospect that is in keeping with his or her wishes and interests; and (4) developing and maintaining timely and accurate records on their prospects and actively encouraging coassigned staff to do the same.

## How to Request Assignment

When a development officer asks for assignment as the primary manager of a prospect, a strategy plan should accompany this request. The strategy plan should include evidence that the development officer has had regular communications with the prospect, as well as with other development officers who also have an interest in this prospect. It is important to include all interested development officers in the design of a strategy because they may all have valuable information that would result in a successful cultivation or solicitation. An example of a sample strategy, as well as a request for assignment, can be found in Exhibits 5.1 and 5.2.

Ultimate responsibility for decisions made regarding this assignment and the clearance levels may rest with a prospect assignment committee. This is usually a small group, but it should be a comprehensively representative group reflecting the composition and nature of the organization's development effort. The primary manager, as well as coassigned staff, acts in accordance with the decisions of this committee.

## Use of a Prospect Assignment Committee

The use of a committee will ensure that a donor's interests are respected and that existing relationships are honored. It encourages accountability for assignments. To work, it requires buy-in and involvement from top management. An assignment committee should be made up of a representative from the research team, donor relations and stewardship staff, major gifts staff, and other development officers who might have a relationship with the prospect. The chair of the committee should provide an agenda of prospects to be reviewed, effectively seek input from all involved at the committee meeting, and provide results to the committee as well as to the staff member requesting assignment. The committee may give approval, denial, or pending status to a request. If the request has been denied or is pending, the reasons for that should be documented along with proposed next actions.

## Planning for Essential Reports

When establishing a system, an organization should plan for the kinds of routine reports needed, as well as for the data it will need to call up at any given moment. Plan for growth, and, if possible, select a system that is flexible enough to allow for modifications and newly identified information needs.

## EXHIBIT 5.2. REQUEST FOR ASSIGNMENT.

REASON FOR REQUEST

____ Identification—(Fill out A only)

| ____ Cultivation* | ____ Solicitation* | ____ Stewardship* |
|---|---|---|
| (Fill out A&B) | (Fill out A,B,&C) | (Fill out A) |
| *Attach strategy plan | *Attach strategy plan | *Attach strategy plan |

DATE OF MOST RECENT VISIT: _____

ARE YOU REQUESTING TO BE THE PRIMARY MANAGER?:   yes ____   no ____

Requested by: _____     Date: _____

College/Dept./Program: _____     Joint Clearance with

_____

(College/Dept./Program)

A. PROSPECT INFORMATION

Prospect ID# _____     Spouse ID# _____

Name _____     Spouse Name _____

Degree/College _____     Degree/College _____

Address (H/B) _____

B. FUNDING OBJECTIVE

Recipient unit/department/special program _____

| OPERATING | ENDOWMENT |
|---|---|
| ____ (bo) bricks/mortar | ____ (be) bricks/mortar |
| ____ (po) professorship | ____ (pe) professorship |
| ____ (fo) fellowship | ____ (fe) fellowship |
| ____ (ro) research | ____ (re) research |
| ____ (eo) equipment | ____ (ee) equipment |
| ____ (so) scholarship | ____ (se) scholarship |
| ____ (smo) seed money | ____ (sme) seed money |
| ____ (spo) special project | ____ (spe) special project |
| ____ (co) chair | ____ (ce) chair |
| ____ (uo) unrestricted | ____ (ue) unrestricted |
| ____ (oo) other (specify) | ____ (oe) other (specify) |
| ____ (mo) miscellaneous (specify) | ____ (me) miscellaneous (specify) |
| _____ | _____ |

C. SOLICITATION AMOUNT   $ _____

4/22/99

[FRONT]

## EXHIBIT 5.2.  REQUEST FOR ASSIGNMENT, Cont'd.

REQUEST FOR PROSPECT ASSIGNMENT

RESULTS

Prospect: _____        Spouse: _____

AFIS id: _____                              AFIS id:  _____

A.  OTHER ASSIGNMENTS

_____

_____

_____

_____


B.  APPROVAL                                                          DATE

____cleared   ____denied   ____pending                _____

C.  COMMENTS: _____

_____

_____

_____


D.  COPIES SENT TO: _____

SIGNATURE: _____
                    Director of Development Services

--------------------------------------------------------------------------------

Points to consider when requesting prospect assignment:

- Identification prospects are assigned to a school or department, rather than being assigned to a specific development officer, as *possible* (suspect) major gift prospects which the school/department will research to confirm.
- Identification prospects will require further clearance by submitting a Request for Prospect Assignment form and a strategy plan before cultivating or soliciting the prospect.
- Primary Manager status can be assigned only for Cultivation, Solicitation, or Stewardship.
- *A strategy plan MUST be attached when requesting cultivation, solicitation or stewardship. If others are assigned to the prospect, evidence of communication must be documented so that strategies are coordinated BEFORE requesting assignment.
- If a request for assignment is not complete, it will be returned with an explanatory note.

4/22/99

[BACK]

The frequency of reports depends on the use and desired outcomes of each. For instance, prospects in cultivation should be reviewed at least annually. If there has been no meaningful contact within that year, the development officer should consider moving the prospect into the research or identification stages until more information is gathered. Generally speaking, there should be at least five meaningful contacts in one year for every prospect in the cultivation stage. According to Panas (in Kelly, 1998), the average cultivation period for a very large gift is about seven years.

For prospects in solicitation, a report should be prepared at least every six months after assignment in order to keep the process moving (see Exhibit 5.3). In the report, the development officer is asked whether to (1) extend the solicitation for another six months, (2) change the level to cultivation or stewardship, or (3) remove the assignment. If no response is received, the prospect should be automatically moved to cultivation.

Successful major gift solicitation results after regular contacts have been made and a positive relationship is established. Nudd (in Kelly, 1998) reports "that a national survey of senior practitioners suggested that an average of nine separate cultivation contacts should take place before a major gift is solicited" (p. 425). Steele and Elder (in Kelly, 1998), who define *cultivation* as "orchestrated involvement," provide the rule of thumb: "The typical major gift requires thirteen contacts over the space of two to three years" (p. 425). Steele and Elder also state: "Donors give if asked to give but do not give if they are not asked. When all is said and done, the number one reason people give is because they are asked" (p. 425). According to Broce (in Kelly, 1998), "The successful fund raiser knows that only when all the earlier steps have been accomplished successfully does solicitation come easily. It is then that the person, foundation, or corporation is meaningfully involved with the organization, understands and appreciates the goals, recognizes their importance, and welcomes the opportunity, when offered, to make [a gift]" (p. 426).

Also helpful is a manager's activity report. This report shows all of the development officers' current assignments, their respective clearance levels, and date assigned. It is helpful to show the most recent contact on this report (see Exhibit 5.4).

Management finds a contact summary report helpful—one that shows the contacts made by each development officer (see Exhibit 5.5). In addition, it lists all the prospects who have been seen in a given period of time.

**Contact Reports.** After every prospect visit, a contact report or trip report should be filed. The more meaningful (as opposed to informational) it is, the more effective the process will be in moving the prospect forward in the cultivation-solicitation cycle. It is vital to keep a record of the prospect's contacts with the organization.

## EXHIBIT 5.3. SAMPLE SOLICITATION EXPIRATION REPORT.

### Solicitation Expiration Report for period 1/1/98–1/31/98

| Staff | Area | Name / Address | TRA | Exp. date |
|---|---|---|---|---|
| _____ | PRIM 46909 | Mr. Gary _____ <br> 5060 _____ Lane <br> _____, IN | S | 01/30/98 |
| _____ | PRIM 48128 | Mr. Larry _____ <br> _____ <br> Winston-Salem, NC | S | 01/30/98 |
| _____ | PRIM 48131 | Mr. Ray _____ <br> _____ <br> Fort Branch, IN 47648 | S | 01/30/98 |
| _____ | PRIM 50314 | Mr. Paul _____ <br> 12057 _____ Drive <br> _____ | S | 01/30/98 |
| _____ | PRIM 50622 | Mr. Jack _____ <br> 16 _____ Lane <br> _____ | S | 01/30/98 |
| _____ | PRIM 5634 | Mr. James _____ <br> _____ <br> Indianapolis, IN 46204 | S | 01/30/98 |
| _____ | PRIM 8899 | Mr. Donald _____ <br> _____ <br> Fort Wayne, IN 46845 | S | 01/30/98 |

## EXHIBIT 5.4. SAMPLE MANAGER'S ACTIVITY REPORT.

| 09/11/2000 | Manager's Activity Report for _____ | | | | Page: 1 |
|---|---|---|---|---|---|
| Prospect Information | Area | Staff Name | Clearance | Asgn Date | Date of most recent contact |
| C1070 | PRIM | | Cultivation | 12/14/1996 | 04/12/2000 |
| | ICC | | Identification | 10/15/1998 | |
| 1 American Square PO Box 368 | LAWI | | Identification | 07/20/1998 | |
| _____, IN | CORP | | Cultivation | 10/31/1997 | |
| | MEDS | | Cultivation | 08/06/1999 | |
| | SBUS | | Cultivation | 06/16/1997 | |
| C24588 | PRIM | | Cultivation | 09/05/1995 | 12/14/1999 |
| | CORP | | Cultivation | 09/05/1995 | |
| Paradise Valley, AZ 85253 | | | | | |
| C72966 | PRIM | | Cultivation | 02/10/1999 | |
| PO Box 368 One American Square | | | | | |
| Indianapolis, IN 46204 | | | | | |
| 151335 | PRIM | | Cultivation | 05/19/1998 | 09/01/2000 |
| | WELS | | Stewardship | 03/27/1998 | |
| 2455 Tamarack Trail #338 | EDUC | | Stewardship | 03/18/1996 | |
| _____, IN | | | | | |

| ID | Address | | Date | Date |
|---|---|---|---|---|
| C84513 | PRIM | Cultivation | 09/07/1999 | 08/25/2000 |
| PO Box 23350 Seattle, WA 98122 | | | | |
| C17251 | PRIM | Cultivation | 05/18/2000 | |
| 311 West Seventh Street Bloomington, IN 47404-3934 | | | | |
| 285017 | PRIM | Stewardship | 06/30/1998 | 06/05/2000 |
| | WELS | Stewardship | 06/30/1998 | |
| | AECB | Identification | 03/13/1998 | |
| Carmel, IN 46032 | | | | |
| 210446 | PRIM | Stewardship | 06/30/1998 | 06/05/2000 |
| | WELS | Stewardship | 06/30/1998 | |
| Carmel, IN 46032 | | | | |
| 365862 | PRIM | Cultivation | 11/07/1995 | 06/15/2000 |
| | WILL | Stewardship | 05/26/1998 | |
| 23268 Shorelane | WELS | Stewardship | 03/30/1998 | |
| | ATHL | Stewardship | 05/19/1994 | |

*Note:* Names have been removed from the Staff/Volunteer Assignment and Prospect Name(s) columns for reasons of confidentiality.

# EXHIBIT 5.5. SAMPLE CONTACT SUMMARY REPORT.

Aug 18 2000 A/FIS: Benefactor Page
CONTACT SUMMARY BY STAFF
07/01/00 to 07/31/00

| Contact ID | Staff/Volunteer Assignment | Prospect Name(s) | Date/Type | Summary of Contact |
|---|---|---|---|---|
| 316678 | | | 07/24/00 Phone call | To invite him to lunch with _____ |
| 316798 | | | 07/31/00 Phone call | Discuss her prospects for the law campaign |
| 316764 | | | 07/21/00 Staff visit | Indianapolis national headquarters of _____ with Community Relations Director |
| 316789 | | | 07/25/00 Staff visit | Visited Dr. _____ in Atlanta before he died |
| 317087 | | | 07/18/00 Other | Dr. _____ sent a letter announcing the funding of a bone cancer grant |
| 317088 | | | 07/24/00 Other | Dr. _____ sent a note to Mrs. _____ as a follow-up to lunch |
| 316848 | | | 07/12/00 Mailing sent | Sent info on endowments; wants to endow $10K history prize |
| 316847 | | | 07/14/00 Phone call | Discussed arrangements for IUB Homecoming campus visit |

| ID | Date / Type | Description |
|---|---|---|
| 316859 | 07/17/00 Phone call | Mrs. _____ must cancel campus visit |
| 316838 | 07/05/00 Staff visit | Had dinner with the _____ to thank them for their gift |
| 316841 | 07/10/00 Staff visit | Keeping in touch |
| 316843 | 07/10/00 Staff visit | Discussed his potential gift to the University |
| 316850 | 7/10/00 Staff visit | Keeping in touch |
| 316851 | 07/10/00 Phone call | Keeping in touch re: his estate plan |
| 316852 | 07/11/00 | Planned giving |

*Note:* Names have been removed from the Staff/Volunteer Assignment and Prospect Name(s) columns for reasons of confidentiality.

A contact report needs to be clear and concise, with a meaningful summary that tells the reader quickly whether this is relevant to his or her specific fundraising activities.

Details of a contact report may include the following:

- Prospect name and system ID number
- Date of contact
- Place and purpose of last contact
- Name of development officer who made the contact
- Results of the contact
- Next steps to be taken
- Staff assigned
- Volunteer(s) assigned

Some examples of meaningful contacts are face-to-face contact initiated by the prospect or development officer, rating or screening sessions, follow-up telephone contact that leads to a gift closure, a solicitation, a high-ranking official's event in a small-group setting (six or fewer guests for lunch or dinner, not a general reception), and the initiation of a planned gift.

Some examples of items or contacts that are informational but not necessarily meaningful (at that time) include attendance at an event, committee meeting, or other reception or similar outing; casual contact; a brief, non-business-related telephone call; and cards or flowers for a birthday, holiday, or anniversary. Even though these events may not be considered meaningful, if the prospect receives them they should be documented in the prospect management program.

Copies of contact reports (see Exhibit 5.6) should be sent to the chief development officer and other development officers who are coassigned to the prospect; they should be placed in the research files and in the files of others who may be important to the success of this prospect's cultivation-solicitation process. (Many organizations have contact reports sent via e-mail, and some database systems can set up the automatic routing of reports to groups or offices.) Every meaningful contact should include a documented next step or reminder.

**_Reminders._** After meetings with major prospects or donors, follow-through is absolutely necessary. One way to accomplish this is to enter a reminder in the prospect management system that could include a task to do within the next week, next month, or even before the end of the year.

Some elements to be included in a reminder may include the

- Prospect's name and system ID number
- Date of next action to be taken
- Action to be taken
- Individual(s) expected to take next action
- Results of the action taken, if any to note at the time

# EXHIBIT 5.6. BLANK CONTACT REPORT FORM.

## PROSPECT TRACKING REPORT

*This is a* confidential *record of [name of organization].*
*It is not subject to disclosure under [applicable code].*

Prospect Name:                           Contact Date:

ID Number:                               Degrees/Years:

Title:                                   Cross Reference

Address:                                 Vol. Name(s)/ID(s):
(Home/Business)

City/State/Zip:                          Reported by:

Phone:                                   Type of Contact: ____ Visit      ____ Phone
(Home/Business)                          (check one)      _____ Other (specify)

Purpose of Contact: ____ Cultivation ____ Solicitation ____ Evaluation ____ Stewardship
(check one)         ____ Feasibility Study ____ Vol. Recruitment ____ Vol. Follow-up
                    ____ Committee Meeting

Summary of Contact
(80 characters or less): _____

Details of Contact:

Reminder(s) & Date(s):

Next Action:

7/98

*Proposals.* It is helpful to know who has been solicited and what gifts might be expected as a result of actual or potential solicitations.

Elements to be considered in the proposal tracking screen might include the

- Prospect's name and system ID number
- Solicitor's name
- Staff member(s) involved in solicitation
- Proposed amount
- Date of proposal
- Type of proposal (verbal or written)
- Expected amount to be received
- Date gift might be received

*Cultivation, Solicitation, and Stewardship Plans.* Planning is an important factor in setting an organization's goals and strategies and in tracking progress and expectations. Obviously, these plans will be ever-changing, depending on the amount of information gathered from conversations with the prospect and the prospect's readiness. Each major gift prospect should be assigned to a member of the staff whose duty it is to see that a personalized plan is enacted to get the best gift possible. This plan will, whenever possible, involve volunteer participation, too. Each staff member becomes an account executive and acts as a catalyst, providing the initiative and the strategy.

## Subsystems in a Prospect Management Program

Five subsystems are usually found in a prospect management system for major donors: (1) a rating system, (2) a priority system, (3) an approach system, (4) an accountability system, and (5) a report system. Each is discussed in the sections to follow.

### Rating System

Step one in a program to obtain extraordinary gifts is identifying priority prospects. This system places a great deal of importance on the research function. Research and rating go hand in hand, and a solid records and research system is the foundation of any fundraising program. If not already in place, a research capability that will yield prospect ratings must be developed. The end result of a rating process should be not one but two rating codes: the prospect's giving capacity and the prospect's interest in the organization. A prospect's giving capacity is a collective "best judgment" (after a review of all the pertinent rating and file information about the prospect) of how much the prospect could contribute to the organization over three to five years, if so inclined. The interest rating is a collective judgment of the prospect's interest in and concern for the organization. This rating is based on personal information, the prospect's giving record, and file information on hand. Tables 5.1 and 5.2 show the numerical rating codes that might be used in a typical system.

## Priority System

By adding the two numerical ratings (capacity and interest), an organization can determine each prospect's priority rating. The higher the rating, the higher the prospect's priority. The higher the prospect's priority, the more cultivation moves (structured contacts designed to bring a prospect closer to making a major gift) an organization will want to make on the prospect in a given period (usually a calendar year).

As a guide to determining how much cultivation a prospect gets, it is recommended that the organization use a cultivation quota—the sum of the two numerical ratings, multiplied by 2. This quota represents the minimum number of cultivation moves an organization should hope to make on a prospect each year. For example, one prospect is rated 3/1 (that is, a capacity rating of 3 and an interest rating of 1); another is rated 1/3; both have cultivation quotas of 8. At the

## TABLE 5.1. PROSPECT RATING CODES FOR NONPROFITS WHOSE LARGEST SINGLE GIFT IS LESS THAN $1 MILLION.

| Giving Capacity Code | Estimated Giving Capacity | Interest Code | Description |
|---|---|---|---|
| 1 | $2,500–5,000 | 1 | Not involved, no record of interest |
| 2 | 5,000–10,000 | | |
| 3 | 10,000–25,000 | 2 | Minimal interest, occasional donor, attends meetings infrequently, and so on |
| 4 | 25,000–50,000 | 3 | Moderately active or formerly very active |
| 5 | 50,000–100,000 | 4 | Very active, major donor, club member, committee person |
| 6 | 100,000–250,000 | 5 | Member of governing board, other boards, or executive groups |
| 7 | 250,000–500,000 | | |
| 8 | 500,000–1,000,000 | | |
| 9 | 1,000,000 or more | | |

## TABLE 5.2. PROSPECT RATING CODES FOR NONPROFITS WHOSE LARGEST SINGLE GIFT IS $1 MILLION OR MORE.

| Giving Capacity Code | Estimated Giving Capacity | Interest Code | Description |
|---|---|---|---|
| 1 | $5,000–25,000 | 1 | Not involved, no record of interest |
| 2 | 25,000–50,000 | | |
| 3 | 50,000–100,000 | 2 | Minimal interest, occasional donor, attends meetings infrequently, and so on |
| 4 | 100,000–250,000 | 3 | Moderately active or formerly very active |
| 5 | 250,000–500,000 | 4 | Very active, major donor, club member, committee person |
| 6 | 500,000–1,000,000 | 5 | Member of governing board, other boards, or executive groups |
| 7 | 1,000,000–2,500,000 | | |
| 8 | 2,500,000–5,000,000 | | |
| 9 | 5,000,000 or more | | |

moment, the first seems a rather unlikely prospect for a $10,000 gift; the other is a fairly likely prospect for a $2,500 gift. Their cultivation quotas tell the organization to plan for eight cultivation moves on each of these prospects in a year. But the organization may have to decide which prospect will get its attention first. With the first prospect, a longer cultivation period may result in a larger gift; with the second, a smaller gift can be more readily realized.

Cultivation quotas are flexible guidelines. Staff and volunteers should have the authority to make more or fewer than the recommended number of contacts, as circumstances may dictate. Another important point is that ratings—and therefore cultivation quotas—can change during the year. To return to the previous example, in the opinion of the organization the person rated 3/1 has a gift potential of $10,000 to $24,999 but has not demonstrated much past interest. Nevertheless, a staff member or volunteer who calls on the prospect discovers that the prospect has become much more interested. This discovery changes the prospect's interest rating to 3, and this change in turn increases the cultivation quota to 12. Therefore four additional contacts will be called for over a year.

It must be clearly understood that, ordinarily, the team's top leaders should be assigned to cultivate and solicit those with both the greatest capacity to give and the greatest interest. It is equally important that the entire team stay focused throughout on the best donor prospects. Little time should be given to prospects rated 1/1, but what about prospects rated 9/1 or 8/2? Should time be spent on them? Yes—but it must be a measured amount of time, and the effort should be disciplined. It usually takes a series of steps to move a prospect from the point of having little or no interest to serving on the organization's governing board. This kind of cultivation is not accomplished in one leap. Hence, even though great ability to give exists, the proclivity to give needs to be developed, and that often takes more time. Leave some time for the long shots, and give some effort to their cultivation, but reserve the bulk of the effort for prospects with major gift potential who are already more involved.

## Accountability System

Each major gift prospect should be assigned to a member of the staff whose duty it is to see that a personalized campaign is waged to get the best gift possible. In order to effectively carry out the responsibility, a strategy needs to be developed for each prospect. A good strategy plan will contain a long-term goal to be achieved with the prospect, including specific steps to be taken toward that goal; the plan should be designed to lead to major gift solicitation and contain an expected solicitation date (refer to Exhibit 5.1).

Each staff member becomes an account executive and acts as a catalyst, providing the initiative and the strategy. The organization should attempt to assign most prospects to one or more staff members or volunteers for cultivation and solicitation, and it should strive to give its volunteers the feeling that they are responsible for their prospects. Every two to four weeks, staff should report on gift prospect assignments. The reports should list all prospects (individuals, foundations, and corporations) for whom the staff person is responsible, the volunteer or volunteers assisting with each prospect, the number of cultivation and solicitation contacts that the master plan indicates should be made with each prospect during the year, and the number of contacts made to date. By reviewing these reports, staff members will readily see which prospects need attention and can plan accordingly.

## Approach System

Types of contact include telephone calls, letters, and personal visits by staff, by the chief executive officer, or by volunteers; attendance by prospects at organizational/institutional functions and leadership retreats; involvement in key issues and programs; publications; firsthand briefings and information on important events; and recognition events. In most systems, contacts are weighted according to significance, importance, and impact. A typical weighted system looks like this:

| *Cultivation Contact* | *Contact Points* |
|---|---|
| Letter from a staff member | 1 |
| Telephone call from a staff member | 2 |
| Letter from a volunteer | 2 |
| Invitation to a major event | 3 |
| Telephone call from a volunteer | 3 |
| Telephone call from the chief executive officer | 3 |
| Visit by a staff member | 4 |
| Letter from the chief executive officer | 4 |
| Attendance at an organizational activity (off-site) | 4 |
| Visit by a volunteer | 5 |
| Attendance at an organizational event (on-site) | 5 |
| Firsthand information about important events | 6 |
| Meeting with the chief executive officer | 7 |
| Personal recognition | 7 |
| Leadership retreat | 7 |

## Report System

Follow-through is absolutely necessary in making contacts with major donor prospects. There is no substitute for persistence and patience. A useful management technique is to require staff members to identify their top ten prospects. During regular staff meetings, each staff member assigned to these prospects should report on what is being done to move them closer to making major gifts, on who has the initiative, and on what the next step is. Then at the next staff meeting, each staff member should report any progress or difficulty in carrying out cultivation plans and should discuss the next sequence of steps to be taken. A call report should also be filed after every telephone call or visit.

◆ ◆ ◆

With its five subsystems, the guidance system for soliciting major donors is a control mechanism ensuring that big gift prospects are rated, given priorities, assigned to staff members and volunteers, cultivated and solicited according to a master plan, and reported on. The system should be designed to help get results, not to stimulate "scoring points" for that sole purpose. It should encourage well-thought-out, appropriate, strategic moves that the organization feels will bring its prospects closer to making major gifts. No one knows for sure how many contacts it will take to bring a prospect to the point of making a gift (the average is generally thought to be seven to ten), but the organization has to use something, such as cultivation quotas, as a guide. It is appropriate to rely on this guidance system as a tool for bringing human factors into play because, after all, human factors are the most important elements in getting the prospect ready to give.

Prospect tracking and management help an organization monitor its involvement with major prospects. Once someone is identified as a prospect, it is imperative that the organization involve that person in its life. Involvement precedes and often begets investment, and investment is the end game.

# Major Gift Fundraising Guidelines

It is desirable to have some expectations for major gift fundraisers. These may be altered by a variety of circumstances identified in guidelines or as agreed upon by the fundraiser and her or his supervisor. Some considerations that may affect the prospect pool that each development officer is expected to maintain are

- Percentage of time spent in major gift solicitation process
- Geographic proximity to prospects
- Complexity and size of gifts being sought
- Campaign and noncampaign mode
- General experience as a development officer
- Nature of constituency

## Productivity

For a full-time major gift officer, it is suggested that he or she manage a pool of no more than 150 individual prospects. This pool should represent a balance of prospects at various stages in the development continuum. As a guideline, the following distribution is recommended, but the mix might change based on the status of a campaign or project:

- Cultivation 65–43 percent
- Solicitation 35–24 percent
- Stewardship 50–33 percent

It is assumed that most or all prospects will fall into one of these categories. Everyone in the pool should receive *at least* one meaningful contact each year. Individuals in the solicitation stage require several substantive, personal contacts yearly, with particular attention paid to the value of the contact in moving the prospect toward closure of a gift.

It has been suggested that full-time major gift officers should make or cause to be made an average of 180 meaningful calls a year. However, other forms of meaningful contacts may be included, each one being tracked and monitored for productivity and reported through the prospect management program.

## Solicitation

Gift officers might also consider making or causing to be made a minimum of thirty major gift solicitations a year; producing fifteen to twenty gifts is a fair measure of productivity. Measuring productivity by meaningful activity, even more than dollars raised, is important. Sustained, meaningful activity over time is the key to producing steady and growing results.

Why is that so? Measuring only by dollars raised can be deceptive and dangerous. What if a major gifts officer operates on the promise of one or two "big hits" a year? What happens in the year when no big hits occur? And who's to say or how can you know in advance whether the donor's major gift capacity is $50,000 or $5 million? Too much focus on short-term success can encourage a short-term-gain mentality that may cause long-term pain. Donors tend to give most generously when they give to what interests them most in a time frame that meets their needs, not the organization's needs. Bad timing, pushing too hard to close a gift on the organization's time line and not the donor's, can lead to gifts of dimes, or no gift at all, when a gift of dollars was possible.

Such factors point to a long-term, steady-as-you-go, keep-working-constantly approach to major gift fundraising. Baseball offers a wonderfully instructional metaphor. Everyone loves to hit home runs; home runs make the headlines. But those who just hit home runs or strike out do not last long, as they strike out far more than they hit homers. The baseball players who call the Hall of Fame their final home hit .300 over their careers. To do that requires getting hits nearly every day and hitting a lot more singles and doubles over a lifetime than home runs.

## Cultivation

Identifying new prospects is also important. Gift officers should qualify fifteen to twenty-five new prospects each year who have the inclination and capability to qualify as major gift prospects. In general, fifty individual contacts should be made to identify and qualify fifteen to twenty new prospects who will replace individuals who have been removed from the prospect pool.

## Stewardship

Full-time major gift officers should make or cause to be made stewardship calls on all donors in the pool. Using the proposed pool distribution, this could require frequency contacts with fifty individuals. The nature of stewardship contacts may take a variety of forms, ranging from individual meetings to invitations to special events. As the major gift officer expands the donor base, it will be essential to rely on a variety of institutional contacts to accomplish the stewardship function.

## Prospect Review Sessions

In small to midsized organizations, it is preferable for the staff to meet together, often with volunteers present, to review the status of prospects and their ongoing management. In larger, more complex organizations, this process must be covered with an umbrella prospect management program. On an as-needed basis, the director of the program, along with a member of the research team, should convene a meeting for the purpose of reviewing current activities with selected major gift prospects and determine how to maximize support from each prospect. Such meetings should be held regularly, especially during large capital campaigns.

The selection of prospects for review should be done by the director of the program, in consultation with members of the development team. Prospects may be selected for review on the basis of their rating, their status as a prospect for a specific project, or for other reasons specified by the chief development officer.

Notification of the staff assigned to a prospect should be sent at least fifteen working days prior to the scheduled review session. Included in this notification should be the names of the prospects to be reviewed.

All staff assigned to prospects being reviewed should attend the meeting to discuss current strategies with each prospect. If attendance is not possible, written comments on each prospect should be sent to the director of the prospect management program at least seven working days prior to the scheduled meeting. A copy of those comments should be sent to the primary manager of each prospect.

Research and the prospect management staff should record the highlights of discussions and the decisions made regarding each prospect reviewed. The prospect management staff should enter this information on the prospect's record and should distribute copies of the meeting summary to all attendees, assigned staff, and others not in attendance but determined as appropriate to receive all or portions of the information.

◆ ◆ ◆

Good development programs do not result from ad hoc practices. Major gifts develop over time and as a result of a series of events and activities. The systematic coordination and orchestration of this process is the key to the long-term vitality of a successful program.

# CHAPTER SIX

# STEWARDING GIFTS

This chapter discusses governing bodies and oversight, as well as administering gift accounts, handling and processing gifts, and complying with donor intent. It is not intended to be a full, complete, in-depth discussion of the intricacies of the IRS codes, applicable federal and state law, or formal accounting procedures. Such a discussion would itself be a book. Rather, this chapter outlines the basics and provides a point of departure for all nonprofits, most particularly for those lacking large professional staffs or having only enough resources to address the basics properly.

## Using a Team Approach

A successful development effort is no longer limited to cultivating and soliciting gifts and then saying thank-you; it is more. Once the gift is received, the process of properly administering the current gift and beginning the cultivation process toward the next gift through proper administrative stewardship begins. Where the work of fundraising often stops, the work of administering the gift begins. A team effort is required. Any organization that truly wants to engage in a successful institutional advancement effort will understand this and will see to it that the activities of the fundraisers, the development services professionals, and the business office are joined in warm embrace. That is the way to ensure a total commitment to a complete, positive, reinforcing experience for the donor.

The donor needs to know that his or her gift is important and does make a difference and that future gifts can be considered with the same confidence and assurance. The modern development effort effectively, cooperatively, and completely involves both the promoting of gifts and their accurate, efficient handling, once received.

The good institutional development program is not contained in silos. A better approach is to see the process of securing gifts in a holistic way, with the donor at its core. Frontline fundraisers need to understand, respect, and comply with the rules, regulations, and requirements imposed on the business officers. By the same token, the business officers need to know, understand, and appreciate that the hoped-for outcome of any gift transaction is a happy donor—one whose experience has been such that the next gift is already on its way. This requires removing any barriers that might exist and silencing any rhetoric about who or what is important organizationally. Such questions are answered by the common thread that runs throughout—the donor—and by satisfying his or her needs. Focus on your donors' needs, and your donors, in turn, will see that the organization's needs are met.

## Considering Donor Needs

There are two additional considerations to weigh in understanding why it's so important to consider donor needs. First, a procedure that ensures checks and balances is necessary and desirable; giving is often more emotional than it is logical and rational. This view, widely accepted, generally focuses on the donor. What is not often considered is that fundraisers can be emotional about their causes as well. Although many mature nonprofits are professionally staffed and managed, many more—practically all the newer ones—are the immediate by-product of a deep personal or religious belief, illness, accident, tragedy, or disaster that moves an individual, a couple, a family, or a group sharing a common cause to seek remedy.

This makes fundraising highly emotional at times for both the donor and the solicitor. In such an environment, even the best intended, most honorable among us can let passion cloud objectivity. The balance needed to ensure donor intent and to protect the nonprofit's integrity is often provided by the objectivity a dispassionate reviewer provides.

Second, it is too often the case that barriers exist between fundraisers and the business operation. Fundraisers sometimes believe that the business office does not understand them or their donors' point of view, and those in business offices have been heard to comment that fundraisers have little appreciation of the rules, regulations, guidelines, policies, and procedures and have even less inclination to honor them. Is it not better to promote an environment in which everyone understands and appreciates each other's roles and works constructively together to eliminate barriers, to increase cooperation—all in the name of serving the best interests of their donors and their organization?

There are two ways to approach the problem of relating the fundraising function and the gift administration operation. One is represented by an organization that approaches gift administration and gift accounting as separate functions, with the former usually residing with the fundraising staff and the latter with the business office. The other approach can be described by the functional title Gift and Account Administration. Here both functions are viewed as coordinated, linked donor services. Either model can work, and each organization must make its own decision as to which approach will serve it best. What is essential, no matter which approach is used, is to provide for bridging the divide between raising funds and administering them, while keeping the focus always on honoring the donor's wishes, satisfying his or her needs, and preparing the way for the next gift.

# Dealing with Governing Bodies

Today there are a plethora of rules and regulations to follow and a gaggle of governmental agencies and professional organizations promulgating and enforcing them. This labyrinth of paperwork makes it mandatory that nonprofits properly document and record gifts and pledges and that due diligence procedures be established to ensure institutional compliance with donor intent now and into the future.

The principal governing bodies that create standards or publications a nonprofit must follow include the Financial Accounting Standards Board (FASB) or the Government Accounting Standards Board (GASB), the IRS, state laws, the Council for Advancement and Support of Education (CASE), the Council for Aid to Education (CAE), and U.S. immigration law.

## FASB and GASB

The FASB and GASB generate professional accounting standards that guide the business side of an organization. Their mission is to establish and improve standards of financial accounting and reporting for the public, including issuers, auditors, and users of financial information.

GASB establishes standards for state and local governmental entities. Many nonprofits that are government entities follow GASB standards; others follow the

FASB standards. In either case, it is important to be familiar with the accounting standards that affect your organization. These standards are essential to the efficient functioning of the economy because decisions about the allocation of resources rely heavily on the credible, concise, and understandable financial information created by these standards. Exhibits 6.1 and 6.2 indicate several standards that these governing bodies have created. For a more detailed listing of the standards issued by either of these groups see their Web sites:

> FASB: rutgers.edu/Accounting/raw/fasb/index.html
>
> GASB: rutgers.edu/Accounting/raw/gasb/index.html

### EXHIBIT 6.1. EXAMPLES OF FASB STANDARDS.

| FASB Statement Name and Number | Issue Date | Purpose |
| --- | --- | --- |
| FASB Statement #117 Financial Statements of Nonprofit Organizations | 6/93 | This statement establishes standards for external financial statements provided by a nonprofit organization. It requires that financial statements provide certain basic information that focuses on the entity as a whole and meets the common needs of external users of those statements. This statement also requires classification of an organization's net assets and its revenues, expenses, gains, and losses based on the existence or absence of donor-imposed restrictions. It requires that the amounts for each of the three classes of net assets, permanently restricted, temporarily restricted, and unrestricted, be displayed in a statement of financial position and that the amounts of change in each of those classes of net assets be displayed in a statement of activities. |
| FASB Statement #116 Accounting for Contributions Received and Contributions Made | 6/93 | This statement establishes accounting standards for contributions and applies to all entities that receive or make contributions. Generally, contributions received, including unconditional promises to give, are recognized as revenues in the period received at their fair values. Contributions made, including unconditional promises to give, are recognized as expenses in the period made at their fair values. Conditional promises to give, whether received or made, are recognized when they become unconditional, that is, when the conditions are substantially met. |

**EXHIBIT 6.1. EXAMPLES OF FASB STANDARDS, Cont'd.**

| FASB Statement Name and Number | Issue Date | Purpose |
|---|---|---|
| | | This statement requires not-for-profit organizations to distinguish between contributions received that increase permanently restricted net assets, temporarily restricted net assets, and unrestricted net assets. It also requires recognition of the expiration of donor-imposed restrictions in the period in which the restrictions expire. |
| FASB Statement #136 Transfers of Assets to a Nonprofit Organization or Charitable Trust That Raises or Holds Contributions for Others | 6/99 | This statement requires an organization that accepts cash or other financial assets from a donor and agrees to use or transfer those assets, the return on investment of those assets, or both to a specified unaffiliated beneficiary to recognize the fair value of those assets as a liability concurrent with recognition of the assets received from the donor. However, if the donor explicitly grants the recipient organization variance power or if the recipient organization and the specified beneficiary are financially interrelated organizations, the recipient organization is required to recognize the fair value of any assets it receives as a contribution received. Not-for-profit organizations are financially interrelated if (a) one organization has the ability to influence the operating and financial decisions of the other and (b) one organization has an ongoing economic interest in the net assets of the other. |

## IRS

The IRS is a regulatory body providing guidance to both the development and the business sides of the organization (see Resource 20). Its mission is to provide U.S. taxpayers (individuals as well as corporations) top-quality service by helping them understand and meet their tax responsibilities by applying the tax law with integrity and fairness to all. The agency has created many regulations that need to be followed and may affect how the charitable organization handles gifts and what may be considered a gift.

Examples of IRS rules, publications, and forms that affect nonprofit organizations include

*Internal Revenue Code 170(f)(8) and 6115; also Publication 1771:* Provide guidance regarding the allowance of certain charitable contributions, the sub-

## EXHIBIT 6.2. EXAMPLES OF GASB STANDARDS.

| GASB Statement Name and Number | Issue Date | Purpose |
|---|---|---|
| GASB Statement #15 Governmental College and University Accounting and Financial Reporting Models | 10/91 | This Statement provides guidance on the accounting and financial reporting models to be used for governmental colleges and universities. Governmental colleges and universities should follow either the AICPA College Guide model or the Governmental model. |
| GASB Statement #20 Accounting and Financial Reporting for Proprietary Funds and Other Governmental Entities That Use Proprietary Fund Accounting | 9/93 | This Statement provides interim guidance on business-type accounting and financial reporting for proprietary activities (that is, proprietary funds and governmental entities that use proprietary fund accounting). Further GASB research is expected to lead to the issuance of one or more pronouncements on the accounting and financial reporting model for proprietary activities. This statement also indicates that the entity is to follow FASB standards as long as they do not contradict GASB pronouncements. |
| GASB Statement #29 The Use of Not-for-Profit Accounting and Financial Reporting Principles by Governmental Entities | 8/95 | This Statement provides interim guidance concerning the use of not-for-profit accounting and financial reporting principles by state and local governmental entities. |
| GASB Statement #34 Basic Financial Statements and Management's Discussion and Analysis for State and Local Governments | 6/99 | This Statement establishes new financial reporting requirements for state and local governments throughout the United States. When implemented, it will create new information and will restructure much of the information that governments have presented in the past. |

stantiation requirements for charitable contributions of $250 or more, and the disclosure requirements for quid pro quo contributions in excess of $75.

*Publication 526 (Charitable Contributions):* Explains how to claim a deduction for your charitable contributions. It discusses organizations that are qualified to receive charitable contributions, the types of contributions you can deduct, how much you can deduct, what records you should keep, and how to report charitable contributions.

*Publication 561 (Determining the Value of Donated Property):* Designed to help donors and appraisers determine the value of the property, other than cash, that is given to a qualified organization. It also outlines how the donor needs to substantiate these types of gifts.

*Publication 515 (Withholding of Tax on Nonresident Aliens and Foreign Corporations):* Outlines tax requirements for withholding agents who pay income to nonresident aliens and foreign corporations should your organization receive gifts that benefit nonresident aliens.

*Publication 520 (Scholarships and Fellowships):* Covers the rules for scholarships, fellowships, and tuition reductions. These amounts are tax-free if they meet the rules discussed in this publication.

*Form 8283 (Noncash Charitable Contributions):* An IRS form donors must attach to their tax return if they give a gift other than cash with a value greater than or equal to $500. The charitable organization must sign this form acknowledging receipt of the gift.

*Form 8282 (Donee Information Return):* An IRS form the charitable organization must complete upon selling a noncash gift with a value greater than or equal to $500 within two years of the original date of the gift.

*Form 1099 MISC (Miscellaneous Income):* An IRS form that defines what the organization must report to the government as taxable income from the vendor payments the organization has made.

*Forms 1042 and 1042S (Foreign Persons Income Reporting Forms):* IRS forms that define what the organization must report as tax withheld on certain income paid to nonresident aliens, foreign partnerships, foreign corporations, and nonresident alien or foreign fiduciaries of estates or trust (see Resource 21).

It is important for the business staff to understand these rules and regulations and to set up procedures accordingly, but it is also important for the fundraising staff to understand these rules. With a close relationship between the business and fundraising staff, the nonprofit can be assured that solicitations to donors, acknowledgments, and gift acceptance all comply with the IRS regulations so that the donor has an allowable tax deduction. Fundraisers who understand these rules may actually be able to enhance current gifts or secure additional gifts by conveying useful tips to their prospects and donors as well. For more information on IRS forms and publications, see its Web site: irs.gov/.

## State Laws

Nonprofits need to be aware of any state laws that may affect them. For instance, in Indiana there is a law called the Uniform Management of Institutional Funds Act: IN code 30-2-12. If adopted by the nonprofit, it is required to make whole a permanent endowment when the market value of the account falls below the amount of the original gift or gifts. In order to adhere to this law, the nonprofit has to set up procedures not only to track the original gift value of a permanent endowment account but to periodically review the accounts and determine whether any remuneration is needed.

State laws may affect the procedures an organization must go through to amend donor intent. They may also provide a framework for what can be acceptable criteria in a gift agreement. For example, a state law may prohibit a donor from restricting his or her gift to a particular race or gender. Therefore it is important to keep current on what is happening with your state legislation in order to determine the effects on your organization and its fundraising and administrative processes and policies.

## CASE

CASE is an international association of education advancement officers that includes alumni administrators, fundraisers, public relations managers, publication editors, and government relations officers.

The purposes of CASE are to develop and foster sound relationships between member educational institutions and their constituencies; to provide training programs, products, and services in the areas of alumni relations, communications, and philanthropy; to promote diversity within these professions; and to provide a strong force for the advancement and support of education worldwide. CASE provides development officers at educational institutions with comprehensive standards and definitions for preparing management reports of yearly fundraising results, as well as management and reporting standards for education fundraising campaigns. For the most part, the fundraising staff follows the standards created by this organization.

These guidelines can be obtained from CASE, 1307 New York Avenue NW, Suite 1000, Washington, D.C. 20005-4701. The following organizations endorse the *CASE Campaign Standards: Management and Reporting Standards for Educational Fund-Raising Campaigns* (Council for Advancement and Support of Education, 1996, p. 91):

American Association of Colleges of Nursing

American Association of Community Colleges

American Association of Fund-Raising Counsel

American Council on Education

American Prospect Research Association

Association of Community College Trustees

Association for Healthcare Philanthropy

Canadian Council for the Advancement of Education

College Board, Council of Graduate Schools

Council of Independent Colleges

Hispanic Association of Colleges and Universities

Lilly Endowment, Inc.

National Association of College and University Business Officers

National Association of Independent Colleges and Universities

National Association of Independent Schools

National Association of State Universities and Land-Grant Colleges

National Council for Resource Development

National University Continuing Education Association

Any organization can look to these guidelines as a model approach, realizing that different circumstances may suggest the need to modify the standards to make them applicable and useful.

The Association of Governing Boards of Universities and Colleges, while supporting the CASE standards, urges institutions to go even further, especially in the area of reporting deferred gifts in fundraising totals. A 1996 statement from that organization said, "The Board of Directors of the Association of Governing Boards [AGB] of Universities and Colleges commends CASE for developing the *CASE Campaign Standards*. AGB endorses the standards except for those provisions addressing testamentary bequests and deferred gifts. AGB urges institutions to count bequests only when actually realized. With regard to deferred gifts, AGB urges that campaign totals be based on present value only" (Council for Advancement and Support of Education, 1996, p. 92).

The point is well taken, but there will be understandable initial reluctance on the part of institutions to take this further step, for three primary reasons. First, over the short haul, changing to these standards will create a series of practical "public relations" problems as the change relates to donors. Donors accustomed to being given credit and public recognition for the face value of deferred gifts will now be credited for smaller gifts. As an illustration, consider the gift of a $100,000 life insurance policy from a fifty-year-old donor. Currently, in most nonprofits the donor is credited and recognized as a $100,000 donor; in terms of the policy's present value, however, the donor's credited gift will be appreciably less. Will this kind of adjustment dampen donors' enthusiasm? And to use another life insurance policy as an example, what is the public relations effect if two fundraiser cochairs each want to give a $100,000 life insurance policy—on the face of it, two equal gifts—but one donor is fifty years old and the other is fifty-eight? In terms of the gifts' present value, the two cochairs will be credited with unequal gift amounts. Again, will this have a harmful effect?

Second, North Americans are intensely competitive; we tend to keep score. This is a far less compelling consideration than the first one, but it is nevertheless real. So which institutions, particularly among those that insist on comparing themselves with others in their sectors, will be the first to step forward and institute these new standards? What type of commitment to the new standards will it take for an institution to tell a potential donor who has multiple philanthropic interests that his $100,000 life insurance policy will be credited at its present value when other institutions are still crediting it at face value?

Third, it is axiomatic that fundraising goals are constantly going higher. When these new standards are implemented, however, it is clearly possible—in fact, it is likely—that fundraising goals, at least for a while, will actually be lower than they are now. What impact, if any, will this development have on the energy and commitment of volunteers who are asked to lead fundraising efforts with seemingly smaller goals? Will it limit the vision of the donors who are asked to support nonprofits, causing them to lower their own sights? It should not matter, but will it? Fundraising goals are not (or at least should not be) established to set records; rather, they should be established to meet legitimate institutional priorities that are consistent with the institution's mission and with its current and future needs.

The further transition that AGB encourages should occur, and governing boards should take the lead in supporting this movement. It is fiscally responsible and intellectually honest to do so. Movement in this direction will take time, however, and it needs to be phased in. One possible way to do that (and some organizations have already done so) is to begin reporting gifts in terms of both face value and present value. This practice can begin the transition to a time when it's acceptable for gift reporting to be based on present value alone.

With these observations and caveats in mind, an institution might consider the guidelines shown in Table 6.1 as a basis for consideration and discussion. It is important to establish such guidelines at the beginning of a fundraising program when they can be considered (and perhaps adopted) in a calm, rational way, without influence from the pressures that often exist when an organization is midstream in its efforts and pressing to achieve success.

These standards differ from the accounting standards established by FASB and GASB, thereby creating a complex environment for administration. Its challenge will be to set up procedures and reports to accommodate both organizations and supply the appropriate information, no matter who is requesting it. For additional information on CASE, see their Web site: case.org/default.cfm.

## TABLE 6.1. FUNDRAISING ACCOUNTING GUIDELINES.

| Type of Gift | Public Value | Internal Value | What Will Count | What Will Not Count |
|---|---|---|---|---|
| Cash | Full amount | Full amount | | |
| Securities | Fair market value of securities on date of transfer | Fair market value of securities on date of transfer | | |
| Real estate | Appraised value at time of gift | Appraised value at time of gift | Real estate received during the campaign | |
| Personal property | Appraised value at time of gift | Appraised value at time of gift | Personal property received during the campaign | |
| Pledges | Full amount | Full amount | Signed pledge card or letter from donor<br>Pledges fulfilled within five-year period | Verbal pledges |
| Bequest expectancies | Face value | Discount based on donor's age | Copy of will or excerpt from will<br>Donor society enrollment<br>Signed gift agreement<br>Letter of intent from donor<br>Letter from donor's attorney or financial adviser | Contact report<br>Contingencies<br>Donor under sixty-five years old |

| | | | | |
|---|---|---|---|---|
| Realized bequests | Full amount | Full amount | Monies actually received from an estate or trust distribution | Gifts that were counted in prior campaigns as bequest expectancies |
| Charitable gift annuities | Face value | Value of charitable remainder interest | Annuity agreement in place | |
| Charitable lead trusts | Face value of annual income received during the campaign and discounted value of annual income after the campaign | Amount of annual income | Copy of trust agreement | |
| Pooled income fund | Full value of contribution to the fund | Discount based on donor's age | Contributions to pooled income fund | |
| Charitable remainder trusts | Face amount | Value of charitable remainder interest | Trust agreement in place Copy of trust agreement (or excerpt) if an outside trust | |
| Retirement plan assets | Face amount | Discount based on donor's age | Signed gift agreement Letter of intent from donor | |
| Insurance | Face value | Discount based on donor's age | Organization as owner of the policy Fully paid-up policy | |

*Note:* In general, the following will not count: gifts or pledges counted previously, investment earnings on gifts, and governmental funds.

## CAE

The Council for Aid to Education (CAE) was established in 1952 to advance corporate support of education. In partnership with corporate leaders, CAE seeks workable solutions to pressing issues in education—the high cost of college, inadequate access for underserved populations, and the disturbing fall-off in quality at many institutions. CAE is also the primary source of information on private funding for colleges and universities. This information is gathered through the Voluntary Support of Education (VSE) survey, which is voluntary and conducted annually. Institutions can use these data to benchmark and improve their fundraising activities. For more information about CAE, check its Web site: cae.org/.

## INS

If your organization accepts gifts that could benefit non-U.S. citizens, regulations issued by the INS (Immigration and Naturalization Service) may be of importance to you. The service is a federal agency within the U.S. Department of Justice that administers the nation's immigration laws. Specifically, the INS regulates permanent and temporary immigration to the United States, including legal permanent residence status, nonimmigrant status (for example, tourists or students), and naturalization. INS rules prohibit or limit payments to non-U.S. citizens, based on the status and type of visa they hold while in this country. If your organization agrees to accept gifts that will benefit non-U.S. citizens (for example, a donor gives money for the purpose of supporting foreign visiting scholars), keeping current with these regulations will help ensure that the donor's intent is met.

## Gift Account Administration

Good gift administration ensures that donor gift accounts are established for the benefit and support of the nonprofit's mission, that they are in compliance with donor intent as well as the organization's policies, and that governing body standards are maintained. Each nonprofit should have a gift acceptance policy as well as a policy on establishing and closing donor gift accounts to ensure that these objectives are met.

The policy on opening new donor gift accounts should contain

- Dollar minimums needed to establish a new account
- The required donor intent documentation
- The qualifications and responsibilities of account administrators who can authorize the use of the funds

- The frequency of reporting on account activity
- Who the account information can be released to
- Consequences for not complying with donor intent

The policy on closing accounts should contain

- The required documentation needed to close the account
- Guidelines as to when an account can be closed
- Final reporting

Within these policies, administration works closely with the development officer responsible for soliciting the gift to document the donor's intent through a gift agreement.

## Gift Agreements

A gift agreement is a legally enforceable document outlining how a gift will be used, what the responsibilities of the nonprofit and recipient of the funds are, and a means to provide for an alternate use of the fund in the future if necessary. The gift agreement can also be used to document the donor's commitment (pledge) to the project or initiative he or she is supporting.

Development officers view the gift agreement as a document that puts the donor's commitment in writing; an agreement should be prepared for each major gift received. Administration, by contrast, views the gift agreement as documentation for how to administer a general ledger gift account in accordance with the donor's intent. It is important to meet both objectives. However, in order to ensure compliance with the donor's intent (from an administrative point of view), it is important to make sure that only one gift agreement is prepared for each gift account. If there are multiple gift agreements for each general ledger gift account with different purposes, it is very difficult for administration to ensure compliance with the donor's intent.

If a donor is making a gift to a gift account that already exists (such as a routine annual fund account or a specific capital fund account), there is no need to prepare a new gift agreement. If this is a major gift and the donor wants a gift agreement, the organization may choose to prepare a separate gift agreement or a gift agreement addendum that addresses *only* the donor's commitment. As for documenting the use of funds, the new agreement or addendum should refer to the original agreement already on file, and a copy of the original should be attached to the new agreement or addendum so that the donor is assured as to how his or her gift will be used. This will help ensure that each gift account has only one purpose, thus making the administration of it easier.

There are several parts to a gift agreement (see Resource 22). At a minimum, the gift agreement should include the following:

*Name of nonprofit.*

*Account name.*

*Parties to the agreement:* Can list one major donor or simply indicate that multiple donors will be supporting this account.

*Department or organization with authorization over the funds.*

*Whereas clauses:* Can be used to outline donors' commitment to projects or initiatives they are supporting, as well as to recognize them (that is, to note their tie to or past support of the organization). This is usually referred to as the "warm and fuzzy" section. Some organizations do not include this section. It is not a requirement, but it is very good for donor relations and stewardship.

*Donor intent (purpose of the fund):* Should contain a clear statement of the donor's intent, including answers to the following questions: Is the gift itself to be spent or only the income from the gift? Do any donor preferences need to be spelled out? Does money have to be spent each year? What happens to any unused money? Is it reinvested in the corpus, or does it remain spendable in future periods?

*Statement as to who has responsibility for managing the use of the funds and the internal operating policies that govern the administration of the funds.*

*Type or duration of account:* Should use language that makes it clear whether the donor funds will be deposited into an endowment or nonendowment account.

*Investment policies or fees charged:* Should reference the investment policies of the organization (that is, any spending policy) or any fees charged. The donor needs to understand how the funds will be managed as well as what will be available for the intended purpose.

*Statement as to the powers or responsibilities the nonprofit and its board have over the gift funds, as well as any future gifts into this account.*

*Statement regarding alternate use procedures should the nonprofit no longer be able to fulfill the donor's original intent.*

*Reference to the fact that the nonprofit's state laws will govern the gift agreement.*

*Signature section for all parties involved:* Should be signature lines for all donors. If several donors are funding the account, this section may include a signature line for a donor representative. If there is no donor representative, only the benefiting entity or recipient responsible for managing the funds and the nonprofit chief executive officer or the board chair would sign the agreement.

Once the gift agreement is drafted, the development officer, the benefiting unit or recipient of the funds, administration, and possibly the legal counsel for the organization should review it. See Exhibit 6.3 for a flowchart describing the gift agreement process.

## EXHIBIT 6.3. GIFT AGREEMENT PROCESS FLOWCHART.

### Step 1

- Development officer works with donor to determine donor intent and drafts gift agreement from organization's template.
- Development officer gets approval from appropriate administrator.
- Standard template may be shown to donor as appropriate. Deviations from the standard template should be approved in Steps 2–4 before being shown to donor.
- Supporting documents (solicitation card and the like) should be forwarded with gift agreement where no donor signature is required (as when there are multiple donors).
- Development officer should make sure new account request is completed and forwarded to Account Administration along with gift agreement.

### Step 2

- Development officer works with Account Administration to review gift agreement and discuss all administrative aspects of the gift.

### Step 3

- Account Administration staff forwards agreement for legal review as necessary.
- Gift agreement is prepared in final form with an original copy for each signer.

### Step 4

- Development officer has final gift agreement signed by donor and appropriate administrator and returns it to Account Administration.

### Step 5

- Account Administration sends gift agreement to chief executive officer for signature.
- Organization's original is filed in Account Administration.
- Remaining originals are sent to development officer for distribution as appropriate internally and to donor.

Many times donors want to put restrictions in place that will either make administering the account difficult or make it unallowable by one of the governing bodies. In working with donors to review gift agreements, the following tips should be kept in mind:

• Avoid specified dollar amounts for scholarships (for example, $500 per recipient), fellowships, prizes, awards, grants, or other donor-stipulated expenses. If the donor is insistent on setting a dollar amount, try to see if it is acceptable to say, for example, "minimum of X dollars or a percentage of the earnings." This takes the donor's wishes into account while giving the nonprofit flexibility to change the numbers in the future as the account grows and as inflation erodes purchasing power.

• Avoid specifying a number of recipients of the funds. If the donor is insistent on setting the number of recipients, try to see if it is acceptable to say, for example, a "minimum number" of recipients. Again, this will take the donor's wishes into account while giving the nonprofit flexibility to change in the future as the account grows.

• Prohibit allowing the donor to control the asset or investment decisions. Per IRS regulations, in order for the donor's money to be considered a charitable contribution, the donor must give up control over the funds.

• Prohibit allowing the donor to select a specific individual recipient. If the donor is insistent, donors can be allowed to serve in a consultative role because the IRS does not allow direct participation. Donors may never constitute a majority opinion in a selection. If that happens, the tax deductibility of the gift could be called into question.

• Avoid letting the donor set up specific requirements that are difficult or impossible to administer over time (for example, requiring the placing of flowers on the donor's grave in perpetuity).

• Avoid letting the donor restrict a fund such that the nonprofit is not able to use the fund on an annual basis (for example, a donor expressing a choice of students from a certain county or small high school). Try to state the donor's wishes as a preference, with a secondary, broader-based criterion in case the preference cannot be met. Remember that the preferences cannot violate the nonprofit's internal policies or be prohibited by law (for example, discrimination by race or religion).

• Encourage donors to support existing accounts if they cannot meet the organization's minimum monetary requirements to open a new account.

• Insert an escape clause in the gift agreement if you feel the donor will not fulfill his or her promise (for example, if the endowment minimum account balance is not met within five years, then the funds will be redirected to an existing account).

- Insert an escape clause if there is a possibility of receiving more money than the amount needed for the project (for example, gifts in excess of what's needed for the designated purpose may be used for other, similar projects).
- Ensure that the donor understands the potential use of funds (scholarship funds such as books, fees, and tuition versus an award, which is nonspecific use of the funds, that has different tax implications for the recipient).

The most important thing to keep in mind in preparing a gift agreement is to clearly state the donor's intentions. That provides clear guidelines as to what the funds can and cannot be used for, along with flexibility as the funds grow or as future changes occur.

## Account Structure

Once the gift agreement is completed, the general ledger account to hold the donated funds should be created. A nonprofit can create its own account structure, keeping in mind that there are two types of accounts: *endowments* and *nonendowments*. *Endowments* are accounts to hold donor funds when the donor gave the money intending that the organization use the investment earnings only to support his or her purpose. The donor's gift must exist in perpetuity. *Nonendowments* are accounts to hold gifts when the donor gives money intending that the organization use it, along with any investment earnings, for expenditures that support the fund's designated purpose. The donor may ask the nonprofit to use the earnings first. However, all the funds given are expendable toward the donor's intended purpose.

The physical account structure can take many different forms, but it is important to keep in mind that you will be asked to categorize accounts for financial reporting purposes, as directed by FASB or GASB. For FASB, this means the accounts will have to be segregated into three categories: permanently restricted, temporarily restricted, and unrestricted. *Permanently restricted* accounts hold funds that are subject to donor-imposed restrictions that can never be removed by the passage of time or by the actions of the nonprofit. *Temporarily restricted* accounts hold funds that are subject to donor-imposed restrictions that expire by the passage of time or can be removed by the actions of the nonprofit. *Unrestricted accounts* hold funds that the nonprofit can use as it sees fit, subject only to the limitations imposed by its mission and its articles of incorporation, by-laws, or similar documents.

Permanent endowment accounts have two parts to the account. One part is the spendable portion—earnings from the endowment. This is considered the temporarily restricted portion. The second part is the gift that will be held in perpetuity. This is considered the permanently restricted portion. One way to account for this is to establish two separate accounts for each permanent endowment. One account is for the permanently restricted amounts (the gifts); the other is for the spendable amounts (investment earnings). If the nonprofit is using some kind of trust software, one account for each permanent endowment would be established with an income (spendable) portion and a principal (permanently restricted) portion.

It may also be important to embed in the account number a code indicating who the benefiting entity or purpose is so that total funds held for that entity or purpose can be easily calculated. Regardless of the physical account structure chosen, the key is to be able to segregate endowment accounts into two parts—what is spendable and what is not.

## Alternate Use

Once the funds are in the established account, there may come a time when the nonprofit has to deal with alternate use. *Alternate use* refers to circumstances where the specific terms of a gift agreement can no longer be complied with, and the governing board of the nonprofit may consider alternatives to the literal donor instructions. Situations that may warrant alternate use include restrictions that become illegal, obsolete, or impossible to perform; restrictions that become contrary to the nonprofit's policy after a policy change; or times when the designated use has ceased to exist. The nonprofit should develop policies as to what warrants an alternate use review, as well as steps the nonprofit will take to approve the alternate use request. Keep in mind that all recommendations for alternate use must retain as close as possible the original charitable goals of the donor. The nonprofit should ask for a written request outlining how the recipient plans to use the funds, as well as the circumstances that prevent using the funds as directed by the donor. The nonprofit's legal counsel or adviser should review these requests, and the governing board should ratify all final recommendations. This will ensure a documented trail as to how and why donor intent was amended.

## Gift Handling and Processing

Now that you have documented donor intent and created a gift account to hold the funds, the next step is the handling and processing of the donated funds. The actual handling of the funds is a pure test of the nonprofit's integrity. Is it doing what it promised? And does it have proper checks and balances in place to ensure compliance with donor wishes and provide verification?

## Charitable Contributions

The IRS defines a *charitable contribution* as a donation or gift to, or for the use of, a qualified organization. A donation or gift is voluntary and is made without getting or expecting to get anything of equal value in return.

Examples of items that are *not* considered charitable contributions are

- A contribution to a specific individual
- A contribution to a nonqualified organization
- The portion of a contribution from which you receive or expect to receive a benefit
- The value of your time or services
- Your personal expenses
- Appraisal fees
- Certain contributions of partial interests in property

According to IRS Publication 526, organizations that are qualified to receive charitable contributions include the following nonprofits: religious, charitable, educational, and scientific or literary groups, or groups that work to prevent cruelty to children or animals.

## Gift Receipts

The gift-receipting process must comply with the IRS substantiation rules. These rules require that the donor substantiate any charitable contributions of $250 or more in order for the amount to be deductible. Because the IRS requires that donors substantiate their donations, it is appropriate for the nonprofit to provide them with appropriate documentation. *Appropriate documentation* means that the nonprofit, as required by the IRS, must provide donors with a written receipt for each contribution of $250 or more, either by the time donors file their tax return or on or before the due date, whichever is earlier.

The gift receipt must address five IRS requirements:

1. The dollar amount of cash contributed must be stated.
2. A description, but not a value, of any property contributed must be included.
3. If the donor received no goods or services in return for the contribution, the acknowledgment must state that.
4. If the donor received goods or services in return for the contribution other than an "intangible religious benefit" or token items of "insubstantial value," the acknowledgment must describe them and provide a "good faith estimate" of their value.
5. If the only benefit the donor has received is an "intangible religious benefit," the acknowledgment must so state.

Nowhere in the IRS requirements does it state that the charity is required to include the donor's name or the date of the gift on the receipt. However, the Tax

Court has disallowed charitable deductions when the donor's receipt did not include the date of the contribution or donor name (Burrell, Jr., T.C. Memo 1994—574)! As for the date of the gift, organizations have two choices. They can use either the date the gift was received or the date the gift was processed. However, for gifts made by credit card, the date of the gift is when the charge was posted to the donor's credit card account. Even though gift receipts are not required on gifts of less than $250, it is good business practice as well as good stewardship to provide gift receipts for all gifts (see Resource 23).

Many times a nonprofit also sends donors an acknowledgment letter with the gift receipt. The acknowledgment letter is a more friendly, enthusiastic correspondence describing the gift received and how it will be used and expressing appreciation. Even though a gift acknowledgment letter and a gift receipt are different, a properly constructed acknowledgment letter can be a receipt for substantiation purposes if it contains the required items that are listed earlier.

## Quid Pro Quo Gifts

One receipt requirement is to list any goods or services received in return for a gift. This is known as a quid pro quo gift—a payment made partly as a contribution and partly for goods or services provided to the donor by the charity. For quid pro quo gifts greater than $75, the IRS requires the nonprofit to (1) inform the donor that the amount of the contribution that is deductible is limited to the excess of any money contributed by the donor over the value of the goods or services provided by the charity and (2) provide the donor with a good faith estimate of the value of the goods or services that he or she received.

The nonprofit must furnish the disclosure statement at the time of solicitation or after the gift is received. Failure to provide this disclosure may cause the IRS to impose a penalty of $10 per contribution, not to exceed $5,000 per fundraising event or mailing.

Here's an example of a quid pro quo gift: A donor pays $65 for a ticket to a dinner dance, knowing through the solicitation material that all the proceeds of the function go to the nonprofit and that the ticket to the dinner dance has a fair market value of $25. The gift receipt must show a total gift received of $65 and an itemized benefit of a dinner in the amount of $25, with a deductible portion of $40.

Another example would be a fundraising auction. A donor contributing an item to be used in a charity auction is eligible for a tax deduction related to the donation and should receive a gift-in-kind receipt (which is discussed later in this chapter). For those who purchase items at the charity auction, only the amount, if any, in excess of the fair market value of the items purchased can be consid-

ered a charitable contribution. The receipt to the individual who purchased something at the auction would indicate the value of the goods received and inform
the donor of the tax deductible portion.

One final type of income that could be labeled as a quid pro quo gift is membership dues. Annual membership benefits offered to a donor in exchange for a
payment of $75 or less per year can be disregarded if the benefits consist of the
following:

> *Any rights or privileges that the donor can exercise frequently during the membership.*
> Examples are free or discounted admission to the organization's facilities,
> free or discounted parking, and discounts on the purchase of goods or
> services.
>
> *Free admission to "members only" events.* This would apply when the cost of the
> event is no higher than the IRS limit of $7.40 (for tax year 2000).

If the benefits received are substantive, commercial-quality publications or
educational programs, special events, or an ability to vote in elections that determine the course of business for the nonprofit, only the amount received above the
value associated with the benefits received can be deducted as a contribution.

An example of a membership dues gift would be this: In December of each
year, Mr. Smith gives the science museum a $50 check for a membership in the
museum. This membership entitles him to free admission to the museum and to
weekly films, slide shows, and lectures. In addition, he receives a monthly non-
commercial-quality newsletter with information about upcoming events and new
exhibits. The museum's receipt to Mr. Smith would state that no goods or services
were provided in exchange for his payment.

Sometimes the value received by the donor is equal to or greater than the
contribution he or she made. An example might be a fundraising event that hosts
a silent auction for various items, with the proceeds being used to support student
scholarships. A donor may submit a bid of $50 for an item that has a fair market
value of $100. In such a case, a gift has not been made. The gift receipt would
indicate the value of the item received at $100 and inform the donor that the tax
deductible portion of the gift is zero.

An exception to the quid pro quo rules is that if the goods or services given
to a donor have an "insubstantial value," the nonprofit does not have to inform
the donor of the value of the goods or services received. What the IRS is saying is
that nonprofits can provide items of token or small value to donors without affecting their tax deductibility. If this is the case, the receipt to the donor should indicate that the value of the benefit received is insubstantial and the full amount of
the gift is allowed.

The benefits received are considered to have insubstantial value, and no disclosure is necessary if either of the following conditions is present:

1. A donor makes a gift to a nonprofit and receives benefits with a fair market value of not more than 2 percent of the gift or $74 (for tax year 2000; adjusted annually for inflation), whichever is less.
2. A donor makes a gift of $37 (for tax year 2000; adjusted annually for inflation) or more to a nonprofit and receives only token items in return.

The items are considered to have insubstantial value if they bear the charity's name or logo and have an aggregate cost to the charity of $7.40 (for tax year 2000; adjusted annually for inflation) or less.

It should also be noted that IRS regulations on substantiation indicate that a donor who has properly rejected a benefit offered by the nonprofit may claim a deduction for the full amount of the gift, and the receipt does not have to show the value of the benefit rejected. The regulations indicate that a proper rejection could be something as simple as the nonprofit offering a check box on the solicitation material provided to the donor that he or she could use to reject the benefit at the time of the gift (Rev. Rul. 67-246, Example 7). However, a proper rejection is not made if the donor simply chooses not to use a benefit that is made available. In this case, the deduction is limited to the amount of the gift in excess of the benefit provided.

## Corporate Sponsorship

In addition to gifts received from individuals, a nonprofit can receive gifts from corporations. Sometimes these are referred to as corporate sponsorships. According to accounting rules, these funds can be treated and recorded as charitable contributions as long as the sponsor receives nothing of substantial benefit in exchange for its gift. According to the IRS guidelines, the nonprofit organization may use or acknowledge the sponsor's name, logo, or product lines in connection with its activities without it resulting in a substantial benefit to the sponsor. This means that 100 percent of the funds given by the corporation is considered a gift. If the gift is acknowledged, it cannot contain any element of advertising such as price information or endorsements or inducements to use the sponsor's product or services. If it contains any of these items, it is considered payment for advertising, not a gift.

## Corporate Matching Gifts

In addition to corporate sponsorships, a nonprofit can receive matching gift funds from a company. These are funds from companies who have agreed to match charitable contributions made by their employees who contribute to a broad range of eligible institutions (see Resource 24). These companies establish their own policies as to

- What contributions qualify; some companies may not match gifts to athletics.
- Who are eligible donors; some companies may not match gifts from spouses.
- Who are eligible institutions or organizations; some will not match gifts to religious organizations.

Basically, this is "free" money to a nonprofit: all it needs to do is remind donors that if they work for a matching gift company, they need to complete the matching gift form (see Resource 25). The forms for this program are available from the company and not the nonprofit organization. The matching gift form requires the employee to complete a section outlining the amount and purpose of the gift. Once the employee completes that portion, he or she is required to send it to the organization that will receive the gift; the recipient must sign the form and return it to the matching gift company. This signature verifies receipt of the gift and, in some cases, that it complies with the matching gift company's policies. In order for a nonprofit to continue to be eligible to receive these types of funds, it must comply with the matching gift company policies. Many times a company will follow up with an audit to ensure that the nonprofit is complying with its policies. Noncompliance can mean loss of future matching gift funds as well as any further corporate support.

## Honoraria and Royalties

The nonprofit may also receive checks from companies that represent honoraria or royalties. It is important to research these checks further due to possible tax consequences.

*Honoraria* are payments made for services rendered, and *royalties* are payments made for copyright services performed or for the use of an invention. If the donor has performed the service that generated the honorarium or royalty, the payment should be made payable to the individual who performed the service. If the donor is interested in using these funds to make a charitable contribution, he or she can then endorse the check over to the nonprofit or issue the nonprofit a separate check. IRS regulations indicate that payments for services rendered are taxable to the individual who performed the service. Therefore the organization that received the services will be required to issue a Form 1099 to the person who performed the service. The Form 1099 should not come to the nonprofit. If it does, it could look as though the nonprofit is involved in some kind of unrelated business. If this is deemed to be the case by the IRS, the nonprofit could be subject to an unrelated business income tax.

## Gifts-in-Kind

In addition to cash gifts, a nonprofit can receive noncash gifts or gifts-in-kind, that is, gifts of nonmonetary items of tangible personal property such as art, collectibles, books, equipment, or automobiles or other assets or materials that represent value to the nonprofit and a furtherance of its mission. Donations of professional or personal services are not allowable by the IRS as a charitable contribution. For example, artists can only deduct the cost of the materials and supplies purchased for artwork they create and donate and not the time they spent creating the artwork. Unreimbursed expenses such as food and limited use of private property are not considered tax-deductible, charitable gifts-in-kind by the IRS.

In the case of a gift-in-kind, the receipt must describe but need not value the property received. Valuation of the donated property is the responsibility of the donor, and IRS Publication 561 is available to help donors determine this value. Donors making gifts of personal property greater than $500 must file Form 8283 (see Resource 21) with their tax return. It is the donor's responsibility to complete this form and get it to the nonprofit so it can be signed by the person who originally received the gift.

Donors making gifts of personal property greater than $5,000 must also file Form 8283 and provide the form to the nonprofit, which is required to sign the form acknowledging receipt of the gift-in-kind. In addition to filing Form 8283, the donor must have an appraisal by a qualified appraiser. For gifts of personal property greater than $5,000, the IRS requires the donor to send a qualified appraisal with his or her tax return substantiating the value claimed as a charitable contribution. The donor should provide a copy of this appraisal to the nonprofit so that the value may be recorded in the gift system and used for insurance purposes.

If the donor does not indicate the value of the gift-in-kind, the nonprofit should determine how it wishes to account for the gift. It may want to record the value of the gift in its gift system at $1 (most systems require a value) or may want to cover the cost of obtaining a value from a qualified outside source. However, the nonprofit would *only* do this in order to reflect a proper value in its gift system and to obtain a value for insurance purposes. It is important to remember that the donor is solely responsible for determining the value of the gift-in-kind and reporting it to the IRS.

If the gift-in-kind is sold by the nonprofit within two years of the date it was received and had a value greater than $500, the nonprofit is required to file Form 8282 (see Resource 21). A copy of the form must be sent to the IRS as well as the donor. The IRS uses this form to verify the validity of the charitable gift amount deducted on the donor's tax return.

## Pledges

Not only do nonprofits receive outright gifts but they may also receive commitments for future charitable contributions. These are referred to as promises-to-give or pledges. The nonprofit should develop a policy outlining requirements needed in order to record a pledge in the gift system. Data elements needed to record a pledge include a donor signature (preferred), the pledge amount, an indication of whether the pledge is conditional or unconditional, installment dates (annually, semiannually, quarterly, monthly, or date certain), installment amount, account name and number, and an indication of whether or not the donor should receive a reminder for future installments due.

A conditional pledge occurs when a donor promises to make a pledge only if specified future and uncertain events or conditions occur. In this case, the pledge can be recorded on the gift system, but it should not be recorded on the financial statements until such time as the condition has been met or waived by the donor. This is because the donor is not bound by the promise until the event or condition occurs. An unconditional pledge occurs when a donor promises to make a pledge that depends only on the passage of time (for example, by a predefined installment due date or at death). In this case, the pledge should be recorded on the gift system as well as in the financial statements.

A nonprofit should not record a verbal commitment for a major gift in the gift system without the accompaniment of signed donor correspondence or a signed memo from the development officer outlining the conversation and commitment. Furthermore, a signed gift agreement, by itself, should not be considered an acceptable document to record a pledge unless it contains all of the necessary data elements listed earlier.

Additional documents an organization could use to record a pledge include a signed pledge card, a signed payroll deduction form, some donor-signed correspondence, an automated clearinghouse (ACH) form, and correspondence or a memo, signed by the development officer, outlining the conversation and commitment of the donor. These examples are all acceptable documents as long as they include all of the necessary data elements.

## Pledge Reminders

Once the pledge has been recorded, a donor reminder system should be established to address billing for future installments. For example, reminders could be sent to the donor thirty days prior to an installment being due. If the installment goes past due, a reminder could be generated thirty, sixty, and ninety days past the installment due date. Not only is a nonprofit responsible for establishing a reminder system, it must also establish a write-off policy for pledges determined to be uncollectible, that is for pledges "X" number of days past due.

The nonprofit can determine its own definition of what is not collectible; one standard could be to write off all unfulfilled annual fund pledges at the end of the nonprofit's fiscal year plus other pledges over 120 days old. Once this definition is set, the nonprofit is required by accounting rules to write these off and reduce the organization's receivables by this amount because these will probably never be received as cash in hand. The nonprofit should also establish an allowance for pledges that remain on the books that may not be collectible. A lot of times, the allowance is calculated based on historical trends (for example, a percentage the nonprofit has not collected over a specified period of time).

## Gift Account Expenditures

The final process in administrating gifts and donor accounts is the expenditure of the funds in accordance with donor intent, the nonprofit's policies, and applicable rules and regulations. In most organizations, this function is not a part of development services. However, it is the final step in compliance with donor intent and thus very important. Development officers need to be familiar with and attentive to this function to ensure that the gifts they accept are actually spent in accordance with their donors' wishes. Attention to this function may also give the development officer guidance as to how to structure the gift to avoid certain tax consequences.

It is the responsibility of the account administrator (usually the nonprofit's recipient and manager of gift funds) to know the restrictions and to request expenditures that comply with the donor's intent. It is the responsibility of the nonprofit to make sure the requested expenditures comply with the donor intent before any funds are released.

When an expenditure is needed, a check request should be completed by the account administrator. The check request must state and document the purpose of the expenditure in order to indicate clearly the benefit to the nonprofit and the way the expenditure meets the donor's intent. All expenditures requested must be reasonable in amount. In addition, sensitivity to the appearance of proper use is expected.

## Scholarships and Fellowships

When it comes to the payment of expenditures, the IRS has established many rules that the nonprofit needs to know and follow. For instance, Publication 520 outlines the rules for scholarships, fellowships, and tuition reductions. These payments are free of any tax if they meet the rules discussed in this publication. The publication also discusses the estimated tax rules and some of the special rules that apply to U.S. citizens and resident aliens who are studying, teaching, or researching abroad under scholarships and fellowships.

If the only restriction a donor has placed on his or her gift is that it be used for scholarships or fellowships with no further criteria or limitation, it is a good idea to follow the IRS definitions of these items. This will minimize the tax consequences to the recipient and the tax reporting for the nonprofit. The IRS defines a scholarship as an amount paid for the benefit of a student at an educational institution to aid in the pursuit of his or her studies. The student may be either an undergraduate or graduate. However, a fellowship is generally an amount paid for the benefit of an individual to aid in the pursuit of study or research. According to the IRS, a qualified scholarship or fellowship that would be free of any tax

- Can be used for tuition and fees paid to enroll in or to attend an educational institution
- Can be used for fees, books, supplies, and equipment that are required for the courses at the educational institution (items must be required of all students in a course of instruction)
- Cannot require a performance of a service

It is a very good idea to have scholarship and fellowship payments applied to the student's bursar bill. This will ensure that the money is used only for allowable expenses, as defined by the IRS. Knowing the IRS definitions will enable the development officers to explain to a donor the types of expenses for which his or her gift funds can be used.

## Payments to Non-U.S. Citizens

Another area where the IRS and the INS have established rules for the nonprofit to follow is in payments to non-U.S. citizens. If your organization receives any gift funds that could be used to support payments to non-U.S. citizens (scholarships, fellowships, honoraria, and so on), you need to be concerned with Publication 515. This publication outlines rules for withholding tax on payments to non-U.S. citizens and requires the nonprofit to file various tax forms.

A non-U.S. citizen may be exempt from withholding if there is a tax treaty in place between his or her country of origin and the United States. Under most tax treaties, pay for independent personal services performed in the United States is exempt from U.S. income tax only if the non-U.S. citizen performs the services during a period of temporary presence in the United States (usually not more than 183 days) and is a resident of the treaty country. Thus the pay is not exempt from U.S. tax if the contractor is a U.S. resident. To claim an exemption from withholding under a tax treaty, non-U.S. citizens must use Form 8233 (see Resource 21). The completed Form 8233 must be sent to the nonprofit, along with a copy of their visa and I94 form. The nonprofit determines if the payment is allowable under the individual's type of visa, as defined by the INS. If everything is acceptable, all the documents are sent to the IRS. The nonprofit must then wait ten days for the IRS to process the documents. If at the end of ten days the nonprofit has not heard from the IRS, it can release the payment.

## Tax Forms

In addition to making sure expenditures comply with donor intent, nonprofit polices, and IRS rules, a nonprofit is responsible for filing several calendar-year-end tax forms; one is the Form 1099 (see Resource 21). This form is used to report miscellaneous income for each person the nonprofit has paid at least $600 (threshold for 2000). The IRS requires organizations to report on Form 1099 the following payments: rents, services, prizes and awards (a payment based on an accomplishment or activity), and other income payments. Therefore it is important that the nonprofit have a form to collect the information needed to complete the Form 1099 at calendar year-end. The critical information to collect is the payee's name, address, and tax ID. The best approach to ensuring that you get this information is to require it before the payment is released; sometimes it is difficult to obtain after the fact. Fees are assessed by the IRS if an organization does not complete Form 1099 with the correct information.

A second annual tax form the nonprofit may be required to file is Form 1042 and 1042-S (see Resource 21). This form is used to report tax withheld on certain income of nonresident aliens, foreign partnerships, foreign corporations, and nonresident alien or foreign fiduciaries of estates or trusts. As discussed previously, IRS Publication 515 outlines what income is subject to withholding. However, organizations must withhold tax at the 30 percent rate on compensation paid to a non-U.S. citizen for labor or personal services performed in the United States, unless that pay is specifically exempted from withholding or subject to graduated withholding. This rule applies regardless of place of residence, place where the contract for service was made, or place of payment.

These are just a few of the rules to be concerned about when expending donor funds. Keep in mind that, as a nonprofit in the fundraising business, you are legally and morally responsible for ensuring compliance with donor intent. This is as much the business of the development staff as it is the business office. Development officers need to know whether the money they have raised is being used or not. In addition, they need to know enough to avoid making promises the nonprofit cannot keep.

## Accountability

Up to this point, this chapter has focused on what the nonprofit needs to do to make sure it is complying with the donor's wishes, the nonprofit's policies, and governing rules and regulations. The next step is to provide accountability. It goes beyond simply administering the gift to ensuring, through dispassionate third-party review, that the gift administration process is not persuaded by institutional or individual staff or board member judgment, or any other factor except the donor's expressed intent. In order to secure future gifts, it is equally important for the nonprofit to inform the donor that his or her wishes have been complied with. This involves accountability. Nonprofits need to be accountable to their donors. Accountability ensures integrity by demonstrating compliance with donor intent. Donors have invested in the nonprofit; now the nonprofit must show that it is responsibly managing their funds.

Nonprofits can do this in many ways. Examples are to

- Provide donors with a statement on their named or endowed account (see Exhibit 6.4).
- Provide calendar-year-end statements to donors indicating their giving history.
- Include donors and recipients of their funds in events.
- Provide regular investment reports in order to show donors how the funds are doing.
- Make sure there is regular communication with donors about what their gift has provided.
- Provide immediate response to donors inquiring specifically about their gift or, more generally, how the funds are managed.

The most important thing is to keep the donor informed and involved. By keeping donors informed, the nonprofit shows them that it is accountable and responsible and that the nonprofit has the appropriate procedures in place to ensure compliance with their wishes.

## Oversight

A final step a nonprofit may want to take to ensure compliance with donor intent is oversight. It is important to establish internal checks and balances to provide even-tempered objectivity to the administration of donor accounts, which can be accomplished by doing any of the following:

## EXHIBIT 6.4. DONOR ACCOUNT STATEMENT.

### Example 1

Name of Organization
Name of Fund
July 1, YEAR through June 30, YEAR

| Description | Disbursements | Income | Balance |
|---|---|---|---|
| July 1, YEAR beginning cash balance | | | $xxxxxx |
| Income | | $xxxxxx | |
| Disbursements | | | |
|    Scholarship/Professorship Award | $xxxxxxx | | |
|    Dues and Subscriptions | xxxxxx | | |
|    Materials and Supplies | xxxxxx | | |
|    Total disbursements | $xxxxxxx | | |
| June 30, YEAR ending cash balance | | | $xxxxxx |
| Market value of investments | | | $xxxxxx |

### Example 2

Endowment Report

Date

*Donor*
*Address 1*
*Address 2*
*City, State Zip*

Dear *Salutation,*

Thank you for your generous support of *(allocation description).* Because of the commitment of loyal friends such as you, the *(organization)* is able to award more than *($ amount)* for *(purpose).* Many *(recipient type)* would not be able to *(activity)* if it were not for this significant financial assistance. You enhance opportunities for future *(activity)*!

Beginning this academic year, we will provide you with an annual update on the recipients. The recipients of the *(fund)* for the *(time period):*

     RECIPIENT(S), HOME TOWN

Currently, the amount of principal in your endowment account is *(amount).* A total of *(amount)* in funding is projected to be available for this year.

Again, thanks for your foresight in supporting the *(organization)* through endowment-related gifts. Please call our office if you have any questions or comments.

Sincerely,


Chief Executive Officer

## Example 3

Name of Endowment Fund

*Endowment Financial Status*

Book Value:       **$$$$**
    (total gifts to fund)

Market Value:     **$$$$**
    (as of date)

---------------------------------------------------------------------------------

Recipient(s)
Major
Class
Hometown
Personal statement from Recipient(s)

---

***Communicating.*** Communication is probably the most important form of oversight a nonprofit can have but the hardest to achieve. All lines of communication must be open. When policies change or solicitations go out, these events need to be communicated to all staff to ensure proper processing, as well as compliance with donor intent.

***Educating Staff.*** All staff internal to the nonprofit, as well as those responsible for administering the funds, need to be made aware of the importance of compliance with donor intent. These individuals also need to understand the procedures in place for compliance and consequences for noncompliance. The nonprofit organization needs to ensure that these individuals receive notice of the gift agreement and any future amendments. It is important to educate staff that if they are in contact with the donor and the donor indicates a desire to change or update the intent, this needs to be communicated and documented.

***Establishing Internal Controls.*** Nonprofit organizations need to make sure they have the proper internal controls in place in order to ensure compliance with donor intent. They may want to begin by asking questions like these: Are accounts properly labeled with a type code that will assist accounts payable in determining if the expenditure is in accordance with donor intent? Are check requests completed properly, indicating the purpose of expenditure, and is this compared to the signed gift agreement? Do those who have the responsibility over the administration of the funds have access to the gift agreement that indicates the donor intent? Does the nonprofit have appropriate people in place reviewing the gift agreements during the draft phase in order to ensure they will be able to comply with donor intent? These are a few of the questions that need to be answered in order to make sure appropriate controls are in place.

*Using the Governing Board.* This group can provide an independent and objective resource to ratify internal decisions and provide the necessary guidance to ensure compliance with donor intent.

*Using External Auditors.* Many times external auditors focus only on the review of financial information. The nonprofit may find that the best oversight it has is to ask the external auditors to perform a disbursement audit. This audit would focus on disbursements made and how they comply with donor intent. The audit may assist the nonprofit in identifying areas that need to be strengthened.

*Establishing an Internal Audit Function.* You could create a separate internal audit function or appoint a staff person to perform this function. In either case, someone should spend dedicated time reviewing transactions processed against documented donor intent and organizational policies. This can serve as a great resource to the nonprofit's board and administration and provide a way to get regular reviews of compliance with donor intent.

*Forming a Compliance Committee.* This is an oversight committee that provides guidance and interpretation for the administration of the donor gift account. It is a way to pull together several resources of an organization (development, administration, and legal) to help with the interpretation and administration of the donor funds, as well as the establishment of policies over these funds. Only larger, more complex organizations use this type of committee.

It does not matter which options an organization chooses. There may even be additional options to consider. What matters is that the organization has some oversight in place to review and assess compliance with donor intent. After all, it is the compliance with donor intent that builds a strong foundation between the donor and the organization and creates an environment in which the donor's only question will be, "What else can I do to help?"

# CHAPTER SEVEN

# STEWARDING DONORS

The prospects have been researched, the cultivation is complete, the happy outcome is a successful solicitation, and gift administration is stewarding the gift. Now fundraising moves to another level, an even higher priority—saying thank-you to the donor for the current gift and preparing the way for the next one. This chapter outlines how to properly create a plan for saying thank-you, showing appreciation, giving recognition, and providing accountability to donors.

*Donor relations* is the descriptive phrase that applies to expressing appreciation to donors. But gone are the days when donor relations, or stewardship, simply refers to hosting non-strategic special events and distributing tokens. As the number of philanthropic organizations grows, nonprofits are seeking many of the same donors. Consequently, as nonprofit organizations establish themselves, this area is becoming a recognized part of a fully formed development program. It is essential that every institution, no matter how small or large, be strategic about the shepherding of current and potential donors.

Some people believe you cannot say thank-you too much. But you can. The purpose of donor relations is to express thanks for what has already been done and to prepare the way for the next solicitation. Too many nonprofits lose sight of the strategic, forward-looking nature of expressions of gratitude and become mired in a repetitious series of non-strategic activities. Donors give because they want to give, and they must be thanked for doing so. But donors who give and enjoy the experience *want* to be asked to give again. Do not deny them this additional pleasure if that is their desire!

An essential component of any follow-through program is the thoughtful, systematic organization of a donor relations effort. And that effort is all about relationships. Although a donor relations or donor stewardship officer can spearhead the overall effort, it is the responsibility of all those involved with the cultivation and solicitation of a gift to guarantee that current donors remain in the organization's embrace. Stewardship effectively begins before the first gift is received. Prospects, volunteers, and donors must be informed regularly, thanked often, and recognized for their generous efforts on an organization's behalf. Once a gift is received, stewardship encompasses a variety of activities centered on the donor, including recognizing, appreciating, and reporting gifts—all of which will further your organization's fundraising efforts measurably.

## Stewardship Plans

Every organization should prepare a written stewardship plan for its best donors. Then follow it; don't file it (see Table 7.1 and Exhibit 7.1). A stewardship plan is simply a written document that outlines and details a complete, systematic, comprehensive approach to managing relationships with donors at the various levels of support a nonprofit deems important.

Before determining the stewardship guidelines, ask the following questions of the organization:

Does the organization have a stated long-range plan or mission statement?

Is the fundraising and stewardship operation guided by that plan?

Will the organization be able to handle stewardship efforts guided by the size and scope of this plan?

Who are the people inside and outside the development office relied upon to make these stewardship options happen?

The flexibility of a stewardship plan begins at inception. The plan can be tailored on an individual basis (for example, to a board member) or done on the basis of recognition societies, or both. It is critical in the development of this plan to consider the organization's location and profile, as well as the characteristics of its donor base.

Effective, long-range strategic plans encompass not only the actual strategies for securing gifts but also the plans for preparing the donor for the next gift. The aim is for donors to remain a part of your continuous lifetime giving program (see Figure 7.1). The key to this is that if a donor specifically requests, either in person, by survey, or in a gift agreement, that certain stewardship requirements be met to retain and maintain loyalty, the organization must comply—willingly and correctly!

## TABLE 7.1. DONOR RECOGNITION AT VARIOUS GIVING LEVELS.

| Gift Levels | $100 | $500 | $1,000 | $2,500 | $5,000 | $10,000 | $25,000 | $50,000 | $75,000 | $100,000 |
|---|---|---|---|---|---|---|---|---|---|---|
| Acknowledgment / Receipt | X | X | X | X | X | X | X | X | X | X |
| Information (for example, newsletters, e-mails) | X | X | X | X | X | X | X | X | X | X |
| Mementos | X | X | X | X | X | X | X | X | X | X |
| Holiday card | | X | X | X | X | X | X | X | X | X |
| Special events (cultural, academic, athletic, black tie) | | | X | X | X | X | X | X | X | X |
| Holiday gift | | | | X | X | X | X | X | X | X |
| Birthday card | | | | X | X | X | X | X | X | X |
| Personal letter / Phone call from key volunteers or staff | | | | | X | X | X | X | X | X |
| Personalized site visit(s) | | | | | X | X | X | X | X | X |
| Personal letter / Phone call from the chief executive officer | | | | | | X | X | X | X | X |
| Reception with chief executive officer and key volunteers | | | | | | X | X | X | X | X |
| Letter from recipient of endowed fund | | | | | | X | X | X | X | X |
| Personal report on endowment | | | | | | X | X | X | X | X |
| Personal report on annual giving amounts and cumulative lifetime giving | | | | | | | | X | X | X |
| Publicity | | | | | | | | X | X | X |
| Personal visit from chief executive officer | | | | | | | | X | X | X |
| Personalized donor recognition event(s) | | | | | | | | | | X |

## EXHIBIT 7.1.  STEWARDSHIP CHECKLIST.

### UNIVERSITY OF FLORIDA FOUNDATION, INC.
*Stewardship Checklist*

The following list will help you choose stewardship next-step activities for donors to your college or unit who have made gifts of $100,000 or more during their lifetimes. Choose as many activities that apply, and enter them into your next activities plans.

---

### *GENERAL RECOGNITION OF THE GIFT*

| STANDARD RESPONSES (*New Gifts Only*) | SPECIAL RECOGNITION OF DONOR |
|---|---|
| Gift acknowledgment (UFF Records Dept) | Article in campus publication |
| Thank you letter from president (President's Council) | Special Event, Opening, Reception* |
| Thank you letter from vice president for development and alumni affairs (President's Council) | Groundbreaking Ceremony* |
| | Commendation |
| Thank you letter from dean/director and department chairman (where applicable) | Permanent recognition (e.g., wall plaque on campus building)* |
| Thank you letter from development officer | |
| Press release (UFF Publications Dept) | |

---

### *STEWARDSHIP SUGGESTIONS FOR ALL GIFTS*

| STEWARDSHIP VISITS | INVITATIONS | OTHER COMMUNICATIONS |
|---|---|---|
| President | President's box (football) | Annual Endowment Report |
| Vice president ODAA | President's area (basketball) | College/unit (newsletters, magazines) |
| Unit vice president | President's Council weekend | |
| Dean/director & dep't chair | Other University events | Birthday card |
| Development officer | College/unit events | Holiday card |
| | | Other |

---

### *STEWARDSHIP POSSIBILITIES BY GIFT KIND*

| EMINENT SCHOLAR CHAIRS/ ENDOWED PROFESSORSHIPS | ENDOWED SCHOLARSHIPS* | BUILDINGS (*New and Extensive Renovations*)* |
|---|---|---|
| Personal contact with chair holder/professor | Thank you letter from scholarship recipient(s) | Invitation to groundbreaking |
| Letter from chair holder/ professor about scholarly work | Letter from president about importance of scholarship | Invitation to dedication |
| Letter from president | Letter from dean/director | Commemorative photo album of building (inside and outside) |
| Letter from dean/director and department chair (where applicable) | Letter from development officer | Letter from president re use of building |
| | Invitation to annual UF scholarship recognition event† | Letter from dean/director and department chair (where applicable) |
| Letter from development officer | Invitation to college's annual scholarship recognition event | Letter from development officer |

---

†Proposed.

*Is there a videotaping opportunity?

### FIGURE 7.1. CONTINUOUS LIFETIME GIVING: THE GIVING LIFE CYCLE.

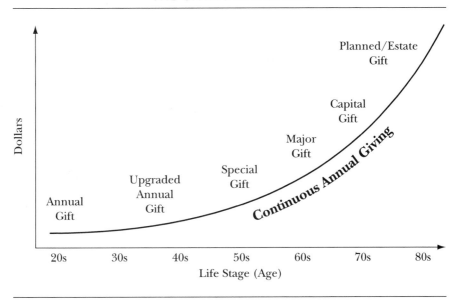

A few ways to craft a solid stewardship program are to do the following:

- Survey donors to discover their preferences and adhere to their wishes.
- Remember birthdays and anniversaries.
- Respect religious holidays, observances, customs, and dietary restrictions.
- Stop by when you are "in the neighborhood" and say hello; make sure you are occasionally in the neighborhood.
- Call occasionally just to say hello and check in.
- Clip and send articles of interest to donors.
- List names in the annual honor roll of donors.
- Send an annual donor statement to those with named and endowed accounts; accompany it with a thank-you letter.
- Provide advance notice of upcoming events and activities; offer to assist with tickets or to provide transportation, as appropriate.
- Offer appropriate courtesies and amenities; a parking pass for use while on campus or in your building is always appreciated.
- Send flowers occasionally; candy, too (except to diabetics).
- Ask donors how they are doing; ask how they think you are doing.
- Always try to find ways to say thank-you, to show appreciation, to remember, to let them know they are valued.

Every donor is special and should be treated as such. That is simple courtesy, and you never know when a $100-a-year donor will bequeath his or her entire estate. That said, there is also the practical side. In development programs that emphasize major gifts and planned giving, 80 to 90 percent of the funds typically come from 10 to 20 percent of the donors. In fiscal year 1999–2000, Indiana University received $109 million in private gifts. Two-thirds of those dollars came from its top two hundred donors (out of a donor base of one hundred thousand donors). Nonprofits that are more focused on annual giving generally find that about 60 percent of their dollars come from 20 to 30 percent of their donors. Even organizations that emphasize special event fundraising find that their financial success is heavily dependent on top-end sponsorships. Even though all donors are special and deserve to be treated well, all should not be treated the same. Treat each one appropriately and proportionally, according to his or her generosity.

Use best practices from the for-profit sector, such as high-end merchandisers like Nordstrom or Neiman-Marcus, who specialize in personal attention and attention to detail, or like the airline industry, which caters to its frequent flyers by knowing their preferences and satisfying them. As an example, send donors with named or endowed accounts an annual statement to show the balance in their fund at the beginning and end of the report period and to show what expenditures have been made. This should be accompanied by a thank-you letter. In it, whenever possible, show how the funds have been used. Tell about the students who have been aided (and wouldn't a letter directly from the scholarship recipient be appreciated!), or buildings built, or laboratories furnished, or children sent to camp, or programs provided. Describe the tangible benefits as well as the financial details (see Exhibit 6.4 in Chapter Six).

When developing a personalized strategy program for either individual donors or groups of donors (for example, all donors of $1,000+), the effective plan should include the components of appreciating, recognizing, and reporting. A successful fundraising program has plans and procedures for promptly acknowledging gifts with the appropriate measures of gratitude. Making a commitment to follow a designated plan for stewardship is a pledge that a donor will be thanked and recognized by an organization in a thoughtful and complete manner.

## Appreciation

No matter the size of the gift, there is nothing more important than acknowledging donors for their generosity. Even more important than thanking a donor is doing it right. Each donor should receive a personal letter of appreciation from the organization, either as a part of the gift receipt or accompanying the receipt.

Keep the following in mind:

- Thank them accurately.
- Thank them promptly.
- Thank them publicly.
- Thank them privately.
- Thank them frequently.
- Thank them appropriately.
- Thank them innovatively.
- Thank them gratefully.

All these elements are critical to the acknowledgment process, but the accuracy and timeliness of showing an organization's gratitude for a gift has proved to be the most important in the eyes of most donors. Correctly using a person's prefix (for example, using the preferred title Dr. instead of Ms.) or being certain the salutation is correct (for example, not addressing Mr. and Mrs. when there has been a divorce) will instill an appreciation and sense of confidence. When addresses are done carelessly, a large misunderstanding can be created that will require apologies later. The timeliness of acknowledging a gift by telephone or letter or in person will provide the donor with the added satisfaction that the organization truly values his or her gift.

## The Thank-You Letter

In composing a simple thank-you letter, make it more than a thank-you; make it personal, informative, and meaty. Tell the donor what is happening, how much has been raised, how the building project is progressing, and what the amount of endowment money is (see Resource 26).

And certain decisions need to be made in reference to the stewardship plan. Who will sign the letters? At what minimum level will institutional administrators and campaign leaders sign? $100? $500? $1,000? More? Is your thank-you letter as simple as a postcard to annual donors (see Exhibit 7.2)? Does your plan call for the institution to ask each volunteer to thank each donor and send the institution a copy of the thank-you letter? It should. For larger gifts, the chief executive officer should certainly provide a personal acknowledgment. The key volunteer working on the solicitation may also choose to communicate with the donor, as may the chair of the board and the chair of the campaign.

Small nonprofits can and should send thank-you letters within twenty-four to forty-eight hours after a gift is received. Larger organizations with layers of management may need longer to respond; a routing or processing procedure will ensure a well-done, continuous flow.

**EXHIBIT 7.2. DONOR THANK-YOU CARD.**

Front

To improve our community for everyone, United Way's goals are...

**Children and Youth will succeed.**

**People will have a second chance.**

**Families and Neighborhoods will be healthy and safe.**

**Seniors will not be alone.**

*Solutions for People*
UNITED WAY OF CENTRAL INDIANA

United Way of Central Indiana
3901 North Meridian Street
P.O. Box 88409
Indianapolis, IN 46208-0409

Nonprofit Org.
U.S. Postage
PAID
Permit No. 7662
Indianapolis, IN

*Solutions for People*
UNITED WAY OF CENTRAL INDIANA

**Thank You**

Back

## EXHIBIT 7.2. DONOR THANK-YOU CARD, Cont'd.

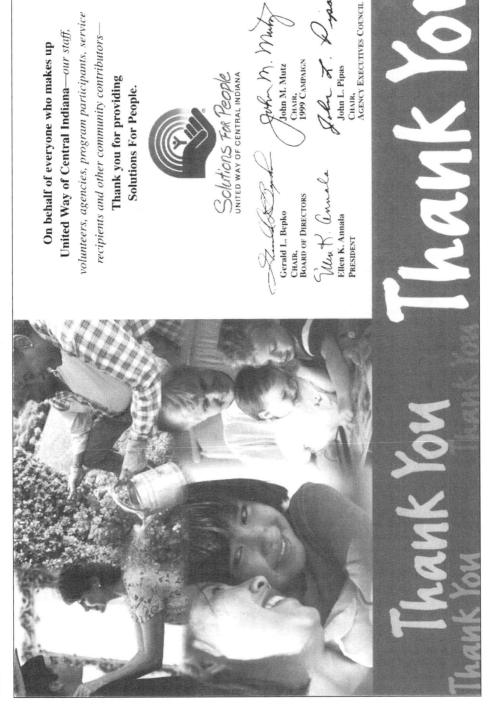

*Source:* Courtesy of United Way of Central Indiana.

An example of a plan for letter processing is as follows:

*Goal: to mail letters within five days of gift receipt*
- Draft to fundraiser within one day of gift date
- Draft approved and returned within one day
- Special letters reviewed by the chief development officer within one day
- Final letters to chief executive officer's office within one day
- Letters mailed within one day

Letters must be meaningful, yet succinct. Use information that the organization already has to further the content in the letters. Save quotations or favorite phrases (see Exhibit 7.3) to use in future letters.

Another suggestion is to build a reference library. Says Kristin V. Rehder (2000), a reference library should contain all or some of the following materials:

- Acknowledgment letters from past years or cycles
- The organization's fact sheet
- Speeches, statements, and letters from the current chief executive officer
- Current fundraising priorities
- List of gift opportunities with "selling price"
- Budget statements
- Treasurers' reports
- Recent reports to the governing board on special topics
- The organization's promotional material
- The inaugural addresses of all the organization's chief executive officers
- Any published histories, collection of letters, or articles about the institution
- *The Elements of Style*
- *Bartlett's Familiar Quotations*
- *The Chicago Manual of Style*

## Going Beyond a Letter

The way most nonprofits choose to say thank-you is very interesting. It is traditional and typical that donors are thanked by letter. This is often motivated by the fact that the thank-you letter also accompanies the gift receipt or serves as the gift receipt and must be done for that purpose, if no other. Thanking by letter, therefore, is a natural, easy thing for all nonprofits to do.

What is equally as interesting, however, is the failure of nonprofits to say thank-you in person or through a telephone call. Fundraisers will tell you that donors respond best to face-to-face appeals, with the telephone being the second-best solicitation technique, whereas direct mail is the technique that generally elicits the least

## EXHIBIT 7.3. PHRASES TO CONSIDER.

I want to thank you personally.

On behalf of all of us, a warm and heartfelt thanks.

Thank you so much for your foresight.

I am very pleased and even a little astounded at your recent addition to the _____ Fund.

These are some of my own highest priorities for the current year.

You and I share a vision of what _____ can accomplish.

Please visit us soon. I'd like for you to see the . . .

I hope we can count on your gift next year.

What we do is costly but well worth the contributions of those who believe in the impact this education can have on our graduates, and through them on the nation and world.

Because private giving has become an increasingly significant resource for us, your donation is extremely important.

Thank you for the personal investment you have made.

We are privileged and grateful to have the support that you so generously give to our institution.

I am a great believer in the strengths of this organization—in our ability to transform people, to give them a sense of direction and the tools to succeed both in the workplace and in their lives. Thank you for believing in us as well.

Our very character depends on our ability to provide scholarship assistance to promising students. Your generosity toward this vital area could not be more welcome, and I can assure you that it serves the institution and its students very well.

By making this gift, you have set an important example for others. Thank you for your leadership.

A college education remains the very best investment that young people make in their lives. Your willingness to invest in the students who come after you represents the spirit of giving in the truest sense.

We are a better community because you have provided funds to make financial aid available.

As always, we will work diligently to use your gift where it is most needed and make certain that all of our resources and energies are devoted to providing the very best education to the enormously talented students who join us each year.

You make it possible for us to place the bar high. I cannot thank you enough for your support.

*Source:* Kristin V. Rehder, CASE Conference, May 2000. Reprinted with permission.

response in terms of average size of gift and percentage of donors responding to the appeal. If this is the pattern in solicitation, will the appreciation factors not be the same when saying thank-you? Wouldn't a personal visit or telephone call be more effective ways of showing appreciation and saying thank-you than a letter? Generally, yes. So why don't more nonprofits incorporate these practices in their appreciation efforts? To be sure, personal visits and telephone calls must be made on a more selective basis than direct mail contacts, but all three techniques should be incorporated into every nonprofit's appreciation program.

## Properly Acknowledging Gifts

Gifts are made individually, and their acknowledgment should be considered individually. If more than one acknowledgment is to be made, the staff should make certain that the acknowledgments are not redundant and that they complement and reinforce each other.

Electronic methods of stewardship are quickly becoming a resource for organizations. The challenge of going high-tech while remaining high-touch vexes institutions around the country. If an organization knows that an individual would like to receive correspondence via e-mail or fax, do it. However, the acknowledgment must still have the personal touch that a stamp and a personalized envelope give.

Acknowledging gifts and thanking donors will be a time-consuming task, so to enable prompt, personal attention to donors, additional secretarial support or word processing capability may be needed. This is an important detail; long delays in acknowledging and thanking donors are unprofessional and make a bad impression. And be creative. This is the organization's chance to shine. Make the most of it.

Donor relations and stewardship efforts necessarily focus on donors, but volunteers must not be forgotten or neglected. Many donors are volunteers as well, and many volunteers will become donors because involvement with a nonprofit is often a precursor to investment in it. Just as with donors, never forget your volunteers and their efforts or fail to appropriately recognize and thank them.

# Recognition

Donor recognition is a distinguishing feature of a successful fundraising program. Recognition takes many forms, from donor recognition walls and honor rolls, to private dinners where accolades are given before an appreciative audience, to simply having the right person say thank-you. Whether or not people say they want to be recognized, the plain fact is that 99 percent of all people love recognition.

Opportunities and guidelines should be established within each nonprofit, with policy guidelines for naming facilities, providing endowments, and placing plaques and other forms of high-visibility recognition. It is more critical that the recognition be of value to the donor than be what suits the organization. A female donor may want a different tribute than a male donor (women are increasingly giving larger gifts in their own name and do not want to be listed with their spouses on a plaque or on an honor roll); corporations and foundations may not want to be listed on a donor wall but would prefer a private audience with the chief executive officer to discuss new initiatives. A series of awards to honor the major donors or volunteers in an organization can be done in a tasteful, meaningful way, particularly if the awards are given special names that embody meaning to the nonprofit.

Major donors need to become a part of a continuing recognition program. If they are properly appreciated in the recognition process, they are likely to make even greater gifts in the future. More and more entities are showering donors with recognition; therefore it becomes crucial to personalize the particular event or piece as much as possible so the organization stands out in the mind of the person being recognized. Public or private, written or spoken—recognition is all about the donor.

## Premiums

T-shirts, key chains, and bookmarks are a few examples of premiums that donors can receive as a result of generosity to a nonprofit (see Exhibit 7.4). Physical tokens of gratitude can range from inexpensive tokens like stickers and magnets to very expensive items like clocks and crystal. And some donors prefer "access" as opposed to a tangible item of thanks. They want access to key officials, parking privileges, upgrading of tickets to special events, and other personalized attention that costs the organization little but provides donors with a feeling of belonging. To ensure that the premium distributed to a donor is fitting for his or her level of contribution (both volunteer and monetary), make the use of premiums a component in the organization's stewardship plan.

Before spending money on a high-priced item, think about the recipient. Will a bookmark be enough? What will the reaction be to an expensive piece of crystal? An organization needs to be able to assure donors that their donated dollars did not help fund the premium they just received at the expense of meeting the needs of the organization. Also remember that the issue of fitting a premium to a donor goes two ways. Some situations and audiences require classy and tasteful, maybe even expensive, items, but they cannot be excessively so. Donors must feel appropriately appreciated but cannot feel that the reason they gave (to provide support) has been diminished. In this area, there is always a delicate balance to be considered. Too much in the donor's eyes can be just as bad as too little.

## EXHIBIT 7.4.  TOKEN COLLAGE.

## Tokens

All nonprofits must consider several implications when designing, purchasing, and giving tangible items.

- *Determine the budget.* Pens and pencils can run as little as $.06 per unit; mid-line items run between $2.00 and $10.00 per unit.
- *Determine the number you will need.* Quantity is not always quality. Plan for the number of pieces, no matter what the cost, before purchasing; buying more pieces to save a few dollars per piece is not always the most economical approach.
- *Get multiple bids.* Specialized marketing companies want a nonprofit's business. Vendors today, both in person and on-line, offer a variety of services that can produce quality premiums for donors. By waging a friendly competition between companies, an organization ensures the best price for any item.

No matter the organization's decision to purchase a certain tangible item, it is crucial to be aware of the limitations of good taste and applicable rules and regulations. Certain rules, such as the NCAA bylaw 1.16.1 or the IRS quid pro quo regulation (see Chapter Six), have been created to offer guidelines for how much can be spent on donor recognition or on certain tangible items.

## Access

Access and special privileges are two items that donors might value and that do not cost the organization a great deal. Parking passes, a special telephone number or contact to call in case questions arise, or upgrades in tickets for certain events create the everlasting feeling of being a part of an institution. Words of caution: do not promise more than you are prepared to deliver. For instance, parking passes to a theater series for donors of a certain giving level are valuable. However, if there are only fifteen parking spaces and three hundred members of a donor society are promised special passes, the recognition is lost and irritability is created instead.

## Walls, Plaques, and Busts

Establishing a recognition wall or mounting plaques or other types of three-dimensional recognition pieces guarantees the immortality of the donor's name in a public space and allows for the recognition of people who have made a significant contribution to the life of an institution. An essential component of establishing a public display of donor recognition is good planning. Here are a few things to consider:

• *Determine who is being recognized.* Is a single donor or couple being recognized? If so, a plaque or bust in an appropriate location (for example, outside a named room) can be created easily. If a large group of people is being honored (for example, in a recognition society), the criteria for having names placed on the plaque must be clearly defined and written out.

• *If it is a large group, plan carefully for space.* The current and projected number of members must be discussed in advance in order to avoid running out of room on a wall. Today companies use more technical expertise designing plaques than in the past and can help plan for growth; they can determine a feasible system for name changes, additions, or deletions.

• *Budget accordingly.* Plaques, walls, and busts are expensive ventures but well worth the money if done correctly. Do some price shopping. Compare the many options vendors will provide. Study the trends in all areas carefully. Plaques can have snap-on or screwed-in nameplates and wooden or laminate bases; many now incorporate a computer kiosk in the design (a great way to honor donors for a lot less money). According to Richard Baum (president of W&E Baum, a full-service recognition firm in Brooklyn, New York), donor recognition walls can cost anywhere from $5,000 to $100,000 (Harrison, 1999).

• *Take time to plan.* A donor recognition piece is expensive, visible, and time consuming to construct and maintain. It should last a lifetime not only on the wall or table itself but in the hearts of donors as an endearing brand. So do it well. Do it right. Consult peers in like organizations: Metal Décor or VisionMark, for example, specialize in constructing three-dimensional recognition pieces. Think through the objective in putting up a wall or plaque. By spending the money to do so, has the organization furthered its mission?

Plaques can also come in smaller, more creative packages. A bookplate, seat plate, or bust can speak volumes to the donor whose philanthropy furthered the nonprofit's mission (see Resource 27). Recognition pieces give an organization an opportunity to thank and publicly salute a donor. Not only that, but if a physical piece is done correctly, it illustrates to future donors the honest gratitude you have toward your donors.

## Recognition Societies

Recognition societies provide the connection and opportunity to engage donors at various giving levels. If an institution does things correctly, a society could be a fortuitous chance to recognize donors who have stepped up to the next level of support in the organization's giving pyramid.

A donor can become a part of a recognition society in one of two ways: (1) by designating a gift specifically earmarked for a certain society (an annual giving society) or (2) by achieving a certain yearly or lifetime giving level that gains automatic entrance. With the latter option, the organization must decide what will qualify a donor to enter, and the name of the society should be appropriate to the organization. Many organizations use a name such as President's Circle to denote that the society is honoring its highest level of donor (see Exhibit 7.5).

## EXHIBIT 7.5. PRESIDENT'S CIRCLE CRITERIA AND BENEFITS.

President's Circle

Criteria and Benefits

*Membership Criteria*

Individuals, households, and private foundations that have irrevocably transferred assets to _____ through the following gift vehicles will qualify for recognition at the designated levels:

- Cash
- Stocks or other securities
- Closely held securities that have a determined value
- Real estate (independent appraisal)
- Tangible personal property (art, books, equipment, etc.)
- Present market value of charitable remainder trusts held irrevocably by the organization or another trustee
- Present value of income interest of charitable lead trust held for the organization or another trustee
- Cash surrender value of life insurance gifts when all incidents of ownership have been given to the organization
- Remainder interest in residence, farm, or business
- Matching gifts
- Joint gifts and other credits (checks written on business accounts)

A person may also become a member of the President's Circle through qualifying support received in his or her honor from one or more contributors. In a similar manner, a person may be named a member in memoriam.

*Membership Levels*

| Level | Cumulative Giving |
|---|---|
| Founder | $10,000 |
| Fellow | $5,000 |
| Benefactor | $1,000 |
| Associate | $500 |
| Patron | $100 |

The Greater Victoria Hospitals Foundation (Recognition Policy, Sept. 1998) has a recognition policy that reflects its goal of providing maximum recognition opportunities for donors. As such, the policy reflects donor gifts in relation to dollar amount and particular target audience.

Four distinct recognition categories have been identified to correspond with GVHF's core target audiences and to address each of their particular recognition needs. Within each category, several divisions of giving have been developed, based on the dollar amount of the donor's cumulative giving history (see Table 7.2).

According to Julia Emlen (in conference notes, 2000), executive director for Development Services and Parent Leadership Programs at Brown University, before structuring a recognition society, an institution must answer the following questions:

What counts?

What is the time period?

How do individuals or couples qualify?

Do matching gifts count?

What transaction types count?

What funding types count (current use, endowment, capital, deferred)?

Will there be multiple levels in one society?

Once criteria for acceptance into the society are complete, determine what premiums will be available to these donors, what piece of three-dimensional recognition will be created, and what special events will set this group apart from the

### TABLE 7.2. DONOR RECOGNITION LEVELS.

| Categories | Gift Divisions (in each category) | |
|---|---|---|
| Corporate Donors | $1,000,000– | Pres. Circle |
| Individual Donors | $75,000–$999,999 | Benefactor |
| Associations & Service Groups | $50,000–$74,999 | Partner |
| Hospital Family (MDs & staff) | $30,000–$49,999 | Patron |
| | $15,000–$29,999 | Fellow |
| | $5,000–$14,999 | Associate |
| | $1,000–$4,999 | Sponsor |
| | $250–$999 | Supporter |
| | $1–$249 | Friend |

*Source:* Greater Victoria Hospitals Foundation Donor Recognition Policy, Sept. 1998.

rest of the donor pool. The society must provide an opportunity for exclusivity and prestige. If the nonprofit chooses to create a recognition society, it must be prioritized among staff and budgeted accordingly. The creation of a donor recognition society does not have to be an expensive venture. Premiums can be access-related privileges rather than tangible tokens, as long as the attention paid to donors in person and by mail or telephone remains of the highest quality. The goal of creating a gift club is to make donors feel as though they are part of an institution that knows them personally.

## Newsletters and Newspapers

Providing information to your constituents and the broader community about donors and gifts can be accomplished by using established communications links. Most organizations publish some form of newsletter. It can and should be used to promote giving, recognize donors, and encourage others to give. Larger nonprofits often have a separate development newsletter (see Resource 28) that focuses on the fundraising process and recognizes gifts, donors, and volunteers.

Newspapers and magazines are also excellent ways to provide recognition and promote the nonprofit to others who are not on the institutional mailing lists or radar screen. Creating media opportunities often requires creativity; in some cases, a story must be positioned for the media—a step beyond providing a media release. Doing this requires understanding that the outlet needs a story it will find appealing. How can you know whether your story would fit? Read the outlet's newspaper; watch or listen to its newscast; even better, ask in person.

Pennsylvania State University had an incredible media opportunity with the $30-million gift it received from William A. Schreyer and his wife, Joan, that created an honor college at the university (see Resource 29). The Schreyers' incredible generosity was documented in a series of publications from internal publications to local media to state and nationwide papers, trade journals, and magazines. Another example of using a donor recognition ad came from the Greater Victoria Hospitals Foundation for the EDS Systemhouse Charity Golf Classic. By announcing the sponsors who supported this event, the level of benefit increased for each entity (see Exhibit 7.6, p. 170).

Smaller, less-well-known nonprofits find media access more difficult to acquire than do larger, more prominent nonprofits. Such variables as size of the fundraising goal, the name value in the community of those leading the fundraising effort, the size of the media market involved, and the level of community interest in the organization are major determinants as to how much, and even whether, media coverage is possible.

### EXHIBIT 7.6.  SPONSORSHIP RECOGNITION.

# Bank of Montreal
## knows books
### are our best investment.

On behalf of the citizens of Vancouver and the Library Square Campaign Leadership Board, John and Kip Woodward, co-chairs, acknowledge the generous contribution Bank of Montreal has made to Library Square.

With their major support, Bank of Montreal has demonstrated their commitment to creating one of the country's finest libraries. Their gift makes it possible to purchase the technology, equipment and furnishings needed for Library Square to ensure universal access to information and education.

We wish to express our sincere thanks to the Bank of Montreal. You are playing an essential role in building a legacy of learning for generations to come.

 **Bank of Montreal**

*Library Square thanks the Vancouver Sun for making this advertisement possible.*

LIBRARY SQUARE

*For the Love of Learning.*

## EXHIBIT 7.6.  SPONSORSHIP RECOGNITION, Cont'd.

# Ronald McDonald Children's Charities wants each child to know the joy of reading.

On behalf of Vancouver and the Library Square Campaign Leadership Board, John and Kip Woodward, co-chairs, acknowledge the generous contribution Ronald McDonald Children's Charities has made to Library Square.

Ronald McDonald Children's Charities of Canada is dedicated to improving the quality of life for children. Their gift makes it possible to purchase information technology and reading equipment for special needs children at Library Square, ensuring universal access to learning and education.

Thank you Ronald McDonald Children's Charities – you are building a legacy of learning for generations to come.

*Library Square thanks the Vancouver Sun for making this advertisement possible.*

LIBRARY
SQUARE

*For the Love
of Learning.*

EXHIBIT 7.6. SPONSORSHIP RECOGNITION, Cont'd.

SUPPORTING COMMUNITY PEDIATRICS. TO A TEE.

Each year, over 600 premature and critically-ill babies are born in our area, some with very unique needs, others weighing as little as one pound. For these budding young Victorians, the mere process of growing can be harder than it seems.

That's why we at EDS Systemhouse and the Greater Victoria Hospitals Foundation wish to thank the many outstanding people who took part in the 3rd Annual EDS Systemhouse Charity Golf Classic, held at Royal Colwood this past September.

As a result of your generosity, the tourney raised $42,000 to purchase an advanced-technology incubator for Victoria General Hospital. This vital equipment will help take away some of the growing pains that our preemies and critically-ill newborns might otherwise face in their earliest travels through life. Thank you for your wonderful show of support! - EDS Systemhouse Inc.

# AUCTION SPONSORS

Aerie Resort
AirBC
Allkat Cut flowers
Anchor Point Bed and Breakfast
Angel Foods
Arbutus Ridge Golf and Country Club
Aveda Concept Salon
BC Ferries Corporation
BC Transit
Beach House on Sunset
Bernard Calibeau
Binners Bed and Breakfast
Black and Lee, Fine Formals For Men
Blackburn Medows Golf Course
Black's Photography Mayfair Shopping Centre
Blandshard St. Winery
Blenkinsop Valley Golf Centre
Blenz on Yates
BSL Business Systems Lustre
Callaway Golf
Canadian Coast Guard Auxiliary Victoria Unit
Canadian Snowmobile Adventures Ltd.
Canadian Tire (Gordon Head)
Canoe Club Restaurant
Cassis
Chapters
Charter's Restaurant at McMorran's Beach House
Chateau Victoria
Cheesecake Café
Chemainus Theatre
Cheryl's Gourmet Pantry
City of Victoria Parks and Recreation (Crystal Pool)
Clarion Hotel
Classic Dry Cleaners
Club Phoenix Health and Fitness

Coast Contract Office Interiors
Coast Victoria Harbourside Hotel and Marina
Cocoon Aesthetics
Coles Books - Mayfair Shopping Centre
Cook St. Village Wines
Cordova Bay Golf Course
Cowichan Golf and Country Club
Dack's Shoes
Deer Lodge - Mt. Washington
Design House
Elaine Lesley
Empire Landmark Hotel - Vancouver
Enterprise Rent-A-Car
Esquimalt Parks and Recreation
F.W. Francis Jewellers Ltd
Fairwinds Golf and Country Club
Fosters
Foxgloves Florist
Galiano Golf and Country Club
Gizmos Computer Exchange
Glen Meadows Golf Club
Golden West Yacht Charters
Gorge Vale Golf Club
Harbour Air Seaplanes
Herald Street Cafe
House Picollo Restaurant
Hummingbird Pub
Hyatt Regency Vancouver
IMAX - National Geographic
Jamie's Whaling Station
Japanese Village
John Phillips Memorial Golf Club
Juan de Fuca Parks and Recreation
Kabuki Cabs
Kitchen Charisma
LA Limosines
LBH Crane
Lush Soap Company

Madrona Lodge
Marina Restaurant
Mayfair Flower Shop
Milestone's Restaurant
Ming's
Mission Hill Winery
Moka House
Moonshadows Guest House
Mazaix Design House
Mt. Washington Resort
Oak Bay Beach Hotel
Oak Bay Recreation Centre
Ocean Centre
Old Spaghetti Factory
Olympic View Golf Club
Ocra Marine
Out of Hand Gallery
Outlooks
PABOOM
Pagliacci's
Peninsula Recreation
Peroklis Greek Restaurant
Prince of Whales Whale Watching
Prism Photofinishing
Quail's Gate Winery
Qualicum Beach Memorial Golf Club
REO Rafting Adventure Resort
Roger's Chocolates
Rosedale on Robson
Royal British Columbia Museum
Royal Oak Golf Club
Russ Hay's the Bicycle Shop
Saanich Commonwealth Place
Salt Spring Island Golf and Country Club
Sea Quest DSV Adventures
Silk Road Tea Company
Sneakers Computers Ltd.
Sony
Sports Traders

Springtide Whale Tours and Fishing Charters
Starbucks (Cook St. Village)
Starbucks (Fort and Blanshard)
Starbucks (Government and Yates)
Starbucks (Oak Bay Ave.)
Stay 'N Save Hotels
Sterling Crane
Surroundings
Suze
Swan's Suite Hotel
Symantic Corporation
Tech Data
That Pine Place
The Country Goose
The Empress Hotel
The Gap
The Keg
The Other Beer Store
Thirsty Vinetner
Tin-Wis Resort Lodge
Toshiba of Canada Ltd.
Uplands Golf Course
Vancouver Island Brewing Co.
Vern Danes
Via Rail Canada, Trade Desk
Victoria Symphony Society
Village Wine Works
Vinoteca
Wal-Mart
Waterford Restaurant
West Coast Crab Bar
West End Gallery
Western Communities-RCMP
Wireless Wave
Woodpecker Furniture
Xircom Corporation
Zellers (Gordon Head)
Zellers (Hillside)

SPECIAL THANKS TO: Acura of Victoria, Fleming Printing Ltd., Hokanson Web Graphic Design, Royal Colwood Golf and Country Club, Times Colonist

Visit our web site at www.eds.com

Visit our golf site at http://www.gvhf.org/edsgolf

In all news releases and stories, whether communicated via organizational publications or released through the media, be certain to coordinate your efforts with the key individuals involved. The idea is to bring favorable notice to the nonprofit and to the donor or volunteer who is the centerpiece of the story. Any attempt at publicity will fail if it does not meet with the approval of its subject. Talk to donors about the information you want to release—what you want to release and why. When you are given approval, conform to the donor's or volunteer's wishes. Some may not want certain details shared, whether about the gift or personal matters. Some may want a spouse included; others may not. Work with your donors in this area to win approval not only for what you are doing but for how you plan to do it. And if a donor doesn't want publicity, don't provide it.

Many donors are at first reluctant to see stories written about them. Many are publicity shy. They do not give to receive notice and are embarrassed by the attention. Some hold religious convictions that strongly suggest the only reward to be expected or received is the personal satisfaction of knowing their gift somehow made a difference. Some have security concerns and don't want personal or family information or photos shared.

So how does the nonprofit bring certain donors to a point where they are comfortable with and agreeable to their stories being told or their names being used? The most forceful, persuasive, winning argument is often a very simple one: the donor's decision to permit this will serve the nonprofit by encouraging others to give. This is another important way the donor can give even more to the important cause he or she believes in deeply and supports generously.

Coverage on radio or television is also highly desirable although seldom achieved. It takes a large event or exceptional gift to catch the attention of the electronic media. Most nonprofits can only dream of such coverage. Nevertheless, when such an opportunity presents itself, be prepared to seize it. The same considerations regarding the clearance of stories with donors apply here.

## Honor Rolls

The creation of an honor roll is an endeavor every organization must take seriously. The compiling and printing of donor names will be as well received as the effort put into the publication. There are, however, some considerations to be weighed:

• *At what level will the nonprofit begin to list names on an honor roll?* Criteria must be established early in the development of an honor roll. By developing guidelines, donors' expectation of whether or not to see their name in print is cemented. This also allows staff to run lists, tally names, and report within certain parameters (for example, publish names of all donors to the local symphony who have given a minimum of $1,000).

- *How will the honor roll be listed?* When planning the layout of the honor roll, the nonprofit must decide how the pages are to be divided. For instance, will people be listed by giving level? By giving society? Alphabetically only? Will it separate corporations and foundations from individuals? How will gifts made in the name of another be treated? The only "right" decision in this area is to be consistent.

- *Will the honor roll be a separate publication or a part of an existing piece?* This will affect the budgeting and the purpose of the pieces written. To do a separate publication costs more money and time but could be more special in the eyes of a donor. However, many nonprofits are finding success in maximizing an existing publication or event program by including the honor roll (see Resource 30).

The honor roll can foster goodwill when written and produced correctly. An organization must invest in staff time to review the correct spelling of names and gift levels; nothing ruins recognition for donors more than being given the wrong title (for example, being called Mr. when Mrs. is correct) or having their name spelled incorrectly. This recognition element for most organizations, large or small, needs to be thoughtfully, thoroughly, and carefully done to guarantee the best results.

## Memorial Program

Honoring a donor posthumously must be done with a delicate hand and a sincere heart. By thanking a donor for generosity during his or her lifetime or a bequest that changed the face of an organization, words printed or verbalized will affect how family, friends, and the knowing public view a nonprofit. Important components of a memorial program are letters thanking individuals for making a contribution in memory of a loved one and the notification to next of kin as to who has made gifts in honor of a loved one (see Exhibit 7.7).

If a deceased person is recognized appropriately and family members are embraced as a part of the institution, an organization has created another level— a new generation of potential donors. One organization in New York personalized an ad in the *New York Times,* January 2000 (see Exhibit 7.8). As with all recognition items, creativity knows no bounds as long as it stays within the realm of good taste.

## Visits and Special Events

A popular way of showing appreciation and expressing gratitude is the special event. Events are a valuable way to reward donors, involve volunteers, and recognize leaders. Such events can be used to build morale, say thank-you, and encourage further involvement and giving.

## EXHIBIT 7.7. MEMORIAL GIFT ACKNOWLEDGMENTS.

**Contribution Given in Memory**

*Date*

*Donor*
*Address_1*
*Address_2*
*Address_3*

Dear *Name of contributor,*

Thank you for your gift in memory of our beloved *(name).* Your contribution to the *(allocation description)* is a wonderful tribute to *(description of person).*

Through your support, *(description of what funds will do). (Name of deceased)*'s leadership and friendship have touched so many lives, and we miss him/her greatly.

Thank you and best wishes.

Sincerely,

Development Officer

---

**Notification to Next of Kin**

*Date*

*Name of Donor*

*Address_1*

*Address_2*

*Address_3*

Dear *Name of next of kin:*

Please accept our deepest sympathy to you and your family on the death of *(relative).* It is said that memories keep the ones we love close to us in spirit and thought and always in our heart.

A memorial gift has been made to the *(fund or account)* as a lasting tribute to your loved one. The *(organization)* has acknowledged this gift that perpetuates the spirit of the organization and sustains valuable programs essential to its vision.

I will forward any additional names to you as I receive them. Do not hesitate to contact me at *(phone number)* if you need further assistance. Please know that we share in your loss.

Sincerely,

Stewardship Associate

Enclosure

## EXHIBIT 7.8.  POSTHUMOUS DONOR RECOGNITION.

Remembering

# ADAM
# YARMOLINSKY

The Ethical Culture Fieldston School community is saddened by the
death of Adam Yarmolinsky '39, alumnus and friend.
Statesman, advocate, educator, and architect of reform,
he was dedicated to the betterment
of our society.

*"The ideal of the School is not the adaptation of the individual to the
existing social environment; it is to develop persons who will be
competent to change their environment."*

Felix Adler, Founder
Ethical Culture Fieldston School

*Source: New York Times,* Jan. 2000. Reprinted with the permission of Ethical Culture Fieldston School.

The planning of special events may fall to the person who does donor relations, or, in larger programs, there may be a staff person responsible for organizing special events. In either case, "The key to any great special event is in the
details," says nationally known events planner Anne Coulter (personal communication, August 1999), "so walking through an event fills in a lot of the detail questions; so does visiting a similar event to see what you like or don't like."

In line with Coulter's advice, Harris (1998) has written a comprehensive book
titled *Special Events: Planning for Success* (2nd edition, CASE Books). She fully details
the planning time line. This resource also contains checklists that the author has
developed. Items include (1) budget, equipment, audiovisual needs, (2) catering, bar,
floral, or décor needs, and (3) the program and VIP list. Any organization can use
these sample forms as a basis for developing its own checklists, such as the example
from the University of Tennessee (see Resource 31). Another resource is *Planning
Special Events* by Jim Armstrong (Jossey-Bass, 2001). This is a workbook, designed
to help readers create a personal "journal" of their own special event planning.

Events should be more than events; they should be special. The invitations
(see Resource 32), which include the description of the programs, and on down
to the name cards, determine the feeling an invitee has about an event. Whatever

the primary purpose, if you are fundraising, friend raising, or expressing appreciation and thanks, plan to make every event individual, personal, and special.

## Stewarding the Investment

Managing funds properly (stewarding the investment) is just as important as stewarding the donor and stewarding the gift. The governing board sets investment and spending policies. As fiduciaries holding a public trust, board members usually adopt investment policies that are designed to maintain purchasing power over time and, in good times, to permit growth. A typical investment mix today is 70 percent in equities (stocks) and 30 percent in fixed-income assets (bonds). Most organizations in today's economic climate pay out 5 percent of income annually on endowed accounts. Also, whether the assets are managed by the organization or by outside managers at the behest of the institution, reasonable and customary administrative and investment fees are paid. The overage, if any, is reinvested in the principal as a hedge against inflation and, in good times, as a way to provide growth beyond inflation. Even funds held short term to be used to meet current needs must be properly managed and invested. Proactive financial management is important to the creditability of the nonprofit and adds to its attractions for donors.

### Reports

Throughout this chapter are references to examples of reports to donors. An honor roll or annual report is a tried-and-true method. Increasingly today, as accountability becomes more of a factor in fundraising, individual reports to donors detailing the activity in individual donor accounts are being provided (see Exhibit 6.4 in Chapter Six). Information about how the money is being spent and, more important, how the institution is benefiting should also be included. How does a dollar given to the annual fund get spent? How do donated dollars fit within the organization's overall budget? How does a dollar given to endowment grow and get spent later? These formal means of reporting are valuable and irreplaceable.

However, just as with a thank-you letter, the less formal, more personal report is coming into fashion. In education, a standard practice is to have recipients of scholarships report to their benefactor. This is often done by letter, but increasingly it is done through face-to-face meetings and telephone calls. If a donor has sponsored camp participation, how about sending taped voice messages from the campers or a home video to the donor before the final report is made? If a piece of equipment is given to a small mission—perhaps a bundling machine that permits it to bundle and sell otherwise unwearable clothing or rags—it would be appropriate to report not only the amount of clothing the equipment has been used to process but how the proceeds are being used to further the organization's mission. And in the case of something like a piece of equipment that will be used for years, don't report just once or twice and drop the reporting. Keep doing this year in and year out. Keep reminding the donor not only of how much the gift meant at the time it was made but of its enduring value. Here again, it is imperative to use multiple ways to say thank-you. You can do it face-to-face, by telephone, direct mail, e-mail, or fax. The idea is to report in order to keep donors informed and indicate to other potential donors the type of sincere, genuine organization you are—one that cares and remembers and one that is both personal enough and professional enough to do proper reporting as a solid business practice and as a caring human practice.

## Reaping the Rewards of Good Stewardship

Justifying a budget allocation for stewardship programs, although sometimes difficult to do in the short term, should be done because of the significant long-term impact on overall fundraising results that comes from this investment. Take into consideration the staff, the equipment, and the physical items needed to establish an effective program. Put together the plan to help determine what the specific needs will be.

Gathering ideas from colleagues offers a creative resource for any type of stewardship recognition and appreciation. One way to garner ideas from peers is to be a part of one or more of several listservs. However, the best method for determining what donors want is simply to ask them. Surveys like the one sent by the Tulip Trace Council of Girl Scouts, Inc. (see Resource 33) should be sent to select groups of donors; the survey will provide the organization with feedback that can be both brutally honest and extremely helpful. As an organization, are you doing a good job? Do they appreciate the way thank-you notes are written? Would they like to attend more or fewer special events? What kinds of events? What do they think is the level of giving at which public recognition should occur (either on a plaque, newspaper, or honor roll)? These are the kinds of questions donors love to be asked. But be prepared to follow through on the answers! This type of audit, done by both the internal and external fans of the organization, can only strengthen the fibers that hold the development program in place.

Stewardship—stewarding donors and their gifts—has evolved into an essential part of any solid development program. Be conscientious about donor needs and wants, but do not promise what cannot be delivered. Careful thought and planning, whether in a small or large shop, can create a powerful recognition, appreciation, and accountability program that will instill gratitude and confidence in the hearts of your donors. This will lead to enhanced fundraising results in the future. A happy, grateful, satisfied donor is any nonprofit's best prospect for its next annual fund, special project, or capital campaign.

PART TWO

# THE DEVELOPMENT SERVICES RESOURCE GUIDE

# RESOURCE GUIDE CONTENTS

# RESOURCE 1

## FINANCIAL REPORT FORMS

NAME OF REPORT:     Comparison Report

DESCRIPTION:        Compares fundraising totals and numbers of donors for the current year and the previous year.

FREQUENCY:          Monthly

## COMPARISON OF TOTAL CONTRIBUTIONS
## TOTAL GIVING FOR ALL SELECTED UNITS

|  | 1998 | | | 1999 | | | INCREASE OR DECREASE | | |
|---|---|---|---|---|---|---|---|---|---|
|  | # DONORS | # GIFTS | AMOUNT | # DONORS | # GIFTS | AMOUNT | # DONORS | # GIFTS | AMOUNT |
| January | 0 | 0 | 0 | 0 | 0 | 0 | 0 | 0 | 0 |
| SUBTOTAL | 0 | 0 | 0 | 0 | 0 | 0 | 0 | 0 | 0 |
| February | 0 | 0 | 0 | 0 | 0 | 0 | 0 | 0 | 0 |
| SUBTOTAL | 0 | 0 | 0 | 0 | 0 | 0 | 0 | 0 | 0 |
| March | 0 | 0 | 0 | 0 | 0 | 0 | 0 | 0 | 0 |
| SUBTOTAL | 0 | 0 | 0 | 0 | 0 | 0 | 0 | 0 | 0 |
| April | 0 | 0 | 0 | 0 | 0 | 0 | 0 | 0 | 0 |
| SUBTOTAL | 0 | 0 | 0 | 0 | 0 | 0 | 0 | 0 | 0 |
| May | 0 | 0 | 0 | 0 | 0 | 0 | 0 | 0 | 0 |
| SUBTOTAL | 0 | 0 | 0 | 0 | 0 | 0 | 0 | 0 | 0 |
| June | 0 | 0 | 0 | 0 | 0 | 0 | 0 | 0 | 0 |
| SUBTOTAL | 0 | 0 | 0 | 0 | 0 | 0 | 0 | 0 | 0 |
| July | 0 | 0 | 0 | 0 | 0 | 0 | 0 | 0 | 0 |
| SUBTOTAL | 0 | 0 | 0 | 0 | 0 | 0 | 0 | 0 | 0 |
| August | 0 | 0 | 0 | 0 | 0 | 0 | 0 | 0 | 0 |
| SUBTOTAL | 0 | 0 | 0 | 0 | 0 | 0 | 0 | 0 | 0 |
| September | 0 | 0 | 0 | 0 | 0 | 0 | 0 | 0 | 0 |
| SUBTOTAL | 0 | 0 | 0 | 0 | 0 | 0 | 0 | 0 | 0 |
| October | 0 | 0 | 0 | 0 | 0 | 0 | 0 | 0 | 0 |
| SUBTOTAL | 0 | 0 | 0 | 0 | 0 | 0 | 0 | 0 | 0 |
| November | 0 | 0 | 0 | 0 | 0 | 0 | 0 | 0 | 0 |
| SUBTOTAL | 0 | 0 | 0 | 0 | 0 | 0 | 0 | 0 | 0 |
| December | 0 | 0 | 0 | 0 | 0 | 0 | 0 | 0 | 0 |
| SUBTOTAL | 0 | 0 | 0 | 0 | 0 | 0 | 0 | 0 | 0 |

*Note:* Figures reported using "cash basis" accounting. Pledges, bequests, and other accruals are not included in these figures.

| NAME OF REPORT: | Pledge Reports |
|---|---|
| DESCRIPTION: | Three separate reports: (1) Pledges with payments currently due and 30–90 days past due; (2) Pledges that are 120–150 days past due; (3) Pledges that are 180 days past due. All receive pledge reminders at each stage if pledge has not been paid. |
| FREQUENCY: | Monthly |

## PAYMENTS DUE 12/31/99–03/31/00 REPORT

| DONOR ID | NAME/ADDRESS | FUND | PLEDGE | PAID | OUTSTANDING | SCHEDULED | PAYMENTS MADE |
|---|---|---|---|---|---|---|---|
| PAYMENTS CURRENTLY DUE AND 30–90 DAYS PAST DUE: | | | | | | | |
| 000000 | Last Name, First Name<br>Address<br>Phone Number | P00CCMP000<br>Fund Name | 000.00 | 00.00 | 00.00 | 00/00/00  00.00 | 00/00/00  00.00 |
| PAYMENTS 120–150 DAYS PAST DUE: | | | | | | | |
| 000000 | Last Name, First Name<br>Address<br>Phone Number | P00CCMP000<br>Fund Name | 000.00 | 00.00 | 00.00 | 00/00/00  00.00 | 00/00/00  00.00 |
| PAYMENTS 180 DAYS PAST DUE: | | | | | | | |
| 000000 | Last Name, First Name<br>Address<br>Phone Number | P00CCMP000<br>Fund Name | 000.00 | 00.00 | 00.00 | 00/00/00  00.00 | 00/00/00  00.00 |

**Resource 1**

NAME OF REPORT:  Completed Pledges Report

DESCRIPTION:  Lists of all completed pledges.

FREQUENCY:  Weekly

# PLEDGES COMPLETED

| DONOR ID | NAME/ADDRESS | ACCOUNT NUMBER/ DESCRIPTION | CAMPAIGN | PLEDGE | PAID | OUTSTANDING | SCHEDULED | PAYMENTS MADE |
|---|---|---|---|---|---|---|---|---|
| 000000 | Last Name, First Name<br>Address<br>Phone Number | 0000000000<br>Description | 000000 | 000.00 | 000.00 | 00.00 00/00/00 | 00.00 00/00/00 | 00.00 |

NAME OF REPORT:       Productivity Report

DESCRIPTION:          Three separate reports: (1) Comparison of gifts in month just
                      completed to same month in previous year; (2) Comparison
                      of year-to-date gifts to same period in previous year; and
                      (3) Comparison of total gifts in past three fiscal years.

FREQUENCY:            Monthly

# MONTH-TO-MONTH TOTAL PRODUCTIVITY COMPARISON FOR THE MONTH OF ___

| | JUNE 1999 | | | JUNE 2000 | | | INCREASE/DECREASE FOR THE MONTH | | |
|---|---|---|---|---|---|---|---|---|---|
| | Documented Gifts and Pledges | Documented Expectancies | Total Raised | Documented Gifts and Pledges | Documented Expectancies | Total Raised | Documented Gifts and Pledges | Documented Expectancies | Total Increase/ Decrease |
| Documented Gifts and Pledges | | | | | | | | | |
| | | | | | | | | | |

# FISCAL YEAR-TO-DATE TOTAL PRODUCTIVITY COMPARISON THROUGH END OF ___

| | YEAR-TO-DATE FISCAL YEAR ___ | | | YEAR-TO-DATE FISCAL YEAR ___ | | | YEAR-TO-DATE INCREASE/DECREASE | | |
|---|---|---|---|---|---|---|---|---|---|
| | Documented Gifts and Pledges | Documented Expectancies | Total Raised | Documented Gifts and Pledges | Documented Expectancies | Total Raised | Documented Gifts and Pledges | Documented Expectancies | Total Increase/ Decrease |
| Documented Gifts and Pledges | | | | | | | | | |
| | | | | | | | | | |

# FISCAL YEAR TOTAL PRODUCTIVITY COMPARISON

| | FISCAL YEAR ___ YTD | | | FISCAL YEAR ___ YTD | | | FISCAL YEAR ___ YTD | | |
|---|---|---|---|---|---|---|---|---|---|
| | Documented Gifts and Pledges | Documented Expectancies | Total Raised | Documented Gifts and Pledges | Documented Expectancies | Total Raised | Documented Gifts and Pledges | Documented Expectancies | Total Increase/ Decrease |
| Documented Gifts and Pledges | | | | | | | | | |
| | | | | | | | | | |

**Resource 1**

NAME OF REPORT:     Giving Analysis

DESCRIPTION:        Provides statistics of numbers of donors and total contributions in various giving levels during the past year.

FREQUENCY:          Annually

## GIVING ANALYSIS REPORT
## TOTAL GIVING FOR ALL SELECTED UNITS

### 07/01/98–06/30/99

| | NUMBER OF GIFTS | NUMBER OF DONORS | DOLLARS |
|---|---|---|---|
| $1–$99 | 000 | 00 | 000,000 |
| $100–$249 | | | |
| $250–$499 | | | |
| $500–$999 | | | |
| $1,000–$2,499 | | | |
| $2,500–$4,999 | | | |
| $5,000–$9,999 | | | |
| $10,000+ | | | |
| TOTAL | | | |

NAME OF REPORT:     5-Year Giving Trends

DESCRIPTION:        Comparison of numbers of donors and total contributions by
                    source of gifts.

FREQUENCY:          Annually

# FIVE YEARS GIVING TRENDS REPORT
## (FISCAL YEARS)

|  | (YEAR 5) | (YEAR 4) | (YEAR 3) | (YEAR 2) | (YEAR 1) |
|---|---|---|---|---|---|
| Individual Donors |  |  |  |  |  |
| Dollars |  |  |  |  |  |
| Corporate Donors |  |  |  |  |  |
| Dollars |  |  |  |  |  |
| Foundation Donors |  |  |  |  |  |
| Dollars |  |  |  |  |  |
| Other Donors |  |  |  |  |  |
| Dollars |  |  |  |  |  |
| Total Donors |  |  |  |  |  |
| Dollars |  |  |  |  |  |

| NAME OF REPORT: | Capital Campaign Reports |
| --- | --- |
| DESCRIPTION: | Status Report, Progress Report, Gift Table Report. |
| FREQUENCY: | Monthly |

## CAMPAIGN STATUS REPORT
### START DATE – CURRENT DATE
### (DOCUMENTED GIFTS, PLEDGES, AND EXPECTANCIES)

| Components | Total Campaign Goal | Documented Gifts and Pledges | Documented Expectancies | Total Raised | Percent of Goal Raised |
|---|---|---|---|---|---|
| | | | | | |

Campaign Total

Period of Campaign: Start Date—End Date

Percent Completed: _____ %

## CAMPAIGN PROGRESS REPORT
### (DOCUMENTED GIFTS, PLEDGES, AND EXPECTANCIES)

| Components | Campaign Goal | Through Current Date | | Through One Month Prior | | Through Six Months Prior | | Through Twelve Months Prior | |
|---|---|---|---|---|---|---|---|---|---|
| | | Total Raised | % of Goal | Total Raised | % of Goal | Total Raised | % of Goal | Total Raised | % of Goal |
| | | | | | | | | | |
| | | | | | | | | | |
| Campaign Total | | | | | | | | | |

## GIFTS NEEDED TO RAISE _____ (AMOUNT OF GOAL)

| Gift Amount | Number of Gifts Needed | Total in Range | Number of Gifts Received to Date | Total Received to Date | Percent of Total Campaign Goal |
|---|---|---|---|---|---|
| | | ___ | ___ | ___ | ___ |
| TOTAL | | | | | |

# RESOURCE 2

## DATA ELEMENTS AND CODES

# GREATER VICTORIA HOSPITALS FOUNDATION

## Data Elements and Codes

*Action Status*
Attended
Invited
Open
Pending Decision/Info
Closed—No Action Required
Not Attended
Accepted
Info Mailed
Active
Closed

*Actions*
Telephone Call
Letter
Recognition Event
Fundraising Event
Proposal
Tour
Request for Information
Recognition
Business Meeting
Home Visit/Meeting
Patrons Council Meeting
Board Meeting
Committee Meeting
Media Interview
Estate Probate Release
1994 Feasibility Study
Prospect. BR Sponsor
Bed Race Sponsor
Solicitation Visit
Letter of Agreement
Donor Meeting
Friend ($1–$249)
Supporter ($250–$999)
Sponsor ($1,000–$4,999)

Associate ($5,000–$14,999)
Fellow ($15,000–$29,999)
Patron ($30,000–$49,999)
Partner ($50,000–$74,999)
Benefactor ($75,000–$999,999)
President's Circle ($1,000,000+)
Volunteer Activity

*Address Info Sources*
Clippings
Patrons Council Member
Board Member
Event
Mailing
Polks Directory
Staff
Phone Book

*Address Types*
Home
Business
Previous Address
Care of
Vacation

*Affiliations*
Board Member
Business
Contact
Customer/Client
Donor
Employee
Executrix
Friend
Honour/Memorial Acknowledgee
Manager

Owner
President
Treasurer
Trustee
Volunteer
Subsidiary
Member
Past Trustee
Chairman
Sponsor
Charitable Interest
City Councilor
Director
Husband
Mayor
Honorary Governor

*Benefits*
Bronze Pin
Certificate
Copper Pin
Donor Rec. Ad in the TC
Donor Wall Plaque
Gold Pin
Gordon Pynn Print
GVHF Quarterly Newsletter
Honorary Board Member
Honorary Patron's Council
   Appointment
Hospital Tour
Invitation to Annual Reception
Leather Bound T. Grant Book
Letter from Executive Director
Linen Bound T. Grant Book
Listing in Newsletter
Lunch Invitation with Chairman
   or CEO
Naming Opportunity
Phone call from Board Member
Phone call from CEO
Phone call from Chairman

Phone call from Vice-Chair
Plaque for display at home/business
Silver Pin
Special Donor profile and photo in
   newsletter
Special Plaque installed prominent
   position
Tax Receipt

*Classifications*
Auxiliary

*Committees*
Executive Committee-Board
Finance Committee
Recognition Committee
TEAM Committee
Visions Committee
Planned Giving Committee

*Constituencies*
CHR Board (CHRB)
GVHF Board (FB)
Patrons Council (PC)
Board Member (Board)
Former Patient (FP)
Media (ME)
Physician (DR)
Hospital Staff (HS)
Business (BUS)
Estates (ES)
Matching Gift Company (MGC)
Committee Member (CM)
Volunteer (VO)
Charity (CH)
Service Club (SC)
Religious Organization (RO)
Union (UN)
Estate Planning Professional (EPP)
Prospect (PR)

Politician (PO)
Government (Gover)
Government Agency (GA)
Former CHR Board (FCHRB)
Former GVHF Board (FFB)
Former Patrons Council (FPC)
Former Physician (FDR)
Former Hospital Staff (FHS)
Former Committee Member (FCM)
Capital Campaign (Capit)
Direct Mail Donor (DMD)
Honour/Memorial (HM)
Honour/Memorial Acknowledgee
   (HMA)
Individual (IND)
Next of Kin (Next)
Organization Contact (ORG C)
Foundation (FDTN)

*Contact Types*
Major Gift Contact
Employee
Event Sponsorship Contact
Pledge Payment Contact
Shareholder
Director
Better Together Prospect
Primary Contact
Secondary Contact
Aware Invitee
Visions Invitee
Visions AucDonor
Owner
Charitable Interest
Employer
Board of Directors

*Credit Cards*
American Express
MasterCard
Visa

*Currency Types*
Cdn Dollars
US Dollars
Pounds

*Degrees*
MBA
Engineering
Dipl.T.
RN

*Descriptions*
Address
Affiliations
Anniversary
Anonymous
Better Together Pledge
Business History
Business Information
Business Name Change
Cancer
Cardiac
CHR Donation
Contact Information
Convert to Individual
Correspondence
Created in Conversation
Deceased Information
Delete from mailing
Diabetes
Direct Mail
Donor Information
Estate Information
Event Contacts
Family Information
Finalist
Financial Health
Financial Info
Former Contractor
Former Sponsorship Contact
Funding Policies

| | |
|---|---|
| Fundraising History | 50 |
| General Information | 65 |
| Gift History | 80 |
| Gift in Kind | |
| Gift of Shares | ***Financial Data Types*** |
| Giving Interests | Bonus |
| Grants | Estimated Net Worth |
| Growth | Inheritance |
| GVHF Board of Directors | Loss |
| Not a duplicate record | Net Income |
| Patron Council participation | Other Real Estate |
| Personal Information | Other Significant Holdings |
| Planned Giving | Primary Residence |
| Power of Attorney | Profit |
| Receipting | Revenue |
| Recognition | Salary |
| Solicitation | Stock Holdings |
| Surgical | Total Compensation |
| Visions | |
| Awards | ***Fund Categories*** |
| Pledge Payment | Internally Restricted |
| Giving History | Externally Restricted |
| Giving Potential | Unrestricted |
| Auction | |
| Capital Equipment Sponsorship | ***Gift Codes*** |
| Creation of "Pegasus Wholesale Inc." | NSF Cheque Payment |
| Level I | Pledge Overpayment |
| Level III | Fee Collection/Payment |
| Level II | Third Party Paid |
| Profession | Cheque (Personal) |
| Previous Address | Cheque (Corporate) |
| Festival of Running | Cash |
| Fashion Show | Visa |
| Company Merger | MasterCard |
| | American Express |
| ***Donor Age Analysis Codes*** | Money Order |
| 20 | Gift in Kind |
| 25 | Other |
| 30 | Payroll Deduction |
| 35 | Deposit Report Code |
| 40 | Pledges |

Payment
Deposited VGH Site
Direct Deposit CIBC
Foreign Currency
Stock

**Gift Size Analysis Codes**
$100,000.00
$50,000.00
$25,000.00
$10,000.00
$5,000.00
$2,500.00
$1,000.00
$500.00
$250.00
$100.00
$50.00
$25.00
$10.00
$0.64
$0.00

**Honour/Memorial Types**
In Honour of
In Memory of
For the Benefit of
For Scholarship of
In Military Honour of
In Wedding Honour of
In Bequest of
To Honour the Memory of
In Special Recognition of
On Behalf of
In Remembrance

**Income**
Under 20,000
20,000–39,999
40,000–59,999

60,000–79,999
80,000–99,999
100,000–150,000
150,001–300,000
300,001–600,000
600,001–900,000
900,000+

**Industries**
Accountants
Administrator
Architects
Artist
Banking
Bus Professionals
Construction
Consultant
Dentists
Dept. National Def.
Doctors
Educators
Lawyers
M.L.A.
Media
MP
Nurses
Pharmacist
Police
Politics
Real Estate
Retail
Social Worker
Foundation
Entertainment
Travel
Healthcare
Hospitality

**Information Requested**
Advocate

Board/Committee Membership
CHR Background
Equipment Needs List
Financial Statements
Memorial Brochure
Planned Giving Brochure
Solicitation—Mail
Letter of Agreement
Annual Report

*Information Sources*
Times Colonist
Business Examiner
Newsgroup Newspapers
Globe and Mail
National Post
Vancouver Sun
Internet
Canadian Business
BC Business
MacLean's
Donor/Prospect
Other Donor/Prospect
Executive Director
Foundation Staff
Board Member
Patrons Council Member
Medical Community Member
Polks Directory
Times Colonist, Earnings Column

*Instruments*
Bequest
Estate
Insurance
Trust
Will

*Mail Types*
Direct Mail Solicitation

Visions Invitation
Newsletter
Pledge Reminders
Visions Auction Donor Thank You
Visions Attendee Thank You
Visions Cash Sponsor Thank You
Visions Combined Thank You

*Marital Status*
Married
Widowed
Divorced
Single
Separated
Unknown
Common-law
Dating

*Media Hosts*
CHEK TV
CFAX Radio
Times Colonist Newspaper
Newsgroup Newspaper
Q100.3 Radio
The Ocean Radio
CBC Radio
Shaw Cable

*Notepad Types*
Volunteers
99 Spring DM Survey Response
Sprint Radio
Proposal
Legacy Goals
Healthcare Information
Giving Constraints
GIK Sponsor
Gift in Kind
General Information
Former Contact

Financial Information

Equipment Sponsorship

Directors Notes

Direct Mail Comments

Created during conversion

Convert Record Type

CHR Donation

Better Together Pledge

Awards/Formal Recognition

Conversion Notes

Visions Sponsor

Contact Information

Gift Details

Business Information

Visions

Major Gift Prospect

99 Fall DM Survey Response

**Participant Status**

Paid

Unpaid

Complimentary

Guest

**Participant Types**

Guest

Sponsor

Volunteer

**Phone Types**

Home

Business

Fax

Email

Cellular

Alternate

Pager

Web Site

Box Office

Cell

Alt. Fax

Direct Line

**Professions**

Doctors

Dentists

Lawyers

Nurses

Bus Professionals

Accountants

Media

Banking

Real Estate

Educators

Social Worker

Architects

Construction

Dept. National Def.

D.M. Finance

C.E.O.

M.L.A.

Politics

Artist

Police

Pharmacist

Administrator

Consultant

MP

Investment Advisor

Service Station

Hospitality

Event Management

Retail

Service Club

Florist

Politician

Sales

Notary Public

Restauranteur

Travel

Esthetics/Beauty
Publishing/Magazine
Communications
Fundraising
Advertising
Jeweller
Computers
Staging
Firefighter
Tourism
Insurance
Non-profit

*Proposal Status*
Accepted
Rejected
Not Approached—See Notes Tab
   (Proposal)
In Progress—Writing
In Progress—Research
Draft—awaiting approval to send
Sent
Decision Pending
Gift Made
Attended
Not Attended
Invited
Open
Closed—No Action

*Prospect Interests*
Healthcare—Greatest Need
Cancer Care
Child/Youth & Maternal
Community Health
Digestive Health
Emergency/High Intensity
Health Restoration
Heart Health
Lung Health

Medical Imaging
Mental Health
Palliative Care
Seniors Health
Surgical Services
Innovation Fund
Patient Comforts
Staff Education—Healthcare
Arts
Disabled
Environment
Minority Cultures
Social Services
Sports
Urban Poor
Women
Youth
Education—General
Heritage Conservation
Religious Organizations

*Purpose for Gift*
Capital Equipment
Minor Equipment
Staff Education
Patient Comforts
Area of Care

*Purposes*
VISIONS (temp)

*Recognition*
Plaque To Be Given
Presentation
Donor Recognition
Geranium
Daffodil
Pansy
NO RECOGNITION
DONOR BOARD

**Resource 2**

*Relationships*

aunt
brother
Business
colleague
Contact
daughter
daughter-in-law
ex-wife
Executor
Executrix
father
granddaughter
grandfather
grandmother
guardian
Honour/Memorial Acknowledgee
husband
Manager
mother
nephew
niece
Owner
parents
President
Self
sister
son
son-in-law
stepdaughter
stepfather
stepmother
stepson
trustee
uncle
unknown
wife
widow
next of kin
sister-in-law
father-in-law

friend
ex-husband
first husband
second husband
Chairman
Director
Charitable Interest
Employer
Employee
Power of Attorney
mother-in-law
baby
baby-son
fiance

*School Types*

Graduate
Undergraduate
Private Grade School
Schools
Simon Fraser University
Queens University
British Columbia Institute of
    Technology
University of British Columbia
Glenlyon Norfolk School
Royal Jubilee Hospital School of
    Nursing

*Solicit Codes*

ALL SOLICITATIONS
DO NOT SOLICIT
SOLICIT FALL ONLY
SOLICIT SPRING ONLY
DO NOT MAIL
DO NOT PHONE
DISBANDED
DECEASED
Tickets VSP'93
Tree sponsor
Annual Campaign

Ticket VSP'94
Annual donation only
Bed Race Sponsor

*Special Codes*
Advocate Mailing
Bequest
Deceased
Foreign
Gorde Hunter Column
Lost Address
Move Notice
Plan. Giv. Prospect
Requested Newsletter
Times Colonist
Tree Designer VSP
Tree Sponsor VSP
Visions Invite Tease

*Special Event Groups*
Visions '99

*Special Event Types*
Marathon
Golf Tournament
Gala Ball
Fashion Show
Gala Fundraiser

*Special Event Units*
1 Ticket
2 Tickets
3 Tickets
4 Tickets
5 Tickets
6 Tickets
7 Tickets
8 Tickets
9 Tickets
10 Tickets
Ticket

*Target*
Under 10
10–24
25–49
50–99
100–249
250–499
500–999
1,000–2,499
2,500–4,999
5,000–9,999
10,000–15,000
15,001–20,000
20,001–25,000
25,001–30,000
30,001–35,000
35,001–40,000
40,001–45,000
45,001–50,000
50,001–75,000
75,001–100,000
100,001–150,000
150,001–300,000
300,001–600,000
600,001–999,999
1,000,000+
A+
A–
B+
B–

*Type of Gift*
Cash
Pledge
Stock
GIK
Auction Item
Event Support (GIK)
Matching Gift/Pledge

# RESOURCE 3

## INFORMATION SERVICES PROJECT LOG

# IU Foundation Project Type Codes for A/FIS Projects

| Project Type Code | Description |
| --- | --- |
| DE | Database Enhancement |
| DI | Database Integrity |
| PI | Process Improvement |
| PR | Programming |
| RD | Research & Development |
| RP | Recurring Project |
| SE | System Enhancement |
| SM | System Maintenance |
| SU | Support |
| SY | Security |
| TR | Training |

# OPEN PROJECTS WITH TYPE

| Staff | Project Type | Assignment Title | Requester | Estimated Hours | Description | Assignment Number |
|---|---|---|---|---|---|---|
| CROSON | DE | 2nd Sybase Member re-write | CROSON | 8.00 | Rewrote sybase membership transfer to speed up process but noticed a lot of useless fields were include in transfer. Jen provided list of those that can be eliminated. Rewrite and possibly run nightly instead of weekly. | 990479 |
| CROSON | DI | Data Integrity—TX.ARCHV | CROSON | 100.00 | Verify integrity of all data pointers in TX.ARCHV. Identify cause for corruption, if any. Write programs to fix existing and prevent future problems. | 990396 |
| PEACOCK | PI | Streamline deposit function | BONK | 0.00 | Review of current procedures and seek out ways to simplify processes. Where possible, eliminate duplication of effort. Possibly incorporate scanning techniques into process for archival needs. Should be examined with current and future lockbox processing services in mind. | 990204 |
| CROSON | PR | Modify Benefactor Security | CROSON | 40.00 | Modify the way in which Benefactor security classes are defined so they are easier to maintain. Write utilities to allow for easy deletion of security classes and/or users from security class. | 990330 |
| MALLORY | RD | Evaluate Exchange Server | MALLORY | 40.00 | Evaluate new exchange server software. Check feasibility of running an IUF exchange server due to several issues (such as address book problems, confidentiality of archives, etc.). | 990511 |

**Resource 3**

## OPEN PROJECTS WITH TYPE, Cont'd.

| Staff | Project Type | Assignment Title | Requester | Estimated Hours | Description | Assignment Number |
|---|---|---|---|---|---|---|
| DOWNS | SE | Corporate edition of NAV | DOWNS | 40.00 | Set up corporate edition of Norton Anti-Virus on a server. Server then checks for updated virus signatures from Symantec site and pushes them to the workstations. | 990490 |
| DOWNS | SM | Rollout workstations | MALLORY | 400.00 | Rollout new workstations (staff and students) with machines running Windows 2000. IUSF will be first; more planning is needed, including a schedule signed by all department heads affected by the rollout. | 990489 |
| BRATCHER | SU | Intranet pages update | MALLORY | 100.00 | Work with intranet design committee to update the AFIS pages on the intranet. | 990497 |
| MALLORY | SY | Select security consultants | MALLORY | 80.00 | Locate reputable security consultants to audit IUF systems; suggest and implement solutions; train staff to maintain and troubleshoot security. | 990407 |
| PEACOCK | TR | Imaging | BONK | 0.00 | Upgrade FP-Multi system to e-Media. Conversion to be done by Van Ausdall and Farrar. | 980280 |

*Note:* This table has been edited.

# RESOURCE 4

## POSITION DESCRIPTIONS

Resource 4

# Hillel: The Foundation for
# Jewish Campus Life Position Description
# Washington, D.C.

| | |
|---|---|
| Title: | Research Associate |
| Supervisor: | Director, Donor Relations |
| Prepared: | June 1, 2000 |

## Work Objectives:

Initiate and provide research on major donors and high level prospects and for other development programs and projects. Assist Development staff in reviewing donor lists and in identifying and analyzing giving potential of current donors and new prospects to Hillel's International Center.

## Responsibilities:

- Provide detailed financial and biographical research on individuals, foundations, and corporations as requested by Development staff and Executive Office staff.
- Proactively research major prospects for Development staff.
- Work with Development staff to review donors and prospects, making recommendations for cultivation and stewardship through visits, invitations to campuses in their communities, and invitations to special Hillel events such as the Renaissance Institute and Hillel's annual leadership and staff conferences.
- Initiate preparation of briefing notes for donor visits and special events, as requested by Development staff, Executive Office staff, and lay leaders, as determined.
- Determine and develop needed forms for trip reports, donor profiles, cultivation visits, etc.
- Document on computer system and in paper files pertinent information on donors and prospects discovered during research. Inform Development staff, on ongoing basis, of relevant information gleaned to assist with cultivation and stewardship (e.g. life cycle events, awards and honors to recognize).
- Contribute to the Development staff team efforts to improve communications and systems in support of the Renaissance Campaign and Endowment Campaign.

- Manage and maintain up-to-date filing system on Board of Governors, major donors, foundations, select members of the Board of Directors, major prospects, and development department's special events.
- Assess the relevance and usefulness of periodicals, newspapers, e-mail newsletter subscriptions for Development staff. Oversee circulation and filing of such materials.
- Seek opportunities for learning. Develop relationships with research colleagues in federations, universities and other organizations as may be helpful for learning and for sharing data.
- Other responsibilities, as determined.

## Qualifications:

College degree required. Organizational experience, as well as demonstrated ability to analyze and develop data helpful for the solicitation of prospects. Experience in development office or non-profits desired. Must have some knowledge of electronic on-line resources. Ability to work under pressure and as a team player. Excellent written and oral communication skills.

# INDIANA UNIVERSITY FOUNDATION
# JOB DESCRIPTION

| Date: | October 26, 2000 | Job Title: | Development Analyst |
|---|---|---|---|
| Department: | Research | Classification: | EXC |
| Supersedes: | | FLSA: | Exempt |

## GENERAL SUMMARY

Identifies and evaluates individual, corporate and foundation major gift prospects and their affiliated organizations. Conducts detailed research using advanced on-line databases, Internet resources, in-house files and data, libraries and other references. Creates written profiles and project summary spreadsheets, compiling and synthesizing information, and oversees appropriate dissemination. Provides analysis of and suggests suitable strategies for prospects in relation to the priorities.

## ESSENTIAL FUNCTIONS

Establish oneself as a knowledgeable staff member by:

- Learning the IUF mission and being knowledgeable about the IUF business and, in particular, the department's responsibilities to that mission.
- Gaining and maintaining proficiency in the use of commercial databases, CD-ROM tools, Internet resources, and IUF computer applications.
- Attending meetings, conferences, and related training opportunities of vendors and professional organizations.

Have a positive impact on Development results by:

- Conducting detailed biographical, business and financial research on individuals and their related organizations using advanced on-line databases, in-house files, library references and other sources; preparing reports synthesizing this information to be used by IU Development staff, University President, and other gift officers.

- Providing corporate intelligence to Development officers; monitoring, analyzing, and reporting on industry trends and business activities of top corporate prospects.
- Identifying alumni, potential donors and friends of the University as new prospects for future research and cultivation and conducting special prospect identification projects in support of specific University objectives.
- Organizing research strategy sessions for proactive research, working with Development officers to qualify prospects and developing strategies for moving new prospects through the IUF solicitation process.
- Serving on campaign and other administrative teams as assigned.
- Contributing to the upkeep of the departmental Internet/World Wide Web site(s).
- Compiling, updating, verifying, and managing electronic files on alumni, donors, friends and prospects to help maintain integrity of internal databases, working with other departments to solve discrepancies in donor and corporate records.

Enhance departmental performance standards and efficiency by:

- Assisting in training of, and serving as mentor to, new Research staff and student help.
- Performing as a team player and fostering a spirit of cooperation.
- Maintaining a high level of reliability and responsiveness.
- Clearly communicating concerns and questions to supervisor.
- Seeking guidance from supervisor and co-workers when uncertainty arises.

Approach each situation with a professional attitude by:

- Following the Research department code of ethics and those prescribed by the IU Foundation.
- Handling confidential materials and situations with respect, sensitivity and discretion.
- Approaching problems with a positive and constructive attitude.

Perform related duties and assist Director with projects as assigned.

## KNOWLEDGE/SKILLS/ABILITIES REQUIRED

- Experience and references demonstrating scrupulous accuracy and superior attention to detail.

- Well-developed interpersonal skills including the ability to function well in a multiple-team setting, ability to prioritize and work independently and responsibly. Ability to meet deadlines and demonstrate excellent oral, face-to-face, and concise written communication skills.
- Ability to handle multiple tasks simultaneously.
- Advanced general computer knowledge of Windows- and network-based environments, ability to use on-line, CD-ROM and electronic databases creatively and effectively, Internet and word processing abilities.
- Experience demonstrating creative and flexible research skills and ability to analyze, interpret, summarize, and present information effectively.
- Working experience with prospect research, or research in an academic or library setting, and/or familiarity with a fund raising or non-profit environment is highly desirable.

## EDUCATION

Baccalaureate degree or commensurate experience.

## MENTAL DEMANDS

Detailed work, reading, confidentiality, problem solving, and verbal and written communication. Ability to cope with interruptions while managing multiple concurrent assignments and deadlines commensurate with a very busy professional office.

## PHYSICAL DEMANDS

Requires little physical effort. Prolonged periods of sitting in front of a computer terminal.

## WORKING CONDITIONS

Typical office working conditions.


Approval:

Supervisor/Date: _____ HR Director/Date: _____

# UNIVERSITY OF WASHINGTON
# OFFICE OF DEVELOPMENT
## Professional Staff Job Description

POSITION TITLE:    Development Services Officer                    Grade: 7

WORKING TITLE:    Research Strategist

BASIC RESPONSIBILITIES

The research strategist identifies and profiles potential major gift donors to the University of Washington, enhancing the University's fundraising efforts. He or she strategizes with development officers, assistant deans and the assistant vice president for development regarding prospect identification, and collaborates with them to develop cultivation and solicitation strategies for major gift donors. The research strategist provides these clients with written reports about specific donors, containing an analysis of information gathered from public sources and recommended courses of action.

CHARACTERISTIC DUTIES

- Assumes primary responsibility for meeting the prospect identification and research needs of a given group of development officers, enabling them to meet fundraising goals. Meets regularly with these individuals, keeping abreast of their activities and the initiatives and programs underway within their schools/colleges/departments.
- Regularly collaborates with development officers to develop prospect identification, cultivation, solicitation and overall fundraising strategies.
- Consults with development officers to determine feasibility of research requests and special projects.
- Negotiates project scopes and deadlines directly with development officers.
- Advises development officers about database segmentation opportunities.
- Independently designs database segmentation strategies and implements them to uncover new prospects.
- Establishes data requirements for database segmentation, downloads or otherwise obtains necessary data from Advance and other databases and analyzes segmentation results so as to make recommendations to development officers.

Resource 4

- Uses both standard and novel prospect research techniques and tools to identify new prospects, including periodical and electronic screening and/or information provided by the prospect or his/her organization. Following established departmental policies, notifies development officers of new potential prospects.
- Creates narrative reports and develops tables, charts, graphs and illustrations as required to describe a prospect or group of prospects.
- As requested by development officers or the vice president for development and alumni relations, provides briefing materials about major donors to the University president, deans, department chairs, foundation board members and other top level executives and volunteers.
- Provides on-the-spot answers to brief, information questions about prospects from development officers.
- Trains research assistants, instructing them in research techniques and educating them about the prospect research office's policies and procedures.
- As appropriate, delegates tasks to a research assistant.
- Reviews the work of research assistants and provides them feedback on areas for improvement.
- Reviews local and national news and business publications, keeping abreast of prospect information and local and regional business developments and economic trends. Sends articles to Development Office central files and other staff as appropriate.
- Notifies Records Maintenance staff when new demographic information is found that updates information residing on the Advance database. When information is important and concerns a high-level prospect, notifies appropriate development staff immediately.
- Safeguards the confidentiality of donor information at all times. Upholds departmental policies regarding confidential information.
- Adheres to ethical and confidentiality guidelines of both the University and the Association of Professional Researchers for Advancement (APRA).

SUPERVISION RECEIVED

General direction is received from the Prospect Research Manager.

SUPERVISION EXERCISED

The research strategist provides general supervision to a research assistant.

MINIMUM QUALIFICATIONS

A qualified candidate must have a bachelor's degree and one year of work experience in development research. One year of work experience in a field with transferable skills or a graduate degree may be substituted for the year of development research experience. Strong written and verbal communication skills, an aptitude for logical thinking, a commitment to professional ethics and the ability to interact with executive level clients are essential. The candidate also must have strong computer skills, including proficiency with Microsoft Office software, CD-ROM products commonly used in prospect research and experience searching on-line databases and the Internet.

ADDITIONAL DESIRABLE QUALIFICATIONS

Other desirable qualifications include two (2) or more years of development research experience, working knowledge of BSR's Advance database, familiarity with Puget Sound and Washington State businesses and VIPs and an interest in professional development.

Resource 4

*Source:* Reprinted with the permission of Lisa A. Thomas, Director of Prospect Research and Tracking, University of Washington.

## UNIVERSITY OF FLORIDA FOUNDATION, INC.

| TITLE: | Research Analyst, Corporate and Foundation Relations Specialist |
|---|---|
| DEPARTMENT: | Research |
| RESPONSIBLE TO: | Director of Research |
| MAJOR FUNCTION: | The incumbent will provide professional research and information services to support the fund raising goals and objectives of the University of Florida Foundation, Inc. which includes the Office of Development and Alumni Affairs. Serves as team member of the Corporate and Foundation Relations staff. |

## DUTIES AND RESPONSIBILITIES:

E 1. Collect, organize and analyze information relating to potential prospects for gifts to the University.

E 2. Utilize a variety of printed reference materials, on-line databases (Dialog, Dow Jones, Internet, AutoTrac, InvestNet, Dun & Bradstreet), CD-ROM products, and governmental or other agency resources (i.e. IRS, court-houses, assessment offices, Foundation Center) to obtain information on prospects or funding sources. Willingness to travel out-of-town for training as needed. Develop comprehensive knowledge of donor database, and retrieval of information from database.

E 3. Prepare thorough, accurate and timely profiles on donor prospects according to Research report guidelines (report type dependent upon cultivation level). Determine gift capacity and inclination of potential donor and ties to UF. Prepare briefing reports on donors and prospective donors as required by the President, development administrators and officers, faculty and staff. Ability to produce biographical profiles on alumni and friends and as well corporate leaders and individuals interested in donating funds to the University. Additionally, prepare background profiles on local, national, and international corporations or foundations, including giving history, philanthropic, financial and historical information about the organization.

E 4. Conduct proactive projects for use by development officers by searching for potential major donor prospects. Read and analyze periodicals and publications.

E 5. Consult with development officers to discuss prospects and projects, and analysis of available data. Present written and oral reports to colleagues on results of electronic screening and integrating other new prospect research information. Educate officers on research resources and policies.

E 6. Contribute to evaluation of research tools and make recommendations to director. Position responsible for evaluation of specialized resources in corporate and foundation research. In addition, participate in professional networking with persons or organizations engaged in specialized corporate and foundation prospect research.

E 7. Serve as liaison between Corporate and Foundation Relations and faculty or administrative officers. Engage in proactive outreach by determining funding needs of college or administrative units, and identifying funding sources. As needed, train administrative/college staff in corporate and foundation resources.

E 8. Serve as team member of Corporate and Foundation Relations staff. Participate in planning and strategy sessions. Contribute to creative ideas and solutions.

9. Other duties as assigned.

*Note:* "E" indicates Essential Functions, which are the functions that this position exists to perform. Any incumbent in this position must be able to perform all of these essential fundamental duties, with or without reasonable accommodations. Management retains the right to modify or add duties at any time.

# QUALIFICATIONS:

Education:

Bachelor's degree in library science, business, journalism, communication, history, or other related field.

Experience and Job Knowledge:

One to three years related work experience, such as financial or legal research, and experience in a non-profit organization is helpful. Knowledge of philanthropy and prospect research desirable. The ability to analyze financial data of corporations and foundations is essential. Must be inquisitive, motivated and flexible. Excellent communication skills; writing and editing ability important, as well as competence in interpreting biographical, corporate and foundation information.

Strong computer skills (Excel and Access knowledge preferred), proficiency with electronic research tools (including Internet) and techniques to gather in-depth information on potential and existing donors desired. Ability to work independently, as well as coordinate projects with others.

# ADDITIONAL CONSIDERATIONS:

The incumbent should be computer literate in these areas:
- Windows 95
- Word Processing (Microsoft Word, Access)
- Some type of World Wide Web browser, preferably Netscape
- Use of e-mail

Accuracy, attention to detail and a service-oriented attitude are important.

## APPROVED BY:

| | |
|---|---|
| _____ | _____ |
| Incumbent | Date |
| _____ | _____ |
| Immediate Supervisor | Date |
| _____ | _____ |
| Personnel | Date |

# NORTHWESTERN UNIVERSITY
## Development Researcher

School or Department:    Development Research

Reports to:    Director, Development Research

Job Function:    Identifies and evaluates individual major gift prospects and their affiliated organizations. Conducts detailed research using advanced on-line databases, Internet resources, in-house files and data, library and other references. Creates written reports compiling and synthesizing this information, and oversees appropriate dissemination. Provides analysis of and suggests suitable strategy for prospects in relation to the University's fundraising opportunities.

Grade Level:    E-05

## Characteristic Duties and Responsibilities

1. Conduct detailed biographical, business and financial research on individuals and their related organizations using advanced on-line databases, in-house files, library references and other sources. Prepare reports (Profiles or other format) synthesizing this information, to be used by NU Development staff, University President and other officers.

2. Identify alumni, potential donors and friends of the University as new prospects for future research and cultivation. Conduct special prospect identification projects in support of assigned University areas' objectives.

3. Develop and maintain an ongoing, communication relationship to advance the prospect requirements of an assigned clientele of Development officers and other front-line fund raisers with particular knowledge about these assigned areas within the University. This particular position works with the Medill School of Journalism and the University Library.

4. Assist in training new Development and Research staff and student help.

5. Compile, update and manage files on alumni, donors, friends and prospects using all available resources.

6. Gain and maintain proficiency in the use of commercial databases, CD-ROM tools, Internet resources, and internal systems. Assist in maintaining internal computer systems and products, including contribution to the upkeep of the departmental Internet/World Wide Web site(s).

Resource 4

7. Gain and maintain awareness of issues within the development profession, and of the goals and activities of Northwestern University and its peer institutions.
8. Attend meetings, conferences, and related training opportunities of vendors and professional organizations.
9. Serve on campaign and other administrative teams in assigned areas.
10. Perform related duties, serve on internal teams/committees, and assist Director with projects as assigned.

## Required Qualifications

1. Bachelor's degree or superior combination of education and experience.
2. Experience and references demonstrating scrupulous accuracy and attention to detail.
3. Well-developed interpersonal skills including ability to function well in a multiple-team setting, ability to prioritize and work independently, responsibly, and meet deadlines, and excellent oral, face-to-face, and concise written communication skills.
4. Ability to apply an ethical code and good judgement, and to handle confidential materials and situations with sensitivity and discretion.
5. Advanced general computer knowledge of Windows- and network-based environments, ability to use on-line, CD-ROM and electronic databases creatively and effectively, Internet and HTML publishing knowledge, and word processing abilities.
6. Experience and references demonstrating creative and flexible research skills and ability to analyze, interpret, summarize and present information effectively.
7. Working experience with prospect research, or research in an academic or library setting, and/or familiarity with a fund raising or nonprofit environment is highly desirable.

# UNIVERSITY OF FLORIDA FOUNDATION, INC.

| TITLE: | Assistant Director of Research |
|---|---|
| DEPARTMENT: | Research |
| RESPONSIBLE TO: | Director of Research |
| MAJOR FUNCTION: | Under the direction of the Director of Research, incumbent will provide assistance with administrative duties in the areas of prospect research and prospect management to support the fund raising goals and objectives of the University of Florida Foundation, Inc., which includes the office of Development and Alumni Affairs. |

# DUTIES AND RESPONSIBILITIES:

## Essential Functions of the Job:

E 1. Serves as the Director of Research in the absence of the Director. In the event of problems with personnel, contact the Director of Human Resources for assistance.

E 2. Assist Director of Research to quantify and measure performance of the Research Department. Assist in policy-making and long term planning and goal setting.

E 3. Provide orientation about research policies, resources and services to development staff, or University administrators as needed.

E 4. Supervise and train new personnel and students. Explain UF Foundation policies and filing system to new research personnel. Train and assist new research personnel in research procedures collectively with other research staff. Coordinate outside on-line training and contact vendors with issues or problems concerning training or access.

E 5. Serve as office liaison with computing service for computer problems, installation of software, and provide technical support and expertise for the department.

E 6. Oversee central files maintenance although day-to-day supervision is the responsibility of the Office Assistant.

Resource 4

E 7.    Review, evaluate, and develop resource acquisition plan for the Research Department, including on-line services, computer hardware and software needs, and print material. Consult co-workers and peers in the profession for input on products and services and comparison of costs.

E 8.    Allocate reading responsibilities and pro-actively distribute relevant articles and information to the appropriate development officer.

E 9.    Assist in evaluation and implementation of new document storage methods, including imaging, or other new technology. Train others in use of new procedures.

E 10.   Implement pro-active and outreach projects with University offices and development staff collectively with research staff. Standardize and refine pro-active reports and procedures. Increase relationships and develop projects with development officers. Integrate electronic screening results and help prioritize prospects. Assist in implementation of specialized research team plan.

E 11.   As needed, produce biographical profiles on alumni and friends, as well as corporate leaders and individuals interested in donating funds to the University. Establish gift capacity and inclination, and ties to UF. Additionally, provide background profiles on local, national and international corporations and foundations, including giving history, financial and historical information about the organization.

12.   Other duties and special projects as assigned. Description is subject to review and revisions as necessary.

*Note:* "E" indicates Essential Functions, which are the functions that this position exists to perform. Any incumbent in this position must be able to perform all of these essential fundamental duties, with or without reasonable accommodations. Management retains the right to modify or add duties at any time.

# QUALIFICATIONS:

### Education:

Bachelor's degree (Master's desirable) in library science, business, journalism, communication, history, or other related field.

### Experience and Job Knowledge:

Minimum of two to four years of experience as a prospect researcher preferably in a higher education development setting. Must be inquisitive, determined, resilient, work well under deadlines and handle multiple priorities. Excellent communication skills; writing and editing ability important, as well as competence in interpreting biographical, corporate and foundation information. Strong computer skills and strong proficiency with electronic research tools (including Internet) and techniques to gather in-depth information on potential and existing donors. Familiarity with electronic screening services a plus. Ability to supervise, manage, delegate, train and mentor research staff including part-time and student workers. Capital campaign experience desirable.

## ADDITIONAL CONSIDERATIONS:

Accuracy, attention to detail and a service oriented attitude are important. Discretion and judgment in working with highly confidential information necessary. Be creative and possess problem-solving skills. Work well with others in busy office. The incumbent should be computer literate in these areas in a PC environment:

- Windows 95
- Microsoft Word
- Microsoft Office 97

- Desktop publishing (for working with graphic designers)
- WWW browsers, preferably Netscape
- E-mail

### SIGNATURES:

_____          _____
Incumbent                                                Date

_____          _____
Immediate Supervisor                                  Date

### Reviewing Authority (as appropriate):

_____          _____
Personnel                                                Date

_____          _____
Name and Title                                         Date

# INDIANA UNIVERSITY FOUNDATION
# JOB DESCRIPTION

| Date: | February 15, 1999 | Job Title: | Director, Research Management and Information Services |
|---|---|---|---|
| Department: | Research | Classification: | |
| Supersedes: | | FLSA: | |

## GENERAL SUMMARY

Manage and coordinate professional and support staff within the IUF Research department with little or no supervision. Provide consulting support to the users of the systems and staff. Analyze staff performance and provide ways to improve department efficiency. Prepare and monitor Research department budget. Continually investigate new book and electronic resources in an effort to maintain high quality of Research services. Make professional, public presentations on the process of prospect research to other units within IU and to national organization when requested.

## ESSENTIAL FUNCTIONS

*Critical features of this job are described below. Nothing in this job description restricts management's right to assign or reassign duties and responsibilities to this job at any time.*

Establish oneself as a knowledgeable supervisor by:

- becoming and remaining current on all IUF policies, procedures and IUF systems
- learning the IUF mission and being knowledgeable about the IUF business and in particular the department's responsibilities to that mission as set forth in the IUF strategic plan
- becoming and remaining current on the latest technologies available for the process of prospect research
- maintaining proficiency in the regularly used IUF software

Manage and coordinate departmental resources by:

- developing annual departmental budget
- effectively monitoring budget compliance on a monthly basis
- ensuring proper cross-training of staff in order to provide depth within the department
- continually monitoring and evaluating the effectiveness of book and electronic resources in order to always have the most up-to-date and efficient tools for prospect research

Manage, coordinate and provide feedback to staff by:

- maintaining a fair and equitable work flow, keeping a log of incoming and completed projects
- assuring availability to answer questions and serve as a mentor
- effectively communicating procedural controls and purpose
- developing clear, concise policies and procedures to assist staff
- performing periodic staff evaluations
- identifying performance inhibitors and providing appropriate training and experiential opportunities designed to correct any performance deficiencies
- holding an annual research staff retreat to develop goals for the department that are in line with the IUF strategic plan
- insuring that the performance goals, as set by the research staff, are being met

Provide support to users, as needed, by:

- assuring availability to orient new employees to the services provided by research and to answer any questions that may arise
- possessing comprehensive knowledge of the process of prospect research as it relates to individuals, corporations and foundations
- maintaining high level of understanding of database systems which store information about IUF's donors and friends
- identifying areas where additional training may be needed

Enhance department communications by:

- receiving, screening, referring and/or responding to inquiries and requests for research (phone and mail), and gathering information and data as required
- timely follow-up with required data and/or information
- meeting and/or coordinating with development officers requesting services from the Research department to maintain clear understanding of what is being requested

- assuring that confidential information remains confidential and is handled with caution to prevent its inadvertent dissemination

Enhance departmental performance standards by:

- performing as a team player
- maintaining level of reliability that generates stability to the department
- meeting or exceeding established departmental performance standards
- fostering a spirit of cooperation

Contribute to departmental efficiency by:

- effectively communicating departmental policy and procedure
- clearly communicating concerns and questions to supervisor
- soliciting guidance from supervisor when uncertainty arises
- assisting in training new employees
- suggesting procedural changes as needed in order to take an active role in improving departmental performance

Approach each situation with a professional attitude by:

- exercising good judgment in discussing issues and results
- maintaining composure and calm demeanor when situations become difficult
- respecting the need for confidentiality of IUF donors, prospects and colleagues
- utilizing a professional presence and demeanor at all times

Perform other related duties incidental to the work described herein.

## EDUCATION

- Bachelor's degree or commensurate experience preferred

## KNOWLEDGE/SKILLS/ABILITIES REQUIRED

- 3–5 years experience in the field of prospect research
- Minimum of 3 years experience in a supervisory or managerial role
- Extensive knowledge of and/or experience with library systems and reference materials (book and electronic) as they pertain to prospect research
- Interpersonal skills and judgment suitable for exercising appropriate discretion and demeanor when dealing with employees and members of the public

- Strong organizational skills
- Ability to exercise good judgment in the handling of confidential information
- Demonstrate ability to use current word processing, spreadsheet, and database software used by the IU Foundation

## MENTAL DEMANDS

- Detailed work, reading, confidentiality, problem solving, and verbal and written communication
- Multiple assignments and deadlines commensurate with a very busy, high-profile office

## PHYSICAL DEMANDS

- Requires very little physical effort. Frequent keyboarding and sitting in front of a computer may occur.

## WORKING CONDITIONS

- Typical office working conditions

Approval:

Supervisor/Date: _____ HR Director/Date: _____

# BUCKNELL UNIVERSITY POSITION DESCRIPTION

POSITION TITLE:   Manager of Prospect Information
DEPARTMENT:       Division of University Relations, Prospect Information
GRADE:            Professional

The Manager of Prospect Information is a full-time professional staff position reporting to the Director of Advancement and Information Services. The Manager is responsible for the planning and management of a comprehensive program of research on individuals, corporations, and foundations that are prospects for significant financial support or can in other ways help to advance the University (e.g., through influence or volunteer activity).

The Manager's role is proactive in expanding the pool of potential prospects and brining to the attention of the development staff those offering the greatest promise of return. The position is also reactive and responsive to research requests from the development and alumni offices, as well as from the office of the president.

The Manager prepares a yearly budget and operating plan and develops long-range plans to support the research needs of periodic capital fund drives. The position includes supervisory responsibility for other professional staff members and student research assistants.

The Manager establishes and maintains standards of quality, accuracy, and timeliness for all work produced by the Office of Prospect Information. The Manager will provide creative leadership of the research team, encouraging innovative and persistent research efforts that are forward-looking and take advantage of emerging new technologies and research sources.

# PRINCIPAL DUTIES AND RESPONSIBILITIES:

The Manager of Prospect Information will:

1. Supervise and/or conduct all research on individuals, corporations, and foundations that are prospects for significant financial support, influence, or volunteer leadership.

2. Allocate the personnel and financial resources of the office in a balanced effort to both expand the pool of identified/researched major prospects and to maintain accurate, up-to-date information on current prospects and past major donors.

3. Establish standardized formats for research in varying degrees of depth to suit a variety of development purposes. Set standards of accuracy, completeness and timeliness for all projects completed by the research staff.

4. Work with the Director of Advancement and Information Services to develop the Benefactor software package, including creating and designing reports, managing information processing, and other system related issues of interest to the mission of the University Relations Division.

5. Supervise and monitor the performances of professional staff members based on established office standards, and conduct regular staff evaluations during which performance and standards issues are discussed; encourage the professional development of these individuals, both in productivity and in job skills.

6. Develop long-range plans to expand research capabilities of the office in support of projected major capital fund drives. Develop methods to estimate the number of prospects required for each level in a campaign scale of gifts and procedures to monitor regular progress of the office in identifying sufficient numbers of prospects.

7. Maintain a current research/reference library of books and periodicals related to research and development; employ database searching services available within the Office of Prospect Information and in the Bertrand Library. Utilize information resources available over the Internet and retain current information on other fee-based data services available in the commercial market.

8. Provide divisional leadership in identifying and screening potential major gift prospects, preparing prospect review agendas, and presenting new information at prospect review meetings.

9. Prepare an annual budget for the Office of Prospect Information and annual operating plans and objectives. Negotiate with vendors of print and electronic information services and monitor expenditures to maximize the University's return on its research investment.

10. Participate in other advancement events and projects as deemed necessary to support the broader goals of the division.

11. Play a leadership role in regional and national professional organizations such as Prospect Researchers of Eastern PA (PREP) and the Association of Professional Researchers for Advancement (APRA).

12. Other duties as assigned by the Director of Advancement and Services.

Resource 4

## QUALIFICATIONS:

The Manager of Prospect Information must:

1. Have a bachelor's degree in humanities, business administration, or the social sciences.
2. Be familiar with a broad range of research techniques, including traditional text and periodical-based research, searching of electronic databases, interviewing, and the use of such other sources as court records, real estate records, the Internet, and census data.
3. Have experience with microcomputers, large databases, and supervisory management. Be computer literate with experience in word-processing, spreadsheet, relational database software, and the Internet. Possess strong problem solving abilities and be able to exercise independent initiative as appropriate. Attention to detail is critical.
4. Have strong interpersonal skills and the ability to communicate effectively and efficiently with co-workers and constituents.
5. Be tactful, discreet, diplomatic, and able to deal with confidential information sensitively.
6. Possess excellent written communication skills, including strong editing, spelling and grammar skills.
7. Have a sense of curiosity and be enthusiastic about learning.

## PREFERRED SKILLS:

1. Familiarity with the philosophy and practices of institutional advancement.
2. Professional experience in a private college setting.
3. Advanced degree in library science or related information fields.
4. Experience with Datatel's Benefactor software.

Resource 4

# RESOURCE 5

## RESEARCH REQUEST FORMS

Resource 5

**243**

# University of Florida Foundation, Inc.
# Department of Research
# Research Request

Date: _____        Submitted by: _____

Requestor: _____        Phone #: _____

College/Unit: _____

Prospect: _____
(Full name, Nickname, Grad. year, Hometown, etc.) If on Advance ID# required

Location: _____
(Address: City, State, Zip, Phone #)

Other Info: _____
(Info pertinent to Research, University staff, or community contact)

Business Affiliation: _____
(Title/Affiliation)

For what/when? _____
(Meeting, Trip, Reception/President, Dean, Director)          (date)

Source of Identification: _____
(Example: Target America, Yahoo Finance)

Type of Request:

    Initial Inquiry _____

    First Visit Scheduled _____     Date: _____

    Cultivation ?, Solicitation ?, Proposal ?, (In-Depth) _____

    Assets of Public Record (property, stock, etc.) _____

    News Search File Information Only _____

    Pro-Active Research Project — (Contact Director) _____

    Funding Search (provide keywords) _____

    Other: _____
    (Please explain)

Date needed: _____
(Please allow 2 weeks for routine requests depending upon current priorities)

Mail to: Research Dept., 2012 W. University Ave. Fax to: 352-846-2754 or Email dmenoher@uff.ufl.edu

Resource 5

# Request for Research
# Duke University Research Department

Name of Requestor [                    ]

Department/Unit [                    ]

Campus Mail
Address [                    ]

Date Submitted [                    ]

Date Needed [                    ]

☐ Individual
Report  ☐ Corporate & Foundation Report

## Individual Report

Prospect's Name: [                    ]

Are you sure of the
spelling?  ○ yes ⦿ no

ADVANCE# [                    ]

Duke Affiliation [                    ]

Address: [                    ▲
                             ▼
          ◄                  ► ]

Do you know this
prospect?  ○ yes ⦿ no

Is there a contact
that can provide
additional
information? If so,
please tell us who: [                    ▲
                                         ▼
                     ◄                   ► ]

|  | ☐ Tier One * Financial Indicators * Other wealth information * Rating |
| Information Needed (Please check all that apply) | ☐ Tier Two * Duke affiliations, boards, and related activities * Giving history |
|  | ☐ Tier Three * Education and employment history * Biographical and family history * Company and/or foundation information * Civic activities and community involvement * Interconnections |

Please list any specific questions you would like to have answered (if possible):

## Corporate & Foundation Report

Name of Organization

Address:

☐ General Overview (Financial Information, Business Activities)
☐ Board Members and Senior Officers
☐ Duke Relationship (Has Duke had any contact with this organization?)

**Corporate (check all that apply):**

☐ Duke Connections (Do any individuals affiliated with the organization have a connection to Duke?)
☐ Current News (recent press releases or articles about the company)

☐ General Overview (Financial Information, Areas of Interest)
☐ Officers and Directors
☐ Application Information

**Foundation (check all that apply):**

☐ Grant Information
☐ Duke Connections
☐ Duke Relationship
☐ Current News

Please list any
other specific
information
you would like:

Submit Survey     Clear the form

Return to the Research home page, without submitting the survey.

# St. Mary's College of Maryland
## RESEARCH REQUEST

*Information above the double line MUST be filled out in order for research to be done.*

**Prospect Name:** _____

**Date Needed:** _____  **Priority:** low    medium    high    *(circle one)*

**Copies To:** _____

**Type of Information Needed:**  *Please select one level and one format.*

Level:  _____ Specific Aspect: _____

_____ Basic *(regular profile)*

_____ Full *(in-depth information—provided when/if needed for solicitation only)*

Format: _____ regular

_____ regular edited *(some details removed for confidentiality)*

_____ other: _____

**Purpose of Research:** *Please select one from each section and provide a date where applicable.*

*1.* Call _____  *2.* Visit _____  *3.* Solicitation _____
*4.* Other _____

*a.* New Prospect   *b.* New profile on existing prospect   *c.* Further info on existing prospect
*d.* Trustee Prospect: preliminary or *e.* ready to share with the Board _____

===

**Pertinent Information:**
Relationship to SMCM:

Occupation/Business:

Board Involvement:

Address:

Family Information:

Contacts for more information:

Other:

**Requestor:** _____    **Request Date:** _____

# UNIVERSITY OF COLORADO
# FOUNDATION, INC.

## REQUEST FOR CORPORATE/FOUNDATION PROSPECT RESEARCH

Date of Request: _____   Date Information Needed: _____   CID #: _____

Complete Name: _____

Address: _____

Phone: ( ) _____   Website: _____

Contact person(s):

**What specific information do you want or need?**

**Who will see/read the information CUF Research provides?**

How was this organization identified as a prospect?

Known information about prospect:

Potential CU giving interests:

Known CU contacts:

Campus connection(s):   ___ Boulder   ___ HSC   ___ Denver   ___ Colorado Springs

---

**How will information be used?**
___ Preparation for major ask    Amount of ask _____   Date of ask _____

___ Appointment/meeting/visit with prospect    Date: _____

Who's attending? _____

___ Qualify potential prospect

___ Other.   Please explain:

---

Originator of request: _____   Return information to: _____

Resource 5

# UNIVERSITY OF COLORADO
# FOUNDATION, INC.

## REQUEST FOR INDIVIDUAL PROSPECT RESEARCH

Date of Request: _____ Date Information Needed: _____ CID#: _____

Prospect: _____ _____
           Last      First      Middle      Nickname         YR–Sch/College

Spouse: _____ _____
           Last      First      Middle      Nickname         YR–Sch/College

Home Address: _____ Business Name: _____

_____ Business Address: _____

_____ _____

Home Phone: ( )_____ Business Phone: ( )_____

Business Title(s) of Prospect:

Campus connection(s): ___ Boulder ___ HSC ___ Denver ___ Colorado Springs

Potential CU Giving Interests:

Known information about prospect:

Known University of Colorado contacts:

Prospect manager name:

___ How will information be used?
___ Preparation for major ask
___ Appointment/meeting/visit with prospect. Date: _____
___ General interest and cultivation
___ Other. Please explain.

How was this person identified as a prospect?

What specific information do you want or need?

Who will see/read the information CUF Research provides?

Indicate appropriate Solicitation Schedule:
___ Scheduled ask, $100,000 or more; date of ask _____ amount _____
___ Scheduled ask, less than $100,000; date of ask _____ amount _____
___ Campaign ask, $100,000 or more
___ Campaign ask, under $100,000
___ Suspect with ability to give $100,000 or more in this campaign
___ Suspect with ability to give $100,000 or more in a future campaign
___ Leadership gift level ($2,500 or more yearly gift)
___ Other: _____

Originator of request: _____ Return information to: _____

# NORTHWESTERN UNIVERSITY—DEVELOPMENT RESEARCH
*2020 Ridge, Rm 305, Evanston 847/491-5363 (FAX 847/491-7095)*

# RESEARCH REQUEST

Prospect's Name: _____ ID #: _____

(First Name/MI/Last Name)

Source of Name: _____

## RESEARCH REQUIRED:

☐ PRP      Category*
(full profile)

_____     _____
                  **Signature of Approving Officer**
                  (VP signature needed for A+ with turnaround
                  requested = under 2 weeks. Exec. Comm. member
                  signature for A with turnaround within 2 weeks.)

Date
Required: _____or _____ At Your Convenience

OR ☐ Particular
Information* _____

Date
Required: _____or _____ At Your Convenience

**BACKGROUND**   *(To help us find information or verify that*
**INFORMATION**  *what we find is about the correct person)*

*Class Year:* _____

*Spouse Name:* _____     *Company:* _____

*Home Address:* _____     *Title:* _____

_____     *Address:* _____

_____

_____

*Phone:* _____     _____

*Work:* _____

*Additional Background Information:*
*(Attach additional sheets if necessary)*

_____

_____

_____

_____

*Today's Date:* _____     *Requested by:* _____

(Name of Development Officer)

*Please see reverse side for PRP categories and other types of available research

**Resource 5**

## *Descriptions of Categories

According to the Vice President's priority definitions as outlined below, taken from his memo summarizing research procedures:

A+:  Turnaround time of under 2 weeks:
     Reserved for super/mega gift prospects where time demands are such that a turn-around time of less than 10 working days is required. These exceptional requests must be approved by the Vice President.

A:   Turnaround time within 2 weeks of Research's receipt; these include:
     - Critical meeting with prospect scheduled in 45 days
     - $100,000 and greater gift potential ($10,000 for annual/reunion gifts)
     - Campaign prospects have priority within Priority A
     - Request must be seen and approved by the development officer's assistant VP or director (Tim Weidmann, Judy Jobbitt, Jon Heintzelman, Penny Hunt, or Edward Paquette)

B:   Turnaround time within 30 days:
     - Significant move (one-on-one contact) anticipated *no later than* six months from the date request received by research office.
     - $50,000 and greater gift potential ($5,000 for annual/reunion gifts)
     - Campaign prospects have priority within Priority B.

C:   Turnaround time within 90 days:
     - Significant move (one-on-one contact) anticipated *no sooner than* six months from the date request received by research office.
     - $50,000 and greater gift potential ($5,000 for annual/reunion gifts).

     *[Note: Do not confuse these research priorities with individual prospect ratings. For example, a triple "A" prospect may have a research priority of C.]*

## *Non-PRP Information Available

If a full PRP is not needed (if you only need a specific piece or pieces of information) we can send you copies of source material or prepare a memo answering your particular questions. For example, we can research a person's education, business and civic affiliations, other family members, indications of wealth, such as income, real estate or stock holdings, publications written by or about the prospect, development contact, etc.

# HILLEL: THE FOUNDATION FOR JEWISH CAMPUS LIFE
## Request for Development Prospect Research (Internal)

Name to research: _____

| | |
|---|---|
| Date of request: | |
| Requested by: | |
| Date research is needed: | |
| Priority: | ☐ high   ☐ med   ☐ low |
| Date of meeting: | |
| Purpose of meeting: | |
| Spelling confirmed? | ☐ yes   ☐ no |
| City (or community), State | |
| Occupation/Business | |
| Hillel Campus Connections | |
| Education: degree & alma mater | |

1. What will the information be needed for (check all that apply)
   ☐ New prospect
   ☐ Update on an established prospect
   ☐ Cultivation activity/event: _____
   ☐ Solicitation

2. Please share any known background information. (list name of prospect's business, position, family relations, hobbies and interests, ties to Hillel, local or regional, Federation relations, professional and community affiliations such as corporate boards and philanthropic boards, contact people, etc. & past major gifts to Jewish and non-Jewish organizations)


3. Please list other persons you have or haven't contacted who may be helpful in this research.


4. Please check the appropriate level of information desired.
   ☐ *I. General Picture + Other Biographical*—includes name, address, occupation, relationship to Hillel, giving history, spouse, parents, birth date & place, education (degree and alma mater), children, interests; community, philanthropic & professional affiliations; company & career background
   ☐ *II. General Picture, Other Biographical + Financial Information*—includes Level I research, salary & other compensation, real estate holdings, stock holdings, & other movable liquid wealth
   ☐ *III. Photograph* (when available)
   ☐ *IV. Other*—Please list the specific information that you are looking for:


\* Please submit form at least two days prior to due date.
\* Please be as specific as possible. The more information you submit, the more information you will receive.

## RESOURCE 6

## RESEARCH ORIENTATION MATERIALS

# RESEARCH FACT SHEET

## STANFORD UNIVERSITY

## Office of Development
## Research Department

# What We Do In Research:

- *Consultation on Topics.* Each individual in the research department has areas of expertise and is available to consult with you on those areas (i.e., wine industry, biotechnology, venture capital).
- *Qualification Research.* Research will qualify prospects to determine the major gift potential of a prospect by looking at key online resources.
- *Responding to Specific Questions.* Most research requests should answer a question. For instance, how much is he/she worth? What might he/she be interested in? What has happened with his/her business or career recently?
- *Full Research Reports.* Research prepares full reports for the use of the university president, trustee's office, and major gift volunteers.
- *Newsletters.* Research sends out the Bay Area Dispatch, The Insider Watch, and In the News on a monthly basis.

# Getting a Head Start:

Reading the central file and viewing the entity profile report in Post Grads will give you a good sense of a prospect prior to requesting research from our department. You may also be interested in checking out some of our top websites used in research:

- *Stanford Research Website* (http://www.stanford.edu/dept/OOD/RESEARCH/). Information on the Research Team, Research Links (portals, search engines, directories, stock quotes, IPO resources, corporate profiles, foundations and non-profits, international resources, top lists), and News Links. The best place to start.

- *CEO Express* (http://www.ceoexpress.com/). Links to news, business, and finance sites.
- *Infospace* (http://www.infospace.com). Great way to look up phone numbers, email addresses, and yellow pages information.
- *Yahoo! Finance* (http://quote.yahoo.com/). Great place to look up company information, stock quotes, monthly or annual stock charts, financial news, and market news.

| THE RESEARCH TEAM | |
|---|---|
| *Randy Lakeman* (5-5526), Director | *Karen Gotchy* (5-4375) *Areas:* Administration, Website, IPOs, Insider Watch |
| *Nanci Olson Gundry* (3-9941) *Areas:* Day-to-Day Operations, Staff Training, Hoover Inst., Venture Capital, IPOs | *Lilly Lim* (5-4277) *Areas:* Asia/Pacific, Europe, Canada, East Coast, Hawaii, Parents |
| *Sharon Hoffman* (3-5192) *Areas:* Northwest, Mid-Continent, Southern California, School of Education, Wine Country, Libraries, Website | *Ginger Ladd* (5-4311) *Areas:* Northern California, Graduate School of Business, School of Engineering, International High-Tech |
| *Lisa Gonzalez* (5-4347) *Areas:* Corporations, Europe, Latin America, IIS | |

Resource 6

# Fundraiser's Guide to the Internet
### Created by Sarah Conner, San Jose State University

## General Reference

- *The Librarians' Guide to the Internet*   http://sunsite.berkeley.edu/InternetIndex/
  A great Internet resource.

- *Internet Sleuth*   http://www.isleuth.com/
  A collection of Internet databases.

## Business & Investment

- *Edgar*   http://www.sec.gov/cgi-bin/srch-edgar
  The Securities Exchange Commission web site. The information on this site is free. It provides access to documents electronically filed by publicly held companies in the US, as required by the SEC. Look for the 10K (annual report) and the DEF14 (Proxy) documents for executive compensation, stockholdings, and biographical information.

- *Edgar Online People Search*   http://people.edgar-online.com/people/
  Search Edgar documents for a specific name. You have to sign up for this service, but accessing proxies is free.

- *Silicon Valley Companies*   http://www.sjmercury.com/svtech/companies/db/
  From the San Jose Mercury News. A database of the top public companies in the Silicon Valley.

- *Money*   http://quote.pathfinder.com/money/quote/qc
  From Money Magazine. An easy-to-use stock quote search engine.

- *Martindale-Hubbell*   http://lawyers.martindale.com/marhub
  Lawyer Look-up. Searchable database by name, law firm, and location.

## Directory Assistance

- *Realnames.com*   http://www.realnames.com/
  For those of you who find it cumbersome to type in the whole http address (and who doesn't) this site simplifies that. Type in the company or product name, and this search engine will find the home page for you.

- *PhoneDisk on-line*   http://fonedisc.lbl.gov/411
  From the Lawrence Berkeley Lab web site.

- *AnyWho*   http://www.anywho.com/
  A new search engine from AT&T indexes telephone numbers and addresses for some 90 million people. "Sounds-like" and reverse searches by phone number are also available.

- *55512121.com*   http://www.555-1212.com/ACLOOKUP.HTML
  Telephone directory, email and Web site directory, and area code look-up.

## San Jose State University Web Sites

- *Campus Home Page*   http://www.sjsu.edu/
  The official SJSU home page.

- *University Advancement*   http://www.sjsu.edu/advancement/dirlist.html
  SJSU University Advancement directory.

- *Supporting San Jose State*   http://www.sjsu.edu/development/index.html
  Raising the level of philanthropy.

- *Electronic Resources*   http://www.library.sjsu.edu/elecres.htm
  Made available through the SJSU Library.

## News

- *San Jose Mercury News*   http://www.mercurycenter.com/
  Today's articles may be accessed for free, but you must pay for archived articles.

- *The Gate*   http://www.sfgate.com/
  The San Francisco Chronicle and the San Francisco Examiner. Includes a searchable archives back to January 1995.

- *The Chronicle of Higher Education*   http://chronicle.merit.edu/
  News and information in academia. You must be a subscriber to access articles on this site.

- *Arts & Letters Daily*   http://cybereditions.com/aldaily/
  A highly recommended resource for news and other interesting links. An exhaustive list of links to mainstream newspapers, literary journals, on-line zines, plus highlighted articles.

## Philanthropy and Fundraising

- *CAE*   http://www.cae.org/
  Council for Aid to Education, a tax-exempt, not-for-profit national organization dedicated both to enhancing the effectiveness of private-sector support in improving education at all levels and to helping education institutions more effectively acquire private support for their programs.

- *NSFRE*   http://www.nsfre.org/
  National Society of Fundraising Executives [now called Association of Fundraising Professionals (AFP)].

- *The Foundation Center*   http://fdncenter.org/index.html
  An independent nonprofit information clearinghouse for grantmakers and grantseekers. Check out their San Francisco office: http://fdncenter.org/library/sanfranc.html

- *The Chronicle of Philanthropy*   http://www.philanthropy.com/
  A good on-line resource for fundraisers.

- *Philanthropy Journal On-line*   http://www.philanthropy-journal.org/
  News and information about fundraising.

# Search Engines

| | |
|---|---|
| *Alta Vista* | *Dog Pile* |
| http://www.altavista.com/ | http://www.dogpile.com/ |
| | the Friendly Multi-Engine Search Tool |

# UNIVERSITY OF FLORIDA FOUNDATION

## Research Department
## Orientation Material

**University of Florida Foundation, Inc.**
2012 W. University Avenue,
PO Box 14425
Gainesville, FL 32604-2425

## Who We Are

Debbie Menoher, Director of Research
    392-8307    dmenoher@uff.ufl.edu

Maria Benton, Assistant Director of Research
    392-9879    mbenton@uff.ufl.edu

Ella Mae Hart, Prospect Tracking Specialist
    846-2750    ehart@uff.ufl.edu

Beth Jordan, Research Analyst
    392-9880    ejordan@uff.ufl.edu

Sue Lautenschlager, Office Assistant
    846-2753    slauten@uff.ufl.edu

Michelle Lovell, Medical Research Analyst
    392-5866    mlovell@uff.ufl.edu

Marilyn Sandbeck, Senior Research Analyst
    392-8306    msandbec@uff.ufl.edu

Jane Spangler, Corporate and Foundation Research Analyst
    392-8305    jspangle@uff.ufl.edu

Peggy Speruggia, File Specialist
    846-3544    psperrug@uff.ufl.edu

Dara Thomas, Research Analyst
    846-2819    dthomas@uff.ufl.edu

RESEARCH FAX NUMBER: 846-2754

# Information Center

Research maintains a library available to all staff; however, we ask that items not be circulated. A copier is available. Resources include newspapers, journals, business directories, Who's Who directories, maps, and more. *New professional book collection circulates.*

Research has a professional collection of books and materials you may borrow upon request. To date the following titles are available:

- The Seven Faces of Philanthropy
- Major Gifts Solicitation Strategies—CASE
- Advancement Services—Research and Technology Support for Fund Raising—CASE
- The Millionaire Next Door
- Developing an Effective Major Gift Program—From managing staff to soliciting gifts
- Askophobia—pamphlet geared toward volunteers
- Guide to Proposal Writing
- Effective committees—The Development Committee—AGB
- Targeting the Powerful—International Prospect Research
- Where the Money Is
- Nuevos Senderos—Reflections on Hispanics and Philanthropy
- Successful Campus Fund Raising—Profile of Award-Winning Fund-Raising Programs
- Building Bridges—Fund Raising for Deans, Faculty and Development Officers

Please ask for assistance in locating information. We'd be happy to help!

# Policies

## Files

Research maintains central donor files for the Foundation. Copies of pertinent gift information, donor activity and correspondence, proposals and guidelines, research reports and clippings are filed. There are individual and corporate/foundation files in the file room, and miscellaneous files are located in the library.

Files may not be removed from the Research Department (with the exemption of Paul Robell, Carter Boydstun and Leslie Bram), although a copier is available in our office.

Retention of file materials is indefinite; however, Research selectively removes materials on a regular basis. Microfilming or other long-term document storage is implemented as necessary, since the files grow at a rapid rate.

Confidentiality of central files is extremely important to the ongoing positive relationship with donors. The research staff has adopted the Ethics Statement of the Association of Prospect Researchers for Advancement.

Information stored in the files shall be for the purposes of fund raising, and only appropriate information is permitted in the files. Research reserves the right to edit/purge inappropriate information.

## Research Requests

Research requests should be submitted on *research request forms only.* You may submit the request form by mail (Research, 2012 Bld.), fax (846-2754) or e-mail (dmenoher@uff.ufl.edu). Give at least two weeks or more for completion time. Exceptions can be made depending upon the urgency of the research. All requests need correctly spelled proper names, middle initial (if available), nickname (if applicable), and ID number if on Advance system. Please *print legibly,* or type request if possible. Include the purpose of the research and any campus or community contacts if available. Lack of above mentioned information causes unnecessary delays in research reports.

Requests are prioritized by receipt date, level of cultivation and current research priorities.

Research provides the type of information appropriate for the level of cultivation. The following are basic definitions of types of reports available.

> *Initial Inquiry* (Health Science Center). These brief overviews include a basic search of standard sources, and a brief cover memo. Copies of information located are attached to the memo. There is no analysis of information. Approximate completion time is 1–2 hours. (Approximate cost $65*)

*Assessment:* The assessment provides a basic overview of information. It does not routinely include stock or other financial information and takes about 2–4 hours for completion. This format includes copies of information found and a brief cover memo. It does not contain analysis of information. (Approximate cost $125*)

*Standard:* A standard report takes about 8–10 hours for completion and includes personal and financial information. We use obvious resources, which includes checking a "standard" list of resources. (Approximate cost $300*)

*In-depth:* An in-depth report is done in special situations that may require information above and beyond a standard report. It may be done for prospects with extensive amounts of information. It contains "everything" we can find; personal, financials, etc. and it takes 10+ hours for completion. We use *every* resource available to the research department. (Approximate cost $300–$500*)

*Special Requests:* If you have a specific request that does not require an entire research report, please feel free to ask us. For example, you may need only property information, stock holdings, a newspaper article, or address update. We have many resources available, and we can probably help!

* *Costs are estimated for demonstration purposes only. These amounts are based upon researchers' time and average cost of resources and standard commercial market prices.* You will not actually receive a bill!

## Services

### Prospect Research

Researchers are professionally trained to strategize and search a multitude of resources, including online services, and to provide reports on prospects. In addition, prospect identification projects are ongoing initiatives of Research.

### Prospect Tracking

The Research Department is your liaison for database issues related to prospect tracking. Our prospect tracking specialist *creates new entity IDs* on the Advance Database, records the assignment and reassignment of prospects (*manager head-*

*ers*), extracts data from contact reports, updates the Prospect Tracking System, analyzes data, and prepares reports for Development Officers and Management on prospect tracking. In addition, this person will provide employee training on prospect tracking management. Any questions or comments on current policies and procedure, Top 100 assignments, and/or database management should be directed to Debbie Menoher (2-8307) or Ella Mae Hart (6-2750).

## Special Projects

Electronic Screening data is maintained in Research. Researchers can assist you with interpreting and utilizing information from Grenzebach's Prospect Profile and Survey, CDA/InvestNet Securities Match, CDA/InvestNet Real Estate Match, Target America, and Prospect Information Network. Research regularly evaluates and implements new screening tools.

### Sources Used in the Research Department

*Dialog.* "Dialog is the world's largest databank of information, providing access to more than 600 different information collections known as databases. Some databases include references and abstracts for published literature, business information and financial data; others contain complete text of articles and news stories; others contain statistical tables and directories." Dialog is accessed through the Internet.

*Dow Jones Interactive.* "Dow Jones provides you with access to more than 55 million articles in the Dow Jones Publications Library of more than 6,000 business, trade and news publications. Dow Jones is the exclusive combined source of The Wall Street Journal, the New York Times, and the Financial Times, The Washington Post, and the Los Angeles Times. Search exclusive newswires and 48 of the top 50 newspapers for global coverage. Now includes Reuters News Service. Access reports on more than 10 million public and private companies and find quotes and data on every major exchange in the world."

The Dow Jones Interactive Custom Clips feature allows you to create a folder, and by using a keyword search, get continuous e-mail updates about individuals and corporations from the 6,000 publications accessed by Dow Jones.

*AutoTrack Plus+ and AutoTrack XP.* AutoTrack (Database Technologies) is used to search a variety of public record information on individuals and companies. Information can be located from both national and state sources including: current and past addresses, neighbors, relatives, drivers' licenses, associates, assets, corporations, real estate, vehicles, death records, and more. AutoTrack can be accessed via a dial-up service or web interface. The same information is available on both versions.

There are several state files and a national file to search. The kind of information available for each state depends upon what information is considered public record in that state. We are fortunate to live in Florida where there is a great deal of information that is considered public record. This is very advantageous when searching for prospects that are Floridians.

*Axciom.* Axciom contains business and residential listings for the entire United States. Searches can be made by name, address, phone number, and SIC code. A prospect's phone number and address can be located, if s/he has a listed phone number. After finding the prospect's address, his or her neighbors can be determined. A list of "wealthy neighborhood" residents can be run. A list of businesses involved in a certain type of industry in a state or city can be found, e.g. a list of all pharmacies in Jacksonville.

### Corporate and Foundation Research Sources

*FC Search.* The Grantmaker File contains records for most active private foundations in the U.S. and numerous corporate giving programs as well as some information on grantmaking public charities like community foundations. It provides: Name, Address and Phone number of the Foundation; Contact; Type of grantmaker (i.e. community foundation); background; purpose and activities; field of interests; geographic focus; application information; limitations; financial data; and selected grants. FC Search contains information on approximately 218,000 officers and directors.

The Sponsoring Company Information provided is: Name; City; State; Description of Business Activities; Number of employees; Assets, Sales, Pre-Tax income; Principal Corporate Officers; and Names and locations of identified subsidiaries, divisions, plants. You can search this file using different search criteria, e.g. Name index, state index, city index, fields of interests index, geographic focus index, types of support index, total giving index, and total assets index.

The Grants File contains records for over 200,000 recent grants of $10,000 or more, awarded by more than 1,300 of the largest foundations listed in the Grantmaker File. It provides information on the recipient, location, type of recipient, grantmaker, grantmaker geographic focus, grant amount, year authorized, duration of the gift, description of the gift, and type of support. You can also search this file by these indices.

*Prospector's Choice.* Provides quick and easy access to detailed profiles of over 10,000 potential donors, including top foundations and corporate direct giving programs. It also includes hard-to-find biographical information on the officers and directors of the organizations.

*UF Sponsored Research Database* on the World Wide Web (http://web.ortge. ufl.edu/cgi-bin/search-awards.perl). Contains all grant awards to the University of Florida since 1975. The UF Sponsored Research Advance System allows the Corporate/Foundation Research Analyst to instantly search by sponsor for any grants awarded to UF.

*Thomson Financial (formerly CDA/InvestNet).* The Thompson Financial Pinpoint Basic service allows researchers to track the actions of insiders and officers of various corporations. Filing information available on Pinpoint Basic is compiled from several Securities & Exchange Commission's forms.

An insider is an officer, director or beneficial owner (holder of 10% or more) of a company's stock. Insiders are both individuals and corporations and are required to report their direct and indirect holdings. Corporate insiders are required to report their non-exempt transactions to the SEC by the 10th of the month following the transaction date. Direct holdings are those held in the name of the insider. Indirect holdings are those controlled by the insider, but held by another entity such as a family member, a trust, a company plan, or even a corporation with which the insider is affiliated.

Pinpoint Basic is updated daily and provides information on trades released by the SEC the prior day, insider trades by stock symbol or company name, and a cross reference of all insider's transactions by name. This is the most commonly used option by the Research Department. It provides a list of all the companies in which the insider has held and/or holds stock that is very useful in determining an individual's assets of public record.

*Duns Link (Dun & Bradstreet).* Dun & Bradstreet maintains the largest business information base in the world with information on more than 10 million US businesses. In addition, D&B maintains information on more than 13 million international firms.

Here at UF Foundation's Research Department, we often request business summaries, and history and operation information. This provides us with background information about a company in a consistent format.

The summary provides basic identification information, such as the legal name and address, the chief executive and the year the company was started or present management took control. Sales and net worth information is either an estimate given by someone affiliated with the company or a figure taken from a financial statement.

The history and operations section gives information on the experience of the principals, the connections of related companies, and the general company structure, including information on the parent company, branches and subsidiaries, the number of accounts, geographic territory, and selling terms.

These portions of the D&B Business Information report help researchers gain knowledge of a company, especially when it is not traded publicly. Complete D&B reports are quite expensive, so they are not ordered or provided on a routine basis.

*Target America.* Target America provides a searchable database of over three million wealthy or influential individuals in the United States. The database contains individuals for whom the company has identified specific assets or income that qualify them as wealthy. The company also includes individuals who have at least one significant business or foundation affiliation or have made a gift of $50,000 or more to another nonprofit.

The information included in the Target America database is retrieved from Professional Association lists, SEC filings, Who's Who publications, census data and various other sources.

The Research Department uses two products from Target America. The first is a web-based product that enables us to search the national database online (http://www.tgtam.com). We can also search a regional database through our screening product at the Health Science Center Development Office. The screening product we use at the Health Science Center functions off a seven-state (CD-ROM) database and runs against the daily admits to the University of Florida affiliated hospitals and clinics. The process identifies wealthy and influential patients for the Grateful Patient program.

*FARES—First American Real Estate Solutions.* The First American Real Estate database contains property records from the United States. Although the database does not include all counties and states, it is a valuable resource for obtaining updated property assessments and descriptions. The Research Department can search the database by the property holder's name, address, zip, the parcel number, or various other identifiers.

Resource 6

## Online Searching Using the Internet

Today's Internet is a global resource containing millions of users that began as an experiment over 20 years ago by the U.S. Department of Defense. Its purpose was to create sustainable communications in case of nuclear attack. Academic and commercial concerns have continued to fuel its explosive growth. There are currently millions of users, adding 2 million new users monthly.

---

**Vocabulary**

*Browser:* an application for viewing pages on the Internet's World Wide Web. For example Netscape or Internet Explorer

*Domain Name:* a text based alias that acts as a link to the unique number assigned to a web site (Internet Protocol or IP address). For example: www.uff.ufl.edu

*HTML:* hypertext markup language; it formats web pages so they are understandable by web browsers.

*Links:* a hypertext connection between web pages that when clicked on, will take you to the linked page.

*Protocol:* a mutually agreed upon method of communication between parties.

*World Wide Web:* an interconnection of computers with groups of pages or web sites accessed over the Internet.

---

Here in the research department, we use the Internet to obtain information on individuals, corporations and foundations. Many times we start with a specific site in mind to look for information, such as the Florida Division of Corporations web site (http://ccfcorps.dos.state.fl.us/index.html) which gives information on corporations and partnerships registered in the state of Florida. However when a specific site is unknown, a "search engine" may be used. One of the more popular search engines for prospect research is Alta Vista. It currently scours over 90% of the web and gives you access to the largest web index available. The web address is (http://www.altavista.com).

Currently there are around 800 million web pages on an estimated 3 million public web sites. So sorting out which sites is useful is no small feat. Our department has enclosed a list of sites we use regularly, our "favorites" so to speak, for you to investigate. One site that you may want to start with is Princeton's Development Research links site located at (http://princeton.edu.one/research/netlinks.html). This site contains an array of useful links specifically geared to the needs of the development professional. Spend a little time "surfing" and you will soon have a list of sites you will use regularly too.

### Some Interesting Web Sites

*Search Engines*

| | |
|---|---|
| Alta Vista | http://www.altavista.com |
| Google | http://www.google.com |
| Hotbot | http://www.hotbot.com |
| Northern Light | http://www.northernlight.com |
| Yahoo! | http://www.yahoo.com/ |

*Individual Research*

| | |
|---|---|
| Anywho | http://www.anywho.com |
| Lycos PeopleFind | http://www.whowhere.lycos.com/Phone |
| Switchboard | http://www.switchboard.com |
| Social Security Death Index | http://www.ancestry.com/search/rectype/vital/ssdi/main.htm |
| Federal Election Commission | http://www.tray.com/fecinfo/indiv.htm |

*Professional Locators*

| | |
|---|---|
| American Medical Association | http://www.ama-assn.org/ |
| Martindale Hubbell | http://www.martindale.com |
| Dental Directory | http://www.catalog.com/cgibin/var/dale/index.html |

*Corporations*

| | |
|---|---|
| Hoover's Online | http://www.hoovers.com/ |
| CEO Express | http://www.ceoexpress.com/ |
| Companies Online Search | http://www.companiesonline.com/ |
| CorporateInformation | http://www.corporateinformation.com |
| EDGAR | http://www.sec.gov/cgi-bin/srch-edgar |
| Financials Online | http://www.10kwizard.com |
| FL Div. of Corporations | http://ccfcorp.dos.state.fl.us/ |
| Tax Exempt Organizations | http://www.irs.ustreas.gov/prod/bus_info/eo/ |

## Stock Information

| | |
|---|---|
| IPO | http://www2.ipo.com/ |
| INVESTools Chart | http://www.investools.com/Services/charts/ |
| Red Herring | http://www.redherring.com/home.html |
| Yahoo Finance | http://finance.yahoo.com |

## Foundations

| | |
|---|---|
| Foundation Center | http://www.fdncenter.org |
| Guidestar | http://www.guidestar.org |
| Internet Non-Profit Center | http://www.nonprofits.org |
| Philanthropy Journal | http://www.philanthropy.com |

## News Sources

| | |
|---|---|
| Gainesville Sun | http://www.sunone.com |
| Miami Herald | http://www.herald.com/ |
| Tampa Tribune | http://www.tampatrib.com/ |
| Orlando Sentinel | http://orlandosentinel.com/ |
| Florida Times-Union | http://www.jacksonville.com |
| Palm Beach Post | http://www.gopbi.com/partners/pbpost/epaper/editions/today/ |
| American City Business Journals | http://www.amcity.com |
| Ecola (Newspapers/Magazines) | http://www.ecola.com/ |
| Florida Trend | http://www.floridatrend.com |

## "Fun"d Stuff

| | |
|---|---|
| Advancement Resources | http://oia.mines.edu/advancement_resources/research/default.htm |
| Prospect Research Links | http://www.presbyterianchurchusa.com/lamb/ |
| Florida Tax Assessor Databases | http://www.appraisers.com/consumer/tax_ass/florida.html |
| Salary Surveys | http://jobsmart.org/tools/salary/sal-prof.htm |
| Wealthy Zipcodes | http://www.usc.edu/dept/source/zipcode/index.htm |

# DUKE UNIVERSITY
# DEVELOPMENT RESEARCH

Office of University Development
2127 Campus Drive
Durham, NC 27708
919-684-2123

## Development Research Staff

Tracy Joseph, 681-0431
Coordinator

Barbara Burig, 681-0481
Researcher, working with Corporate and Foundation Relations
and the Southeast Region

William Conescu, 681-0480
Researcher, working with the South and North Carolina/So. Virginia Regions

Chris O'Neill, 681-0482
Researcher, working with the Midwest and West Regions

Jill Range, 681-0484
Researcher, working with the Northeast and DC/MD/VA Regions

Regina Rice, 681-0446
Secretary

Caroline Vaughan, 681-0483
Researcher, working with the Triangle and New York City Regions

## What We Do
(In a nutshell)

Assist university-wide development staff with the identification and research of potential donors.

1. Respond to *requests for research* from development officers across the university, except for the Medical Center, which has its own Research Department. See attached request form AND PLEASE VISIT OUR ON-LINE REQUEST FORM AT:

http://devcomm.duke.edu/research/request.html
This site is password protected. You will need to use:
id: research
password: seek

2. Assign a gift *rating* (see p. 3) on ADVANCE to individuals identified through the BOND screening program and other resources to discover "new" prospects. We then move these prospects through the Prospect Management system for assignment to the various units/schools. Prospects rated at $25,000 will be automatically assigned by the coordinator based on Prospect Management Policies and Procedures. Prospects rated as $100,000+ will come before the Prospect Management Committee.

3. Compile and distribute materials for the *Prospect Management Committee* meetings. The committee consists of the directors of development from the various units/schools, and the meetings are held the third Wednesday of every month. Research gathers requests for assignment (see attached form) from the various units/schools and writes the agenda for the meetings. The coordinator and a researcher attend the meetings, take notes, make the necessary changes on the ADVANCE system, and then write and distribute the minutes.

4. Prepare *the President* for her meetings with key donors by working with development officers from across the university to develop strategy as well as provide in-depth personal background and connections to Duke.

5. Maintain *files* on alumni, parents, and friends. These files are divided into two sections, major prospect and miscellaneous. The major prospect files are those on individuals who have been identified as having the capability to make a $25,000+ gift. Both sets of files include trip reports, letters, research reports, and newspaper/magazine articles as well as internal memorandums. If you would like a tour of our filing system, please contact *Regina at 681-0446.*

## Determining Gift Ratings—The Process

The Research Department assigns gift ratings to roughly 300 prospects a month. We receive these prospect's names through various sources, including staff referrals, newspaper and magazine articles, and our peer screening program, BOND (Building Our National Donorbase). We then run the prospects through numerous sources to identify assets. Among others, these sources include: SEC filings, The Foundation Center, *Forbes 400, The Rich Register, The Junior Rich Register, Guide to Private Fortunes, New Fortunes,* and *Who's Wealthy in America.* We also obtain property assessments on each prospect, if available.

If Research can verify an individual's assets, we use a table to estimate his or her net worth. The table lists the findings of Internal Revenue Service researchers Barry W. Johnson and Marvin Schwartz, who compiled data from 1989 tax returns for their 1993 study of personal wealth and how that wealth is held (source: Robert Millar, "How Much is that Donor in your Records?," CASE *Currents,* July 1995, pp. 38–41).

Once we have an estimate of the prospect's net worth, we can calculate his/her giving ability based on the universal formula, 5% of net worth = total giving capability to ALL charities. For instance, if a prospect has an estimated net worth of $2 million, he/she can make an outright gift of $100,000 (payable over five years). We assign a gift rating on our alumni database, based on the following scale:

| RATING | TRANSLATION (low end of range) |
|---|---|
| 1.4 | $100 million+ |
| 1.3 | $50 million |
| 1.2 | $25 million |
| 1.1 | $10 million |
| 1 | $5 million |
| 2 | $1 million |
| 3 | $500,000 |
| 4 | $250,000 |
| 5 | $100,000 |
| 6 | $25,000 |
| 98 | Unable to confirm gift potential |
| 99 | Not a major gift prospect |

# AN OVERVIEW OF PROSPECT RESEARCH AND ITS PLAN IN DEVELOPMENT FOR CALIFORNIA STATE UNIVERSITY NORTHRIDGE

Effective fundraising begins with a need. Prospect research supports the act of raising funds to fill the identified need.

In order to raise funds effectively, the fundraiser must be fully aware of specifics of the need and have a very good idea of who he or she is going to approach to provide the funds. The fundraiser who knows something of the background, interests, and giving capacity of a prospective donor will be much more successful in bringing in the money to meet the need than the one who is unprepared.

Good prospect research needs to be done in an organized, methodical fashion. When the development officer gives a name to the researcher, the researcher must have a plan. The plan must include many resources of information for analysis to aid in the cultivation, solicitation and stewardship of prospective donors.

All information concerning donors and prospective donors, including the identity of donors and prospective donors who have not been publicized by the University or the Foundation, is confidential information and shall not be used for any purpose other than Foundation and University Development business consistent with these Policies and Procedures, nor shall it be disclosed by any Foundation or University personnel except as required by law or in connection with Foundation or University Development business, and then only on a "need-to-know" basis and with appropriate precautions to protect the strict confidentiality of the information. See sections on "Confidentiality" and "Ethics" below.

## Background

The Manager of Prospect Research is responsible for providing timely prospect information to development department staff members, with an emphasis on determining a prospect's financial resources, philanthropic tendencies and identification of appropriate contacts. In each instance this involves the creation of a prospect profile of varying depth, depending on the amount of information needed, the estimated level of a prospect's giving capacity, the volume of requests received, and the time constraints of the requester.

With limited staff, and a large volume of prospects to be researched, it is critical that research be requested primarily on prospects for whom vital information is necessary to help create the background for a successful cultivation/solicitation strategy.

Prospect research should be viewed as a vital stop on the record-keeping trail. Including the researcher in identification, cultivation, solicitation and stewardship insures that vital data on donors will be tracked and preserved over the coming years.

# The Process

The actual process of prospect research involves many facets: preliminary research in examining existing donor files, giving histories, scanning multitudes of periodicals in print, keeping abreast of current business trends, reading society and entertainment publications, searching through library reference collections, conducting on-line database searches, and engaging in active listening sessions with staff members and volunteers who have knowledge of donors and prospects. Thus, the more information provided by other development staff members to the researcher, the better!

# Requesting Research

To manage a large volume of requests from a variety of development officers, it is necessary to use a system with request forms to aid in the prioritization, tracking and process of researching prospects.

There are three forms—one for an individual prospect, and one for a corporate or foundation prospect, and one for identification of prospects for a specific project or program. The forms ask for the name of requester, date submitted, campaign or program the prospect is being considered for, and an estimated gift amount. The priority of research is rated, with date needed and justification to be included for high priority requests. The depth of research is as follows:

- Quick (includes checking in-house hard copy resources, donor files, giving history)
- In-House (similar to quick research that is put into a hard copy profile or memo format)
- Full Basic (in-house + library reference search, on-line database search)
- In-Depth (full basic + all available resources, hall of records search, courthouse and any other specialized searches)

Next on the form is the information checklist. This is a method to "streamline" the research process by avoiding searching for information already known to the requester or solicitor, and information not deemed necessary for the cultivation/ solicitation strategy. Careful consideration in making these selections makes the research process efficient and effective.

It is extremely important to fill out the request with as much clear information as possible—including any data known by the requester about the prospect.

## Prioritization

All requests for research made in writing using the appropriate form will be considered important. Requests for research should be sent or given directly to the researcher—with the knowledge that each request will be reviewed and thoughtfully prioritized with approval of the Director of University Development prior to any research activity. If a deadline is established for the need of the results, every attempt will be made to accommodate the request. Please be mindful of the issue of "planning ahead" to avoid frustration!

## Confidentiality

*Requests for information regarding donors or prospective donors are accepted from College and Program Development Directors.* All requests for prospect research are considered confidential and will be treated as such by the development department staff. Any research materials produced, including confidential profiles, contact reports, and memos are held in the strictest of confidence. *No donor or prospective donor information will be released to anyone other than College and Program Development Directors without written approval of the Director of University Development.* All research documentation not being maintained for a specific purpose in donor/prospect files, will be disposed of by the use of a mechanical shredder. At no time should any confidential information be disposed of in any other manner.

Hard copy files containing confidential donor and prospective donor information are kept in the Central Development office under lock and key. Computer files containing confidential donor and prospective donor information are kept in a password-restricted environment by the Manager of Prospect Research. Confidential donor and prospective donor information should not be transmitted by e-mail, fax or modem. Cellular and cordless telephones are considered insecure and should not be used to discuss confidential donor and prospective donor information.

When an employee who has access to confidential donor and prospective donor information leaves the organization, the employee should be asked in an exit interview to sign a written memorandum acknowledging that confidential donor information was made available to them or collected by them while employed by the University or the Foundation and that the Information is to remain with the organization. The interviewer should have a third employee present during the interview to witness the signature.

Any incidents of unauthorized use or disclosure of confidential donor information will be followed up on by the Manager of Prospect Research and reported to the Director of University Development. Failure to take reasonable steps to stop such use or disclosure is the equivalent of allowing it to continue.

## Ethics

The most useful information in prospect research is hard facts. Each person involved in development activities should use his or her best judgment as to whether a particular item of information should be included in a donor's file. The relevance of the item to the development process must be balanced against the donor's reasonable expectations of privacy. Derogatory information without factual basis or a weak factual basis should be included in a donor's file only if it is directly related to a current development effort, and the development office's need to include the information should be recorded at the same time.

## Contact Reports

Contact reports are an efficient method of transmitting information from one source to another. The objective is to summarize an exchange of information from a staff member, board member or volunteer solicitor with a donor or prospective donor, to put the exchange on record. The information contained in these reports is used to track the cultivation, solicitation and stewardship and to assist the researcher in preparation of an accurate donor profile. All information included in a contact report should be done in a professional and responsible manner, and only appropriate language used.

The transmission of contact reports should be handled in a confidential manner. Given the fact that they contain information regarding cultivation and solicitation of a prospect, these reports should not be left on desktops, or out in "public" view. When sending a contact report through inter-office mail, the word CONFIDENTIAL should be clearly marked. Contact reports should not be sent via e-mail. As with prospect profiles, information contained in contact reports will be treated with the utmost respect. Information contained in contact reports should be released internally on a "need-to-know" basis.

# Samples

Sample research request forms for individual and corporate/foundation prospects and specific projects or programs follow, along with the preferred form to use for contact reports. Please begin using these forms immediately. Additional copies of forms are available from the Manager of Prospect Research.

# Results

As the Manager of Prospect Research, my goal is to do everything possible to support the fundraising efforts of California State University Northridge. With much effort on my part, and the cooperation of the development staff and volunteers, I will be able to effectively and efficiently produce prospect research profiles that will enable the most successful fundraising strategies to unfold.

# Prospect Management System

The Prospect Management System was created to track the prospecting, cultivation and stewardship of funding sources for California State University Northridge. The system resembles a typical large corporation's national sales account system: it focuses the limited resources of a staff on a small number of individuals, corporations and foundations that comprise the majority of gifts.

Just as many large corporations have for years designated one person to act as the liaison between the company and the University (e.g. Boeing, IBM, GE), so too do we designate a liaison with select individuals, foundations and corporations. These University liaisons are referred to as "prospect managers." All prospects are directed to one of three types of accounts: Key, Lead and Open.

## Key Accounts

Key Accounts represent the University's top prospects, those with $100,000 or more potential and/or those corporations and foundations that have requested centrally-coordinated proposals rather than repeated, multiple asks from the University. Most Key Account corporations and foundations will be managed by the Director of Corporate and Foundation Relations unless otherwise designated.

Those accounts designated to others will be based on a significant history of giving to one particular college and/or a personal relationship with the Director or Dean. Individual Key Accounts will be assigned based on alumni status, past giving, and/or personal relationships.

## Lead Accounts

Lead Accounts represent prospects that are to be solicited within a six-month period or that already are in the midst of a large multi-year pledge schedule.

## Open Accounts

Open Accounts represent all individuals, foundations and corporations not appearing as a Key or Lead Account on the monthly listing of prospects. No Development Director is assigned to these accounts. Development Directors are strongly encouraged to "upgrade" these individuals, foundations and corporations to Lead Account status.

## Responsibilities of Prospect Managers

The Prospect Manager is the University's campus authority on:

- how the individual/foundation/corporation makes funding decisions
- our relationship with the prospect (board connections, research, philanthropy)
- the specific corporate culture
- for individuals, know their areas of interest, key relationships, background
- managers naturally will represent the interest of their individual colleges and units foremost, and be willing to seek other appropriate opportunities for the good of the University as a whole

## Determination of Prospect Manager

Assignment of a particular prospect is made to a prospect manager in the following way:

- a request is sent to the Manager of Prospect Research by the Development Director asking to be assigned as the prospect manager
- names are presented by the Manager of Prospect Research and a review and discussion are held during the next meeting of Development Directors and

final approval of assignment of prospect manager is granted by the Director of University Development

If unsure about whether or not a Prospect Manager has been assigned to a prospect, a call to the Manager of Prospect Research will provide the most current information.

Each assignment of a Lead Account is for a period of six months, or in some cases longer, when in the midst of a large multi-year pledge schedule. An additional six-month extension may be granted by the Director of Corporate and Foundation Relations and the Director of University Development. The extension may be requested by calling the Manager of Prospect Research.

## Criteria for Preliminary Assignment of Prospects

The following criteria are set forth to aid in the determination of the most effective process for the identification, cultivation and stewardship of obtaining funding for the California State University Northridge:

### Individuals

- giving patterns
- college affiliations
    self
    spouse
    children
- personal relationship with campus
- athletic participation
- a current profession
- philanthropic interest (includes board participation)
- other campus activities
- time and circumstances of initial contact

### Foundations/Corporations

- giving pattern
- personal relationship with campus
- philanthropic interest
- giving guidelines
- time and circumstances of initial contact

## What Is Expected in Management of a Prospect?

A preliminary cultivation plan must be submitted in writing to the Manager of Prospect Research within six weeks of the prospect being assigned, on all prospects in categories I-V. The prospect rating categories are defined as follows:

a  =  $1,000–4,999
b  =  $5,000–9,999
c  =  $10,000–24,999
I  =  $25,000–49,999
II  =  $50,000–99,999
III  =  $100,000–499,999
IV  =  $500,000–999,999
V  =  $1,000,000 and above

*Note:* categories a–c are annual gift prospects, I–V are major gift prospects.

The first contact with the prospect must be made within eight weeks of the prospect being assigned. All contacts must be reported in writing as made, and submitted to the Manager of Prospect Research within five working days of the contact.

Following the first contact, the interest expressed by the prospect may result in a reassignment. It is the responsibility of the Development Director to propose this reassignment.

A review of the prospect assignment may result in an extension being granted by the Director of University Development for an additional six-month period. Extension will be based on preparation of a plan and review of initial moves. (In a situation where the cultivation plan is not being followed, and/or contacts are not being made or reported in writing in a timely manner, a review of the prospect management assignment may result in the assignment being terminated.)

## Information Flow

Copies of all germane correspondence (letters, reports, proposals, etc.) should be directed to both College and Central Development files (copies directed to Central Development files should be sent to the Manager of Prospect Research for handling). If in the process of cultivating a prospect managed by someone else, copies of correspondence should also be sent to that person for their information. Confidential donor and prospective donor information should not be transmitted by e-mail, fax, modem, cellular or cordless telephone (refer to "Confidentiality" section).

## Status Changes

Changes in the status of a prospect should be called into the Manager of Prospect Research. Changes will be reflected in the current Prospect Management System. Each Director of Development will receive a copy of the updated Prospect Tracking List at the meeting of the Development Directors on the first Tuesday of each month from 9:00–11:00 A.M. in the University Relations conference room. Prospect account activity will be discussed during these meetings, and additional changes may be made with the Manager of Prospect Research at this time.

# ST. MARY'S COLLEGE OF MARYLAND
# OFFICE OF DEVELOPMENT

## Research Procedures for the Novice

These procedures are intended for use by members of the Office of Development when the Prospect Researcher is not available.

1. Make a note of what information is needed by whom for the Prospect Researcher's records.
2. You may find it helpful to review the Statement of Ethics and Confidentiality for Prospect Research.
3. Check any *relevant* hard copy and electronic sources. See pages 2–4 for lists of sources, where they are located, and what information can be found in them. Also, use the disk with Internet bookmarks to easily locate useful websites. You may find it helpful to make a note of what resources you have checked.
4. Create a profile by compiling the information found and organizing it into a readable format. A blank profile form is included on the disk of Internet bookmarks.
5. Make sure the month and year are noted on the profile, and make sure to put your name on the profile so that it is known who compiled the information.
6. Make sure to appropriately mark all profiles "Confidential."
7. If a profile is going outside of the Office of Development, the President's Office or the Governance Committee (i.e. to volunteers working on behalf of the Office of Development, the Board of Trustees, etc.), details of giving history and detailed financial information must not be included. General statements such as ". . . has been a consistent supporter . . ." ". . . is capable of a gift in the _____ range . . ." are acceptable.

## Select Prospect Research Resources

### Resources in Prospect Researcher's Office

- Washington 99 and Baltimore/Annapolis 97–98
  Board membership, information about groups

- Social Register, Social List of Washington DC (green book), and Blue Book (Baltimore Society Visiting List)
  Address, some college and club information, children

- Who's Wealthy in America
    Vol. 1 – residence
    Vol. 2 – stocks

- Major Donors

- DC/Baltimore Donors and National Capital Campaign Donors (Donor Series on CD)

- Guide to Private Fortunes, New Fortunes (I use these less frequently, but sometimes you get lucky)

- The American Almanac of Jobs and Salaries

- Corporate Public Affairs (most current in Office of Corporate and Foundation Relations)
    information about philanthropy of companies

- Guide to Greater Washington DC Grantmakers, The Association of Baltimore Area Grantmakers, Index of Private Foundation Reports (kept in the Prospect Researcher's Office and in the Foundation and Corporate Relations office)
    information about philanthropy of foundations, etc.

- The Foundation Directory (current edition available in Office of Foundation and Corporate Relations)
    information about philanthropy of foundations

- FC Search (CD-ROM)
    information about foundations

- Prospector's Choice (CD-ROM)
    information about foundations

## Resources on the Internet *(See the disk of bookmarks for useful Internet sites.)*

- University of Virginia Prospect Research Page
    http://www.people.Virginia.edu/~dev-pros/(Click on "Web Resources.")

    *Contains*

    Biographical Info:
        rich lists (Forbes, Fortune, etc.)
        campaign contributions
        directories for doctors, lawyers, etc.

Corporate Info:

> Hoover's (company capsules) and Marketguide (snapshots) provide summary info on public companies
>
> Dun & Bradstreet ($20 business background reports—useful for private companies)
>
> links to places to get stock quotes
>
> Edgar (SEC filings – proxy reports for companies)

Financial Info:

> Stockholdings (Edgar and Edgar People – can search proxy reports by company or by person's name)
>
> Real Estate (links to tax assessors pages – the Maryland Real Property system can only be searched by address on the Internet)

Foundations/Grants Info:

> Foundation Center

Other Info:

> including links to finding addresses (Switchboard, Anywho, etc., city to county look-up)

- SMCM Library

  http://www.smcm.edu/library/ (Click on "Online Databases" or "Reference Resources.")

  *"Online Databases" Contains*

  Academic Universe Lexis/Nexis – news information

  > select "Reference" and "Biographical"

  Academic Elite EbscoHost – citations to (with some full text) journal articles

  *"Reference Resources" Contains*

  > Gale Biography and Genealogy Master Index (BGMI) – search by name, get list of citations (includes Who's Who series, Dun & Bradstreet, Standard & Poor, etc. (which are available in the library); (does not contain citations for the current year)

- Web Pages

  AltaVista search engine: www.altavista.com

  To find web pages for companies – click on "Advanced" at the right; select "English" for language, then in the "Boolean expression" field type: *title: "Company Name"* and search; if you get no hits, remove *title:* and try again

## Personal Information

*Address*

- (P) Social Register
- (P) Social List of DC
- (P) Blue Book – Baltimore Society Visiting List
- (I) Switchboard

*Family, Education*

- (L/I) Who's Who*
- (I) Lexis-Nexis
- (I) BGMI
- (I) AMA
- (I) Martindale-Hubbell

## Professional Activity

- (L/I) Who's Who*
- (I) Lexis-Nexis
- (I) BGMI
- (L/I) Maryland Manual
- (L) Contemporary Authors
- (L) Standard & Poor's

## Business Information

- (I) Edgar
- (I) Hoovers, Marketguide
- (I) Internet – company home pages
- (L) (Reference section in library)
- (I) Lexis-Nexis
- (P) Corporate Giving Directory
- (P/F) Corporate Public Affairs
- (I) Dun & Bradstreet ($20, info on private companies)

## Board Activity

- (P) Washington 99
- (P) Baltimore/Annapolis 97/98
- (P) Social Register (clubs)
- (L/I) Who's Who*

## Financial Information

*Income*

- (P) American Almanac of Jobs and Salaries
- (I) Proxy Reports (Edgar)

*Home*

- (I) Tax Assessor Database (or visit office in Leonardtown)
- (I) City to County Lookup
- (P) Who's Wealthy in America

*Assets*

- (P) Who's Wealthy in America
- (P) Guide to Private Fortunes, New Fortunes
- (I) Internet
- (I) Edgar People
- (I) Rich Lists

## Giving History

- (P) Major Donors
- (P) Donor Series on CD
- (P/I) Annual Reports
- (I) FEC (Federal Campaign Contributions)
- (I) Maryland Campaign Contributions

## KEY:

(P) = Prospect Researcher's Office

(I) = Internet (most are available through the University of Virginia Prospect Research page and the SMCM Library page – use disk with bookmarks

(L) = Library

(F) = Office of Foundation and Corporate Relations

* Who's Who entries are sometimes available through Lexis Nexis.

# UNIVERSITY OF CALIFORNIA, BERKELEY

## Who Does What?

| | Fundraiser | Researcher |
|---|:---:|:---:|
| Articulate research needs | • | |
| Determine best format to meet needs | • | • |
| Provide essential background info | • | |
| Establish timeline | • | • |
| Define methodology and search strategy | | • |
| Gather information | | • |
| Analyze data | | • |
| Present report or summary | | • |
| Provide contact summary | • | |
| Debrief research project | • | • |
| Follow up on additional questions | | • |

## How to Contact Us

*Site Address:*

2505 Channing Way, Suites 5 and 9      Fax: 643-2154
[Names of contacts have been omitted here]

## DEVELOPMENT RESEARCH
## New Strategies for a New Millennium

In the age of information, or more precisely, information overload, Research's pivotal functions have changed and continue to evolve dramatically. The most substantive change is that we have gone from information collectors to information managers. Our real value is realized when we add thoughtful context to data point after data point, which requires us to understand the specific purpose for the information and the larger process of fundraising. In order to align ourselves with the changing needs of the campus and the progress of our profession, Research will . . .

- *serve* as the key campus contact for information on major donors, prospects, and distinguished alumni by providing high-quality analyzed donor/prospect data.

- *identify* new, untapped prospects among Cal alumni and friends.

- *track and monitor* new wealth generated by venture capital, IPOs, and Mergers and Acquisitions.

- *produce* regular editions of *The Prospector* for campuswide fundraisers, highlighting newly uncovered prospects and updating information on known/managed prospects.

- *collaborate* with the major gift development staff and campus development officers in the formulation of solicitation strategies for identified major gift prospects.

- *provide* campuswide consultation regarding financial capacity of donors, cultivation and solicitation strategy, or funding sources for unit initiatives.

- *engage* campuswide development officers in an account-management model with individual researchers in order to facilitate a more effective fundraising effort.

- *employ* state-of-the-art technology to facilitate collection and analysis of relevant information.

- *educate* the campus about our resources, capabilities, and policies.

- *assume* a strategic role in the planning and implementation of fundraising campaigns.

- *fulfill* clients' requests for profiles on potential individual, corporate, and foundation donors within a standard response time.

## Prioritization of Research Services and Requests

1. *Identification* of new and previously unknown prospects—including analysis of large-scale electronic screening projects

2. *Ad Hoc requests* for specific questions—by email or phone (should be limited to one question at a time and be of immediate use to the requestor)

3. *Strategic analytical projects* to assess regions, industries and pools of potential prospects and to develop target lists for leadership committees, volunteer assignments, or event invitations

4. *Training and consultation* to fundraisers or their assistants so that each fundraising program is able to conduct basic, preliminary research on their own

5. *Major Gift Prospect* research requests:

   | | |
   |---|---|
   | Solicitation requests | 1–2 weeks turnaround |
   | Cultivation requests | 2–3 weeks |
   | Discovery requests | 3–4 weeks |

   *Solicitation* research is targeted to the fundraiser's need depending on the individual donor and the details of the particular solicitation. Profiles are likely to include a confirmation or update of previously ascertained information including wealth and changes in the donor's financial situation, any current news items, or information about personal changes that might affect the donor's gift—most of which is defined in meetings between researcher and fundraiser.

   *Cultivation* research includes information on the prospect's career, financial capacity, connections to the University, other philanthropic interests and any current news items about the prospect. Cal's Alumni Development Database (CADS) will be the primary source for biographical information, giving history and Cal connections and should be used to supplement research profiles.

   *Discovery* research will be done on prospects who are defined as probable major gift donors but are not yet qualified as a major gift donor. These profiles will be brief and will address the question of capacity (wealth indicators). Again, please consult CADS for Cal information.

6. *Lists of names,* possible donors and those with no previous relationship to campus will take 4–6 weeks or longer depending on work load.

7. *Award and Nomination profiles* for the UCBF Board of Trustees, Haas International Awards, and The Haas Public Service Award on an annual basis.

## What You Can Do Before, During, and After Your Research Request

Ongoing:

- Define major gift level for your fundraising program.
- Select top prospects and clear them through campus prospect management procedures.
- Share prioritized cultivation and solicitation prospect lists with your researcher.
- Explain your research needs based on your fundraising goal(s).
- Include your researcher in research strategy meetings.
- Maintain ongoing communication with your researcher.

Before your project:

- Consult CADS to see if there is information that answers your specific questions about a prospect.
- Ascertain whether or not your prospect already has a primary manager, and consult with that person.
- Check Central Files for previous research performed.
- Confirm information that you or another manager may already have on an individual, such as correct spelling of name, home address, business address, relationships, etc., and share this information with your researcher.

During your project:

- As early on as possible, collaborate with your researcher to determine a feasible timeline.
- Clearly articulate the objective of your request.
- Determine, with the help of your researcher, the level of research you will need.
- Return prospect file to Central Files for researcher's use.
- Communicate any new information on prospect to your researcher.
- Let your researcher know of any development that could alter the schedule of the research project, including change in strategy, postponed meeting, cancellation or delay of solicitation, or cancellation of research need.

After your project:

- Discuss with your researcher what worked and what did not work during the research process.
- Make a copy of your Contact Report available to your researcher.
- Ask your researcher to follow up on any questions that resulted from your contact with the prospect.

*Source:* Copyright UC Regents. Reprinted with the permission of Brooke J. Conner, Director of Research, UC Berkeley.

# RESOURCE 7

## VISION AND MISSION STATEMENTS

## INDIANA UNIVERSITY FOUNDATION RESEARCH DEPARTMENT

### Vision

To provide Indiana University and Indiana University Foundation with relevant, high-quality information and analysis in an effective and proactive manner to help build the foundation necessary to achieve maximum private sector support for Indiana University.

### Mission

The IU Foundation Research Management & Information Services Department discovers, manages and disseminates information to assist in the development of lifetime donor relationships. This is accomplished by:

- Continually identifying potential donors and following-up on information gathered and distributed;
- Providing consistent and accurate information on prospects based on the principle of linkage, ability and interest;
- Providing analysis of information gathered on a prospect and working with development staff (gift officers) to determine the best strategy for moving forward;
- Working with others to maintain the integrity of our database and files.

# THE UNIVERSITY OF FLORIDA FOUNDATION RESEARCH DEPARTMENT

## Mission

The mission of the Research Department of the UF Foundation, Inc. is to efficiently provide timely and responsive information services to support the fundraising efforts of the foundation. Research upholds the principles of the APRA Code of Ethics, which address confidentiality, accuracy, relevance, accountability, honesty, recording and maintenance, use and distribution of donor information.

Resource 7

# RESOURCE 8

## RESEARCH DEPARTMENT PROCEDURES

**Resource 8**

# ST. MARY'S COLLEGE OF MARYLAND
# OFFICE OF DEVELOPMENT

## Research Procedures

The Prospect Researcher does research for members of the Office of Development, the President's Office and other volunteers working on behalf of the Office of Development to raise funds. The Prospect Researcher will track research done in hard copy and in an electronic database.

## Research Request Forms

1. A research request form must be received in order for research to be done. Request forms are available in the Prospect Researcher's office in a box on the side of the filing cabinet near the door. The Prospect Researcher can also e-mail forms to those who need a copy. If a request form is received, proceed to step 5. If not, proceed to step 2.
2. If the request for research is made via e-mail, telephone, in person, or is (for example) a copied check with a name circled, it must be qualified as a brief request or a normal request. A brief request is one that will take no more than 15 minutes (e.g. retrieving a letter from a file, checking a piece of information in a profile, providing a fresh copy of a profile). If the request qualifies as a brief request, proceed to step 3. If not, proceed to step 4.
3. In the case of a brief request, answer the request, fill out the brief research request form, print it out and file it in the research request binder. The request must also be logged in the research request database and identified as a "brief request."
4. If the request received via e-mail, telephone, in person, or otherwise not on a research request form qualifies as a normal request, attach the information received to a research request form and return it to the requestor.
   a) In some cases, the request may be very urgent. In those cases, the Prospect Researcher, at his/her discretion, may determine that the request form should be filled out in the research office. It will be noted in the bottom right hand corner of the form that it was filled out by the researcher.
   b) The Prospect Researcher, at his/her discretion, may decide to proceed with a request prior to receiving the research request form back from the requestor.

5. When the research request form is received, log the request in to the research request database.
6. Requests will be prioritized based on when they are needed and by whom. In the event that several requests are received and cannot all be done in the allotted time, contact the requestor and ask for a prioritization.

## Conducting Research

1. In conducting research, relevant hard copy and online sources will be checked. The resources are not specifically listed here because there are too many, and each profile may require different resources. Refer to the "Research Procedures for the Novice" for a list of resources available and the information in them.
2. When conducting research, (especially if only a small amount of information is given) if no good information is found after 15 minutes, return the research request form to the requestor with a request for more information or attempt to contact the person(s) listed under "contacts for more information."
3. While conducting research, keep track of what resources have been checked on the form at the bottom of the profile. Also note if they yielded any information in the "Comments" section.
4. Make copies of relevant materials for the files.

## Profiles

1. When the profile is completed:
   a) provide a copy without the list of resources attached to each person listed on the research request form.
   b) put a copy with the resource list attached in the file.
   c) save the profile in the appropriate folder(s) on the C and G drives. The C drive should be copied to the G drive quarterly to make sure there is a back-up.
2. All profiles must be appropriately marked "Confidential." Hard copies should be stamped with red ink; e-mailed profiles should be done on the form with "CONFIDENTIAL" in red at the top.
3. If a profile is going outside of the Office of Development, the President's Office or the Governance Committee (i.e. to volunteers working on behalf of the Office of Development, the Board of Trustees, etc.), details of giving history and detailed financial information must not be included. (General statements such as ". . . has been a consistent supporter . . ." ". . . is capable of a gift in the _____ range . . ." are acceptable.)

## Finishing Research

1. When the profile has been sent out, update the research request database to reflect that the research is complete. (Make sure to include the date.)
2. Write the date completed in the top right hand corner of the research request form and file in the research request binder.

# BUCKNELL UNIVERSITY RELATIONS
# AIS MANAGEMENT CONTROLS MANUAL

## Research Profile Procedures

| | | |
|---|---|---|
| *SECTION* | *ISSUED* | *SUPERCEDES* |
| Office of Prospect Information | 09/15/99 | |
| *SUBJECT* | *APPROVED* | *PAGE* |
| Research Profile Procedures | | 1 of 9 |

## PURPOSE:

This procedure outlines the standard format and research techniques used for full research. Modifications can easily be made to this format for other profile types.

## SCOPE:

The procedure is utilized primarily by staff in the office of prospect information, including professional, casual, and student research staff.

## PROCEDURE:

*Note: Before research begins, the "Before, During, and After Research" procedure should be reviewed.*

The most difficult part of responding to a proactive or reactive research need is determining the exact nature of the research task and, therefore, what product should be created to meet the need. There are several important things to consider when making this decision.

### *For reactive research requests, the following items should be considered:*

Who is making the request? What are the requestor's expectations?

Is the request related to a visit, and if so, when is the visit scheduled to occur?

In what stage of cultivation is the prospect currently in?

Has the prospect been researched before? If so, when, and to what level?

What is the current prospect rating? Do we believe it to be accurate?

What else do we already know about the prospect?

*For proactive projects, the following items should be considered:*

How long will this project take?

What will be gained by this research?

Can a student research assistant be utilized in part of this research?

What is an appropriate deadline to set for this project?

Once the researcher determines the appropriate level of research for the request or project, the next step is determining the appropriate research product. A conversation with the requestor is an important part of this decision-making process. There are many ways that research can be presented, and every researcher has the right to create a new product to meet a specific need. However, it is helpful to fit the product into one of the following categories when possible:

*Full Profile (Individual or Organization).* This profile includes all the relevant biographical and financial information that is appropriate for a presidential or vice-presidential visit. This profile should always include cultivation history, although the format of this section can be detailed or brief, according to the need.

*Qualification Profile (Individual or Organization).* This profile includes all the information and research related to the qualification of an individual as a major prospect.

*Qualification Research (Individual).* This research records information gathered on an individual during the prospect qualification process.

*Qualification Research (Group).* This research records information gathered on a prospect group during the prospect qualification process.

*Biographical Research.* This research includes all of the relevant biographical information on an individual. Often, information is summarized in a memo or placed into the appropriate BEN screens.

*Basic and Preliminary Nuggets.* Basic nuggets are prepared by administration support staff with research assistance for development and alumni program events.

*Expanded Nuggets.* Expanded nuggets are prepared for lengthy events that the President attends.

*Update.* A research update is conducted when the previously completed research is out-of-date but the product format stays the same.

*Upgrade.* A research upgrade is conducted when the previously completed research is out-of-date and the format of the new research will be more inclusive.

*Summary Profile.* This research is a prose summary of relevant information for the specific need, usually limited to one page.

## Profile Format

The following format is for a full profile, but can be modified easily for qualification (no cultivation history), preliminary (no cultivation history, financial information, or analysis) or summary (see below) research. An important thing to remember is the importance of *making the best use of your time and knowing when to stop.* Although researchers are in the habit of following a format and gathering specific, factual information, each research project calls for a careful assessment of what is relevant to the cultivation process.

The header format for these profiles *is* standard and should always be completed as much as possible, but the rest of the profile should only include details that are relevant to the specific research request. It is important that each researcher has the flexibility to incorporate the facts he or she feels are important.

The most important part of the research product is the interpretation of the data, which falls under the *Analysis* section. Once all of the relevant data has been gathered, the analysis should be written to explain how the information works together to provide a picture of the prospect's capacity and inclination. More on the analysis section can be found below.

The following annotated profile should be used as a *guideline,* not a template. There will often be times when additional resources are needed.

*The Header* The header is the section of the profile that identifies the prospect in question. All of the information contained in the header can be found in Benefactor (using ADRI, BIOI, ACAI, and SRK screens) except information about preparatory schools and the birth place. This information can only be found on alumni prospects and is located in the paper file on the prospect's matriculation card.

<<Name>> <<Source>>
other graduate schools, year
Prepared at
(Born on x/x/x in City, State)

| *Business:* | *Home:* |
|---|---|
| Title | Home Address |
| Business Name | City, State, Zip |
| Business Address | Home Phone |
| Business City, State, Zip | Home E-mail |
| Business Phone | |
| Business E-mail | |

*Qualification Summary* If the profile format is a qualification summary, then this section is utilized. This format allows the researcher to provide a prose summary of the information that has been gathered, followed by an analysis section. The order of information included in the summary should loosely follow the order in which the information would appear in a more detailed (or outline) qualification profile. The analysis section, if included, should be separate and follow the summary.

*Family Information* This section includes information about the prospect's family, including his or her current spouse (SPOI, XNBU, Who's Who CD-ROM), children (RELI, SRK, Who's Who CD-ROM), and other Bucknell relatives (RELI). Previous spouses should be included if past cultivation has included them or if they are Bucknellians. Information on children who are currently attending Bucknell should include current activities and declared major if possible (Student's ACAI screen, Bucknell Web page search, call to the registrar's office and/or athletics coaches).

 If the prospect is related to Bucknellians who are also major prospects, it is helpful to include basic information on those family members (hometown, state, employment information, prospect rating, and brief cultivation summary).

### Bucknell Activities

*Alumnus.* AFFI screen, trip reports (MPC), paper file, and interview with gift officer

*Student.* ACAI screen, yearbook, trip reports (MPC), paper file, and interview with gift officer

*Fraternity/Sorority.* ACAI screen, yearbook, trip reports

**Cultivation History** Cultivation history is a *summary* of the cultivation that has occurred to date on the prospect in question. This section should be no more than one medium paragraph long in most cases. The summary should not include information that could otherwise be placed in other sections of the profile. For example, information about country club membership belongs in Non-Bucknell Activities, information about the value of a car or home belongs in Financial Information, etc. The goals of this section are to summarize cultivation activity ("Joe Smith has met with President Adams three times since last spring") and to report on the general attitude the prospect has towards the University ("Joe Smith is still upset with Bucknell over their decision to paint the Geology Building orange").

This information is gathered from the paper file, the MPC screen, the MPT and MPTD screens, an interview with the current gift officer and interviews with the university relations staff who have worked with the prospect in the past.

### Non-Bucknell Interests and Activities

*Philanthropic.* Other nonprofit activities, trusteeships, etc.

*Other.* This can include hobbies, honorary degrees, interests, social club memberships, political activity, non-professional awards, etc.

If the prospect (or the prospect's spouse and/or children) attended other colleges/universities, the researcher should contact these institutions for giving information. In most cases, it is best to request a report of gifts from the institution in question, rather than ask about the specific prospect and risk identifying them to the other institution.

If the prospect is affiliated with a foundation, summarize the foundation information (including foundation assets, purpose or sample grants, prospect's position in or connection to the foundation).

Resources for this section can include, but are not limited to: Who's Who CD-ROM; The Donor Series CD-ROM; Lexis/Nexis News and Biographic searches, Northern Light Searches, Reunion Questionnaire information (statistical and biographic); file notes and trip reports; FC Search CD-ROM; Prospector's Choice CD-ROM; Grants on Disc CD-ROM.

*Gifts to Bucknell* This section should include total gifts to Bucknell and a breakdown of how gifts have been designated to different schools, departments, etc. If gifts were made through a foundation or corporate matching gift program, this information should be noted. If the prospect has made gifts to create a named fund, scholarship, etc., this section should include information on when the fund was created and what the fund guidelines are. Patterns of giving (or not giving) should also be noted here.

The information on giving is found in the GPSI and GPDI screens. Some researchers prefer to use the XFIN report as a tool for this section. Foundation and corporate matching/foundation information can be located in the CFPI, CFPM, GPDI screens.

**Career History** Career history should be summarized briefly in chronological order if it is easily researched. In a new paragraph, details about the prospect's current employment should be provided.

*Directorships.* Of public companies

*Memberships.* Professional societies and business related activities, etc.

*Company Name.* In separate and indented paragraphs, include brief descriptions of the prospect's current employer(s) and other current corporate affiliations. Information to include: summary of business activities, location of business, size of business (number of employees, sales, etc.), sales figures, and relevant news information.

Sources for this section include, but are not limited to: BEN, Prospect File, Who's Who CD-ROM, Walkers CD-ROM, Standard and Poors' Directories, L/N Company News, Company Financial, and Biographic searches, Northern Light, Company Web Pages, Hoovers, Wall Street Journal, Thomas Register, Companies Online, Corporate Annual Reports, AM City Business Journals, and CEO Express.

*Financial Information* This section should include a bulleted list of all financial information that is relevant to prospect qualification. The list should start with more general indicators of wealth (lifestyle information) and move toward more specific, factual financial data (value of a home, financials related companies, stock holdings, etc.). If detailed stock holding information is available, the guidelines and stock chart (below) should be followed.

As a general rule, stock information should be reported *simply* and *accurately.* It is not always possible, however, to obtain a clear picture of individual stock ownership from publicly accessible resources. Researchers follow these guidelines when reporting stock ownership and then use the format below for including this information in the profile.

*Note: It is not important to have every minute detail about stock ownership in the profile. Only the relevant information should be included—what kind of stock does the prospect own and how much money does he or she have based on that stock ownership. If it is important to include other information in the file, a File Memo or notes will suffice. Footnotes should be used when possible to keep the Profile narrative clean and easy to follow.*

When researching stocks, the researcher should:

- Use today's stock market information to calculate stock value based on current ownership (Stockmaster.com or Nasdaq.com).
- When the status of ownership is not known (i.e. you know the person owned the stock at one time, but you do not know if the person still owns the stock), use a footnote to state this.
- If you are updating a profile, use a footnote to indicate older values of the same stock. Only include this information in the body of your text if the difference is a large increase or decrease in value.
- Direct stock should be listed and included in the total values accessible to the prospect.
- Indirect stock should be listed, but not included in the total values accessible to the prospect unless the prospect has access to the stock (i.e. it is owned by his/her company and he/she is president and owner of the company).
- Beneficial stock should be listed, but not included in the total values accessible to the prospect unless the prospect has access to the stock (i.e. it is not in trust for children/grandchildren).
- *Never discard copies of Proxy Statements and other SEC documents.* Instead, highlight relevant sections, discard unnecessary pages, make note of what the document is, and keep it in the file. You never know if you will be able to find that document again.

Be careful to keep the narrative explanation of stock ownership simple and *focus on interpretation rather than straight reporting.* It is our job to make sense of the jumble for others. Try to avoid copying directly from the proxy. If you must, include that information in a footnote when possible.

| Company Name | Type of Stock | # of Shares | Value/Exercise Price |
|---|---|---|---|
| Company Name $00.00 per/share as of 00/00/00 | Direct | XX,XXX | Today's Value |
| | Indirect | Today's Value | |
| | Beneficial | Today's Value | |
| | Options (Date) | Exercise Price | |

*Analysis* All profiles are different, and the analysis that goes with them will be different too. However, there are some specific issues that each profile should try to address in the Analysis section.

- Rating
- Rating changes and justification
- Specific ask range recommendations
- Specific designation recommendations
- Analysis of assets (including health of business, personal assets such as homes and cars, and collections) and how this information affects capacity and/or inclination
- Analysis of previous and future cultivation
- Relationships to Bucknell and with Bucknellians
- Problem areas or concerns

Points of Discussion is the part of the analysis that is a bulleted list of possible discussion points for the next personal visit with the prospect. Any questions that the researcher has that might be answered during a personal visit should be included here.

*Profile History* This section details the history of the profile, including who the profile was prepared by and for, the level of the research completed, and the date it was completed. If only a portion of the profile was updated, that is noted here.

cc:   Central Files
       Moves Manager or MG Officer responsible for that region
       Program Director

*Sources*: This is a list of sources utilized during the most current research. Complicated searches should include searching methodology {i.e., Lexis/Nexis (Bio Information: Paul Smith; Company Information: ABC Company; Company New: ABC Company and XYZ Company)}. Phone numbers and names of people spoken with should be included if phone calls were made.

*No information located in*: This is a list of sources utilized that did not result in any new information.

# RESOURCE 9

## STATEMENTS OF ETHICS

Resource 9

# Association of Professional Researchers for Advancement (APRA) Statement of Ethics

Association of Professional Researchers for Advancement (APRA) members shall support and further the individual's fundamental right to privacy and protect the confidential information of their institutions. APRA members are committed to the ethical collection and use of information. Members shall follow all applicable federal, state, and local laws, as well as institutional policies, governing the collection, use, maintenance, and dissemination of information in the pursuit of the missions of their institutions. APRA members shall respect all people and organizations.

## Code of Ethics

Prospect researchers must balance the needs of their institutions to collect, analyze, record, maintain, use, and disseminate information with an individual's right to privacy. This balance is not always easy to maintain. The following ethical principles apply, and practice is built on these principles:

I. Fundamental Principles
  A. Confidentiality
     Confidential information about constituents (donors and non-donors), as well as confidential information of the institutions in oral form or on electronic, magnetic, or print media are protected so that the relationship of trust between the constituent and the institution is upheld.
  B. Accuracy
     Prospect researchers shall record all data accurately. Such information shall include attribution. Analysis and products of data analysis should be without personal prejudices or biases.
  C. Relevance
     Prospect researchers shall seek and record only information that is relevant and appropriate to the fund-raising effort of the institutions that employ them.
  D. Accountability
     Prospect researchers shall accept responsibility for their actions and shall be accountable to the profession of development, to their respective institutions, and to the constituents who place their trust in prospect researchers and their institutions.
  E. Honesty
     Prospect researchers shall be truthful with regard to their identity and purpose and the identity of their institution during the course of their work.

II. Suggested Practice
   A. Collection
      1. The collection of information shall be done lawfully, respecting applicable laws and institutional policies.
      2. Information sought and recorded includes all data that can be verified and attributed, as well as constituent information that is self-reported (via correspondence, surveys, questionnaires, etc.).
      3. When requesting information in person or by telephone, it is recommended in most cases that neither individual nor institutional identity shall be concealed. Written requests for public information shall be made on institutional stationery clearly identifying the inquirer.
      4. Whenever possible, payments for public records shall be made through the institution.
      5. Prospect researchers shall apply the same standards for electronic information that they currently use in evaluating and verifying print media. The researcher shall ascertain whether or not the information comes from a reliable source and that the information collected meets the standards set forth in the APRA Statement of Ethics.
   B. Recording and Maintenance
      1. Researchers shall state information in an objective and factual manner; note attribution and date of collection; and clearly identify analysis.
      2. Constituent information on paper, electronic, magnetic or other media shall be stored securely to prevent access by unauthorized persons.
      3. Special protection shall be afforded all giving records pertaining to anonymous donors.
      4. Electronic or pager documents pertaining to constituents shall be irreversibly disposed of when no longer needed (by following institutional standards for document disposal).
   C. Use and Distribution
      1. Researchers shall adhere to all applicable laws, as well as to institutional policies, regarding the use and distribution of confidential constituent information.
      2. Constituent information is the property of the institution for which it was collected and shall not be given to persons other than those who are involved with the cultivation or solicitation effort or those who need that information in the performance of their duties for that institution.
      3. Constituent information for one institution shall not be taken to another institution.
      4. Research documents containing constituent information that is to be used outside research offices shall be clearly marked "confidential."

5. Vendors, consultants, and other external entities shall understand and agree to comply with the institution's confidentiality policies before gaining access to institutional data.

6. Only publicly available information shall be shared with colleagues at other institutions as a professional courtesy.

III. Recommendations

1. Prospect researchers shall urge their institutions to develop written policies based upon applicable laws and these policies should define what information shall be gathered, recorded and maintained, and to whom and under what conditions the information can be released.

2. Prospect researchers shall urge the development of written policies at their institutions defining who may authorize access to prospect files and under what conditions. These policies should follow the guidelines outlined in the CASE Donor Bill of Rights, the AFP Code of Ethical Principles, and the Association for Healthcare Philanthropy Statement of Professional Standards and Conduct.

3. Prospect researchers shall strongly urge their development colleagues to abide by this Code of Ethics and Fundamental Principles.

*Source:* Association of Professional Researchers for Advancement (APRA), Sept. 30, 1998, http://www.aprahome.org/apra_statement_of_ethics.htm. Printed with permission from APRA.

**Resource 9**

# Council for Advancement and Support of Education (CASE) Mission and Statement of Ethics

## MISSION

The purposes of CASE are to develop and foster sound relationships between member educational institutions and their constituencies; to provide training programs, products, and services in the areas of alumni relations, communications, and philanthropy; to promote diversity within these professions; and to provide a strong force for the advancement and support of education worldwide.

## STATEMENT OF ETHICS

Institutional advancement professionals, by virtue of their responsibilities within the academic community, represent their colleges, universities, and schools to the larger society. They have, therefore, a special duty to exemplify the best qualities of their institutions and to observe the highest standards of personal and professional conduct.

In so doing, they promote the merits of their institutions, and of education generally, without disparaging other colleges and schools.

Their words and actions embody respect for truth, fairness, free inquiry, and the opinions of others.

They respect all individuals without regard to race, color, sex, sexual orientation, marital status, creed, ethnic or national identity, handicap, or age.

They uphold the professional reputation of other advancement officers and give credit for ideas, words, or images originated by others.

They safeguard privacy rights and confidential information.

They do not grant or accept favors for personal gain, nor do they solicit or accept favors for their institutions where a higher public interest would be violated.

They avoid actual or apparent conflicts of interest and, if in doubt, seek guidance from appropriate authorities.

They follow the letter and spirit of laws and regulations affecting institutional advancement.

They observe these standards and others that apply to their professions and actively encourage colleagues to join them in supporting the highest standards of conduct.

The CASE Board of Trustees adopted this Statement of Ethics to guide and reinforce our professional conduct in all areas of institutional advancement. The statement is also intended to stimulate awareness and discussion of ethical issues that may arise in our professional activities. The Board adopted the final text in Toronto on July 11, 1982, after a year of deliberation by national and district leaders and by countless volunteers throughout the membership.

*Source:* Copyright 2000 by the Council for Advancement and Support of Education. Reprinted with permission.

# Association of Fundraising Professionals (AFP) Code of Ethical Principles and Standards of Professional Practice

## STATEMENT OF ETHICAL PRINCIPLES

### Adopted November 1991

The Association of Fundraising Professionals (AFP) exists to foster the development and growth of fund-raising professionals and the profession, to promote high ethical standards in the fund-raising profession and to preserve and enhance philanthropy and volunteerism. Members of AFP are motivated by an inner drive to improve the quality of life through the causes they serve. They serve the ideal of philanthropy; are committed to the preservation and enhancement of volunteerism; and hold stewardship of these concepts as the overriding principle of their professional life. They recognize their responsibility to ensure that needed resources are vigorously and ethically sought and that the intent of the donor is honestly fulfilled. To these ends, AFP members embrace certain values that they strive to uphold in performing their responsibilities for generating philanthropic support.

### AFP members aspire to:

- practice their profession with integrity, honesty, truthfulness and adherence to the absolute obligation to safeguard the public trust;
- act according to the highest standards and visions of their organization, profession and conscience;
- put philanthropic mission above personal gain;
- inspire others through their own sense of dedication and high purpose;
- improve their professional knowledge and skills in order that their performance will better serve others;
- demonstrate concern for the interests and well being of individuals affected by their actions;
- value the privacy, freedom of choice and interests of all those affected by their actions;
- foster cultural diversity and pluralistic values, and treat all people with dignity and respect;
- affirm, through personal giving, a commitment to philanthropy and its role in society;
- adhere to the spirit as well as the letter of all applicable laws and regulations;

- advocate within their organizations, adherence to all applicable laws and regulations;
- avoid even the appearance of any criminal offense or professional misconduct;
- bring credit to the fundraising profession by their public demeanor;
- encourage colleagues to embrace and practice these ethical principles and standards of professional practice; and
- be aware of the codes of ethics promulgated by other professional organizations that serve philanthropy.

## STANDARDS OF PROFESSIONAL PRACTICE

### Adopted and incorporated into the AFP
### Code of Ethical Principles November 1992

Furthermore, while striving to act according to the above values, AFP members agree to abide by the AFP Standards of Professional Practice, which are adopted and incorporated into the AFP Code of Ethical Principles. Violation of the Standards may subject the member to disciplinary sanctions, including expulsion, as provided in the AFP Ethics Enforcement Procedures.

### Professional Obligations

1. Members shall not engage in activities that harm the member's organization, clients, or profession.
2. Members shall not engage in activities that conflict with their fiduciary, ethical, and legal obligations to their organizations and their clients.
3. Members shall effectively disclose all potential and actual conflicts of interest; such disclosure does not preclude or imply ethical impropriety.
4. Members shall not exploit any relationship with a donor, prospect, volunteer or employee to the benefit of the member or the member's organization.
5. Members shall comply with all applicable local, state, provincial, federal, civil and criminal laws.
6. Members recognize their individual boundaries of competence and are forthcoming and truthful about their professional experience and qualifications.

### Solicitation and Use of Charitable Funds

7. Members shall take care to ensure that all solicitation materials are accurate and correctly reflect the organization's mission and use of solicited funds.

8. Members shall take care to ensure that donors receive informed, accurate and ethical advice about the value and tax implications of potential gifts.

9. Members shall take care to ensure that contributions are used in accordance with donors' intentions.

10. Members shall take care to ensure proper stewardship of charitable contributions, including timely reports on the use and management of funds.

11. Members shall obtain explicit consent by the donor before altering the conditions of a gift.

## Presentation of Information

12. Members shall not disclose privileged or confidential information to unauthorized parties.

13. Members shall adhere to the principle that all donor and prospect information created by, or on behalf of, an organization is the property of that organization and shall not be transferred or utilized except on behalf of that organization.

14. Members shall give donors the opportunity to have their names removed from lists that are sold to, rented to, or exchanged with other organizations.

15. Members shall, when stating fundraising results, use accurate and consistent accounting methods that conform to the appropriate guidelines adopted by the American Institute of Certified Public Accountants (AICPA)* for the type of organization involved. (*In countries outside of the United States, comparable authority should be utilized.)

## Compensation

16. Members shall not accept compensation that is based on a percentage of charitable contributions; nor shall they accept finder's fees.

17. Members may accept performance-based compensation, such as bonuses, provided such bonuses are in accord with prevailing practices within the members' own organizations, and are not based on a percentage of charitable contributions.

18. Members shall not pay finder's fees, commissions or percentage compensation based on charitable contributions and shall take care to discourage their organizations from making such payments.

*Amended October 1999*

Resource 9

# RESOURCE 10

## CASE EDUCATIONAL PARTNERS VENDOR LIST

*Source:* Reprinted with permission from the 2000–01 *CASE Educational Partners Yellow Pages.*

## Computer Services Consultants

### DataProse, Inc.
*Bronze Level Affiliate*

1451 N Rice Avenue
Suite A
Oxnard, CA 93030
(800) 927-7634
(805) 278-7430
Fax: (805) 278-7420
E-mail: bmurray@corp.dataprose.com
Web: www.dataprose.com

6012 Campus Circle Drive, Suite 260
Irving, TX 75063
(800) 876-5015
(972) 550-0190
Fax: (972) 550-8907

Bill Murray, VP, Sales

When your organization needs an ambitious direct marketing program, DataProse can help you reach your goals. We have helped hundreds of clients achieve results with cutting-edge technology, experience, know-how and superior service. All of which has earned us satisfied clients, repeat business and a reputation for providing fresh ideas and smart solutions. At DataProse, we offer a comprehensive range of services to fulfill your direct marketing needs, including consulting, database, and direct mail services. DataProse has offices in Los Angeles, Dallas, Seattle, Denver, San Francisco, and Ft. Lauderdale. Call (800) 927-7634 for the office in your area, or see us online at www.dataprose.com.

### Educational Marketing Group Inc.
*Bronze Level Affiliate*

PO Box 440832
Denver, CO 80014-0832
(303) 743-8298
Fax: (303) 727-6822
E-mail: bbrock@emgonline.com
Web: www.emgonline.com

Bob Brock, President

Educational Marketing Group Inc. provides brand development and integrated marketing services for colleges and universities nationwide. We custom-design services to match your institution's needs. Our seasoned consultants and creative specialists combine award-winning experience in corporate and consumer marketing with a thorough understanding of higher education and its unique mission. *New Educational Partner*

## KPMG Peat Marwick

*Bronze Level Affiliate*

700 Louisiana
Houston, TX 77002
(713) 319-2504
Fax: (713) 319-2488
E-mail: rweiner@kpmg.com
Web: www.us.kpmg.com/ps/he_nfp.html

Robert Weiner, Manager

KPMG's Fundraising and Advancement Services consulting group provides fundraising operations with the ability to assess and transform the effectiveness of their fundraising efforts and support services. The practice assists institutions with strategic planning for advancement services, selection and implementation of alumni and donor information systems, workflow analysis and process redesign, operations and staffing assessments, development of policies and procedures, evaluation of gift management and stewardship, and facilitation of fund raiser–support staff interaction.

## R. I. Arlington

*Bronze Level Affiliate*

806 West King Road
PO Box 1414
Malvern, PA 19355
(610) 647-2648
Fax: (610) 647-8168
E-mail: hunsaker@riarlington.com
Web: www.riarlington.com

Charles Hunsaker, President

Independent and objective consultant with 25+ years of systems experience. The last 10 years, we have focused on alumni & development systems including work with most of the major A&D vendor systems. We have assisted many CASE members with system projects covering audits, procedures, requirements definition, selection, contracting, implementation management, etc.

### Williamson Consulting, Inc.

*Bronze Level Affiliate*

25 Farrar Road
Lincoln, MA 01773
(781) 259-0091
Fax: (781) 259-3447
E-mail: jim@williamsonconsulting.com
Web: www.williamsonconsulting.com

Jim Williamson, President

With over 30 years' experience working exclusively with nonprofit organizations, Jim Williamson brings a unique combination of skills and experience to his consulting practice. Well known as a conference speaker, fundraising software designer, and consultant, Jim has helped hundreds of organizations grapple with the complex technical and management issues related to development information systems.

## *Computers*

### Bentz Whaley Flessner

*Gold Level Affiliate*

7251 Ohms Lane
Minneapolis, MN 55439
(952) 921-0111
Fax: (952) 921-0109
E-mail: bwf@bwf.com
Web: www.bwf.com

5272 River Road
Suite 500
Bethesda, MD 20816
(301) 656-7823
Fax: (301) 656-2156

Bob Burdenski, Senior Associate, Annual Giving
Diane R. Crane, Managing Associate, Systems & Technology

M. Bruce Dreon, Partner
Bruce W. Flessner, Principal
Karen L. Greene, Managing Associate, Prospect Research
Lisa Grissom, Senior Associate
Michael Hammerschmidt, Senior Associate
Sandra K. Kidd, VP for Institutional Advancement
William R. Lowery, Managing Associate
Jack F. McJunkin, Partner
Donna Merrell, Senior Associate
Ann Neitzel, Senior Associate
Bobbie J. Strand, Principal
William D. Tippie, Principal

Bentz Whaley Flessner's team of seasoned specialists offers a comprehensive range of services including advancement audits, feasibility studies and campaign implementation, prospect research and evaluation, electronic hardware and software analysis, and annual giving program analysis and planning and staff training. The integration of diverse advancement services and customized approaches to individual client requirements create productive partnerships. These are the kinds of relationships that promote clear understanding of institutional goals and the need for philanthropic dollars.

## Lucent Technologies Foundation

*Silver Level Affiliate*

600 Mountain Avenue
Room CF-418
Murray Hill, NJ 07974
(908) 582-7910
Fax: (908) 582-6985
E-mail: foundation@lucent.com

Florence Demming, Director Employee Programs
David S. Ford, President
Deborah Stahl, Executive Director
Phyllis McGrath, Vice President Foundation Programs

Lucent Technologies designs, develops, manufactures and markets communications systems and technologies ranging from microchips to networks. We're a $23 billion company launched in 1996 operating in more than 94 countries. The Lucent Technologies Foundation's matching gift program provides a one-to-one match for K–16 education and arts.

## *Donor Recognition*

### Ameropean Corporation

*Bronze Level Affiliate*

7 Corporate Drive, Suite 109
North Haven, CT 06473
(203) 239-0448
Fax: (203) 234-8820
Web: www.leatherbookmarks.com

Guy M. Bigwood, President

Ameropean Corporation markets custom designed top quality leather bookmarks. They are elegant recognition or thank you gifts to support fundraising programs.

### GreatGiftsForGrads.Com

*Bronze Level Affiliate*

PMD 150, 1100 Hammond Drive
Suite 410A
Atlanta, GA 30328
(770) 512-7138
Fax: (770) 512-7139
E-mail: don@GreatGiftsforGrads.com
Web: www.GreatGiftsforGrads.com

Don Kennedy, President

A much easier way for schools to shop! More products at lower prices than mail order catalogs but with personal service like a local rep. Search for gifts by budget, event, program, or alphabetically. All product information in standardized, easy-to-read format. Save an extra 5 or 10% on multiple product orders!

### Honorcraft Incorporated

*Bronze Level Affiliate*

292 Page Street
Stoughton, MA 02072
(781) 341-0410
Fax: (781) 341-8460
E-mail: awards@honorcraft.com
Web: www.honorcraft.com

Sharon M. Rabesa, National Marketing Coordinator

For 40 years Honorcraft has been designing and fabricating unique donor walls and individual recognition awards while providing unmatched customer service. Our offices are located in Massachusetts, Illinois, and New York. *New Educational Partner.*

## Medallic Art Company Ltd

*Bronze Level Affiliate*

80 Airpark Vista Blvd.
Dayton, NV 89403
(775) 246-6000
Fax: (775) 246-6006
E-mail: minted@medallic.com
Web: www.medallic.com

Robert W. Hoff, President

Medallic Art, America's oldest and largest private mint, makes the most distinguished medals, awards, chains of office, ceremonial maces and donor recognition awards and plaques.

## Metal Décor

*Bronze Level Affiliate*

PO Box 19452
Springfield, IL 62794
(217) 523-4565
Fax: (217) 753-8502
E-mail: info@metal.decor.com
Web: www.metaldecor.com

Dan Marshall, National Sales Manager

Specializing in donor displays, personalized annual giving gifts and custom signage, Metal Décor designs and manufactures the most innovative donor recognition in the market place.

## Recognition Products International

*Bronze Level Affiliate*

8706 Commerce Drive, Suite 6
Easton, MD 21601
(410) 820-0022
Fax: (410) 820-5044
E-mail: info@recognitionproducts.com
Web: www.recognitionproducts.com

Brian K. Gearhart, VP

Designers and producers of custom recognition products; specializing in die struck Bronze, Silver and Gold medallions, cast bronze plaques, awards in crystal, as well as premium specialty items for special events such as Graduation Awards, table favors for Gala events, board Member Gifts, Alumni Awards, Building Dedications, and Anniversary Milestones.

### VisionMark, Inc.

*Bronze Level Affiliate*

PO Box 4219
2309 Industrial Drive
Sidney, OH 45365-4219
(937) 492-3100
Fax: (937) 492-3108
Web: www.donorrecognition.com

Angela M. Speelman, National Sales Manager

VisionMark forms a partnership with all the clients we serve. Our objective is to accomplish your recognition goals while ensuring the finest quality, timeliness and value in the profession. Our resourcefulness results in an unlimited scope of materials available to you, your board and your donors. The result is a testimony to your belief in the value of philanthropy and the importance of donor recognition.

## Enrollment Management

### Adams Associates

*Bronze Level Affiliate*

Paoli Executive Green I
41 Leopard Road
Paoli, PA 19301-1549
(610) 407-4500
Fax: (610) 407-4504
E-mail: aapubrel@aol.com

Francis T. Adams III, VP of Production
Francis T. Adams Jr., President

For 37 years we have created innovative programs that significantly broaden development (especially annual giving), admissions, marketing, and communications activities. We conduct market research and manage outstanding special events, such as anniversaries, symposiums and inaugurations. Equally important, as a full service company, we provide cost effective visuals through graphic design, photography and video as individual or package projects. Call us about our exciting new full-motion interactive video technology for CD-ROMs.

## Art & Science Group, Inc.

*Bronze Level Affiliate*

6115 Falls Road
Suite 101
Baltimore, MD 21206
(410) 377-7880
Fax: (410) 377-7955
E-mail: consult@artsci.com
Web: www.artsci.com

Richard A. Hesel, Principal

Provides strategic marketing and communications planning for enrollment management and institutional advancement; market research and modeling of prospect behavior; financial aid and pricing analysis; institutional positioning and marketing; and creation of promotional materials for student recruitment, capital campaigns, and other advancement purposes.

## Crane MetaMarketing Ltd.

*Bronze Level Affiliate*

9020 Laurel Way
Alpharetta, GA 30022-5900
(888) 642-2400
Fax: (770) 642-9404
E-mail: cranes@cranesnest.com

Patti Crane, Founder and President
Jennifer Joseph, Senior Consultant

We deliver successful positioning campaigns that are individually tailored, grounded in institutional values, targeted through insightful market research, and expressed through compelling communications. We can help you distill and convey your identity, attract your best-fit audiences, define and capture your market position, and initiate needed change.

## Creative Communication of America, Inc.

*Gold Level Affiliate*

16 Sage Estate
Albany, NY 12204
(518) 427-6600
Fax: (518) 427-6679
E-mail: viewbook@aol.com

Ed McKeown, Senior Creative Assoc
Pam Orr, President
Joe Orzechowski, Chief Executive Officer
Charles Wagner, Senior Writer
Ray Witkowski, Dir of Marketing

We work exclusively in recruitment communications, creating publications, Web sites, and related materials for colleges and universities of all types and sizes. Let our service-minded marketing consultants, researchers, writers, designers, photographers, and production specialists help you acquire fresh, affordable new recruitment tools that will deliver the measurable results you want.

## George Dehne & Associates, Inc.

*Silver Level Affiliate*

3331 Cotton Field Drive
Mt. Pleasant, SC 29466
(843) 971-9088
Fax: (843) 971-7759
E-mail: topher@dehne.com
Web: www.gddais.com

1401 Spyglass Drive
Austin, TX 78746
(512) 347-9737
Fax: (512) 347-0235
E-mail: marilyn@dehne.com

33 Main Street, Suite F
Old Saybrook, CT 06475
(860) 388-3958
Fax: (860) 388-0595
E-mail: topher@dehne.com

3174 Arbour Lane
Yorktown Heights, NY 10598
(914) 245-5955
Fax: (914) 245-9610
E-mail: gdatr@dehne.com

202 Nottingham Drive
Huntersville, NC 28078
(704) 947-8428
Fax: (704) 948-4362
E-mail: steve@dehne.com

David Broidigan, Managing Director for Research
Gina Campbell, Director for GDA Telerecruiting
Steve Cloniger, Managing Director for Student Recruitment Counseling
George Dehne, President
Marilyn Mock, Managing Director for Public Relations Counseling
Christopher Small, Executive VP

George Dehne & Associates specializes in market research, developing marketing strategies, and communications programming to meet the student recruitment needs of colleges and universities. Professional Development Service offers training plus mentoring in the fields of admissions, public relations, financial aid and institutional research. GDA Telerecruiting uses former admissions professionals to assist in an institution's student recruitment telemarketing effort. Public Relations Counseling provides planning and implementation services in support of advancement and student recruitment.

## The Lawlor Group, Inc.

*Silver Level Affiliate*

6106 Excelsior Blvd.
Minneapolis, MN 55416
(612) 922-6291
Fax: (612) 922-7980
E-mail: tlg@thelawlorgroup.com
Web: www.thelawlorgroup.com

Carole Arwidson, VP
John T. Lawlor, Founder and President
Jennifer Britz, Editor, The Lawlor Review

The Lawlor Group (TLG) is a premier, full-service higher education marketing communications firm specializing in institutional marketing, brand building and enrollment management. Since its founding in 1987, TLG has provided intelligent, creative and affordable marketing solutions to over 100 college clients. TLG's services include research, planning and communications development, including strategic planning for the Internet and the development and design of Web sites. TLG also publishes the critically acclaimed *Lawlor Review* and sponsors professional development seminars through The Lawlor Institute.

### Lipman Hearne, Inc.

*Bronze Level Affiliate*

303 East Wacker Drive
Suite 1030
Chicago, IL 60601
(312) 946-1900
Fax: (312) 946-1922
E-mail: rmoore@lipmanhearne.com
Web: www.lipmanhearne.com

Thomas D. Abrahamson, Managing Partner
Robert F. Lipman, President
Robert Moore, Managing Partner
Michael Stoner, VP of New Media

Marketing and communications to build stronger institutions: institutional repositioning, enrollment management, market research, marketing plans, direct mail, media relations, new media, communications audits, case statements, advertising, editorial and design services. A leader in total institutional marketing with a 30-year track record. Call for complimentary case studies of our work.

### The Lorish Company

*Bronze Level Affiliate*

922 Penn Avenue
Wyomissing, PA 19610
(610) 373-2200
E-mail: lorishco@fast.net

Lee Kershner, VP

Award-winning, results-oriented communication solutions delivered on time and on budget since 1979. Our client partners benefit from dynamic creativity that produces tangible results in enrollment management and advancement. Work with hands-on professionals who value your business and care about your success. Call us for complimentary case studies.

## Maguire Associates, Inc.

*Bronze Level Affiliate*

135 South Road
Bedford, MA 01730
(781) 280-2900
Fax: (781) 280-2909
E-mail: mail@maguireassoc.com
Web: www.maguireassoc.com

Patricia Casey, Senior Vice President

Maguire Associates is a comprehensive market research and consulting firm that provides educational clients with highly effective research-based marketing strategies. Maguire Associates' services include strategic planning, institutional positioning, enrollment management consulting. Web-based research, student satisfaction/retention studies, and financial aid analysis and predictive modeling.

## North Charles Street Design Organization

*Gold Level Affiliate*

222 West Saratoga Street
Baltimore, MD 21201
(410) 539-4040
Fax: (410) 685-0961
E-mail: info@ncsdo.com
Web: www.ncsdo.com

Douglass B. Forsyth, VP
Douglas B. Hutton, VP
Jill A. Jasuta, Account Manager
Clifford Lull, President
Susann T. Studz, VP
Bernice A. Thieblot, Founding Creative Director

Since 1972, some of the best and the most interesting colleges, universities, and schools in America have made us continuing partners in their management of the ever-changing scene. With them, we have created powerful marketing communications for enrollment and institutional advancement. Our efforts together have been marked by extraordinary success.

### Stein Communications

*Bronze Level Affiliate*

1255 Williams Street NW
Atlanta, GA 30309-2811
(404) 875-0421
Fax: (404) 872-8814
E-mail: jwilliams@steincommunications.com
Web: www.steincommunications.com

Lynn Donham, Associate VP
Rich Fleming, VP
Robert Glass, VP
Brian Scales, Account Executive
Jay R. Williams, President

Experienced. Creative. Successful. Partnering with clients in higher education since 1965 to achieve their marketing, enrollment and advancement goals. Comprehensive, tailored services include qualitative and quantitative market research, creative concept development, design, copywriting, photography, all phases of electronic pre-print and print production, as well as Web site and interactive media development.

### Waldinger/Birch, Inc

*Bronze Level Affiliate*

1025 Saint Paul Street
Baltimore, MD 21202
(410) 361-6161
Fax: (410) 361-6164
E-mail: mark@waldingerbirch.com
Web: www.waldingerbirch.com

Mark Shippe, Creative Dir

Waldinger/Birch is a creative services business providing a full range of marketing communications services: strategic positioning, educational marketing, eMedia, branding and overall message development.

## *Event Management Software*

### SunGard BSR Inc.

*Gold Level Affiliate*

1000 Winter Street
Waltham, MA 02451
(781) 890-2105
Fax: (781) 890-4099
E-mail: Sales@sungardbsr.com
Web: www.sungardbsr.com

Bonnie Burns, Marketing Communication Manager
Brad Goodman, SmartCall Account Executive
Geoff Knue, Senior Account Executive
Fred Weiss, Vice President, Sales & Marketing
James Werner, Senior Account Executive

SunGard BSR Inc. supports the advancement efforts of higher education and other not-for-profit organizations. Our client list numbers more than 140 major institutions worldwide.

- Advance: Establish, maintain, and manage relationships with friends, donors, and prospects.
- Advance Express: Get all the features of Advance in a turnkey system for streamlined implementation.
- SmartCall: Manage your call center for more successful telefundraising.
- Special Events: Plan and manage events more effectively.
- Web Access: Provide distributed access to your data on a "need-to-know" basis.
- Advance Web Community: Communicate more productively with your constituents.
- Services: Consulting, training, and outsourcing.

## *Fundraising Analysis*

### Target Analysis Group Inc.

*Bronze Level Affiliate*

1030 Massachusetts Avenue
Cambridge, MA 02138
(617) 876-2275
Fax: (617) 354-0895
E-mail: info@targetanalysis.com
Web: www.targetanalysis.com

Beth Filippone, Director, Sales Account Manager

Offers analytical benchmarking and predictive modeling services for non-profit development professionals. Our clients include leading universities, secondary schools, public broadcasting stations, museums, hospitals, and health service organizations. *New Educational Partner*

## Fundraising Consultants

### Adams Associates

*Bronze Level Affiliate*

Paoli Executive Green I
41 Leopard Road
Paoli, PA 19301-1549
(610) 407-4500
Fax: (610) 407-4504
E-mail: aapubrel@aol.com

Francis T. Adams III, VP of Production
Francis T. Adams Jr., President

For 37 years we have created innovative programs that significantly broaden development (especially annual giving), admissions, marketing, and communications activities. We conduct market research and manage outstanding special events, such as anniversaries, symposiums and inaugurations. Equally important, as a full service company, we provide cost effective visuals through graphic design, photography and video as individual or package projects. Call us about our exciting new full-motion interactive video technology for CD-ROM's.

### Alexander Haas Martin & Partners, Inc.

*Bronze Level Affiliate*

133 Carnegie Way
Suite 1200
Atlanta, GA 30303
(404) 525-7575
Fax: (404) 524-2992
E-mail: ahmp@ahmp.com
Web: www.ahmp.com

G. Douglass Alexander, President
Del Martin, VP
David Shufflebarger, Assoc VP

We know what it takes to be successful in today's competitive philanthropic marketplace. We have over a 95% success rate in hundreds of campaigns. Large enough to service a $200-million-plus campaign, and small enough to give personal attention to a $2-million project, AHM&P is a national firm headquartered in Atlanta. AHM&P: Strategists in Philanthropy.

## Art & Science Group, Inc.

*Bronze Level Affiliate*

6115 Falls Road
Suite 101
Baltimore, MD 21206
(410) 377-7880
Fax: (410) 377-7955
E-mail: consult@artsci.com
Web: www.artsci.com

Richard A. Hesel, Principal

Provides strategic marketing and communications planning for enrollment management and institutional advancement; market research and modeling of prospect behavior; financial aid and pricing analysis; institutional positioning and marketing; and creation of promotional materials for student recruitment, capital campaigns, and other advancement purposes.

## Barnes & Roche, Inc.

*Bronze Level Affiliate*

919 Conestoga Road—Bldg. 3
Suite 110
Rosemont, PA 19010-1375
(610) 527-3244
Fax: (610) 527-0381
E-mail: consult@brnsrche.com

John P. Butler III, President
Jeanne B. Jenkins, Senior Consultant
Allen L. Martineau, Senior Consultant
Mary H. Wade, VP
H. Sargent Whittier, Senior Consultant

Barnes & Roche, Inc. provides a comprehensive approach to institutional advancement and resource management. The firm offers a full range of fundraising and consulting services. In addition, related services include communications, public relations, market research, prospect research and information systems consulting. To respond to the changing dynamics of financing, B&R encourages its clients to adopt a total resource management approach—maximizing all income opportunities while identifying cost containment measures.

### Bentz Whaley Flessner

*Gold Level Affiliate*

7251 Ohms Lane
Minneapolis, MN 55439
(952) 921-0111
Fax: (952) 921-0109
E-mail: bwf@bwf.com
Web: www.bwf.com

5272 River Road
Suite 500
Bethesda, MD 20816
(301) 656-7823
Fax: (301) 656-2156

Bob Burdenski, Senior Associate, Annual Giving
Diane R. Crane, Managing Associate, Systems & Technology
M. Bruce Dreon, Partner
Bruce W. Flessner, Principal
Karen L. Greene, Managing Associate, Prospect Research
Lisa Grissom, Senior Associate
Michael Hammerschmidt, Senior Associate
Sandra K. Kidd, VP for Institutional Advancement
William R. Lowery, Managing Associate
Jack F. McJunkin, Partner
Donna Merrell, Senior Associate
Ann Neitzel, Senior Associate
Bobbie J. Strand, Principal
William D. Tippie, Principal

Bentz Whaley Flessner's team of seasoned specialists offers a comprehensive range of services including advancement audits, feasibility studies and campaign implementation, prospect research and evaluation, electronic hardware and software analysis, and annual giving program analysis and planning and staff training. The integration of diverse advancement services and customized approaches to individual client requirements create productive partnerships. These are the kinds of relationships that promote clear understanding of institutional goals and the need for philanthropic dollars.

## Brakeley, John Price Jones Inc.

*Silver Level Affiliate*

86 Prospect Street
Stamford, CT 06901
(203) 348-8100
Fax: (203) 978-0114
E-mail: brakeleyct@aol.com
Web: www.brakeley.com

Paramount House
162-170 Wardour Street
London, United Kingdom W1V 4AB
44 (0) 207-287-3361
Fax: 44 (0) 207-287-8705

George A. Brakeley III, President
John M. Carter Jr., Managing Dir, Western United States
John G. Kelly, Managing Dir, Brakeley Europe

A full-service organization providing fundraising consulting, planning and management services in the fields of education, health, culture and the arts, community, religious and civic organizations, and national associations throughout the world.

## Browning Associates, Inc.

*Bronze Level Affiliate*

209 Cooper Avenue
Suite 5A
Upper Montclair, NJ 07043
(973) 746-5960
Fax: (973) 746-0189
E-mail: browninga@aol.com
Web: www.browning-associates.com

Elizabeth Alling Sewall, Consultant
Cecile D. Banner, Assoc
Gregory Floyd, Vice-President
William A. Griffin, President

Total development for the independent school, including strategic planning, retreats, admissions, capital and annual fundraising, head searches, research, office studies, and administrative surveys.

**Resource 10**

## Campbell & Company

*Silver Level Affiliate*

One East Wacker Drive
Suite 2525
Chicago, IL 60601
(312) 644-7100
(877) 957-0000
Fax: (312) 644-3559
Web: www.campbellcompany.com

Eastern Regional Office
85 Eastern Avenue #305
Gloucester, MA 01930
(978) 281-1235
Fax: (978) 281-1248

Ohio Office
25825 Science Park Drive #100
Beachwood, OH 44122
(216) 766-5730
Fax: (216) 766-5731

Western Regional Office
24451 Ridge Route Drive #200
Laguna Hills, CA 92653
(949) 470-4555
Fax: (949) 470-4556

William Hausman, Senior VP and Eastern Regional Manager
Kenneth W. Johnson, VP and Regional Manager
Suzanne Mink, Vice President
Russell G. Weigand, Co-President

Founded in 1976, Campbell & Company is a national philanthropic consulting firm offering a full range of services, including capital and endowment campaign counsel and management, annual and planned giving program counsel, feasibility studies and development audits, volunteer and staff training, marketing and communications plans and materials, case statements, board development, and executive search. Our firm prides itself on helping to build stronger institutions and stronger philanthropic partnerships. With over two decades of service to more than 600 institutions nationwide, our team of senior professional has the insight, skills and experience to meet a range of client needs.

## Cargill Associates, Inc.

*Bronze Level Affiliate*

1701 Altamesa Blvd.
Fort Worth, TX 76133
(817) 292-9374
Fax: (817) 292-6205
E-mail: institution@cargillfw.com
Web: www.cargillassociates.com

Wayne Vaughn, CFRE, President, Institution Division

A full-service fundraising consulting firm specializing in major gifts campaign management, feasibility studies, development audits, annual giving, and pre- and post-campaign counseling. In 24 years, the firm has become one of the largest in America, raising over $3 billion for their clients.

## Carol O'Brien Associates

*Silver Level Affiliate*

120 West State Street
Ithaca, NY 14850-5441
(607) 272-9144
Fax: (607) 272-9180
E-mail: cobaithaca@aol.com

Carol O'Brien, President
Paula P. Sidle, Senior Assoc

Carol O'Brien Associates offers development counsel to strategically position and strengthen institutions through services in evaluation and implementation (e.g., feasibility studies; internal assessment); individual (annual, major and planned), corporate and foundation giving programs; alumni and constituent programs; communications and research; staff and volunteer; governing board development and training.

## ChangingOurWorld.com

*Bronze Level Affiliate*

420 Lexington Avenue, Suite 2458
New York, NY 10170
(610) 429-0161
Fax: (610) 430-3552
E-mail: smuldoon@changingourworld.com
Web: www.changingourworld.com

Susan Muldoon, Director

The goal of ChangingOurWorld.com is to use the power of the Internet to increase the amount of philanthropy worldwide. Founded by non-profit executives, fundraising professionals, and Internet experts, our core business is providing fundraising counsel to both non-profits and for-profits via professional consultation on all aspects of philanthropy.

## Community Counselling Service Co., Inc.

*Silver Level Affiliate*

350 Fifth Avenue, Suite 7210
New York, NY 10118
(212) 695-1175
Fax: (212) 967-6451
E-mail: ccsnewyork@ccsfundraising.com
Web: www.ccsfundraising.com

David Gallagher, VP
Thomas F. Hanrahan Jr., VP
Frederic J. Happy, VP, Managing Dir, Western
Michael Infurnari, VP
Robert Kissane, Executive VP
Joseph F. X. Lee, VP
Patrick W. Moughan, President, Midwest
Carmel Napolitano, Dir of Research Services
Brian Nevins, VP
Robert B. Rice, VP
Dennick Skeels, VP

For over 50 years, CCS has provided fundraising counsel and management services to outstanding institutions of higher education worldwide.

Today, CCS is a leader in designing innovative campaigns to advance the mission of public and private colleges, universities, academic systems, and specialized research and training institutions.

With a permanent staff of more than 150 high-skilled professionals, CCS can provide outside counsel, resident campaign management, and comprehensive support services include:

- Development audits
- Feasibility studies
- Strategic campaign planning
- Trustee orientation and development
- Capital campaign counsel and management
- Major gifts counsel

- Planned giving programs
- Annual giving
- Case statement development
- Development publications
- Electronic research services

## Copley Harris Company, Inc.

*Bronze Level Affiliate*

106 High Street
Danvers, MA 01923
(978) 750-1028
Fax: (978) 750-6709
E-mail: chc@copleyharris.com
Web: www.copleyharris.com

Betty Ann Copley-Harris, President

Copley Harris Company, Inc. provides counsel to non-profit health care, educational, cultural and social service organizations seeking to advance philanthropy. We strive to provide our clients with services that yield measurable returns and generate essential resources to support their charitable missions.

## Coxe, Curry & Associates

*Bronze Level Affiliate*

50 Hurt Plaza, Suite 630
Atlanta, GA 30303
(404) 525-4821
E-mail: acurry@coxecurry.com

Ann Q. Curry, President

Coxe Curry and Associates is an Atlanta-based fundraising consulting firm with over 40 associates serving various not-for-profit clients, including local independent schools, colleges and universities.

## Craigmyle & Co. Ltd.

*Silver Level Affiliate*

The Grove
Harpenden, Herts AL5 1AJ
United Kingdom
01582 762441
Fax: 01582 461489

E-mail: craigmyle@cwcom.net
Web: www.craigmyle.org.uk

Trevor Barton, Director
Geoff Howard, Director
Mark Jefferies, Managing Director

The company provides advisory, managerial, research, editorial, tax, and charity law (governance) consultancy to the charity sector. Services include: appeal direction; strategic consultancy; recruitment and training; feasibility studies; marketing and communications strategies; tax and legal advice. *New Educational Partner*

## Crane MetaMarketing Ltd.
*Bronze Level Affiliate*

9020 Laurel Way
Alpharetta, GA 30022-5900
(888) 642-2400
Fax: (770) 642-9404
E-mail: cranes@cranesnest.com

Patti Crane, Founder and President
Jennifer Joseph, Senior Consultant

We deliver successful positioning campaigns that are individually tailored, grounded in institutional values, targeted through insightful market research, and expressed through compelling communications. We can help you distill and convey your identity, attract your best-fit audiences, define and capture your market position, and initiate needed change.

## DataProse, Inc.
*Bronze Level Affiliate*

1451 N Rice Avenue
Suite A
Oxnard, CA 93030
(800) 927-7634
(805) 278-7430
Fax: (805) 278-7420
E-mail: bmurray@corp.dataprose.com
Web: www.dataprose.com

6012 Campus Circle Drive, Suite 260
Irving, TX 75063
(800) 876-5015
(972) 550-0190
Fax: (972) 550-8907

Bill Murray, VP, Sales

When your organization needs an ambitious direct marketing program, DataProse can help you reach your goals. We have helped hundreds of clients achieve results with cutting-edge technology, experience, know-how and superior service. All of which has earned us satisfied clients, repeat business and a reputation for providing fresh ideas and smart solutions. At DataProse, we offer a comprehensive range of services to fulfill your direct marketing needs, including consulting, database, and direct mail services. DataProse has offices in Los Angeles, Dallas, Seattle, Denver, San Francisco, and Ft. Lauderdale. Call (800) 927-7634 for the office in your area, or see us online at www.dataprose.com.

## Datatel
### *Gold Level Affiliate*

4375 Fair Lakes Court
Fairfax, VA 22033
(703) 968-9000
Fax: (703) 968-4540
E-mail: mktg@datatel.com
Web: www.datatel.com

Datatel, Inc.
100 Spear Street, Suite 1410
San Francisco, CA 94105
(415) 957-9002
(800) 969-9002
Fax: (415) 957-9554

Jill Doran, Benefactor Application Consultant
Diane Dunlap, Manager, Benefactor Technical Support
Amy Houy, Benefactor Application Consultant
Kyran Kennedy, Product Manager
Nancy McAndrew, Manager, Benefactor and Core Srvcs

Benefactor, Datatel's strategic planning and management tool designed specifically for fundraising professionals, provides your organization with a competitive edge in its quest to identify and solicit the funds needed for success. Benefactor not only keeps complete and accurate records of your organization's fundraising activities and efforts, but it also collects, calculates, and manipulates data to provide forecasts, progress reports, and prospect identification.

Benefactor's features and functions provide the information access and tools necessary to effectively and efficiently manage a development staff while increasing the level of contribution and participation from donors. Benefactor tracks and stores detailed records on individuals and organizations, and then ties that information together to identify the personal and business relationships so crucial to successful fundraising. Benefactor also automates gift and pledge processing, tracking of matching contributions, identification and tracking of major prospects, campaign management, and scheduling and coordination of activities and events, so that all aspects of fundraising are integrated in one system. By consolidating financial and demographic data, Benefactor provides you with the ability to generate reports and perform analyses that help make informed decisions and develop future fundraising strategies.

## Demont & Associates, Inc.

*Bronze Level Affiliate*

477 Congress Street, Fifth Floor
Portland, ME 04101
(207) 773-3030
Fax: (207) 773-5213
E-mail: demontassociates@compuserve.com
Web: www.demontassociates.com

Robert D. Demont, CFRE, President

Demont & Associates provides comprehensive fundraising counsel, institutional advancement counsel, and other related services to private and public colleges and universities; independent, parochial and quasi-public schools; and other nonprofit organizations throughout the Northeast. Demont promotes organizational and fundraising success through a tailored partnership of client personnel, volunteers, and counsel.

## The Dini Partners, Inc.

*Silver Level Affiliate*

3400 Carlisle, Suite 348
Dallas, TX 75204
(214) 754-9393
Fax: (214) 754-9363
E-mail: kfriend@dinipartners.com

3724 Jefferson, Suite 302
Austin, TX 78731

4820 East Michigan Avenue
Scottsdale, AZ 85252

2727 Allen Parkway, Suite 700
Houston, TX 77019

Katherine L. Friend, Senior Consultant
David B. Jones, Principal and Managing Partner
David K. Northington, PhD, Senior Consultant
Rick Miller, Of Counsel

The Dini Partners provides professional services that build upon the existing strengths of an institution and help our clients achieve their fundraising and management objectives. Services include: fundraising, strategic direction, leadership development, quality performance, communications management, constituent surveys, marketplace analysis, financial and fund policy analysis, executive search, event management.

## DirectLine Technologies, Inc.

*Silver Level Affiliate*

1600 N. Carpenter Road, Bldg. D
Modesto, CA 95351-1145
(800) 448-1200
Fax: (209) 491-2091
E-mail: martha_connor@directline-tech.com
Web: www.directline-tech.com

Wayne Choate, National Sales Director
Gary Connor, Chief Technologist
Martha Connor, President
David Murzi, National Account Executive

DirectLine Technologies Inc. specializes in cost-effective telemarketing fundraising campaigns for colleges and universities nationwide. DirectLine provides full alumni membership acquisition and renewal campaigns as well as surveying services.

## Donald E. Craig & Associates, Inc.

*Bronze Level Affiliate*

206 Southpoint Drive
Suite 100
Williamsburg, VA 23185-4440

Resource 10

(757) 259-4421
Fax: (757) 259-4439
E-mail: deca@infi.net

Donald E. Craig, President

A full-service national fund development consulting firm. We specialize in assisting volunteers and staff in making effective personal calls, and helping faculty and
professional staff redefine projects and programs for funding.

### eAdvancement.org

*Bronze Level Affiliate*

1301 21st NW
Washington, DC 20036
(202) 463-7310
Fax: (202) 318-1093
E-mail: theodore@eAdvancement.org
Web: www.eAdvancement.org

7812 SE 78th Street
Mercer Island, WA 98040
(206) 236-8062
Fax: (206) 232-4370
E-mail: Stanton@eAdvancement.org

37 Hawthorne Avenue
Princeton, NJ 08540
(410) 770-3171
Fax: (253) 423-9269
E-mail: white@eAdvancement.org

6 Rockland Park
Branford, CT 06405
(203) 481-8710
Fax: (203) 481-8177
E-mail: holcombe@eAdvancement.org

Jolanne Stanton, Principal
Eustace Theodore, Principal
Dan White, Principal
Terry M. Holcombe, Principal

**Resource 10**

A consortium of independent consultants providing strategic guidance in alumni relations, communications, and development. Full information may be found at www.eAdvancement.org. *New Educational Partner*

## Focus Direct

*Bronze Level Affiliate*

9707 Broadway
PO Box 17568
San Antonio, TX 78217-0568
(800) 299-9185
Fax: (210) 804-0477
E-mail: darwins@focusdirect.com
Web: www.focusdirect.com

Darwin Sparkman, Univ Program Manager

Direct mail expertise and a track record of on-time performance for our clients. Printing, lasering, creative graphics, and data processing services available. Effective fundraising and membership growth packages with namestickers, bookmarks, and more to complement your appeal programs.

## Ford & Associates

*Bronze Level Affiliate*

1372 Peachtree Street, NE
Suite 207
Atlanta, GA 30309
(404) 897-3456
Fax: (404) 897-3452
E-mail: info@fordassociates.com
Web: www.fordassociates.com

Rocky Ford, President
Becky Ross, Consultant

Ford & Associates offers comprehensive development counsel for independent schools exclusively. Our clients are located throughout the US and overseas. For more information, call us at (404) 897-3456, or visit our web site at www.fordassociates.com.

### Fund-Raising and Management Counsel, Inc.

*Bronze Level Affiliate*

2900 Chamblee-Tucker Road, Building 16
Atlanta, GA 30341
(770) 457-5077
Fax: (770) 457-5177
E-mail: marketing@frmc-inc.com
Web: www.frmc-inc.com

Janet Dorado, President

Fund-Raising and Management Counsel, Inc. offers professional consulting and management services for annual giving programs and capital campaigns, personalized direct mail programs, and telephone campaigns.

### The Galler Group

*Bronze Level Affiliate*

52 Page Road
Newton, MA 02460
(617) 965-0922
Fax: (617) 969-5862
E-mail: gallergroup@usa.net

Susan Galler, President

The Galler Group is a full-service consulting firm that works in partnership with nonprofit organizations to maximize their performance and help them achieve revenue and programmatic goals.

### Gonser Gerber Tinker Stuhr

*Bronze Level Affiliate*

400 East Diehl Road
Suite 380
Naperville, IL 60563
(630) 505-1433
Fax: (630) 505-7710
E-mail: info@ggts.com

Mary A. Chicoine, Consultant
Charles P. Cushman, Partner
M. Jane Eaves, Partner

Ronald D. Gunden, Consultant
Charles H. Kayton, Partner
Douglas D. Mason, Partner
Salvatore F. Polizzoto, Partner
Calvin H. Stoney, Partner

Since 1950, Gonser Gerber Tinker Stuhr has provided full-service development consulting in the areas of development, public relations, fundraising, and student recruitment.

## Goodale Associates, Inc.

*Bronze Level Affiliate*

509 Madison Avenue
Suite 1112
New York, NY 10022
(212) 759-2999
Fax: (212) 759-7490
E-mail: tkgassoc@aol.com
Web: www.tkgoodale.com

Alex Shalom, Consultant

Development and management consulting for nonprofits. Specializing in capital campaigns for colleges and independent schools, annual giving campaigns, foundation and corporate donor strategies, individual prospect research, feasibility studies, and specialized volunteer training.

## Grenzebach Glier & Associates, Inc.

*Silver Level Affiliate*

55 West Wacker
Suite 1500
Chicago, IL 60601
(312) 372-4040
Fax: (312) 372-7911
E-mail: gga@grenzglier.com

212 Piccadilly
London, W1V 9LD, UK
44 (0) 20-7917 1758
Fax: 44 (0) 20-7439 0262

G. Robert Alsobrook, Senior Consulting Vice President
J. Barry Brindley, Senior Consulting Vice President
Lyn Britt, Prospect Profile Director
Richard M. Carter, Senior Vice President and Managing Director
William J. Conner, Vice President and Managing Director
Charlotte Davis-McGhee, Senior Counsel, Information Technology
G. David Gearhart, Senior Consulting Vice President
John J. Glier, President and CEO
Martin Grenzebach, Chairman
Robert J. Haley, Senior Consulting Vice President
Virginia Ikkanda-Suddith, Senior Consulting Associates
Kathleen Kavanagh, Senior Executive Vice President and Managing Director
John M. Kudless, Senior Executive Vice President and Managing Director
James K. Looney, Senior Vice President and Managing Director
Barbara Macpherson, Senior Consulting Associate, GGE
Jill Pellew, Vice President and Managing Director, CGE
Dave Powers, Senior Consulting Vice President
Barbara Rose, Senior Consulting Associate
Roger J. Schifferli, Senior Consulting Vice President and Managing Dir
Patrice W. Schulze, Consulting Vice President
William Simmons, Senior VP and Managing Dir
Bill Squire, Chairman, Grenebach Glier Europe
Dominic Varisco, Senior Consulting Vice President
Leslie Ford Weber, Senior Consulting Associate
Brigitte Warning Watkins, Senior VP and Managing Dir
Patrice Welch-Schulze, Consulting VP
Donna L. Wiley, Senior Consulting Vice President
Lori F. Yersh, Senior Consulting Associate

With more than 35 years experience, Grenzebach Glier & Associates provides counsel to educational, medical, cultural, and other not-for-profit organizations throughout the United States, Canada, and Europe. Current client campaign goals surpass $8 billion. Services include: feasibility, planning, and market studies; information technology consultation: full-scale campaign consultation and management; annual fund analyses; communications services; constituency surveys; pre- and post-campaign audits; and PROSPECT PROFILE geodemographic screening. Headquartered in Chicago; offices also in the United Kingdom. GG&A is a member of the American Association of Fund-Raising Counsel (AAFRC).

Resource 10

## Hayes Briscoe Associates

*Bronze Level Affiliate*

322 West Bellevue Avenue
San Mateo, CA 94402-1104
(650) 344-8883
Fax: (650) 344-3387
E-mail: hbaconsult@aol.com
Web: www.hbaconsult.com

Marianne G. Briscoe, PhD, ACFRE, Founding Principal

Consultants to public and independent schools, colleges, and universities for governance, planning, fund development, and capital campaigns. Offices: California, New York, Florida, Connecticut and Wisconsin.

## Helen Colson Development Associates

*Silver Level Affiliate*

4725 Dorset Avenue
Chevy Chase, MD 20815
(30) 652-7819
Fax: (301) 652-7916
E-mail: hcolson@hcda.com
Web: www.helencolson.com

Helen A. Colson, President

Development and management consultants for independent schools. Services include institutional plans; programs assessments; annual, capital and planned gift counsel; governance counsel; board retreats; and executive search.

## Iain More Consultants

*Bronze Level Affiliate*

Inverlaw House, 48 Albany Terrace
Dundee, Scotland DD3 6HR
+ 44 (0) 1382 224730
Fax: + 44 (0) 1382 204934
E-mail: iain@iainmore.demon.co.uk
Web: www.im-consultants.co.uk

Iain More, Principal Consultant

Established for ten years. Large portfolio of clients in higher education and other sectors in the UK, Ireland, Italy, France, and the United States. *New Educational Partner*

## J. F. Smith Group

*Bronze Level Affiliate*

PO Box 1197
165 Magnolia Avenue, Suite 225
Auburn, AL 36831-1197
(334) 502-5374
Fax: (334) 502-5370
E-mail: jfsg@mindspring.com
Web: www.jfsg.com

Sheila Eckman, VP
Jerry F. Smith, President
Jerri Wortham, VP

J. F. Smith Group, Inc. is a full service fundraising consulting firm, serving a wide variety of nonprofit organizations, Christian schools and universities throughout the Southeast.

## J. M. Perrone Co., Inc.

*Bronze Level Affiliate*

105 Research Road
Hingham, MA 02043
(781) 741-2200
Fax: (781) 741-8028
E-mail: pbarry@jmperrone.com
Web: www.jmperrone.com

Paul Barry, VP

A complete direct mail production facility under one roof. Services include: laser personalized letters with merged data text, matching response forms and envelopes, creative design, desktop publishing, in-house printing (sheet-fed and web), bindery, CASS certification and Group 1 Software, automation postal discounting, and high-speed mail processing. We provide exceptional service: call for client references.

## John B. Cummings Co., Inc.

*Bronze Level Affiliate*

2911 Turtle Creek Blvd.
Suite 300
Dallas, TX 75219

(214) 526-1772
Fax: (214) 523-9001

John C. Carr, Senior Consultant

Founded in 1974. A major portion of the firm's clientele are educational institutions. Cummings Company, a full-service firm, specializes in providing counsel for strategic planning, major gifts, including corporation and foundation grants, and planned giving. The firm also offers executive recruitment services for development and communications professionals.

## Johnson, Grossnickle & Associates
*Bronze Level Affiliate*

PO Box 576
Franklin, IN 46131
(317) 736-1985
Fax: (317) 736-1983
E-mail: jga@jgacounsel.com
Web: www.jgacounsel.com

Ted R. Grossnickle, CFRE, President
Kris W. Kindelsperger, Ed.D, Senior Associate
Ernest Vargo II, CFRE, Senior Assoc
Angela E White, CFRE, Senior Assoc

JGA serves as guides in advancement, helping your organization build the programs and relationships that will allow it to reach a new level of philanthropic aspiration. JGA works with clients as partners to achieve superior results in campaign planning and management; annual giving analysis and program development; long-range and strategic planning; development program capacity building; board development and dynamics; and program evaluation.

## Ketchum, Inc.
*Silver Level Affiliate*

Three Gateway Center
Suite 1726
Pittsburgh, PA 15222
(412) 281-1481
Fax: (972) 450-4477
Web: www.rsi-ketchum.com

12770 Merit Drive, Suite 900
Dallas, TX 75251

Fax: (2214) 450-4477

Robert E. Carter, CFRE, President
Elliott S. Oshry, Executive VP
Frank Pisch, Senior VP
Mark J. Zachary, VP

Ketchum, Inc., founded in 1919, is a full-service fundraising counseling firm. We offer development audits, studies to facilitate campaign planning and to determine fundraising potential, access to research, campaign management, major gift and planned gift development, board and volunteer leadership development, communications counsel, staff development, strategic and long-range development planning, annual giving programs, funding proposals, presentations to foundations and corporations, donor relations and stewardship development, pledge-collection systems, and post-campaign counsel.

## Lipman Hearne, Inc.

### Bronze Level Affiliate

303 East Wacker Drive
Suite 1030
Chicago, IL 60601
(312) 946-1900
Fax: (312) 946-1922
E-mail: rmoore@lipmanhearne.com
Web: www.lipmanhearne.com

Thomas D Abrahamson, Managing Partner
Robert F. Lipman, President
Robert Moore, Managing Partner
Michael Stoner, VP of New Media

Marketing and communications to build stronger institutions: institutional repositioning, enrollment management, market research, marketing plans, direct mail, media relations, new media, communications audits, case statements, advertising, editorial and design services. A leader in total institutional marketing with a 30-year track record. Call for complimentary case studies of our work.

## Marts & Lundy, Inc.

### Silver Level Affiliate

1200 Wall Street West
Lyndhurst, NJ 07071
(201) 460-1660

Fax: (201) 460-0680
E-mail: jolly@martsandlundy.com
Web: www.martsandlundy.com

Michael F. Sinkus, Chair
Charlie P. Howland, President
Richard T. Jolly, Vice President

Marts & Lundy's experienced staff of consultants offers counsel on development programs including capital campaigns; annual funds; planned giving; audits; studies; and prospect research, screening, and rating. ELECTRONIC SCREENING Prospect Identification Process with POTENTIAL PLUS is offered as a separate service.

## Membership Management Services

*Bronze Level Affiliate*

6849 Old Dominion Drive
Suite 320
McLean, VA 22101
(703) 749-3130
Fax: (703) 749-0967
E-mail: mmsinfo@memberdiscounts.com
Web: www.memberdiscounts.com

Kim E. Way, Program Manager

Membership Management Services provides membership benefits to alumni organizations by offering special discounts on car rentals, hotels, plastic membership cards, and other reduced rate programs. We also offer full direct mail production and fundraising services.

## MyAssociation.com

*Bronze Level Affiliate*

50 W. Broadway #400
Salt Lake City, UT 84101
(801) 363-0193
Fax: (801) 363-0645
E-mail: info@myassociation.com
Web: www.myassociation.com

Brian Kelley, Dir of Marketing

Resource 10

MyAssociation.com advances your cause by using its unique member benefits technologies to add value to your alumni, raise funds, and help you operate more efficiently.

### The Osborne Group, Inc.

*Bronze Level Affiliate*

70 West Red Oak Lane
White Plains, NY 10604
(914) 697-4921
Fax: (914) 697-4899
E-mail: karen@theosbornegroup.com
Web: www.theosbornegroup.com

Karen E. Osborne, Principal

A results-oriented, hands-on, full-service management and consulting firm specializing in development, marketing, staff and volunteer training. Board development and strategic planning.

### Oxford Philanthropic Limited

*Bronze Level Affiliate*

36 Windmill Road
Headington, Oxford OX3 7BX
England
(01865) 744300
Fax: (01865) 744600
E-mail: consult@oxphil.com

Dr. H. M. Drucker, Dir
H. New, Dir

To aid a small number of educational, artistic, scientific and charitable enterprises in creating and managing development programmes including capital campaigns and thorough executive search.

### Phillips & Associates

*Bronze Level Affiliate*

10877 Wilshire Blvd.
Suite 708
Los Angeles, CA 90024
(310) 208-7772
Fax: (310) 208-7066

Susan Pearce, Senior VP

Phillips & Associates is a professional management consulting firm focusing on organizational planning, financial planning and fundraising counsel for not-for-profit institutions and organizations.

## Pierpont & Wilkerson

*Bronze Level Affiliate*

1111 Route 9, The Stone House
PO Box 179
Garrison, NY 10524-0179
(845) 737-4435
Fax: (845) 737-7352
E-mail: info@pierpont-wilkerson.net
Web: www.pierpont-wilkerson.net

G. Steven Wilkerson, President and CEO

Senior professionals experienced in comprehensive advancement and development programs, capital and endowment campaigns, fundraising management, board development, staff training, campaign planning and pre-campaign studies.

## R. Gordon Talley Communication for Institutional Advancement

*Bronze Level Affiliate*

25 Magazine Street
Cambridge, MA 02139-3960
(617) 497-7490
Fax: (617) 497-2545
E-mail: info@rgtalley.com
Web: www.rgtalley.com

R. Gordon Talley, Principal

Strategic counsel for nonprofit communications. Our CASE award-winning materials and campaign case statements in print and electronic media have helped raise more than $725 million. Clients include MIT, Tuck School of Business at Dartmouth, Phillips Academy, Dana-Farber Cancer Institute, the Redwood Library, and the Boston Symphony Orchestra.

## Raybin Associates, Inc.

*Bronze Level Affiliate*

275 Madison Avenue, Suite 1811
New York, NY 10016
(212) 490-0590

Fax: (212) 986-2731
E-mail: araybine@aol.com
Web: www.raybinassociates.com

Nancy L. Raybin, Managing Partner

A full-service fundraising and management consulting firm offering creative problem solving for gift-supported institutions. Has assisted more than 350 clients with capital campaign design and implementation, annual fund and planned giving programs, strategic planning, marketing studies, and board development. Member of AAFRC.

### Ross, Johnston & Kersting, Inc.

*Bronze Level Affiliate*

3326 Durham Chapel Hill Blvd.
Suite C-220
Durham, NC 27707
(919) 286-0721
Fax: (919) 402-9199
E-mail: rjkinc@mindspring.com

Tod T. Lindsley, VP
J. David Ross, President

Ross, Johnston & Kersting, Inc. provides development counseling for non-profit organizations. We offer clients a variety of services including internal studies, long-range planning, staff and volunteer training, feasibility studies, capital campaign counsel, and personnel searches (for client institutions). Each client receives specialized counsel tailored to their specific needs.

### RPA, Inc.

*Bronze Level Affiliate*

951 Westminster Drive
Williamsport, PA 17701
(800) 992-9277
Fax: (570) 321-7160
E-mail: rpainc@epix.net

Richard Allen Page, President

In our second decade of service to education, RPA Inc. provides institutionally tailored executive search and fundraising consulting for our national and international clients.

## RuffaloCODY & Associates

*Silver Level Affiliate*

221 3rd Avenue, SE
Cedar Rapids, IA 52406-3018
(319) 362-7482
Fax: (319) 362-7457
E-mail: djasper@ruffalocody.com
Web: www.ruffalocody.com

Stan Campbell, CFRE, VP and Senior Consultant
Duane Jasper, President
Bart Showalter, VP, CAMPUSCALL®

RuffaloCODY provides off-site and on-campus fundraising, membership, and enrollment management solutions. We specialize in contacting your constituents via the telephone, and our calling software, CAMPUSCALL®, is the leading call center automation software technology in the industry. We pride ourselves in developing long-term partnerships with our clients.

## Seeberg & Associates, Inc.

*Bronze Level Affiliate*

11 Old Lyme Road
Pittsford, NY 14534
(716) 234-1034
Fax: (716) 383-1273
E-mail: seebergms@aol.com

Mark S. Seeberg, President

We provide advisement on all aspects of philanthropic marketing, including strategic planning and visioning, board development, case positioning, and fundraising. We help our clients build and sustain comprehensive advancement programs in which annual, capital, and planned giving are integrated to serve their needs and those of their benefactors.

## The Sheridan Group

*Bronze Level Affiliate*

2700 South Quincy Street
Suite 230
Arlington, VA 22206
(703) 931-7070
Fax: (703) 931-6249

Nelson Cover, President

The Sheridan Group provides full-service fundraising/management consulting including: planning/feasibility studies, situation analysis, campaign management, strategic planning, major gifts programs, planned giving, and annual funds.

### Sinclair, Townes & Company

*Bronze Level Affiliate*

230 Peachtree Street, NW
Suite 1601
Atlanta, GA 30303-1505
(404) 688-4047
Fax: (404) 688-6543
E-mail: info@sinclairtownes.com
Web: www.sinclairtownes.com

Nancy Hubbard, Senior Consultant

Founded in 1980, the firm provides comprehensive fundraising, planned giving, and capital campaign counseling for colleges, universities, and independent schools locally, regionally, and nationally.

### Staley/Robeson®

*Bronze Level Affiliate*

733 Summer Street, Suite 204
Stamford, CT 06901
(800) 659-7247
(203) 358-9252
Fax: (203) 358-9262
E-mail: uwin@staleyrobeson.com
Web: www.staleyrobeson.com

Joseph L. Staley, President and CEO

Comprehensive, customized fundraising counsel to not-for-profit organizations, worldwide. Round-the-clock accessibility and hands-on personal guidance is our reputation and guarantee. Member AAFRC.

### Staley/Robeson/Ryan/St. Lawrence, Inc.

*Bronze Level Affiliate*

635 West Seventh Street
Suite 308
Cincinnati, OH 45203

(513) 241-6778
Fax: (513) 241-0551
E-mail: mail@staley-robeson.com
Web: www.staley-robeson.com

J. Patrick Ryan, President

Fundraising counsel to educational and other nonprofit organizations. Services include planning studies, counsel and management of capital, annual and planned giving programs; research POW&R; and editorial services. Serving the United States and the world. U.S. offices in Atlanta, Chicago, Cincinnati, Dallas, Phoenix, St. Louis and Washington, D.C. Member of Downes Ryan International.

## Waldinger/Birch, Inc

*Bronze Level Affiliate*

1025 Saint Paul Street
Baltimore, MD 21202
(410) 361-6161
Fax: (410) 361-6164
E-mail: mark@waldingerbirch.com
Web: www.waldingerbirch.com

Mark Shippe, Creative Dir

Waldinger/Birch is a creative services business providing a full range of marketing communications services: strategic positioning, educational marketing, eMedia, branding and overall message development.

## Washburn & McGoldrick, Inc.

*Bronze Level Affiliate*

8 Century Hill, Suite 1
Latham, NY 12110
(518) 783-1949
Fax: (518) 783-4001
E-mail: info@wash-mcg.com

Dr. Peter McE. Buchanan, Associate
William P. McGoldrick, Partner
Cindy G. Sterling, Associate
Susan L. Washburn, Partner

Washburn & McGoldrick, Inc., offers customized services that focus on building relationships to enhance philanthropic support: comprehensive counsel; campaign planning/readiness/feasibility studies; program audits; board, staff, volunteer development programs and retreat facilitation; major gift programs and strategies; counsel on building stronger volunteer boards.

### Whaley LeVay

*Bronze Level Affiliate*

790 E. Colorado Blvd., 9th Floor
Pasadena, CA 91101
(626) 568-0267
Fax: (626) 568-0367
E-mail: info@whaleylevay.com
Web: www.whaleylevay.com

Julie H. LeVay, Partner
John C. Whaley, Partner

Whaley LeVay offers a full range of consulting services in institutional advancement and philanthropy. The firm is comprised of seasoned professionals with firsthand experience managing sophisticated advancement programs. Whaley LeVay helps institutions plan for and reach their immediate fundraising goals with an eye to stability and long-term growth.

### William L. Jaques & Co., Inc.

*Bronze Level Affiliate*

Liberty Square
Danvers, MA 01923
(978) 777-2289
Fax: (978) 777-4758
E-mail: info@wljco.com

William L. Jaques, President
Nancy Sullivan-Skinner, Principal
Linda A. Welter, Principal

Fundraising counsel and related services for educational and other non-profit organizations, including overall development program counsel; program audits/ planning studies; pre-campaign feasibility studies; campaign planning and execution; top prospect management; planned giving; and improvement of annual fund performance.

### Witzleben & Associates

*Bronze Level Affiliate*

1516 East Franklin Street, Suite 103
Chapel Hill, NC 27514
(919) 942-0260
Fax: (919) 942-1640
E-mail: wcw@witzleben.com
Web: www.witzleben.com

W. Charles Witzleben, Principal

Witzleben & Associates is a full-service firm providing counseling services at every stage of institutional advancement—internal assessments; organizational and support systems design; annual giving, individual major gifts, corporate and foundation programs; staff and volunteer leadership training; pre-campaign studies and prospect evaluation; and campaign counsel.

## *Fundraising Software*

### Ascend Technologies, Inc.

*Bronze Level Affiliate*

2658 Crosspark Road, Suite 200
Coralville, IA 52241
(319) 626-5490
Fax: (319) 626-5491
E-mail: info@ascend-tech.com
Web: www.ascend-tech.com

Cindy Knight, VP Sales and Marketing

ASCEND is a fully integrated fundraising database that maintains donor information, gifts and pledges, prospect management, campaigns, planned giving and alumni membership.

### Blackbaud Inc.

*Bronze Level Affiliate*

4401 Belle Oaks Drive, Suite 400
Charleston, SC 29405-8530
(800) 443-9441
(843) 740-5400

Fax: (843) 740-5410
E-mail: sales@blackbaud.com
Web: www.blackbaud.com

Monica McDonald, Media PR Coord
Glenn Raus, Conference Coord

Blackbaud is the leading supplier of fundraising, accounting and administrative computer systems designed specifically for nonprofit and philanthropic organizations.

## Connectys, Inc.

*Bronze Level Affiliate*

120 North Green Street, Suite 705
Chicago, IL 60607-2625
(312) 733-3434
Fax: (312) 733-3036
E-mail: info@connectys.com
Web: www.connectys.com

1100 East Hector Street, Suite 200
Conshohocken, PA 19428
(610) 567-2940
Fax: (610) 567-0433

Sandra Bogle, Chief Strategy Officer
Malia Huff, Director of Marketing

Designed for development directors at universities and other educational institutions who are dissatisfied with the high cost and low response rates of direct mail and telethons. Connectys is a permission-based e-mail marketing ASP that allows development directors and volunteers to create and manage fundraising campaigns via e-mail and the Internet. Beyond Critical Path and other general-purpose e-mail ASPs, Connectys provides the full suite of information and services needed to support e-mail-based fundraising and communication campaigns. *New Educational Partner*

## Datatel

*Gold Level Affiliate*

4375 Fair Lakes Court
Fairfax, VA 22033
(703) 968-9000

Fax: (703) 968-4540
E-mail: mktg@datatel.com
Web: www.datatel.com

Datatel, Inc.
100 Spear Street, Suite 1410
San Francisco, CA 94105
(415) 957-9002
(800) 969-9002
Fax: (415) 957-9554

Jill Doran, Benefactor Application Consultant
Diane Dunlap, Manager, Benefactor Technical Support
Amy Houy, Benefactor Application Consultant
Kyran Kennedy, Product Manager
Nancy McAndrew, Manager, Benefactor and Core Srvcs

Benefactor, Datatel's strategic planning and management tool designed specifically for fundraising professionals, provides your organization with a competitive edge in its quest to identify and solicit the funds needed for success. Benefactor not only keeps complete and accurate records of your organization's fundraising activities and efforts, but it also collects, calculates, and manipulates data to provide forecasts, progress reports, and prospect identification.

Benefactor's features and functions provide the information access and tools necessary to effectively and efficiently manage a development staff while increasing the level of contribution and participation from donors. Benefactor tracks and stores detailed records on individuals and organizations, and then ties that information together to identify the personal and business relationships so crucial to successful fundraising. Benefactor also automates gift and pledge processing, tracking of matching contributions, identification and tracking of major prospects, campaign management, and scheduling and coordination of activities and events, so that all aspects of fundraising are integrated in one system. By consolidating financial and demographic data, Benefactor provides you with the ability to generate reports and perform analyses that help make informed decisions and develop future fundraising strategies.

## DirectLine Technologies, Inc.

*Silver Level Affiliate*

1600 N. Carpenter Road, Bldg. D
Modesto, CA 95351-1145
(800) 448-1200
Fax: (209) 491-2091

E-mail: martha_connor@directline-tech.com
Web: www.directline-tech.com

Wayne Choate, National Sales Director
Gary Connor, Chief Technologist
Martha Connor, President
David Murzi, National Account Executive

DirectLine Technologies Inc. specializes in cost-effective telemarketing fundraising campaigns for colleges and universities nationwide. DirectLine provides full alumni membership acquisition and renewal campaigns as well as surveying services.

## Institutional Memory, Inc.

*Bronze Level Affiliate*

559 Solon Road
Chagrin Falls, OH 44022-3334
(440) 247-2957
Fax: (440) 247-7056
E-mail: lange@giftedmemory.com
Web: www.giftedmemory.com

Scott R. Lange, President

The GiftedMemory prospect management system organizes your major gift program. It serves as a companion to your gift accounting system to integrate research profiles with action plans and contact reports. You can even travel with Gifted Memory-Remote for instant access to your top prospects.

## JSI FundRaising Systems, Inc.

*Silver Level Affiliate*

4732 Longhill Road
Suite 2201
Williamsburg, VA 23188
(800) 574-5772
Fax: (757) 565-4546
E-mail: millen@jsifrs.com
Web: www.jsifrs.com/millennium

Farnsworth Street
Boston, MA 02210
(800) 521-0132

Fax: (617) 482-0617
Web: www.jsifrs.com/frs

Lori Combs, Sales Consultant
Blake Jacobson, Sales Consultant
Sabre Leek, Senior Consultant
Nancye Milam, Dir, Millennium Sales and Marketing
John Murphy, Dir of Marketing and Sales
Jeffery R. Shy, President
Susan Stewart-Kelley, Sales Consultant

JSI FundRaising, providing development information systems to non-profit organizations since 1978, offers two distinct products—Millennium and Paradigm.

Millennium—A comprehensive development information system designed to meet demanding and diverse development needs. Biographical, events, membership, gift and pledge information are integrated with a top prospect tracking system that includes features to manage all areas of the major gift process: research, ratings, interests, proposals, planned giving, and contact history. For campaign management, Millennium's idea (intuition-driven executive analysis) module incorporates the use of on-line analytical data analysis, drill-down reporting, mapping software, English Query Language tools, notification alerts of prospect and campaign activity and a Palm VII for accessing and/or downloading constituent database information. Choice of user interfaces: Windows or Browser and database engines: SQL Server or Oracle. For more information on Millennium, contact our Williamsburg office at (800) 574-5772 or millen@jsifrs.com.

Paradigm—the one with the Index Card design, effectively manages the needs of small to mid-sized development programs. The aesthetic index card and file folder design present information in a clean, efficient and familiar visual metaphor. Donor and prospect tracking, gift processing, mail merge, special events, volunteer management, reporting, data import/export utilities and user-definable fields—everything you need at a price you can afford. Paradigm's on-line help, sample database and Getting Started tutorial will get most users up and running without any training. For more information on Paradigm, contact our Boston office at (800) 521-0132 or frs@jsifrs.com.

### KPMG Peat Marwick

*Bronze Level Affiliate*

700 Louisiana
Houston, TX 77002
(713) 319-2504

Fax: (713) 319-2488
E-mail: rweiner@kpmg.com
Web: www.us.kpmg.com/ps/he_nfp.html

Robert Weiner, Manager

KPMG's Fundraising and Advancement Services consulting group provides fundraising operations with the ability to assess and transform the effectiveness of their fundraising efforts and support services. The practice assists institutions with strategic planning for advancement services, selection and implementation of alumni and donor information systems, workflow analysis and process redesign, operations and staffing assessments, development of policies and procedures, evaluation of gift management and stewardship, and facilitation of fund raiser–support staff interaction.

## Lucent Technologies Foundation

*Silver Level Affiliate*

600 Mountain Avenue
Room CF-418
Murray Hill, NJ 07974
(908) 582-7910
Fax: (908) 582-6985
E-mail: foundation@lucent.com

Florence Demming, Director Employee Programs
David S. Ford, President
Deborah Stahl, Executive Director
Phyllis McGrath, Vice President Foundation Programs

Lucent Technologies designs, develops, manufactures and markets communications systems and technologies ranging from microchips to networks. We're a $23 billion company launched in 1996 operating in more than 94 countries. The Lucent Technologies Foundation's matching gift program provides a one-to-one match for K–16 education and arts.

## MyAssociation.com

*Bronze Level Affiliate*

50 W. Broadway #400
Salt Lake City, UT 84101
(801) 363-0193
Fax: (801) 363-0645

E-mail: info@myassociation.com
Web: www.myassociation.com

Brian Kelley, Dir of Marketing

MyAssociation.com advances your cause by using its unique member benefits technologies to add value to your alumni, raise funds, and help you operate more efficiently.

## PeopleSoft

*Silver Level Affiliate*

6903 Rockledge Drive
Suite 1100
Bethesda, MD 20817
(301) 571-5922
Fax: (301) 581-2133
E-mail: rachel_cayelli@peoplesoft.com
Web: www.peoplesoft.com

4460 Hacienda Drive
Pleasanton, CA 94588-8618
(925) 694-4010

Robb Eklund, Advancement Product Strategy
Laura King, Higher Education Marketing Dir
MichaelKohmescher, Product Strategy Manager
Karen Willett, Marketing Communication Higher Education

PeopleSoft Advancement is an integrated and comprehensive software solution for philanthropic and nonprofit management. PeopleSoft Advancement supports all your fundraising needs with eight functionally rich modules: Constituent Information, Gift and Pledge, Prospect Manager, Event Manager, Campaign Manager, Volunteer Manager, Membership Manager, and Planned Giving.

## Prospect Information Network, LLC

*Bronze Level Affiliate*

501 N. Grandview Avenue
Suite 203
Daytona Beach, FL 32118
(888) 557-1326

Fax: (904) 226-1154
E-mail: info@prospectinfo.com
Web: www.prospectinfo.com

Maggie Cowlan, Executive Vice President
Jennifer Wachtel, Production Assistant

Prospect Information Network's full-file computerized research and Profile Building Software enables fundraisers to efficiently find, profile and monitor the wealth on their prospect database.

## RuffaloCODY & Associates

*Silver Level Affiliate*

221 3rd Avenue, SE
Cedar Rapids, IA 52406-3018
(319) 362-7482
Fax: (319) 362-7457
E-mail: djasper@ruffalocody.com
Web: www.ruffalocody.com

Stan Campbell, CFRE, VP and Senior Consultant
Duane Jasper, President
Bart Showalter, VP, CAMPUSCALL®

RuffaloCODY provides off-site and on-campus fundraising, membership, and enrollment management solutions. We specialize in contacting your constituents via the telephone, and our calling software, CAMPUSCALL®, is the leading call center automation software technology in the industry. We pride ourselves in developing long-term partnerships with our clients.

## SCT

*Silver Level Affiliate*

4 Country View Road
Malvern, PA 19355
(610) 647-5930
Fax: (610) 578-7564
Web: www.sctcorp.com

Jason Buckley, Sales Consultant
David Carey, Solutions Manager
Veronica Chappelle-McNair, Senior Consultant
Ed Hauser, General Manager Solutions Strategy
David Killip, Functional Consultant
Ron Rasmussen, Vice President of Sales

SCT enables colleges and universities around the world to achieve breakthrough results by leveraging key relationships with their students, prospects, alumni, faculty, donors, and other constituents. SCT Education Solutions provides relationship leverage solutions to more than 1,100 colleges and universities in 27 countries worldwide, representing more than 8 million students.

## SeniorSystems

*Bronze Level Affiliate*

15915 Katy Freeway
Suite 230
Houston, TX 77094
(877) 890-2583
Fax: (281) 398-1046
E-mail: info@bsmginc.com
Web: www.bsmginc.com

Richard Ellis, Sales/Marketing

Senior Systems is a Windows based, integrated, student information management system designed exclusively for independent schools. Modules include Admissions, Business Office, Registrar and Alumni Development.

## SPO America

*Bronze Level Affiliate*

650 Worcester Road
Framingham, MA 01701
(508) 875-9900
Fax: (508) 875-5177
E-mail: web@spo-us.com
Web: www.spo-us.com/npo/index.htm

Ruth Ann Fisher, Business Development Coordinator

SPO America is an international Software Solutions provider and Consulting firm, specializing in SAP's R/3 products. It became one of the first National Implementation Partners and participated in over 70 implementations nationwide. With the MFP Fundraising and Membership solution, SPO America introduces an extremely versatile R/3 based package which integrates many years of industry experience in the fundraising sector with the most powerful enterprise system in the world.

## SunGard BSR Inc.

*Gold Level Affiliate*

1000 Winter Street
Waltham, MA 02451
(781) 890-2105
Fax: (781) 890-4099
E-mail: Sales@sungardbsr.com
Web: ww.sungardbsr.com

Bonnie Burns, Marketing Communication Manager
Brad Goodman, SmartCall Account Executive
Geoff Knue, Senior Account Executive
Fred Weiss, Vice President, Sales & Marketing
James Werner, Senior Account Executive

SunGard BSR Inc. supports the advancement efforts of higher education and other not-for-profit organizations. Our client list numbers more than 140 major institutions worldwide.

- Advance: Establish, maintain, and manage relationships with friends, donors, and prospects.
- Advance Express: Get all the features of Advance in a turnkey system for streamlined implementation.
- SmartCall: Manage your call center for more successful telefundraising.
- Special Events: Plan and manage events more effectively.
- Web Access: Provide distributed access to your data on a "need-to-know" basis.
- Advance Web Community: Communicate more productively with your constituents.
- Services: Consulting, training, and outsourcing.

## Viking Systems, Inc.

*Bronze Level Affiliate*

236 Huntington Avenue
Boston, MA 02115
(617) 267-0011
Fax: (617) 425-0009
E-mail: rfrench@vikingsys.com
Web: www.vikingsys.com

Robert French, National Accounts Manager

Viking Systems, Inc. produces a powerful, flexible, full-featured, development system used in colleges and universities throughout the United States and Canada.

# Phone Number Lookup

## Executive Marketing Services, Inc.

*Silver Level Affiliate*

184 Shuman Blvd., Suite 300
Naperville, IL 60563-1258
(630) 355-3003
Fax: (630) 355-3090
E-mail: mhaumesser@emsphone.com
Web: www.emsphone.com

Karen Beechler, Business Development Manager
Fred Haumesser, Sales Executive
Monica Reimer, Marketing
Gretchen Rot, Major Accounts Manager

Executive Marketing Services specializes in telephone number lookups, mail processing services, and finding lost alumni. EMS has 13 years experience serving the college and university market.

# Prospect Management Systems

## Institutional Memory, Inc.

*Bronze Level Affiliate*

559 Solon Road
Chagrin Falls, OH 44022-3334
(440) 247-2957
Fax: (440) 247-7056
E-mail: lange@giftedmemory.com
Web: www.giftedmemory.com

Scott R. Lange, President

The GiftedMemory prospect management system organizes your major gift program. It serves as a companion to your gift accounting system to integrate research profiles with action plans and contact reports. You can even travel with Gifted Memory-Remote for instant access to your top prospects.

## JSI FundRaising Systems, Inc.

*Silver Level Affiliate*

4732 Longhill Road
Suite 2201
Williamsburg, VA 23188
(800) 574-5772
Fax: (757) 565-4546
E-mail: millen@jsifrs.com
Web: www.jsifrs.com/millennium

Farnsworth Street
Boston, MA 02210
(800) 521-0132
Fax: (617) 482-0617
Web: www.jsifrs.com/frs

Lori Combs, Sales Consultant
Blake Jacobson, Sales Consultant
Sabre Leek, Senior Consultant
Nancye Milam, Dir, Millennium Sales and Marketing
John Murphy, Dir of Marketing and Sales
Jeffery R. Shy, President
Susan Stewart-Kelley, Sales Consultant

JSI FundRaising, providing development information systems to non-profit organizations since 1978, offers two distinct products—Millennium and Paradigm.

Millennium—A comprehensive development information system designed to meet demanding and diverse development needs. Biographical, events, membership, gift and pledge information are integrated with a top prospect tracking system that includes features to manage all areas of the major gift process: research, ratings, interests, proposals, planned giving, and contact history. For campaign management, Millennium's idea (intuition-driven executive analysis) module incorporates the use of on-line analytical data analysis, drill-down reporting, mapping software, English Query Language tools, notification alerts of prospect and campaign activity and a Palm VII for accessing and/or downloading constituent database information. Choice of user interfaces: Windows or Browser and database engines: SQL Server or Oracle. For more information on Millennium, contact our Williamsburg office at (800) 574-5772 or millen@jsifrs.com.

Paradigm—the one with the Index Card design, effectively manages the needs of small to mid-sized development programs. The aesthetic index card and file folder design present information in a clean, efficient and familiar visual metaphor. Donor and prospect tracking, gift processing, mail merge, special

**Resource 10**

events, volunteer management, reporting, data import/export utilities and user-definable fields—everything you need at a price you can afford. Paradigm's on-line help, sample database and Getting Started tutorial will get most users up and running without any training. For more information on Paradigm, contact our Boston office at (800) 521-0132 or frs@jsifrs.com.

## PeopleSoft

*Silver Level Affiliate*

6903 Rockledge Drive
Suite 1100
Bethesda, MD 20817
(301) 571-5922
Fax: (301) 581-2133
E-mail: rachel_cayelli@peoplesoft.com
Web: www.peoplesoft.com

4460 Hacienda Drive
Pleasanton, CA 94588-8618
(925) 694-4010

Robb Eklund, Advancement Product Strategy
Laura King, Higher Education Marketing Dir
MichaelKohmescher, Product Strategy Manager
Karen Willett, Marketing Communication Higher Education

PeopleSoft Advancement is an integrated and comprehensive software solution for philanthropic and nonprofit management. PeopleSoft Advancement supports all your fundraising needs with eight functionally rich modules: Constituent Information, Gift and Pledge, Prospect Manager, Event Manager, Campaign Manager, Volunteer Manager, Membership Manager, and Planned Giving.

## SCT

*Silver Level Affiliate*

4 Country View Road
Malvern, PA 19355
(610) 647-5930
Fax: (610) 578-7564
Web: www.sctcorp.com

Jason Buckley, Sales Consultant
David Carey, Solutions Manager

Veronica Chappelle-McNair, Senior Consultant
Ed Hauser, General Manager Solutions Strategy
David Killip, Functional Consultant
Ron Rasmussen, Vice President of Sales

SCT enables colleges and universities around the world to achieve breakthrough results by leveraging key relationships with their students, prospects, alumni, faculty, donors, and other constituents. SCT Education Solutions provides relationship leverage solutions to more than 1,100 colleges and universities in 27 countries worldwide, representing more than 8 million students.

## SunGard BSR Inc.

### Gold Level Affiliate

1000 Winter Street
Waltham, MA 02451
(781) 890-2105
Fax: (781) 890-4099
E-mail: Sales@sungardbsr.com
Web: ww.sungardbsr.com

Bonnie Burns, Marketing Communication Manager
Brad Goodman, SmartCall Account Executive
Geoff Knue, Senior Account Executive
Fred Weiss, Vice President, Sales & Marketing
James Werner, Senior Account Executive

SunGard BSR Inc. supports the advancement efforts of higher education and other not-for-profit organizations. Our client list numbers more than 140 major institutions worldwide.

- Advance: Establish, maintain, and manage relationships with friends, donors, and prospects.
- Advance Express: Get all the features of Advance in a turnkey system for streamlined implementation.
- SmartCall: Manage your call center for more successful telefundraising.
- Special Events: Plan and manage events more effectively.
- Web Access: Provide distributed access to your data on a "need-to-know" basis.
- Advance Web Community: Communicate more productively with your constituents.
- Services: Consulting, training, and outsourcing.

## Prospect Research

### Bentz Whaley Flessner

*Gold Level Affiliate*

7251 Ohms Lane
Minneapolis, MN 55439
(952) 921-0111
Fax: (952) 921-0109
E-mail: bwf@bwf.com
Web: www.bwf.com

5272 River Road
Suite 500
Bethesda, MD 20816
(301) 656-7823
Fax: (301) 656-2156

Bob Burdenski, Senior Associate, Annual Giving
Diane R. Crane, Managing Associate, Systems & Technology
M. Bruce Dreon, Partner
Bruce W. Flessner, Principal
Karen L. Greene, Managing Associate, Prospect Research
Lisa Grissom, Senior Associate
Michael Hammerschmidt, Senior Associate
Sandra K. Kidd, VP for Institutional Advancement
William R. Lowery, Managing Associate
Jack F. McJunkin, Partner
Donna Merrell, Senior Associate
Ann Neitzel, Senior Associate
Bobbie J. Strand, Principal
William D. Tippie, Principal

Bentz Whaley Flessner's team of seasoned specialists offers a comprehensive range of services including advancement audits, feasibility studies and campaign implementation, prospect research and evaluation, electronic hardware and software analysis, and annual giving program analysis and planning and staff training. The integration of diverse advancement services and customized approaches to individual client requirements create productive partnerships. These are the kinds of relationships that promote clear understanding of institutional goals and the need for philanthropic dollars.

**Resource 10**

## Campbell Research

*Bronze Level Affiliate*

218 W Carmen Lane
Suite 110
Santa Maria, CA 93458
(888) 7Campbell
Fax: (805) 922-3909
E-mail: info@campbell-Research.com
Web: www.campbell-Research.com

Jim McGee, VP

The professionals at Campbell Research specialize in marketing research for colleges and non-profits. Maximize your marketing and fundraising potential by developing marketing intelligence about your constituents. Receive a customized research plan to reveal the attitudes, perceptions and motivations of your:

- Donors
- Prospective Students
- Current Students
- Parents
- Alumni
- Local Community
- Guidance Counselors

Campbell Research uses methods such as:

- Prospect Research
- Phone Surveys
- Mail Surveys
- Focus Groups
- Depth Interviews
- Competitive/Perception Analysis
- Interpretive Statistical Analyses

You receive results tempered by experience, as Campbell Research staff has aided dozens of colleges and universities. Campbell Research publishes *The College Report.*

## Community Counselling Service Co., Inc.

*Silver Level Affiliate*

350 Fifth Avenue, Suite 7210
New York, NY 10118
(212) 695-1175
Fax: (212) 967-6451
E-mail: ccsnewyork@ccsfundraising.com
Web: www.ccsfundraising.com

David Gallagher, VP
Thomas F. Hanrahan, Jr., VP
Frederic J. Happy, VP, Managing Dir, Western
Michael Infurnari, VP
Robert Kissane, Executive VP
Joseph F. X. Lee, VP
Patrick W. Moughan, President, Midwest
Carmel Napolitano, Dir of Research Services
Brian Nevins, VP
Robert B. Rice, VP
Dennick Skeels, VP

For over 50 years, CCS has provided fundraising counsel and management services to outstanding institutions of higher education worldwide.

Today, CCS is a leader in designing innovative campaigns to advance the mission of public and private colleges, universities, academic systems, and specialized research and training institutions.

With a permanent staff of more than 150 high skilled professionals, CCS can provide outside counsel, resident campaign management, and comprehensive support services include:

- Development audits
- Feasibility studies
- Strategic campaign planning
- Trustee orientation and development
- Capital campaign counsel and management
- Major gifts counsel
- Planned giving programs
- Annual giving
- Case statement development
- Development publications
- Electronic research services

## DataProse, Inc.
*Bronze Level Affiliate*

1451 N Rice Avenue, Suite A
Oxnard, CA 93030
(800) 927-7634
(805) 278-7430
Fax: (805) 278-7420
E-mail: bmurray@corp.dataprose.com
Web: www.dataprose.com

6012 Campus Circle Drive, Suite 260
Irving, TX 75063
(800) 876-5015
(972) 550-0190
Fax: (972) 550-8907

Bill Murray, VP, Sales

When your organization needs an ambitious direct marketing program, DataProse can help you reach your goals. We have helped hundreds of clients achieve results with cutting-edge technology, experience, know-how and superior service. All of which has earned us satisfied clients, repeat business and a reputation for providing fresh ideas and smart solutions. At DataProse, we offer a comprehensive range of services to fulfill your direct marketing needs, including consulting, database, and direct mail services. DataProse has offices in Los Angeles, Dallas, Seattle, Denver, San Francisco, and Ft. Lauderdale. Call (800) 927-7634 for the office in your area, or see us online at www.dataprose.com.

## Marts & Lundy, Inc.
*Silver Level Affiliate*

1200 Wall Street West
Lyndhurst, NJ 07071
(201) 460-1660
Fax: (201) 460-0680
E-mail: jolly@martsandlundy.com
Web: www.martsandlundy.com

Michael F. Sinkus, Chair
Charlie P. Howland, President
Richard T. Jolly, Vice President

Marts & Lundy's experienced staff of consultants offers counsel on development programs including capital campaigns; annual funds; planned giving; audits; studies; and prospect research, screening, and rating. ELECTRONIC SCREENING Prospect Identification Process with POTENTIAL PLUS is offered as a separate service.

## SunGard BSR Inc.

*Gold Level Affiliate*

1000 Winter Street
Waltham, MA 02451
(781) 890-2105
Fax: (781) 890-4099
E-mail: Sales@sungardbsr.com
Web: ww.sungardbsr.com

Bonnie Burns, Marketing Communication Manager
Brad Goodman, SmartCall Account Executive
Geoff Knue, Senior Account Executive
Fred Weiss, Vice President, Sales & Marketing
James Werner, Senior Account Executive

SunGard BSR Inc. supports the advancement efforts of higher education and other not-for-profit organizations. Our client list numbers more than 140 major institutions worldwide.

- Advance: Establish, maintain, and manage relationships with friends, donors, and prospects.
- Advance Express: Get all the features of Advance in a turnkey system for streamlined implementation.
- SmartCall: Manage your call center for more successful telefundraising.
- Special Events: Plan and manage events more effectively.
- Web Access: Provide distributed access to your data on a "need-to-know" basis.
- Advance Web Community: Communicate more productively with your constituents.
- Services: Consulting, training, and outsourcing.

**Resource 10**

## Special Events

### Adams Associates

*Bronze Level Affiliate*

Paoli Executive Green I
41 Leopard Road
Paoli, PA 19301-1549
(610) 407-4500
Fax: (610) 407-4504
E-mail: aapubrel@aol.com

Francis T. Adams III, VP of Production
Francis T. Adams Jr., President

For 37 years we have created innovative programs that significantly broaden development (especially annual giving), admissions, marketing, and communications activities. We conduct market research and manage outstanding special events, such as anniversaries, symposiums and inaugurations. Equally important, as a full service company, we provide cost effective visuals through graphic design, photography and video as individual or package projects. Call us about our exciting new full-motion interactive video technology for CD-ROM's.

### Consort Corporation

*Bronze Level Affiliate*

2129 Portage Road
Kalamazoo, MI 49001
(616) 388-4532
Fax: (616) 388-2018
E-mail: info@consortcorp.com
Web: www.consort.com

John May Jr., Vice President and General Manager

Consort Corporation manufactures KBW™ exterior and interior vertical banners, BannersFlex® light pole hardware, Messenger® PT BannerStands for exterior, and the Display One™ Exhibit System for interior use. *New Educational Partner*

### I.D.E.A.S. Inc.

*Bronze Level Affiliate*

340 W. 57th Street, Suite 9A
New York, NY 10019
(212) 246-9697

Fax: (212) 246-3703
E-mail: herson@attglobal.net
Web: www.ideasinc.org

M. J. Herson, President

I.D.E.A.S. Inc. creates and produces events and experiences that communicate great ideas for:

- Capital Campaigns
- Inaugurations
- Alumni Events
- Annual Meetings
- Reunions

Recent clients include: Duke, Harvard, Yale, Cornell, Chicago, University of Dayton, Trinity and Siena College. Our new division, LiveWiredEvent.com, designs live and interactive Internet events. *New Educational Partner*

## JSI FundRaising Systems, Inc.

*Silver Level Affiliate*

4732 Longhill Road
Suite 2201
Williamsburg, VA 23188
(800) 574-5772
Fax: (757) 565-4546
E-mail: millen@jsifrs.com
Web: www.jsifrs.com/millennium

Farnsworth Street
Boston, MA 02210
(800) 521-0132
Fax: (617) 482-0617
Web: www.jsifrs.com/frs

Lori Combs, Sales Consultant
Blake Jacobson, Sales Consultant
Sabre Leek, Senior Consultant
Nancye Milam, Dir, Millennium Sales and Marketing
John Murphy, Dir of Marketing and Sales
Jeffery R. Shy, President
Susan Stewart-Kelley, Sales Consultant

JSI FundRaising, providing development information systems to non-profit organizations since 1978, offers two distinct products—Millennium and Paradigm.

Millennium—A comprehensive development information system designed to meet demanding and diverse development needs. Biographical, events, membership, gift and pledge information are integrated with a top prospect tracking system that includes features to manage all areas of the major gift process: research, ratings, interests, proposals, planned giving, and contact history. For campaign management, Millennium's idea (intuition-driven executive analysis) module incorporates the use of on-line analytical data analysis, drill-down reporting, mapping software, English Query Language tools, notification alerts of prospect and campaign activity and a Palm VII for accessing and/or downloading constituent database information. Choice of user interfaces: Windows or Browser and database engines: SQL Server or Oracle. For more information on Millennium, contact our Williamsburg office at (800) 574-5772 or millen@jsifrs.com.

Paradigm—the one with the Index Card design, effectively manages the needs of small to mid-sized development programs. The aesthetic index card and file folder design present information in a clean, efficient and familiar visual metaphor. Donor and prospect tracking, gift processing, mail merge, special events, volunteer management, reporting, data import/export utilities and user-definable fields—everything you need at a price you can afford. Paradigm's on-line help, sample database and Getting Started tutorial will get most users up and running without any training. For more information on Paradigm, contact our Boston office at (800) 521-0132 or frs@jsifrs.com.

## Montreat Conference Center

*Bronze Level Affiliate*

402 Assembly Drive
PO Box 969
Montreat, NC 28757
(828) 669-2911
Fax: (828) 669-2779
E-mail: emiled@montreat.org
Web: www.montreat.org

Emile H. Dieth Jr., President

Montreat, a national Presbyterian Church (USA) conference center, offers a year-round schedule of conferences, as well as meeting, housing, dining and recreational facilities, comfortably accommodating groups as large as 1,250.

## StarLink Productions

*Bronze Level Affiliate*

6477 Almaden Expressway

Suite D2B4
San Jose, CA 95120
(408) 268-9688
Fax: (408) 268-9724
E-mail: k@starlinkproductions.com
Web: www.starlinkproductions.com

Katrina Sussmeier, Executive Producer

Make your fundraising concerts, golf tournaments, speaking events and personal appearance events as successful as possible!! StarLink will make sure you have the absolute lowest price for your celebrity and help you with sponsorship and event planning too! Everything from committee meetings to the event itself go great with StarLink! Make sure you make the most money you can! *New Educational Partner*

## SunGard BSR Inc.
### *Gold Level Affiliate*

1000 Winter Street
Waltham, MA 02451
(781) 890-2105
Fax: (781) 890-4099
E-mail: Sales@sungardbsr.com
Web: ww.sungardbsr.com

Bonnie Burns, Marketing Communication Manager
Brad Goodman, SmartCall Account Executive
Geoff Knue, Senior Account Executive
Fred Weiss, Vice President, Sales & Marketing
James Werner, Senior Account Executive

SunGard BSR Inc. supports the advancement efforts of higher education and other not-for-profit organizations. Our client list numbers more than 140 major institutions worldwide.

- Advance: Establish, maintain, and manage relationships with friends, donors, and prospects.
- Advance Express: Get all the features of Advance in a turnkey system for streamlined implementation.
- SmartCall: Manage your call center for more successful telefundraising.
- Special Events: Plan and manage events more effectively.
- Web Access: Provide distributed access to your data on a "need-to-know" basis.
- Advance Web Community: Communicate more productively with your constituents.
- Services: Consulting, training, and outsourcing.

# RESOURCE 11

## ESTIMATING NET WORTH

# ESTIMATING NET WORTH:
# ONE ORGANIZATION'S SEARCH FOR TRUTH

Several months ago, the Research Department here at the University of Virginia decided to take a closer look at how we estimated an individual's net worth. Although many in our field will agree that an accurate determination of net worth is impossible (and some believe futile), here at Virginia we find it to be a necessary step in our attempts to segregate our exceptionally large database of prospects. By calculating potential gift capability based on the total known assets of an individual, we are able to assign to each a rating, ranging from $10,000 to $10 million plus. These ratings then allow us to provide a more selective solicitation strategy that is appropriate to the gift range into which each prospect falls.

For several years prior we relied upon two very straightforward formulas to arrive at these ratings. If stockholdings were an individual's largest asset, the following would apply:

Total known direct stock holdings $\times$ (1–3) = estimated net worth
5% of estimated net worth = estimated gift capability

We felt comfortable with this formula. By using a multiplier of anywhere from 1 to 3, the researcher was able to use her/his discretion as to how many unknown assets the prospect probably owned. If we believed that we had found the majority of an individual's assets, we multiplied his/her holdings by a lower number. If we felt that what we had found was just the tip of the iceberg (i.e., the prospect was a private investor), we applied a multiplier of 3. We chose to leave this formula as it was.

The problem, in our eyes, was in determining a prospect's net worth based solely on his/her real estate holdings. Our old formula for this situation was as follows:

Total real estate holdings $\times$ 5 = estimated net worth
5% of estimated net worth = estimated giving capability

While we felt that we were getting fairly accurate numbers for individuals with large real estate holdings, we believed that those with houses assessed at lower values were receiving disproportionately high ratings. Can a Professor of Architecture with a $200,000 house really afford a gift of $50,000?

In an effort to discover how our formulas for arriving at net worth compared to those of our colleagues around the country, we posted a query on PRSPCT-L. The results were quite varied and included the following:

20 × level of consistent annual giving = giving ability (over 5-year period)

10% of annual income = giving ability (over 5 years)

.5%–1.5% of liquid assets = giving ability

5% of total known assets (real estate + stock holdings +
annual income for 5 years) = giving ability (5 years)

However, after applying these formulas to examples from our database, we found that none of the above were truly feasible for us. Unless our prospect was listed on a proxy, we usually did not have his/her annual income or stockholdings. In fact, 75%–80% of the time, real estate holdings are our only source on which to base our estimates.

So we turned in a different direction. By far the most popular source recommended to us for determining net worth was an article by Rob Millar, Director of Development Services at Boston College, titled "How Much Is That Donor in Your Records?" (*Case Currents,* July/August 1995). The solution provided in this article was attractive to us for a number of reasons.

To begin, it suggests a formula based upon statistical averages obtained from the Internal Revenue Service. Compiled into percentage tables, these averages represent a breakdown of total assets drawn from tax returns for deceased individuals with estates of $600,000 or higher in 1989. This study determined what percentage each asset was of the total net worth of the estate, on average. Different percentages are also provided for estates of varying sizes. To use the tables, you simply plug in the asset you are working with and calculate a net worth.

Here is an example: you know that your prospect has real estate valued at $200,000. Looking at the table, you see that for an individual whose estate falls between $600,000–$1 million, real estate will, on the average, comprise 27.6% of his/her overall wealth. If $200,000 is 27.6% of your prospect's wealth, then she/he has an estimated net worth of $724,638 ($200,000/.276).

But once again, after applying several case studies from our database to these tables, we found that our initial problems remained unresolved. While the estimates obtained from this table initially seemed reasonable, it made no provision for individuals with estates of less than $600,000, a category into which a number of our prospects fell. Also, we were bothered by the fact that the table was based upon statistics from 1989. The Dow Jones Index has quadrupled since 1989, a fact that could dramatically alter the average amount of an individual's stockholdings in relation to his/her overall wealth. This, alone, was enough to make us wary.

In the end, we chose to improvise. Because our estimates for wealthier individuals were comparable to, if not more conservative than, those arrived at by several of the formulas used by other institutions, we decided to address only the issue of prospects with lower real estate holdings. The University of Virginia, currently in a capital campaign, is focusing its efforts on major gift prospects (gifts of $100,000 and above). We therefore drew the line at real estate holdings of $400,000 and above. Those falling in this category, based upon our old formulas (5 × real estate = net worth and 5% of net worth = gift capability), were qualified as major gift prospects, and we felt fairly confident of their capability to give.

We took a closer look at our prospects that fell below the $400,000 mark. We compared the original ratings that we had assigned to these prospects based upon real estate to the actual amounts they eventually gave. We decided that our best alternative would be to lower our multiplier to 3 for those with property totaling less than $400,000:

$$\text{Total real estate holdings} \times 3 = \text{estimated net worth}$$
$$3\% \text{ of estimated net worth} = \text{estimated giving capability}$$

These figures presented a much more accurate reflection of wealth and ability at this level than our previous numbers.

It was a long journey, but an important one. Although estimating net worth for individuals is still a nebulous practice at best, it is still a necessary one for many organizations. The solution ultimately adopted by the University of Virginia will undoubtedly not be appropriate for all, but I hope that our process of reaching it will prove helpful and informative to those of you who are facing similar challenges.

*Source:* Angela Vaughan, Senior Development Researcher, University of Virginia, January 1998. Copyright 1998 The Rector and Visitors of the University of Virginia. This article was initially published in the Winter 1998 issue of the official publication of the Virginia APRA.

# RESOURCE 12

## WEB-BASED RESEARCH

**It's All Out There . . .**

*I need everything there is about Bob Jones. It's all out there on the web somewhere, right? Just pull it together for me by tomorrow.*

No one reading this newsletter would make (or accept) such an ill-considered request; however, here's a strategy for finding "it all" on the web. As an added bonus, everything here is a free site (although some may require you to register, and some may offer "premium" services for a fee), and they are all public records or published information.

Here's what I would do first if I got that request:

• Breathe into a brown paper bag, and
• Find out what you can from the requestor about why they think Bob Jones is a potential prospect.

With some luck, they already know something—where Bob lives or where he works. If they know nothing other than his name and, presumably, his likelihood of caring about your cause, then I offer some strategies at the end of the article. Let's be optimistic first, and assume you have some basic leads to follow. You know his address—what can you find out about him? You can almost certainly establish whether he owns or rents, how much the property is worth, what it has sold for, and when it sold. County assessors are increasingly on-line. Go to http://pubweb/acns.nwu.edu/~cap440/assess.html for a list of assessors sorted by state, then by county. It also provides phone and fax numbers. Locally, having a prospect in Greene County is a bonus. Go to http://www.co.greene.oh.us/ gismapserver.htm where you can search by address or by owner and get back a wealth of detail (down to the number of bathrooms). Finding out an address's county is essential for using assessors successfully, and it's easy to find—ask the Post Office at http://www.usps.gov/ncsc/lookups/lookups.htm. With a zip code or partial address, they'll return full mailing information (including carrier codes and ZIP+4 which can be useful to those with access to marketing information) and the county in which the address is.

If the county assessor is not on-line, and you don't want to call or fax them, there is an alternative: web-based real estate tools are common, but are less reliable and may be out of date. The classic site is http://realestate.yahoo.com/ realestate/homevalues/ which lets you search by exact address, street address ranges (e.g. everyone on the block), and price range (e.g. all sales in Dayton over $250,000). Don't forget to search Florida and South Carolina for holiday homes.

If you know where Bob works, his employer's website is a great starting point. More often than not, simply typing www.bobscompanyname.com will get you there. If not, some browsers, Netscape for example, will return a list of near matches, and it's very likely to have what you need there. If not, a quick trip to your favorite search engine should solve the problem. Try Yahoo.com, your browser's own home site, www.askjeeves.com, www.google.com, http://www.altavista.com/, and many more. I personally like www.dogpile.com because it searches a variety of other engines and compiles their results for you. Also excellent and fast is www.ragingsearch.com—no extraneous material, and results without ads. General search techniques could fill a book, so I suggest you go to www.about.com and check out their Internet articles; however, four quick tips that help me on-line are

- Know what search parameters your chosen engine uses. Click on their tips button to see what they want. Some are more user-friendly than others and let you use intuitive language, symbols (+ or &), or phrases in quotations; others want strict Boolean.
- Once at a site, use the site map—who knows where a webmaster decides is the right place for the info you want? Clicking on their site map reveals their filing hierarchy and lets you click straight to your area.
- Using Netscape, once at a promising site, click the button labeled "What's Related" for an instant list of other sites to explore.
- Bookmark sites you find useful, and organize the bookmark folder into sub-directories. Bookmark names are often opaque, so filing them in an appropriate directory (e.g. real estate resources, local companies, search engines) can rescue you from fruitless clicking.

Back to bobscompany.com—once at the site, you can try a variety of techniques depending on the type of company and his position. A megacorp's site may be so generic and vast that Bob isn't going to show up unless he's the CEO, but you can get a feel for how he earns his bread. If Bob ranks highly, go to "investor relations" which will get you their annual report (on-line or downloadable—getting a free copy of Acrobat Reader is vital) and corporate compensation and director bios. A search of their PR archive may get the announcement of his hiring or promotion—these usually contain education and career histories, which give you yet more leads to follow on the web. A smaller private company site often includes the history of the company and/or the founding family.

For information about companies try Hoovers (http://hoovweb.hoovers.com/) or for more financial information on public companies, visit the SEC at http://people.edgar-online.com/people/ where you can search for insider trading, IPOs, and their major filings. If Bob's a director, his stock holdings will show up here. Going to a career site such as www.nationjob.com will often give a summary of the company's own take on themselves. Two sites that are great starting points are www.business.com and http://www.ceoexpress.com.

Bob's not a corporate type? If Bob's a professional, run a search (at www.ask jeeves.com for example) to find his professional, or accrediting, organization, which may maintain searchable lists of its members. For example, the AMA gives details about areas of specialization and which medical school a doctor attended. (Go to http://www.ama-assn.org and choose Doctor Finder.) If Bob requires a license from the state to practice, the state site will often provide information. In Ohio, accountants, architects, dentists, doctors, nurses, optometrists, social workers, engineers, and more are at http://www.state.oh.us/ohio/license.htm.

Whatever Bob does, you'll want to know how much he earns. There's a variety of salary sites to look at. Try www.salary.com or http://www.jobsmart.org/tools/salary/sal-surv.htm. Feeling brave? Try the Department of Labor's Occupational Outlook Handbook: http://stats.bls.gov/ocohome.htm.

After this searching, you may know where Bob went to school. His alma mater's site is likely to have an alumni section, have an internal search function, or have a searchable set of press releases. If Bob is a notable alumnus, you may well find some excellent material here.

Need to know his political affiliation? Donations reported to the FEC are at http://www.tray.com/fecinfo/_indiv.htm. As a bonus, you can click to an image of the filing form that often shows a donor's home address and employer.

Newspapers and local community sites are indispensable: Business News not only has a Dayton edition at http://www.bizjournals.com/dayton (which lets you hunt through its archives for free), but it also lets you link to its other markets nationwide. Suburban Newspapers of Dayton gives a good local look at our community-level newspapers: http://www.sndnews.com/. Likewise, look at Active Dayton: http://www.activedayton.com—in particular their lists of the top local companies under http://www.activedayton.com/business/localbusiness/mv100/ (for public companies) or http://www.activedayton.com/business/localbusiness/mv50/ (for private companies). To find equivalent sites by region, and all the news sites you could ever want: http://gwis2.circ.gwu.edu/~gprice/newscenter.htm.

What can you do if your requestor knows nothing other than "Bob Jones gave money to XYZ so I'm sure he'll like ABC." If they can't give you an employer, a home address, or some strong lead to his whereabouts, then the reasons for their request become a) suspect, and b) essential in your quest, as they'll shape your search strategy. For example, if Bob is on their radar because of his membership in other organizations, or giving to a particular cause, then surfing over to those organizations' sites may well be your best starting point. For example, The Dayton Foundation (www.daytonfoundation.org) lets you download their annual reports.

If you have no address for Bob, try http://www.555-1212.com. This offers some of the best techniques for finding an address, including a reverse look-up (for when you have just a phone number). Another good choice is http://www.whohere.lycos.com/. An obvious problem with "Bob Jones" is his name. If you know nothing else about him, you do have a problem, but one technique is to search for his spouse (with any luck, she's called Eudoxia) and hope to track him down that way. Knowing another family member's name can be a vital cross check.

There are myriad sites out there of varying usefulness and reliability: to check a site's reliability, run a search on yourself and see what turns up. As a last resort (and often one that renews faith in serendipity), go to a general search engine (see sites suggested under searching for www.bobscompany.com), enter "Bob Jones," and see what kind of gold pans out from your prospecting. Perhaps you'll find the perfect link that begins "Bob Jones has his own university. . . ."

For more information, or refutation, please e-mail sarah.mcginley@wright.edu. Sarah McGinley is a research analyst at Wright State University.

*August 2000*

# RESOURCE 13

## RESEARCH PROFILE FORMATS

# NORTHWESTERN UNIVERSITY

**CHARTER TRUSTEE**
*(if applicable)*

### Confidential—for Internal Use Only
**PROSPECT RESEARCH PROFILE**
December 14, 2000

Presidential Prospect
*(if Trustee)*

Preferred Reunion Year: 20xx
*(sometimes people have a
preference for a reunion year
other than the one in which
they graduated)*

| Prospect | NU School/Year | ID NO |
|---|---|---|
| **JOHN Q. PROSPECT** | WCAS 'xx | A00000000 |
| Spouse: Jane Prospect (nee: Doe) | WCAS 'xx | A00000001 |

**BORN:** *Full name—date of birth, in City, State*

**EDUCATION:**

| School/Year | Degree (Major) |
|---|---|
| NU WCAS 'xx | BA (Basket weaving) |
| oe's College 'xx | MBA |

**NU Selected Student Activities**
National Basket Weaving Society
Debate Team
Alpha Beta Chi (social fraternity)

**HOME:**
*Home Street*
*Home City, State Zip*
*Home phone number; Home fax number*
*(note if not verifiable through Directory Assistance)*
*Personal e-mail address*
*Include second/summer home, if applicable*

**BUSINESS:**
*Title, Business Name, Business Street*
*Business City, State Zip*
*Business phone; Business fax*
*Business e-mail address*

**FAMILY FOUNDATIONS:**
*John Q. and Jane Prospect Foundation*
*Address, phone*
*Any historical, asset, or giving history information available*
*Foundation phone; Foundation fax*

JOHN Q. PROSPECT
December 14, 2000
Page 2

## BUSINESS BACKGROUND & CORPORATE OR FOUNDATION AFFILIATIONS

| Date | Affiliations |
| --- | --- |
| 19xx–present | Mr. Widget Manufacturing, the nation's largest widget manufacturer (1999 sales $1 million billion), 4000 employees |

- President (19xx–xx)
- Vice president of operations (19xx–xx)
- Manager, Northeast sales (19xx–xx)

Mr. Widget Manufacturing was founded by Mrs. Prospect's grandfather, Joe Doe, and was on the verge of bankruptcy when Mr. Prospect became VP of operations; he spearheaded a reorganization which helped the company become "one of the hottest manufacturing concerns in the nation" according to *Forbes* in 1998. Local trade papers have recently mentioned that Mr. Prospect is expected to gradually relinquish control of day-to-day duties to his executive vice president, (Joe Blow, NU L 'xx) and Mr. Prospect will probably be named Chairman by 2001, Mr. Blow succeeding him as President.

A 19xx article noted that Mr. Widget Manufacturing had been investigated by the US House Intelligence Committee due to the company's sale of widgets to Iraq, which might have had connections to arms manufacturing. The company's former president and Mr. Prospect's predecessor, Michael Smith, had stepped down because of a scandal involving this investigation and its connection to his service with a US government corporation. The Committee investigation remains classified and no action has been taken since it occurred.

| 19xx–xx | Some Other Company |
| --- | --- |

- Salesman

| 19xx–xx | United States Army |
| --- | --- |

Mr. Prospect sits on the board of the Mr. Widget Foundation, Widget International, Widget Byproduct Company, and Guns and Butter, Inc.

## CIVIC AND PROFESSIONAL AFFILIATIONS AND AWARDS

| Date | Civic Affiliations |
| --- | --- |
| 19xx | Lyric Opera of Nowhere |
| 19xx | Nowhere Zoo |
| 19xx | Nowhere Symphony Orchestra |

Resource 13

**JOHN Q. PROSPECT**
December 14, 2000
Page 3

| Date | Professional Affiliations |
|------|---------------------------|
| Since 19xx | Widgetmakers of America (chairman 19xx–xx) |

| Date | Awards |
|------|--------|
| 19xx | Golden Widget (Widgetmakers of America) |
| 19xx | Nowhere's Most Prominent Businessman (Nowhere Chamber of Commerce) |

## FAMILY MEMBERS

**Father:**     *(family members, names and any historical information, including*
**Mother:**     *date and place of birth, schools attended, marriage dates, occupations,*
**Spouse:**     *relationships to NU, etc.)*
**Children:**
**Siblings:**
**Other:**

## INDICATIONS OF WEALTH

**Most Recent Salary/Family Income:**

Alumni Questionnaire/Annual Income Survey:     *(if available, latest reported income range from alumni surveys)*

Other: *(any other indications, such as articles about compensation, information from proxy statements, rules of thumb for professions, American Almanac of Jobs and Salaries)*

**Current Stock Holdings, per Mr. Widget proxy filed 3/11/99:**

*Company (date of last transaction)—shares held—direct [D]/indirect[I] × close/open price [date] = Total*

Widget Int'l—2,000[D] × $33.43 [12/14/00] = $66,860
Widget Int'l—1,000[I]

**Per Thomson Financial**

Guns and Butter Inc. (7/20/98)—1,000[D] × $75 [12/14/00] = $75,000

**Other Stock Holdings:**

Mr. and Mrs. Prospect reportedly own 95% of the capital stock of Mr. Widget Manufacturing.

—— **CONFIDENTIAL** ——
*FOR INTERNAL USE ONLY*

**JOHN Q. PROSPECT**
December 14, 2000
Page 4

## Other:

*Information about net worth from magazines, value of real estate holdings, large gifts to other charities, family wealth of note, "interests of wealth" such as yachting, or other information pointing to significant wealth, such as kidnappings for ransom (I'm not making this up) etc.*

### GIVING ABILITY

### Range

Annual: $*(usually from giving to date)*
Major (3–5 years): $ *(usually from 10% of income, 10–15% of stockholdings,
        15% of real estate, other formulae)*
Ultimate: $(bequest, entire estate, if applicable)

### Lifetime Giving (c 1988):

Peer ratings from 1988 program

### Peer Ratings (c 1998):

Peer ratings from 1997–98 program

### Development Ratings:

Ratings by Development staff

### Rationale:

*Explanation of the factors that went into the researchers' estimation of their giving ability ranges. For example, if a prospect has mentioned that they're very committed to his/her spouse's old school or charity, or that they didn't like giving to higher ed, but they might give to NU in a smaller amount; or if their business is in transition; basically, where the numbers come from.*

### SELECTED ACTIVE PLEDGES AND GIFTS TO THE UNIVERSITY

*FILLED IN AS NECESSARY AND AVAILABLE, all other sections deleted*

*Selected Active Individual Pledges*

| Pledge Date | Amount | Purpose | Balance Due |
|---|---|---|---|
| | 0 | | 0 |
| | 0 | $ | 0 |

—— **CONFIDENTIAL** ——
*FOR INTERNAL USE ONLY*

Resource 13

**JOHN Q. PROSPECT**
December 14, 2000
Page 5

*Selected Individual Gifts*

| Total Amount | # of Gifts | FY | Purpose |
|---|---|---|---|
| $ 0 | 0 | | |
| $ 0 | 0 | | |

*Selected Active Corporation Pledges*

| Pledge Date | Amount | Purpose | Balance Due |
|---|---|---|---|
| | 0 | | 0 |

*Selected Corporation Gifts*

| Total Amount | # of Gifts | FY | Purpose |
|---|---|---|---|
| $ 0 | 0 | | |

*Selected Active Foundation Pledges*

| Pledge Date | Amount | Purpose | Balance Due |
|---|---|---|---|
| | 0 | | 0 |

*Selected Foundation Gifts*

| Total Amount | # of Gifts | FY | Purpose |
|---|---|---|---|
| $ 0 | 0 | | |

*Matching Gift Company Connections*

*Are they affiliated with a matching gift company, and if so, how much does the company match and at what ratio?*

*Total Contributions to NU:*

| | | |
|---|---|---|
| John Q Prospect: | $ | 0 |
| Jane Prospect: | $ | 0 |
| J&J Prospect Fdn: | $ | 0 |
| **GRAND TOTAL** | $ | 0 |

**CURRENT AND SIGNIFICANT NU MEMBERSHIPS AND AWARDS**

| Date | Membership/Award |
|---|---|
| Since 19xx | John Evans Club |
| 19xx | WCAS Visiting Committee |

—— **CONFIDENTIAL** ——
*FOR INTERNAL USE ONLY*

**JOHN Q. PROSPECT**
December 14, 2000
Page 6

## PERSONAL RELATIONSHIPS

| Name | Tie |
|------|-----|
| Joe Blue (L 'xx) | Executive vice president of Mr. Widget under Mr. Prospect |
| Jim Nobody (WCAS 'xx) | Mr. Prospect's roommate at NU |
| Jill Nobody (WCAS 'xx) | Mrs. Widget's roommate at Joe's Law School |
| Professor Science | NU Professor invited to make presentation on manufacturing processes at Mr. Widget |

## NU AREAS OF INTEREST

Athletics, Library, WCAS *(alphabetized, unless there's a clear priority of interests)*

## DEVELOPMENT CONTACT

*Most Recent 3 Years*

- *Month, year—Development Staff Member did thus and so to contact Mr. Prospect, and learned thus and so information and had thus and so results*
- *Etc., etc.*

*Other Previous Significant Contact*

- 

## NOTES

Resource 13

## Most Current Reunion Survey/Alumni Questionnaire Ratings

Mr. -[Survey/Questionnaire]:
    Ranked NU:
    Evaluated NU Education:
    Characterized Attitude About NU:
    Noted:

—— **CONFIDENTIAL** ——
*FOR INTERNAL USE ONLY*

**JOHN Q. PROSPECT**
December 14, 2000
Page 7


Mrs. -[Survey/Questionnaire]:
    Ranked NU:
    Evaluated NU Education:
    Characterized Attitude About NU:
    Noted:

## Outside Interests

Sailing, racquetball. Mr. and Mrs. Prospect have also expressed an interest in attending every basket weaving conference in the country in their Winnebago. They also enjoy rehabbing homes. Mrs. Prospect is a self-described "health nut."

## Research Analysis

*A summary of salient points in this report, including information about wealth and attitudes toward NU and anything that might affect the prospect's giving and mindset about NU, what to expect. The place for narrative if something just doesn't fit into any of the above categories perfectly.*

**Researcher:**    *Who wrote this*
**Requested by:**    *Who asked for it (Research, if proactive)*

## CURRENT PROSPECT ASSIGNMENTS

*All this is as reported in our prospect management system in BSR Advance*

**Primary Officer:**
**Secondary Officer:**
**PMG:**
**Other:**

**or:**

******Not Currently Assigned******

**PMG Territory Officer:**

**CURRENT PROSPECT STAGE:**

# COLORADO UNIVERSITY FOUNDATION

## CUF RESEARCH CORPORATE PROFILE

### —Confidential—

**CORPORATE NAME:**                                        CID#:
Address:
Telephone:                                                          Fax:
E-mail Address:
Website Address:

CEO—Name and Title:

Business Description:

Financial Information:

Officers & Directors:

Corporate History:

Corporate Giving to CU:
Lifetime Giving:
Total Giving FY (present year) – all campuses:
Outstanding Pledges and Designations – all campuses:
Largest Gift and Designation:
Top 5 or 6 Total Giving Designations and Amounts:

Non-CU Philanthropic Interests:
Known Corporate Relationships with CU:
Alumni/Friends:
Departmental:
Development Staff:
Faculty:
Project:

Cultivation Highlights:

Recent Noteworthy Events:

**FOUNDATION NAME:**                    CID#:
Address:
Telephone:                    Fax:
E-mail Address:
Website Address:

Contact:

Purpose:

Limitations:

Foundation Type:

Interest and Support Areas:

Financial Data:

Officers & Directors:

Policies & Guidelines:

Foundation Giving to CU:

Known Relationships with CU:
Alumni/Friends:
Departmental:
Development Staff:
Faculty:
Project:

Cultivation Highlights:

Recent Noteworthy Events:

**NAME:**                                                     CID#:
CU Campus/Year/School or College/Major:
Home Address:                                    Business Address:
Phone:
E-mail Address:


Employment Information:
Current:
Career History:


Corporate Directorships:
Current:
Previous:


Non-Profit Affiliations:


CU Activities and Affiliations:
As a student:
As an alumnus/non-alumnus:
Awards and honors:


Cultivation Highlights:


Noteworthy Relationships:


Non-CU Philanthropic Interests:

Giving to CU:
Lifetime giving total:          Last Gift:                    Date:
Largest single gift/pledge:
Years of giving:
Areas of support/interest:

Known Assets:
Bonus:                          Source:                       Date:
Household income:               Source:                       Date:
Property:                       Source:                       Date:
Salary:                         Source:                       Date:
Securities:                     Source:                       Date:
Stock Options:                  Source:                       Date:

Known Liabilities:

Ratings:
Campaign:                       Source:                       Date:
Lifetime:                       Source:                       Date:
Net Worth:                      Source:                       Date:
Peer:                           Source:                       Date:
PPR:                            Source:                       Date:
Readiness:                      Source:                       Date:
Real Estate:                    Source:                       Date:
Research:                       Source:                       Date:
Securities:                     Source:                       Date:
Staff:                          Source:                       Date:
Wealth Estimate:                Source:                       Date:
(CDA Wealth Estimate is not considered reliable as a major gift rating.)

Financial Summary:

Personal Information:
Birthdate:                      Place:
Non-CU Education:
Family:     Spouse
            Children
            Others
Interests/Hobbies:
Other:

Comments/Recommendations/Miscellaneous:

# RESOURCE 14

## WALL STREET TERMINOLOGY YOU NEED TO KNOW

Resource 14

# GLOSSARY OF WALL STREET TERMS

## Directly Held Stock

When an individual owns stock directly, they have sole voting and investment powers of over their shares including the authority to gift the shares.

## Indirectly Held Stock

When an individual owns stock indirectly, they share the voting and/or investment power. It is very important to investigate whether the individual has access to these shares before including them in an analysis of their financial capability. Shares owned by family members, foundations, trusts, and pension plans are examples of shares claimed by individuals as indirectly owned by them.

## Restricted Stock

Restricted Stock is stock which has been acquired in a non-public transaction and has not been registered with the SEC. Companies are increasingly providing their top management and directors with grants of restricted stock. Unlike options, where the individual must buy the stock before owning it, restricted stock is given to the individual at no cost. Like an option, the individual must wait a period of time (at least one year) before gaining voting and investment powers over the shares. When the shares are sold they are subject to Rule 144 (Intention To Sell) filing requirements. While the individual does not own the stock, he or she does receive any dividend income produced by the shares while they are restricted. An individual that receives Restricted Stock may elect to pay taxes on the stock based on the market value on the day it was granted. The market value becomes the cost-basis for any future gains. If the taxes are not paid, then the tax liability occurs at the time the restrictions are lifted. Some companies pay the tax obligation for their executives and directors.

## Bonds

Bonds are promissory notes or IOUs issued by a corporation or government to its lenders. They are usually issued in multiples of $1,000 or $5,000, although $100 and $500 denominations are available.

A bond is evidence of a debt on which the issuing company usually promises to pay the bondholders a specified amount of interest for a specified length of time, and to repay the loan on the expiration date. In every case a bond represents debt—its holder is a creditor of the corporation and not a part owner as is the shareholder.

## Convertible Bonds

Convertible Bonds are a hybrid of bonds and stocks. They offer the fixed-interest income of bonds and the price appreciation potential of stocks. Owners of Convertible Bonds can convert them into the stock of the issuing company at a pre-determined price.

The terms of the Convertible Bond specify how many shares of stock the bond can be converted for.

## Warrants

Warrants give you the right to buy a share of common stock for a specified price within a specified time. Warrants usually have five, ten or twenty year expiration dates. There are also some "perpetual" warrants which have no expiration date.

The warrant's exercise price is set well above the stock price at the time it is issued. For this reason warrants sell for a fraction of the cost of stocks, with many under $5 each. Warrant owners are speculating that the stock will rise above the exercise price before the warrant expires.

Warrants offer both a larger potential for gain and a larger potential for loss. They offer no current income in the form of interest or dividends from the underlying stock.

## Preferred Stock

Stockholders who own Preferred Stock are given preferential treatment over Common Stock owners. Preferences include having dividends distributed to them before other stockholders and in the event of the issuing company being liquidated. Preferred Stockholders are entitled to receive compensation first. Many companies issue Preferred Stock with special rights for major shareholders that enable them to stop an unfriendly take-over.

Resource 14

## Options

Options are the most common form of non-salary/benefit executive compensation. The net value of an option is the difference between the exercise price and the current market price.

There are two dominant types of options granted: Non-Qualified and Incentive Stock Options. When an individual exercises a Non-Qualified option he or she incurs a tax liability (amounting to the difference between the exercise price and market price) on the day of the exercise whether or not the underlying shares are sold or held. When Incentive Stock Options are exercised the tax liability is incurred only when the underlying shares are ultimately sold.

# U.S. SECURITIES AND EXCHANGE COMMISSION (SEC) TERMS

## Fund-Raising and Prospect Research Applications

As a development professional, why should I use these documents?

- SEC corporate files are open to the public.
- Several types of documents contain a record of what public company *officers and directors* earn each year, including:

  salary
  bonus
  stock awards and incentives
  options
  retirement benefits
  and other forms of compensation, such as low-interest loans.

- Certain documents disclose the securities-based holdings of *beneficial owners and affiliated people* and entities, including *spouses and family trusts*.
- Some documents contain:

  biographical information
  career histories
  professional affiliations
  and charitable affiliations

  for corporate officers and directors.

## Annual Reports to Shareholders

The familiar glossy, often illustrated annual reports are not required, official SEC filings. Consequently, companies have considerable license in what types and amounts of information the report can contain and how it is presented. The SEC does, however, require an annual report known as a 10-K.

### 10-K

The annual disclosure provides a comprehensive overview of the registrant (publicly traded company). The report must be filed within 90 days after the close of the company's fiscal year. Covers:

I.  principal businesses, products, services, markets and distribution;
    top divisional and subsidiary officers;
    locations and facilities;
    legal proceedings pending;
    matters pending vote by stockholders;
II. market for registrant's Common Stock;
    financial performance data; covers five years;
    management's analysis of financial data and results of operations;
    audited two-year balance sheets, three-year statements of income, and
        statement of cash flow;
III.* name, office, term and background on each director and executive officer;
    remuneration of directors and officers;
    security ownership of beneficial owners of 5 percent or more of a
        registrant's stock;
    amount and percent of each class of stock and options held by officers and
        directors;
    relationships and related transactions, including loans to officers and
        directors;
IV. complete, audited annual financial information and a list of accompanying
    exhibits filed; also, any unscheduled material events and corporate
    changes not filed in an 8-K during reported fiscal year.

## *Proxy Statements

A proxy statement officially notifies designated classes of shareholders of matters to be brought to vote, generally at the shareholders annual meeting. Proxy votes are solicited for items such as changing company officers and directors.

Executive compensation and stock ownership disclosures normally made by proxy statement may in some instances be made using Part III of Form 10-K.*

## 20-F

The Annual Report/Registration Statement, filed by foreign issuers of securities trading in the U.S., covers most categories found in 10-K's, including directors, officers and their respective compensation packages.

# Periodic Reports

## 8-K

Reports on corporate changes and unscheduled material events considered important to shareholders or to the SEC. 8-K's must be filed within 5 to 15 days of an event. Covers:

changes of control of registrant;
acquisition or disposition of assets;
bankruptcy or receivership;
changes in registrant's certifying accountant;
other materially important events;
resignation of registrant's directors;
financial statements and exhibits;
changes in fiscal year.

## 10-Q

This is an unaudited quarterly financial report filed by most companies. 10-Q's must be filed within 45 days after the end of each fiscal year quarter. Also covers:

legal proceedings;
changes in securities;
defaults on payments;
voting matters;
other materially significant events.

## Tender Offer/Acquisition Reports

### 13-D

13-D's are required for equity owners of 5 percent or more within 10 days of acquisition. Covers:

  security and issuer:
  identity and background of person(s) filing statement;
  source and amount of funds;
  purpose of transaction;
  interest in securities of the issuer;
  contracts, arrangements or relationships with respect to securities
    of the issuer.

### 14-D1

A tender offer filing made with the SEC at the time an offer is made to holders of equity securities of the target company, if acceptance of the offer would give the bidder over 5 percent ownership of the subject securities.

### 13-E3

Statement of public company or affiliate going private.

## Security Holdings by Insiders and Institutions

### 13-F

A quarterly report of equity holdings required of all institutions with equity assets of $100 million or more. This includes banks, insurance companies, investment firms, investment advisors and large internally managed endowments, foundations and pension funds.

### 13-G

An annual filing which must be filed by all reporting persons (primarily institutions) meeting the 5 percent equity ownership rule within 45 days after the end of each calendar year. Covers:

name and address of issuer;
identification of reporting person(s);
amount of shares beneficially owned;
percent of class outstanding;
sole or shared voting power;
sole or shared power of disposition;
ownership of 5 percent or less of a class of stock;
ownership of more than 5 percent on behalf of another person.

## FORM 3

Initial statement which identifies holdings of company's securities owned by directors, officers and 10 percent shareholders. A Form 3 must be filed within 10 days after the transaction.

Form 3 is also required for anyone becoming an insider whether or not they own stock.

## FORM 4

Amendment to Form 3 reporting a disposition (sale or gift) or acquisition of a company's securities. A Form 4 must be filed by the 10th day of the month following the month during which the transaction occurred.

Form 4 also records the actual granting and schedule of options to an insider.

## FORM 5

New as of May 1, 1991, Form 5 is a required annual filing which reflects stock gifts, splits and options. Form 5's also include an exit notice indicating when an insider is no longer an insider with the registrant firm.

## FORM 144

Notice of Proposed Sale of (Restricted) Securities lists the stockholder's broker and often a secondary address which could be the insider's home or other previously unknown address.

# Registration of Securities

## REGISTRATION STATEMENTS

### OFFERINGS

Offering registrations are used to register securities before they are offered to investors. Part 1 of the registration, a preliminary prospectus or "red herring," contains preliminary information including:

> selling security holders;
> interests of named experts and counsel;
> description of business;
> directors and executive officers;
> security ownership of beneficial owners and management;
> management compensation.

Red herrings, which include initial public offerings (IPO's), can be obtained from the registrant's underwriter often before they are available at the SEC. Red herrings offer the public its first opportunity to examine a private company's financial statements, including executive compensation and ownership data.

### PROSPECTUS

The SEC-approved offering which must be made available to investors before the sale of the stock is initiated. A prospectus also contains the actual offering price.

# Sources

| | |
|---|---|
| CDA/Investnet, Ft. Lauderdale, FL | (800) 933-4446 (insider filings) |
| Disclosure, Inc., Bethesda, MD | (800) 843-7747 (SEC filings) |
| Q-Data Corp., St. Petersburg, FL | (813) 522-9491 (SEC filings) |

*Resource 14*

# CORPORATE FILINGS

# GUIDE TO CORPORATE FILINGS

The following is a short description of the most common corporate filings made with the SEC; many of these filings are now made on EDGAR and thus available on the Commission's Web Site. The staff organization within the SEC responsible for interpreting the rules, regulations and forms used in connection with the filing also is identified.

This guide cannot take the place of the Commission's official rules and regulations. It is not to be used as a legal reference document. Please refer to the federal securities laws and the rules and regulations thereunder (Title 17 of the Code of Federal Regulations, Parts 200 to End) for the official description of the forms mentioned. These are available at most law libraries. They may also be ordered through:

> Superintendent of Documents
> Government Printing Office
> Washington, D.C. 20402
>
> or
>
> Securities and Exchange Commission
> Publications Unit
> Mail Stop C-11
> 450 Fifth Street, N.W.
> Washington, D.C. 20549

## Form ADV

This form is used to apply for registration as an investment adviser or to amend a registration. It consists of two parts. Part I contains general and personal information about the applicant. Part II contains information relating to the nature of the applicant's business, including basic operations, services offered, fees charged, types of clients advised, educational and business backgrounds of associates and other business activities of the applicant.

*Interpretive Responsibility:*

Division of Investment Management—Office of Chief Counsel

# Annual Report to Shareholders

The Annual Report to Shareholders is the principal document used by most public companies to disclose corporate information to shareholders. It is usually a state-of-the-company report including an opening letter from the Chief Executive Officer, financial data, results of continuing operations, market segment information, new product plans, subsidiary activities and research and development activities on future programs.

*Interpretive Responsibility:*

Division of Corporation Finance—Office of Chief Counsel

# Form BD

This form is used to apply for registration as a broker or dealer of securities, or as a government securities broker or dealer, and to amend a registration. It provides background information on the applicant and the nature of its business. It includes lists of the executive officers and general partners of the company. It also contains information on any past securities violations.

*Interpretive Responsibility:*

Division of Market Regulation—Office of Chief Counsel

# Form D

Companies selling securities in reliance on a Regulation D exemption or a Section 4(6) exemption from the registration provisions of the '33 Act must file a Form D as notice of such a sale. The form must be filed no later than 15 days after the first sale of securities.

For additional information on Regulation D and Section 4(6) offerings, ask for a copy of the Regulation and the pamphlet entitled: "Q & A: Small Business and the SEC" from the Commission's Publications Unit or see the Small Business Section of the Commission's Web Site.

*Interpretive Responsibility:*

Division of Corporation Finance—Office of Small Business Policy

# Form 1-A

Regulation A provides the basis for an exemption for certain small offerings (generally up to $5 million in any twelve month period). Companies selling securities in reliance on a Regulation A exemption from the registration provisions of the 1933 Act must provide investors with an offering statement meeting the requirements of Form 1-A.

For additional information on Regulation A, ask for a copy of the Regulation and the pamphlet entitled "Q & A: Small Business and the SEC" from the Commission's Publications Unit or see the Small Business section of the Commission's Web Site.

*Interpretive Responsibility:*

Division of Corporation Finance—Office of Small Business Policy

# Form MSD

This report is used by a bank or a separately identifiable department or division of a bank to apply for registration as a municipal securities dealer with the SEC, or to amend such registration.

*Interpretive Responsibility:*

Division of Market Regulation—Office of Chief Counsel

# Form N-SAR

This is a report to the Commission filed by registered investment companies on a semi-annual and annual basis, at the end of the corresponding fiscal periods. Unit investment trusts, however, are required to file this form only once a year, at the end of the calendar year. The form contains information about the type of fund that is reporting sales charges, 12b-1 fees, sales of shares, identity of various entities providing services to the investment company, portfolio turnover rate, and selected financial information.

*Interpretive Responsibility:*

Division of Investment Management

# Prospectus

The prospectus constitutes Part I of a 1933 Act registration statement. It contains the basic business and financial information on an issuer with respect to a particular securities offering. Investors may use the prospectus to help appraise the merits of the offering and make educated investment decisions.

A prospectus in its preliminary form is frequently called a "red herring" prospectus and is subject to completion or amendment before the registration statement becomes effective, after which a final prospectus is issued and sales can be consummated.

*Interpretive Responsibility:*

Division of Corporation Finance—Office of Chief Counsel (or)
Division of Investment Management

# Proxy Solicitation Materials (Regulation 14A/Schedule 14A)

State law governs the circumstances under which shareholders are entitled to vote. When a shareholder vote is required and any person solicits proxies with respect to securities registered under Section 12 of the 1934 Act, that person generally is required to furnish a proxy statement containing the information specified by Schedule 14A. The proxy statement is intended to provide security holders with the information necessary to enable them to vote in an informed manner on matters intended to be acted upon at security holders' meetings, whether the traditional annual meeting or a special meeting. Typically, a security holder is also provided with a "proxy card" to authorize designated persons to vote his or her securities on the security holder's behalf in the event the holder does not vote in person at the meeting. Copies of definitive (final) proxy statements and proxy card are filed with the Commission at the time they are sent to security holders. For further information about the applicability of the Commission's proxy rules, see Section 14(a) of the 1934 Act and Regulation 14A.

Certain preliminary proxy filings relating to mergers, consolidations, acquisitions and similar matters are non-public upon filing; all other proxy filings are publicly available.

*Interpretive Responsibility:*

Division of Corporation Finance—Office of the Chief Counsel

## 1933 Act Registration Statements

One of the major purposes of the federal securities laws is to require companies making a public offering of securities to disclose material business and financial information in order that investors may make informed investment decisions. The 1933 Act requires issuers to file registration statements with the Commission, setting forth such information, before offering their securities to the public. (See Section 6 of the Securities Act of 1933 for information concerning the "Registration of Securities and Signing of Registration Statement"; Section 8 of the Securities Act of 1933 for information on "Taking Effect of Registration Statements and Amendments Thereto.")

The registration statement is divided into two parts. Part I is the prospectus. It is distributed to interested investors and others. It contains data to assist in evaluating the securities and to make informed investment decisions.

Part II of the registration statement contains information not required to be in the prospectus. This includes information concerning the registrants' expenses of issuance and distribution, indemnification of directors and officers, and recent sales of unregistered securities as well as undertakings and copies of material contracts.

(Investment companies file 1933 Act registration statements that are, in many cases, also registration statements under the Investment Company Act of 1940. For descriptions of registration statements filed by these issuers, see the following section.)

### Interpretive Responsibility:

Division of Corporation Finance—Office of Chief Counsel.
(Except for the foreign forms [e.g., F-1 and F-2], for which the Office of International Corporate Finance should be consulted.)

The most widely used 1933 Act registration forms are as follows:

S-1     This is the basic registration form. It can be used to register securities for which no other form is authorized or prescribed, except securities of foreign governments or political sub-divisions thereof.

S-2     This is a simplified optional registration form that may be used by companies that have been required to report under the 1934 Act for a minimum of three years and have timely filed all required reports during the twelve calendar months and any portion of the month immediately preceding the filing of the registration statement. Unlike Form S-1, it permits incorporation by reference from the company's annual report to stockholders (or annual report on Form 10-K) and periodic reports. Delivery of these incorporated documents as well as the prospectus to investors may be required.

S-3    This is the most simplified registration form and it may only be used by companies that have been required to report under the '34 Act for a minimum of twelve months and have met the timely filing requirements set forth under Form S-2. Also, the offering and issuer must meet the eligibility tests prescribed by the form. The form maximizes incorporating by reference information from '34 Act filings.

S-4    This form is used to register securities in connection with business combinations and exchange offers.

S-8    This form is used for the registration of securities to be offered to an issuer's employees pursuant to certain plans.

S-11   This form is used to register securities of certain real estate companies, including real estate investment trusts.

SB-1   This form may be used by certain "small business issuers" to register offerings of up to $10 million of securities, provided that the company has not registered more than $10 million in securities offerings during the preceding twelve months. This form requires less detailed information about the issuer's business than Form S-1. Generally, a "small business issuer" is a U.S. or Canadian company with revenues and public market float less than $25 million.

SB-2   This form may be used by "small business issuers" to register securities to be sold for cash. This form requires less detailed information about the issuer's business than Form S-1.

S-20   This form may be used to register standardized options where the issuer undertakes not to issue, clear, guarantee or accept an option registered on Form S-20 unless there is a definitive options disclosure document meeting the requirements of Rule 9b-1 of the '34 Act.

Sch B   Schedule B is the registration statement used by foreign governments (or political subdivisions of foreign governments) to register securities. Generally, it contains a description of the country and its government, the terms of the offering, and the uses of proceeds.

F-1    This is the basic registration form authorized for certain foreign private issuers. It is used to register the securities of those eligible foreign issuers for which no other more specialized form is authorized or prescribed.

Resource 15

F-2     This is an optional registration form that may be used by certain for-
        eign private issuers that have an equity float of at least $75 million
        worldwide or are registering non-convertible investment grade securi-
        ties or have reported under the '34 Act for a minimum of three years.
        The form is somewhat shorter than Form F-1 because it uses delivery of
        filings made by the issuer under the '34 Act, particularly Form 20-F.

F-3     This form may only be used by certain foreign private issuers that have
        reported under the '34 Act for a minimum of twelve months and that
        have a worldwide public market float of more than $75 million. The
        form also may be used by eligible foreign private issuers to register
        offerings of non-convertible investment grade securities, securities to
        be sold by selling security holders, or securities to be issued to certain
        existing security holders. The form allows '34 Act filings to be incorpo-
        rated by reference.

F-4     This form is used to register securities in connection with business
        combinations and exchange offers involving foreign private issuers.

F-6     This form is used to register depository shares represented by American
        Depositary Receipts ("ADRs") issued by a depositary against the
        deposit of the securities of a foreign issuer.

F-7     This form is used by certain eligible publicly traded Canadian foreign
        private issuers to register rights offers extended to their U.S. share-
        holders. Form F-7 acts as a wraparound for the relevant Canadian
        offering documents. To be registered on Form F-7, the rights must be
        granted to U.S. shareholders on terms no less favorable than those
        extended to other shareholders.

F-8     This form may be used by eligible large publicly traded Canadian for-
        eign private issuers to register securities offered in business combina-
        tions and exchange offers. Form F-8 acts as a wraparound for the
        relevant Canadian offering or disclosure documents. The securities
        must be offered to U.S. holders on terms no less favorable than those
        extended to other holders.

F-9     This form may be used by eligible large publicly traded Canadian for-
        eign private issuers to register non-convertible investment grade securi-
        ties. Form F-9 acts as a wraparound for the relevant Canadian offering
        documents.

F-10    This form may be used by eligible large publicly traded Canadian for-
        eign private issuers to register any securities (except certain derivative

securities). Form F-10 acts as a wraparound for the relevant Canadian offering documents. Unlike Forms F-7, F-8, F-9, and F-80, however, Form F-10 requires the Canadian issuer to reconcile its financial statements to U.S. Generally Accepted Accounting Principles ("GAAP").

F-80    This form may be used by eligible large publicly traded Canadian foreign private issuers to register securities offered in business combinations and exchange offers. Form F-80 acts as a wraparound for the relevant Canadian offering or disclosure documents. The securities must be offered to U.S. holders on terms no less favorable than those extended to other holders.

SR      This form is used as a report by first time registrants under the Act of sales of registered securities and use of proceeds therefrom. The form is required at specified periods of time throughout the offering period, and a final report is required after the termination of the offering.

# Investment Company Registration Statements

Investment companies also register their securities under the 1933 Act. However, many of the forms used are also used as registration statements under the Investment Company Act of 1940.

Mutual funds, the most common type of registered investment company, make a continuous offering of their securities and register on Form N-1A, a simplified, three-part form. The prospectus, or Part A, provides a concise description of the fundamental characteristics of the initial fund in a way that will assist investors in making informed decisions about whether to purchase the securities of the fund. The statement of additional information, Part B, contains additional information about the fund which may be of interest to some investors but need not be included in the prospectus. Part C contains other required information and exhibits.

Closed-end funds, unit investment trusts, insurance company separate accounts, business development companies and other registered investment companies register their securities and provide essential information about them on other registration forms, as listed below. All the forms listed are used for registration under both the 1933 Act and 1940 Act unless otherwise indicated.

*Interpretive Responsibility:*

Division of Investment Management

N-lA    This form is used to register open-end management investment com-
        panies ("mutual funds").

N-2     This form is used to register closed-end management investment com-
        panies ("closed-end funds").

N-3     This form is used to register insurance company separate accounts
        organized as management investment companies offering variable
        annuity contracts.

N-4     This form is used to register insurance company separate accounts
        organized as unit investment trusts offering variable annuity contracts.

S-6     This form is used to register securities issued by unit investment trusts
        (1933 Act only).

N-14    This form is used to register securities issued by investment companies
        in connection with business combinations and mergers (1933 Act only).

## Other Securities Act Form: Form 144

This form must be filed as notice of the proposed sale of restricted securities or
securities held by an affiliate of the issuer in reliance on Rule 144 when the
amount to be sold during any three month period exceeds 500 shares or units or
has an aggregate sales price in excess of $10,000.

*Interpretive Responsibility:*

Division of Corporation Finance—Office of Chief Counsel

## 1934 Act Registration Statements

All companies whose securities are registered on a national securities exchange,
and, in general, other companies whose total assets exceed $10,000,000 ($10
million) with a class of equity securities held by 500 or more persons, must register such securities under the 1934 Act. (See Section 12 of the '34 Act for further
information.)

This registration establishes a public file containing material financial and business information on the company for use by investors and others, and also cre-

ates an obligation on the part of the company to keep such public information current by filing periodic reports on Forms 10-Q and 10-K, and on current event Form 8-K, as applicable.

In addition, if registration under the 1934 Act is not required, any issuer who conducts a public offering of securities must file reports for the year in which it conducts the offering (and in subsequent years if the securities are held by more than 300 holders).

The most widely used 1934 Act registration forms are as follows:

10     This is the general form for registration of securities pursuant to section 12(b) or (g) of the '34 Act of classes of securities of issuers for which no other form is prescribed. It requires certain business and financial information about the issuer.

10-SB     This is the general form for registration of securities pursuant to Sections 12(b) or (g) of the '34 Act for "small business issuers." This form requires slightly less detailed information about the company's business than Form 10 requires.

8-A     This optional short form may be used by companies to register securities under the '34 Act.

8-B     This specialized registration form may be used by certain issuers with no securities registered under the'34 Act that succeed to another issuer which had securities so registered at the time of succession.

20-F     This is an integrated form used both as a registration statement for purposes of registering securities of qualified foreign private issuers under Section 12 or as an annual report under Section 13(a) or 15(d) of the '34 Act.

40-F     This is an integrated form used both as a registration statement to register securities of eligible publicly traded Canadian foreign private issuers or as an annual report for such issuers. It serves as a wraparound for the company's Canadian public reports.

*Interpretive Responsibility:*

Division of Corporation Finance—Office of Chief Counsel
(Except for Form 20-F, as to which the Office of International Corporate Finance should be consulted.)

## Other Exchange Act Forms

### Form TA-1

This form is used to apply for registration as a transfer agent or to amend such registration. It provides information on the company's activities and operation.

*Interpretive Responsibility:*

Division of Market Regulation—Branch of Stock Surveillance

### Form X-17A-5

Every broker or dealer registered pursuant to Section 15 of the Exchange Act must file annually, on a calendar or fiscal year basis, a report audited by an independent public accountant.

*Interpretive Responsibility:*

Division of Market Regulation—Branch of Financial Reporting

### Forms 3, 4 and 5

Every director, officer or owner of more than 10 percent of a class of equity securities registered under Section 12 of the '34 Act must file with the Commission a statement of ownership regarding such security. The initial filing is on Form 3 and changes are reported on Form 4. The annual statement of beneficial ownership of securities is on Form 5. The forms contain information on the reporting person's relationship to the company and on purchases and sales of such equity securities.

*Interpretive Responsibility:*

Division of Corporation Finance—Office of Chief Counsel

### Form 6-K

This report is used by certain foreign private issuers to furnish information: (i) required to be made public in the country of its domicile; (ii) filed with and made public by a foreign stock exchange on which its securities are traded; or (iii) distributed to security holders. The report must be furnished promptly after such material is made public. The form is not considered "filed" for Section 18 liability purposes. This is the only information furnished by foreign private issuers between annual reports, since such issuers are not required to file on Forms 10-Q or 8-K.

*Interpretive Responsibility:*

Division of Corporation Finance—Office of International Corporate Finance

## Form 8-K

This is the "current report" that is used to report the occurrence of any material events or corporate changes which are of importance to investors or security holders and previously have not been reported by the registrant. It provides more current information on certain specified events than would Forms 10-Q or 10-K.

*Interpretive Responsibility:*

Division of Corporation Finance—Office of Chief Counsel

## Form 10-C

This form must be filed by an issuer whose securities are quoted on the Nasdaq interdealer quotation system. Reported on the form is any change that exceeds 5 percent in the number of shares of the class outstanding and any change in the name of the issuer. The report must be filed within ten days of such change.

*Interpretive Responsibility:*

Division of Market Regulation—Office of Chief Counsel

## Form 10-K

This is the annual report that most reporting companies file with the Commission. It provides a comprehensive overview of the registrant's business. The report must be filed within 90 days after the end of the company's fiscal year.

*Interpretive Responsibility:*

Division of Corporation Finance—Office of Chief Counsel

## Form 10-KSB

This is the annual report filed by reporting "small business issuers." It provides a comprehensive overview of the company's business, although its requirements call for slightly less detailed information than required by Form 10-K. The report must be filed within 90 days after the end of the company's fiscal year.

*Interpretive Responsibility:*

Division of Corporation Finance—Office of Chief Counsel, Office of Small Business Policy

## Form 10-Q

The Form 10-Q is a report filed quarterly by most reporting companies. It includes unaudited financial statements and provides a continuing view of the company's financial position during the year. The report must be filed for each of the first three fiscal quarters of the company's fiscal year and is due within 45 days of the close of the quarter.

*Interpretive Responsibility:*

Division of Corporation Finance—Office of Chief Counsel

## Form 10-QSB

The Form 10-QSB is filed quarterly by reporting small business issuers. It includes unaudited financial statements and provides a continuing view of the company's financial position and results of operations throughout the year. The report must be filed for each of the first three fiscal quarters and is due within 45 days of the close of the quarter.

*Interpretive Responsibility:*

Division of Corporation Finance—Office of Chief Counsel, Office of Small Business Policy

## Form 11-K

This form is a special annual report for employee stock purchase, savings, and similar plans, interests in which constitute securities registered under the 1933 Act. The Form 11-K annual report is required in addition to any other annual report of the issuer of the securities (e.g., a company's annual report to all shareholders or Form 10-K).

*Interpretive Responsibility:*

Division of Corporation Finance—Office of Chief Counsel

## Form 12b-25

This form is used as a notification of late filing by a reporting company that determines that is unable to file a required periodic report when first due without unreasonable effort or expense. If a company files a Form 12b-25, it is entitled to relief, but must file the required report within five calendar days (for a

Form 10-Q or 10-QSB) or within fifteen calendar days (for a Form 10-K, 10-KSB, 20-F, 11-K, or N-SAR).

*Interpretive Responsibility:*

Division of Corporation Finance—Office of Chief Counsel

## Form 13-F

This is a quarterly report of equity holdings by institutional investment managers having equity assets under management of $100 million or more. Included in this category are certain banks, insurance companies, investment advisers, investment companies, foundations and pension funds.

*Interpretive Responsibility:*

Division of Investment Management—Office of Chief Counsel

## Form 15

This form is filed by a company as notice of termination of registration under Section 12(g) of the '34 Act, or suspension of the duty to file periodic reports under Sections 13 and 15(d) of the '34 Act.

*Interpretive Responsibility:*

Division of Corporation Finance—Office of Chief Counsel

## Form 18

This form is used for the registration on a national securities exchange of securities of foreign governments and political subdivisions thereof.

*Interpretive Responsibility:*

Division of Corporation Finance—Office of International Corporate Finance

## Form 18-K

This form is used for the annual reports of foreign governments or political subdivisions thereof.

*Interpretive Responsibility:*

Division of Corporation Finance—Office of International Corporate Finance

## Schedule 13D

This schedule discloses beneficial ownership of certain registered equity securities. Any person or group of persons who acquire a beneficial ownership of more than 5 percent of a class of registered equity securities of certain issuers must file a Schedule 13D reporting such acquisition together with certain other information within ten days after such acquisition. Moreover, any material changes in the facts set forth in the schedule generally precipitates a duty to promptly file an amendment on Schedule 13D.

The Commission's rules define the term "beneficial owner" to be any person who directly or indirectly shares voting power or investment power (the power to sell the security).

### Interpretive Responsibility:

Division of Corporation Finance—Office of Tender Offers

## Schedule 13G

Schedule 13G is a much abbreviated version of Schedule 13D that is only available for use by a limited category of "persons" (such as banks, broker/dealers, and insurance companies) and even then only when the securities were acquired in the ordinary course of business and not with the purpose or effect of changing or influencing the control of the issuer.

### Interpretive Responsibility:

Division of Corporation Finance—Office of Tender Offers

## Schedule 13E-3

This schedule must be filed by certain persons engaging in "going private" transactions. The schedule must be filed by any company or an affiliate of a company who engages in a business combination, tender offer, or stock purchase that has the effect of causing a class of the company's equity securities registered under the 1934 Act (1) to be held by fewer than 300 persons, or (2) to be de-listed from a securities exchange or interdealer quotation system. The filer must disclose detailed information about the transaction, including whether the filer believes the transaction to be fair.

### Interpretive Responsibility:

Division of Corporation Finance—Office of Tender Offers

## Schedule 13E-4

This schedule (called an Issuer Tender Offer Statement) must be filed by certain reporting companies that make tender offers for their own securities. In addition, Rule 13e-4 under the 1934 Act imposes additional requirements than an issuer must comply with when making an issuer tender offer.

*Interpretive Responsibility:*

Division of Corporation Finance—Office of Tender Offers

## Schedule 13E-4F

This schedule may be used by a Canadian foreign private issuer that makes an issuer tender offer for its equity shares (provided that U.S. holders hold less than 40 percent of the class of shares subject to the offer). It serves as a wraparound for the relevant Canadian disclosure documents. The Canadian issuer must comply with relevant Canadian tender offer regulations.

*Interpretive Responsibility:*

Division of Corporation Finance—Office of International Corporate Finance

## Information Statement (Regulation 14C/Schedule 14C)

Schedule 14C sets forth the disclosure requirements for information statements. Generally, a company with securities registered under Section 12 of the '34 Act must send an information statement to every holder of the registered security who is entitled to vote on any matter for which the company is not soliciting proxies. (If the company solicits proxies, Regulation 14C/Schedule 14A may be required.)

*Interpretive Responsibility:*

Division of Corporation Finance—Office of Chief Counsel

## Schedule 14D-1

Any person, other than the issuer itself (see Schedule 13E-4), making a tender offer for certain equity securities registered pursuant to Section 12 of the '34 Act, which offer, if accepted, would cause that person to own over 5 percent of that class of the securities, must at the time of the offer file a Schedule 14D-1. This schedule must be filed with the Commission and sent to certain other parties, such as the issuer and any competing bidders. In addition, Regulation 14D sets forth certain requirements that must be complied with in connection with a tender offer.

*Interpretive Responsibility:*

Division of Corporation Finance—Office of Tender Offers

## Schedule 14D-1F

Any person making a tender offer for securities of a Canadian foreign private issuer may use this schedule if U.S. holders hold less than 40 percent of the class of securities that is the subject of the offer and if the bidder extends the tender offer to U.S. holders on terms that are at least as favorable as those extended to any other holder. The schedule serves as a wraparound for the relevant Canadian disclosure documents. In addition, the tender offer must comply with relevant Canadian requirements.

*Interpretive Responsibility:*

Division of Corporation Finance—Office of International Corporate Finance

## Schedule 14D-9

This schedule must be filed with the Commission when an interested party, such as an issuer, a beneficial owner of securities, or a representative of either, makes a solicitation or recommendation to the shareholders with respect to a tender offer which is subject to Regulation 14D.

*Interpretive Responsibility:*

Division of Corporation Finance—Office of Tender Offers

## Schedule 14D-9F

Schedule 14D-9F may be used by a Canadian foreign private issuer or by any of its directors or officers when the issuer is the subject of a tender offer filed on Schedule 14D-1F. The schedule is used to respond to tender offers. The schedule serves as a wraparound for the relevant Canadian disclosure documents. In addition, the filer must comply with all relevant Canadian requirements.

*Interpretive Responsibility:*

Division of Corporation Finance—Office of International Corporate Finance

# Trust Indenture Act of 1939—Forms

T-1   This form is a statement of eligibility and qualification of a corporation to act as a trustee under the Trust Indenture Act of 1939.

T-2   This form is basically the same as Form T-1 except it is to be used for individual, rather than corporate trustees.

T-3   This form is used as an application for qualification of indentures pursuant to the Trust Indenture Act of 1939, but only when securities to be issued thereunder are not required to be registered under the Securities Act of 1933.

T-4   This form is used to apply for an exemption from certain provisions of the Trust Indenture Act.

T-6   This form is used by a foreign corporation as an application to act as sole trustee under an indenture qualified under the Trust Indenture Act.

### Interpretive Responsibility:

Division of Corporation Finance—Office of Chief Counsel

# Additional Material on Filings and Forms

- Additional EDGAR forms and further details on EDGAR forms
- Filing Acts and Related Form Types
- Selected non-EDGAR forms

http://www.sec.gov/info/edgar/forms.htm
Modified: 05/24/1999

*Source:* EDGAR Database of Corporate Information.

RESOURCE 16

---

## CORPORATE RESEARCH RESOURCES

---

# FAVORITE BOOKS AND CD-ROMS
# FOR CORPORATE RESEARCH
### (supplied by Vicky Martin, IU Foundation)

## Books and CDs

*The Corporate Directory of US Public Companies,* Walker's: Provides information on more than 10,000 publicly held US corporations.

*Corporate Giving Directory,* TAFT: Provides information on corporate philanthropy including program priorities; cash, nonmonetary, and corporate sponsorship giving; corporate matching gift and company-sponsored volunteer programs; corporate operating locations; geographic giving preferences; corporate and foundation officers and directors; application procedures and evaluative criteria; and recently awarded grants.

*Corporate Giving Yellow Pages,* TAFT: Provides contact information for over 3,500 corporate foundations and giving programs, including companies that operate difficult-to-research direct giving programs.

*Directory of Corporate Affiliations* (also available on CD-ROM titled *Corporate Affiliations Plus*), National Register Publishing: Details the relationship among domestic parent companies and their divisions, subsidiaries and affiliates, whether located in the US or overseas.

*Million Dollar Directory* (also available on CD-ROM titled *Million Dollar Disk*), Dun & Bradstreet: Offers extensive coverage of public and private companies, easy cross-referencing, primary and secondary lines of business, and the names and titles of key decision makers, along with brief bios on each. The top 160,000 US companies are profiled.

*National Directory of Corporate Giving,* The Foundation Center: Provides basic descriptions of large and small corporations with foundations and structured giving programs or whose past contributions activities demonstrate an interest in supporting nonprofit organizations.

*International Directory of Company Histories,* St. James Press: Provides accurate and detailed information on the historical development of some of the world's largest and most influential companies. The companies chosen for inclusion in the directory have either achieved a minimum of two billion US dollars in annual sales and/or they are a leading influence in a particular industry or geographical location.

*Standard & Poor's Register of Corporations, Directors and Executives,* McGraw-Hill: This is a three volume set, with Volume 1 featuring corporate listings of over 75,000 corporations, including address, telephone number, Internet address; names, titles and functions of approximately 437,500 officers, directors, and other principals; names of company's primary accounting firm, bank and law firm; stock exchange(s) on which a company is traded; ticker symbol; description of company's products/services; Standard Industrial Classification (SIC) codes; annual sales and number of employees where available; division names and functions; subsidiary listings separate with reference to parent companies; principal business affiliation and address of officers, if other than the subject company. Volume 2 highlights brief, biographical sketches of over 72,000 individuals serving as officers, directors, trustees, partners, etc. Volume 3 provides an indices, broken into various sections.

*Corporate Affiliations Plus,* National Register Publishing: This is the CD-ROM version of *Directory of Corporate Affiliations* and provides much of the same information, but offers much more flexibility in searching.

*Standard & Poor's Corporation On Disk:* While this is also available in print version, the CD-ROM is a much more efficient and searchable medium. The CD-ROM provides balance sheet information on public firms; 12,000 public and 34,000 private companies can be searched by name, industry, sales, or number of employees. Selective information on private business is made available. Facts and figures about key executives can also be searched.

## Fee-Based Databases

Bloomberg (www.bloomberg.com): Provides access to a worldwide financial network of news, data, and analyses of financial markets and business as well as being the definitive source of data for all securities, statistics, indices, and research.

Dow Jones Interactive, now known as Factiva (www.factiva.com): Provides access to 65 million documents from more than 6,000 publications, 92 percent of which are full text, access to detailed company and industry reports on thousands of companies, and contains the latest news on virtually any subject.

Dun & Bradstreet (www.dnb.com): Excellent source of corporate information, particularly private companies. Most valuable information found in History & Operations section of Business Information Report, such as key officers, brief biographical information about the key officers, as well as the percentage of the company they own.

Global Access, PRIMARK (www.primark.com): Provides full-text SEC filings, scanned images of US and international company annual reports submitted to US and foreign exchanges, US public company debt and equity offerings, and downloadable financial statements for US and international companies.

Hoover's (www.hoovers.com): Free company and industry news and press releases, as well as brief company capsules. For a fee, more in-depth corporate reports are available. Direct links to corporate web sites and SEC filings available at the free site.

Prospect Research Online (PRO), iWave (www.rpbooks.com): Contains comprehensive profiles on corporations, foundations, and prospects, along with other great information. Added perk: if you can't find what you need, e-mail your request to PRO and within 24–48 hours, it will e-mail you back indicating if your requested information is found and where to go on the PRO site to find it.

## Fee Internet Sites

Search for information on over 900,000 public and private companies. Provides snapshot information and links to company websites. Dun & Bradstreet reports can be purchased directly at this site.

Business Credit USA (www.businesscreditusa.com)

Free credit ratings on 12 million businesses. Full credit reports on any business for $3.00.

Hoovers (www.hoovers.com)

Free company snapshots and links to company web sites. Full company profiles available with subscription.

EDGAR (www.edgar-online.com/overview.asp)

SEC filings, people search, IPO information, compensation and insider trader information, news, stock quotes, and more.

Corporate Information (www.corporateinformation.com)

Over 350,000 company profiles indexed, offering a list of sites that cover the company for which information is sought. Research available on countries around the world, as well as by state.

Thomas Manufacturers Directory (www.thomasregister.com)

Information on over 156,000 manufacturing companies in the United States and links to available company web sites.

Bank Online (www.bankonline.com/fidirectory.htm)

Information on banks, credit unions and other financial institutions around the world. Links directly to the institution's web site.

American Journalism Review NewsLink (ajr.newslink.org)

Outstanding site for news. Includes 18,000 links to newspapers, magazines, broadcasters and news services worldwide.

Insider Trader (www.insidertrader.com)

Provides detailed information on the activities of corporate insiders, along with an alert service for activities to be monitored.

This list is by no means comprehensive, but does contain some of the more popular tools for conducting research on public companies.

## Private Companies

Researching private companies is not nearly as easy since they are not required to file with the SEC. However, there are several good resources to consult when researching private companies:

### Books

*Directory of Corporate Affiliations, US Private Companies,* National Register Publishing

*Million Dollar Directory,* Dun & Bradstreet

*Manufacturers Directory,* Harris Publishing (by state or region)

*Standard & Poor's Register of Corporations, Directors and Executives,* McGraw-Hill

*Ward's Private Company Profiles,* Gale Research, Inc.

Many of the references for public company research provide information on private companies, due in large part to these books, databases and web sites offering a wide range of corporate information. However, when the books, databases and web sites don't seem to offer much insight into a private company, other excellent resources include:

Secretary of State Corporation Division: all companies, public or private, must register with this division in any state where it conducts business. The information found here is minimal, but usually includes the address, phone and principal officers.

National Association of Secretaries of State: http://www.nass.org/sos/sosflags.html

Chambers of Commerce: http://www.worldchambers.com/frnote.shtml

Finally, always try to determine if the company, public or private, has its own web site. There is a web site that will allow you to plug in a company name and will search for a possible web site for that company: http://www.websense.com/locator.cfm.

# RESOURCE 17

## NONPROFIT KEYWORD SEARCH

Adolescent health issues
African American affairs
After-school/enrichment programs
Agricultural education
AIDS/HIV
Air/water quality
Alzheimer's disease
Animal protection
Art history
Arthritis
Arts and humanities general
Arts appreciation
Arts association and councils
Arts centers
Arts festivals
Arts funds
Arts institutes
Arts outreach
Arts/humanities education
Asian American affairs
At-risk youth
Ballet
Bible study/translation
Big Brothers/Big Sisters camp
Botanical gardens/parks
Business education
Business/free enterprise
Business-school partnerships
Cancer
Chambers of commerce
Child abuse
Child welfare
Children's health/hospitals
Churches
Civic and public affairs
Civil rights
Clinics/medical centers
Clubs
Colleges and universities
Community arts

Community centers
Community foundation
Community service organizations
Community/junior colleges
Continuing education
Counseling
Crime prevention
Criminal rehabilitation
Dance
Day care
Delinquency
Diabetes
Dioceses
Domestic violence
Economic development
Economic education
Economic policy
Education
Education associations
Education funds
Education reform
Elementary education (private)
Elementary education (public)
Emergency relief
Emergency/ambulance services
Employment/job training
Energy
Engineering education
Environment
Ethnic and folk arts
Ethnic organizations
Eyes/blindness
Faculty development
Family planning
Family services
Film and video
First Amendment issues
Food/clothing distribution
Foreign arts organizations
Foreign education

Forestry
Gay/lesbian affairs
Geriatric health
Gifted and talented programs
Health
Health and physical education
Health care/hospitals (international)
Health funds
Health organizations
Health policy/cost containment
Heart
Hispanic affairs
Historic preservation
History and archaeology
Home care services
Homes
Hospice
Hospitals
Hospitals (university-affiliated)
Housing
Human rights
Inner-city development
International
International affairs
International development
International environmental issues
International exchange
International law
International organizations
International peace and security
    issues
International relations
International relief efforts
International studies
Jewish causes
Journalism/media education
Kidney
Law and justice
Leadership training
Legal aid

Legal education
Libraries
Literacy
Literary arts
Long-term care
Lung
Medical education
Medical rehab
Medical research
Medical training
Mental health
Ministries
Minority education
Missionary activities (domestic)
Missionary/religious activities
Multiple sclerosis
Municipalities/town
Museums/galleries
Music
Native American affairs
Nonprofit management
Nursing services
Nutrition
Observatories/planetariums
Opera
Outpatient health care
Parades/festivals
People with disabilities
Performing arts
Philanthropic organizations
Prenatal health issues
Preschool education
Preventive medicine/wellness
    organizations
Private and public education
    (precollege)
Professional/trade associations
Protection
Public broadcasting
Public health

Public policy
Recreation/athletics
Refugee assistance
Religion
Religious education
Religious organizations
Religious welfare
Research
Research/studies institutes
Resource conservation
Rural affairs
Safety
Sanitary systems
Science
Science exhibits/fairs
Science museums
Science/mathematics education
Scientific centers/institutes
Scientific labs
Scientific organizations
Scientific research
Secondary education (private)
Secondary education (public)
Seminaries
Senior services
Sexual abuse

Shelters/homeless
Single-disease health associations
Social science education
Social services
Social/policy issues
Special education
Speech and hearing
Student aid
Substance abuse
Synagogues/temples
Theater
Trade
Transplant networks/donor banks
Trauma treatment
United Funds/United Way
Urban/community affairs
Veterans
Visual arts
Vocational/technical education
Volunteer services
Watershed
Wildlife protection
Women's affairs
YMCA/YMHA/YWCA/YWHA
Youth organizations
Zoos/aquariums

# USEFUL BOOKMARKS FOR DOING ON-LINE RESEARCH

# VICKY'S BOOKMARKS

## Address/Phone/ZIP Sites

AmeriCom Area Decoder (http://decoder.americom.com)

AnyWho: Telephone number, e-mail, home page URL, fax, toll-free number, and address (http://www.anywho.com)

Directory Assistance (http://www.555-1212.com)

ZIP Code Lookup and Address Information (http://www.usps.gov/ncsc)

## News Sites

American Journalism Review News Link (http://www.ajr.org)

@BRINT: The Premier Network for Business, Technology, and Knowledge Management: Forums, articles, magazines, events, resources, analyses, and news (http://www.brint.com)

Business Wire 1999 (http://www.businesswire.com)

CFO Magazine and Treasury and Risk Management (http://www.cfonet.com)

Dow Jones Reuters Business Interactive LLC (http://www.bestofboth.com/index.html)

Folio: The Magazine for Magazine Management (http://www.foliomag.com)

Gebbie Press: PR Media Directory: Newspapers, radio, TV, magazines, press releases, faxes, e-mail, publicity, freelance, journalism, marketing (http://www.gebbieinc.com/index1.htm)

Minority Business Entrepreneur Magazine (http://www.mbemag.com)

NewsDirectory: Newspapers and media (http://newsdirectory.com)

News Headlines from Interlope News (http://www.interlope.com)

NewsHub—Headline news every 15 minutes (http://newshub.com)

PointCast download page (http://www.pointcast.com)

Wall Street Reporter.com (http://www.wallstreetreporter.com)

# Corporate Information Sites

CEO Express (http://www.ceoexpress.com)

CommerceInc (http://www.commerceinc.com/index.shtml)

Company Sleuth (http://www.companysleuth.com)

Corporate Information (http://www.corporateinformation.com)

CorpTech Database of 50,000 U.S. Technology Companies
(http://www.corptech.com)

Dun & Bradstreet (http://www.dnb.com/dnb/dnbhome.htm)

Financials.com: Annual reports, stock quotes, and more
(http://www.financials.com)

FirmFind (http://udese.state.ut.us/cgi/foxweb.exe/firmfind)

Global Corporate Information Services (http://www.gcis.com)

Hoover's Online (http://www.hoovers.com)

Industry.net (http://www.industry.net)

InvestorGuide: The Leading Guide to Investing on the Web
(http://investorguide.com)

Online Investor (http://192.41.31.102/onlineinvestor.index.html)

Search SEC EDGAR Archives (http://www.sec.gov/cgi-bin/srch-edgar)

10K Wizard Quick Search Menu (http://www.tenkwizard.com)

Thomas Register of American Manufacturers: Industrial manufacturing supplies,
equipment, plastics, valves, fasteners, motors, compressors, engineering,
CAD/CAM, sheet metal fabricating (http://www.thomasregister.com)

WSRN.com: Financial research (http://www.wsrn.com)

# Investor and Insider Information Sites

Quicken.com—Insider Trading (http://quicken.com/investments/insider)

Stock Quotes (http://www.streetnet.com/quote.html)

Stock Splits (http://www.stocksplits.net)

Thomson Financial Wealth Identification (http://www.wealthid.com)

Yahoo! Finance (http://finance.yahoo.com/)

## Foundation Information Sites

The Foundation Center (http://fdncenter.org)

GuideStar: The Donor's Guide to Nonprofits and Charities (http://www.guidestar.org)

Quality 990: Improve IRS Form 990 Reporting (http://www.qual990.org)

## Biographical Information Sites

American Medical Association Doctor Finder (http://www.ama-assn.org)

Ancestry.com: Online Genealogy (http://www.ancestry.com)

Indiana Biography Index Overview (http://199.8.200.90:591/ibioverview. html)

International Directory of Finance and Economics Professionals (http://linux.agsm.ucla.edu/dir)

FindLaw West Legal Directory: Lawyers and information about the law (http://directory.findlaw.com)

Martindale-Hubbell Lawyer Locator (http://www.martindale.com)

Outstanding Americans (http://oyaawards.com)

## General Information Sites

The Careful Donor (http://donors.philanthropy.com)

Chambers of Commerce and Other Related Associations on the Internet (http://www.indychamber.com/chambers.htm)

Council for Advancement and Support of Education (CASE) (http://www.case.org)

Guide to Understanding Financials (http://www.ibm.com/FinancialGuide)

Indiana University Libraries Online Resources (http://www.indiana.edu/~libfind)

KPMG Knowledge Management
(http://kpmg.interact.nl/publication/survey.html)

Lexis-Nexis Academic Universe (http://web.lexis-nexis.com/universe)

Librarians' Index to the Internet (http://sunsite.berkeley.edu/InternetIndex)

Price's List of Lists (http://gwis2.circ.gwu.edu/~gprice/listof.htm)

Primary Source Media: City Directories Online
(http://citydirectories.psmedia.com/index.html)

Prospect Research Online (http://www.rpbooks.com)

Travelocity: Online airfares, hotel, and car reservations
(http://www.travelocity.com)

Travelweb: Hotel Reservations and Flight Reservations
(http://www.travelweb.com)

University of Virginia Prospect Research (http://www.people.virginia.edu/
~dev-pros/index.html)

Yahoo! Real Estate: Home Values
(http://realestate.yahoo.com/realestate/homevalues))

## Search Engines

Alta Vista (http://altavista.digital.com)

Dogpile (http://www.dogpile.com)

Google (http://www.google.com)

Resource 18

RESOURCE 19

# PROSPECT MANAGEMENT PROTOCOLS

Resource 19

# UNIVERSITY OF BRITISH COLUMBIA
# PROSPECT COORDINATION PROTOCOL

## Responsible Unit

Faculty Fund-Raising Unit

## Protocol

The Prospect Coordination Program (PCP) is a method of ensuring that UBC's prospects are cultivated and solicited in a well-planned, coordinated fashion by the appropriate personnel to enable the university to attract the highest value gift. This is the principle of the optimum gift. The key to the success of the program is open communication, close cooperation and good will, which will result in successful fund-raising for the university.

## Purpose

Prospective donors have a right to expect UBC to coordinate efforts so that they are not approached several times by various parts of the university. UBC has the obligation to avoid duplication of effort and to resolve competing claims on prospective donors in order to secure the greatest possible support from each potential donor for the university's priorities. The purpose of this protocol is to develop and administer a fair and consistent process for the orderly approach to prospects and is not intended to inhibit or discourage informal exploratory inquiries in an effort to locate possible outside sources of support. No one at the university has the authority to formally solicit gifts on behalf of the university without the knowledge and approval of the president or designated development professional through the Prospect Coordination Program. Gifts also include sponsorships.

## Procedure Summary

The program acts as the central clearing file for all such prospects, and it enhances the communication between development professionals, faculty and volunteers that is critical when two or more individuals are working with the same prospect(s). The procedure ensures:

- the reservation of prospects and donors by UBC development professionals for purposes of cultivation and solicitation;

- information sharing and accurate and complete records of approaches, responses and giving to UBC;
- focused activity on priority prospects;
- one system to coordinate gift activity;
- consensus for prospect assignment;
- authorized and coordinated cultivation and solicitation activity; and
- active cultivation of prospective donors.

## Detailed Procedures

### 1. When do we do it?

when planning any fund-raising activities

### 2. Which prospects?

President's Circle ($250,000+)
Chancellor's Circle ($25,000–$249,000)
Wesbrook members ($1,000–$24,999)
those capable of giving a $50,000 or more outright gift
those capable of giving a $25,000 pledge over 5 years
community groups of 100 or more, regardless of amount

### 3. Who is involved?

PCP is managed by the Faculty Fund-Raising Unit
PCP is implemented by the PC Committee (see Appendix IV)
the Manager, Faculty Fund-Raising Unit, is responsible for monitoring the entire
    process to ensure the university's prospects, particularly the Chancellor's Cir-
    cle, are being cultivated appropriately on a regular basis and ultimately
    solicited for approved UBC case statement projects
the Manager, President's Circle/International, ensures that the President's Circle
    prospects are being cultivated and solicited appropriately

### 4. How do we do it?

a. *Clearance Factors*

current potential as a prospective donor
affiliation with UBC
interest in a particular area of the university
giving history to UBC
current solicitation activity (other approaches, pledge status)
the amount to be requested
the purpose and priority of the project for which he/she/it is to be solicited

the prospect's philanthropic giving history external to UBC

corporate/foundation giving policies

the last time they were solicited by UBC

b. *Multiple Projects*

A prospect may be cleared for more than one university-approved case statement project for cultivation purposes. A prospect is cleared for solicitation for more than one initiative during the same time period only when there is rationale and a plan to do so. It is the responsibility of the development officers in question to coordinate the timing and the approach of the solicitation and declare the plan to the PCP committee.

c. *Multiple Requests for Clearance of Single Prospects*

If a development officer requests clearance for a prospect who is currently cleared for another project, as a general practice, the solicitation for which the earliest clearance has been given will take precedence. Clearance for another solicitation will be withheld until the first solicitation has been completed/ resolved.

d. *Appeals*

If clearance for a prospect cannot be agreed upon by the Prospect Coordination Committee then the Manager, Faculty Fund-Raising Unit, will convene a meeting with the appropriate development officers to resolve the coordination issue.

If an agreement is still not reached, the president or designate will be called upon to determine, in consultation with the interested parties, the order of access. In some cases, the prospect will be cleared for both faculties and will be cultivated/solicited on behalf of both interested parties. The donor will be given a choice.

e. *Time Limits*

The development officers are accountable for a deadline-oriented program of cultivation/solicitation; clearance is not given in perpetuity. Clearance for cultivation or solicitation activities is eligible up to a maximum of six months, with review after three months. If action is not taken within the specified time on a cleared prospect, and others are seeking clearance for the same prospect, a new coordination decision should be made, weighing all factors involved.

If solicitation of a prospect takes place and is declined, that prospect will no longer be considered cleared for re-solicitation by that faculty unless open-ended clearance has been given or circumstances resulting from the initial solicitation warrant renewed solicitation. If solicitation has not taken place within the specified time frame, clearance should be reconfirmed.

f. *Open-Ended Clearance*

In some cases, a prospect may be cleared on an open-ended basis for a particular faculty. This means that a prospect can be cultivated/solicited by the faculty at any time for approved projects. This clearance will be given when there is no evidence of potential conflict with other faculties and their approved case statement projects.

If a situation should arise that calls into question the previously granted open-ended clearance, the clearance may be reviewed, revised or reconfirmed.

g. *Declines*

If a solicitation of a prospect takes place and is declined, that prospect is no longer cleared for that faculty and must be formally cleared again through the Prospect Coordination Program for another project. A decline is reported to the Faculty Fund-Raising support staff and entered on the solicitation text screen on Advance. The clearance expiry date is brought forward to the current date on the advance system.                    November 28, 1996

## Prospect Coordination Protocol Detail

1. The prospect coordination forms are submitted to the Faculty Fund-Raising Unit support staff before the semi-monthly deadlines, which are predetermined dates. Contact the Faculty Fund-Raising Unit support staff for these dates.
2. The Faculty Fund-Raising Unit support staff reviews and collates the prospect coordination forms, ensuring that the information is complete. Incomplete forms will be returned to the applicant.
3. The collated prospect coordination forms are then reviewed and discussed in the bi-monthly Prospect Coordination Committee meeting. Decisions are made with further input as needed from appropriate parties such as: Presidents Circle, Planned Giving, Annual Fund & Awards. When the committee requires more information in order to make a clearance decision, the chair will defer the decision and determine the necessary follow-up.
4. The prospect coordination report, which summarizes the recommendations, is prepared by the Faculty Fund-Raising Services support staff and distributed within two working days.
5. The assigned clearances are entered on the Advance System by the Faculty Fund-Raising Unit support staff within two business days following the meeting.

6.  The Faculty Fund-Raising Unit support staff returns copies of the prospect co-ordination request to the originator, once a decision is reached.

7.  The original forms are filed in a binder by the Faculty Fund-Raising Unit support staff and kept in her/his office at Mary Bollert Hall.

8.  Copies of the finalized prospect coordination report are sent to:
    Director of Development
    Director, Advancement Services
    Manager, Annual Fund & Awards
    Manager, Faculty Fund-Raising Unit
    Manager, President's Circle
    Faculty Development Officers
    President's Circle Committee Rep

9.  The faculty development officers are responsible for maintaining accurate and current information on the solicitation text screen of the Advance System, including key meetings with the prospect, correspondence relating to proposals and solicitations, solicitation responses, recognition, declines and other relevant information.

10. Significant modifications to the solicitation strategy for which clearance was granted must be brought to the attention of the Prospect Coordination Chair & Committee.

11. Prospect Coordination is required for a group of alumni for solicitation purposes, and development officers must coordinate their plans and activities with the Manager, Annual Fund & Awards.

12. If a prospect is not on the Advance System when requesting clearance, the development officer forwards the basic information to Records, Information Services requesting (a) that it be entered on Advance and (b) that the Faculty Fund-Raising Unit support staff be notified when this is done. The information required by Records includes the individual name or organization and contact name, address and telephone numbers as well as other available information such as preferred title, affiliation to UBC and spouse's name.

                                                            November 28, 1996

# PROSPECT COORDINATION FORM:
## DONORS, PROSPECTIVE DONORS & VOLUNTEERS

| Development Officer | Faculty | Date |
|---|---|---|
| | | |

**A. Prospect Information**

| Prospect Name | Corp/Org Affiliation | Prospect ID |
|---|---|---|
| | | |

Region    (check one)

| East | West | International |
|---|---|---|
| | | |

**B. Clearance Requested (check one)**    *(solicmod)*

| Cultivation | Solicitation | Feasibility Study | Volunteer/FR Committee |
|---|---|---|---|
| | | | |

Presently Cleared For    *(solsminq)*

| N/A | Project | Faculty/Unit | School Clearance Code | Expiry Date    *(solacinq)* |
|---|---|---|---|---|
| | | | | |

**C. Clearance Requested For**

| Project | Solicitation Code | | | School Clearance Code |
|---|---|---|---|---|
| | F | / | / | |
| | Faculty | Project | Method | |

| Donor Initiated? | Academic Approval Date | By Whom |
|---|---|---|
| Yes        No | | |

**D. Campaign Plan**

| Amount currently required ($) | Ask amount ($) | Is this the lead gift? | Comment |
|---|---|---|---|
| | | Yes        No | |

**E. Prospect Detail**

Activities & timing to secure gift/participation _____

_____

Individual's affiliation to UBC/Faculty    *(alactinq)*

Known interests/giving policies relevant to your project    *(soltxinq/textinq)*

Other philanthropic/volunteer activities

| Lifetime giving amount    *(gsuminq)* | Largest gift/pledge amount | Date received | Account/Designation (gftsminq/pldsminq) |
|---|---|---|---|
| | | | |

Most recent Giving Club & last year of membership    *(gclubinq)*

| Chancellor's Circle | Wesbrook Society | Heritage Circle |
|---|---|---|
| | | |

**F. Types of Clearance**        (FOR DEVELOPMENT OFFICE USE ONLY)

| Cleared | Conditional | Coordinated | Declined |
|---|---|---|---|
| | | | |

| Clearance Review Date | Clearance Expiry Date |
|---|---|
| | |

Committee's comments

_____

_____

| Chair's signature | Solicitation code entered by |
|---|---|
| _____ | _____ |
| Date | Date |
| _____ | _____ |

# Appendix II—Prospect Coordination: Renewal Process

## Rationale:

Prospect coordination clearances are currently valid for a maximum of 6 months. When a prospect clearance expires, the PROSPECT COORDINATION RENEWAL form provides the opportunity for the FDO to extend the clearance for cultivation and/or solicitation of a prospect.

When clearances expire, the Advance Prospect Tracking is distributed by Unit FDO support staff to the appropriate FDO:

(I) to be aware of approaching expiry dates, both for their own prospects and for prospects cleared to others, who may now be re-entering the "pool" and;

(II) to complete and submit the PROSPECT COORDINATION RENEWAL form to the Unit Support staff for a decision by the Prospect Coordination Committee before the expiry date.

Incomplete forms will not be reviewed, but will be returned to the FDO.

## Process:

1.  Complete Prospect Coordination Renewal Form.

    *The Renewal Form should contain:*

    renewal period requested (up to a maximum of 6 months)

    reasons for the delay in the original cultivation/solicitation strategy

    the rationale for continuing cultivation/solicitation

    new plan of action

    $ amount currently required for the project

    the new ask amount

2.  Attach copy of the original Prospect Coordination Form.

3.  Forward to Faculty Fund-Raising Unit support staff.

4.  Decision will be made at next meeting of Prospect Coordination Staff.

5.  Extension will be granted if there is a valid reason and no one else is requesting clearance for this prospect.

6.  Process continues as per protocol; the Unit Secretary will make necessary changes to update the Advance System, and will record the new clearance expiry dates on the update report.

# PROSPECT COORDINATION RENEWAL FORM

| Development Officer | Faculty | Date |
|---|---|---|

**A. Prospect Information**

| Prospect Name | Corp/Org Affiliation | Prospect ID |
|---|---|---|

Region   (check one)

| East | West | International |
|---|---|---|

**B. Clearance Requested (check one)**   *(solicmod)*

| Cultivation | Solicitation | Feasibility Study | Volunteer/FR Committee |
|---|---|---|---|

Presently Cleared For   *(solsminq)*

| N/A | Project | | Faculty/Unit | School Clearance Code | Expiry Date   *(solacinq)* |
|---|---|---|---|---|---|

**C. Clearance Requested For**

| Project | | Solicitation Code | School Clearance Code |
|---|---|---|---|
| | | F _____ / _____ / _____<br>Faculty    Project    Method | |
| Donor Initiated?<br>Yes ___   No ___ | Academic Approval Date | By Whom | |

**D. Campaign Plan**

| Amount currently required ($) | Ask amount ($) | Is this the lead gift?<br>Yes ___   No ___ | Comment |
|---|---|---|---|

**E. Rationale For Renewal/New Activities & Timing Planned**

_____

_____

_____

_____

_____

_____

_____

**F. Types of Clearance**        (FOR DEVELOPMENT OFFICE USE ONLY)

| Cleared | Conditional | Coordinated | Declined |
|---|---|---|---|

| New Clearance Review Date | New Clearance Expiry Date |
|---|---|

Committee's comments

_____

_____          _____
Chair's signature                         Solicitation code entered by

_____          _____
Date                                          Date

FDO: Please attach a copy of original Prospect Coordination Form.

Revised May 1995
P–CO–FM3

## Appendix III—President's Circle Prospects/Donors

1. Identified President's Circle donors and prospects are *NOT* available for prospect coordination. All approaches to these prospects and donors are made directly to/through the PC Unit.
2. Submit a President's Circle Notification Form to *both* the Manager of President's Circle and the Prospect Coordination Committee via the Faculty Fund-Raising support staff.
3. The President's Circle representative will address the status of the President's Circle prospect at the following Prospect Coordination Committee meeting. This information will appear on the PC Report.
4. The FDO is responsible to meet with the President's Circle staff to plan strategy, if appropriate, for a President's Circle Unit approach.

November 28, 1996

**Resource 19**

# PRESIDENT'S CIRCLE NOTIFICATION FORM
## FOR CURRENT PC MEMBERS AND PC UNIT–IDENTIFIED PROSPECTS

| Development Officer | Faculty | Date |
|---|---|---|
| | | |

**A. Prospect Information**

| Prospect Name | Corp/Org Affiliation | Prospect ID |
|---|---|---|
| | | |

Region   (check one)

| East | West | International |
|---|---|---|
| | | |

**B. Activity Requested (check one)**   *(solicmod)*

| Cultivation | Solicitation | Feasibility Study | Volunteer/FR Committee |
|---|---|---|---|
| | | | |

**C. Campaign Plan**

| Amount currently required ($) | Ask amount ($) | Is this the lead gift? Yes ☐  No ☐ | Comment |
|---|---|---|---|
| | | | |

**D. Rationale For Approach including known interests, other philanthropic/volunteer activities and affiliation to UBC**

_____

_____

_____

_____

_____

_____

_____

_____

_____

President's Circle Unit's comments

_____

_____

_____
President's Circle Unit's signature

_____
Date

FDO: forward this request to 1. Manager, President's Circle and 2. Faculty Fund-Raising Unit Secretary for Prospect Coordination Committee/Records
President's Circle Unit: complete comments and forward copies to 1. FDO and 2. Faculty Fund-Raising Secretary

Revised May 1995
P–CO–FM2

**Resource 19**

# Appendix IV—Prospect Coordination Committee

1. COMMITTEE
   A. Mandate
      1. to coordinate prospect-related UBC Development activities
      2. to ensure that the process of prospect coordination continues to meet the needs of the various constituents in a timely, efficient and equitable manner
      3. to make adaptations, refinements and changes to the protocol and procedures as necessary
   B. Membership
      Chair—FDO (3 mo. rotating basis)
      1. Development Officer responsible for Chancellor's Circle and Eastern: FDO 3 mo. rotating basis
      2. Manager or delegate, President's Circle/International Unit
      3. Development Officer responsible for Chancellor's Circle and Eastern
   C. Roles & responsibilities
      Chair:
        schedules and chairs Prospect Coordination meetings
        has final call on committee recommendations
        ensures timely communication of results
        brings issues to appropriate Development unit(s) for problem solving as necessary
        oversees rewrites/changes to the protocol and procedures
      Committee members:
        review submissions, identify issues arising, recommend action
      President's Circle/Int & Eastern reps:
        inform chair/committee of current & past activity about requests re: President's Circle Notification Forms

The following material is from the *UBC Prospect Management Handbook:*

# MOVES MANAGEMENT TRACKING

1. When fundraising is done well, it's an Art. And when it's carefully carried out, it brings terrific joy to both the new donor and the institution receiving the gift. But, before that happy day is realized, fundraising is a bit of a chess game requiring careful research, discussions, strategies, *"moves"* (phone calls, introductions, meetings, letters, discussions, tours, proposals, etc.). Each and every strategy and "move" takes management. And tracking. *Lots of it.*

2. It takes a number of "moves" to help a prospect progress through each "stage of development." The following are the "status codes" we use to identify these stages:

   1) Identification/Research   . . . potential/links verified but no contact yet
   2) Cultivation   . . . meet, greet, interest and involve the prospect
   3) Solicitation   . . . we know their interests, and offer a proposal(s)
   4) Pending   . . . a proposal has been made; we await response, or tailor an ask
   5) Committed   . . . in writing
   6) Stewardship/Probate   . . . thanks, recognition, and plans for continued involvement!
   7) Declined   . . . not this time, thanks
   8) Withdrawn   . . . not the right fit for this project/faculty

3. No one can remember the myriad of details required to make hundreds of moves on hundreds of prospects in various stages of cultivation, solicitation, recognition, and stewardship! Therefore, it's *absolutely critical* that individual moves specifying the date, type of contact, purpose, outcome and next steps, as well as changes to "status code" be constantly and immediately updated on the Viking System.

4. The many reports currently available and under development will become Development Officer's bibles. As well, they are critical to directors and managers who must constantly monitor overall fundraising progress and quantitative "moves management" analyses.

# EVALUATION & REASSIGNMENT

1. As a rule, prospect assignments will stay with their PRIMARY if a reasonable level of activity is demonstrated in Viking's prospect management reports.

2. However, the Donor and the University will always take precedence if tough decisions arise.

3. The following are some reasons why names might be brought back to a PMC meeting for evaluation or reassignment discussion:

- The 6-month "lease" on a prospect has expired, and insufficient cultivation activity has taken place.
- The Development Officer voluntarily withdraws from the prospect because of a poor alignment and/or stated lack of interest on the part of the prospect.

## PRIMARY ACCOUNT MANAGER *("PRIMARY")* RESPONSIBILITIES

1. *Manage* the complete prospect file. . .
2. *Research* & *Qualify* the account.
3. Develop & document *overall account strategy* and *particular "Moves Management"* steps.
4. Ascertain when a *partnered approach strategy* will be beneficial, or at minimum, non-harmful, to UBC's relationship with the donor.
5. Work with *"Account Partners"* when advantageous to furthering a prospect's interests in UBC or securing a larger or greater number of gifts.
6. Proactively *chair strategy meetings* with all Account Partners.
7. Develop and discuss particular *"rules of engagement" each* Partner must adhere to regarding the cultivation & monitoring of his or her PRIMARY Accounts. (e.g. Once the PRIMARY & Partner have determined that they will partner on an account, and have decided what the cultivation strategy will be, the PRIMARY should *confirm* who is responsible for implementing & reporting on the cultivation; who is responsible for ensuring the right number of proper moves are made; if the partner has to vet every contact through the PRIMARY, or only those directly leading toward solicitation; at what level of detail does the PRIMARY want the Partner to report progress to him or her, etc.)
8. Ensure all Account Partners *share key prospect information* with one another.
9. Ensure *all "cultivation" contacts\** with prospect are appropriately *coordinated.*
10. Ensure all *solicitations* are timely and in line with overall account strategy.
11. Ensure meaningful *recognition* activities are planned and implemented (self & partners).
12. Develop and document *stewardship* activities (with assistance of Partners).
13. Regardless of who is making an actual solicitation at a specific time, it's the PRIMARY who is responsible for the *happiness of the prospect,* and the *securing of the eventual gift.* If the PRIMARY doesn't want this responsibility, the account should be reassigned.

\*PRIMARY Account Managers don't *always* have to know about *each* contact made with a prospect. But, they *are* responsible for ensuring everyone's "cultivation contacts" (contacts made with a prospect in order to eventually solicit and secure a gift) are coordinated—so that *all Partners* know "who's on base with what strategy at what moment"—*in advance of any moves.*

# PROSPECT MANAGEMENT COMMITTEE

## 1. THE TEAM

The Prospect Management Committee (PMC) is where the magic, fun and hard reality of teamwork happen. It's never easy. But it should be profitable . . . in terms of both UBC dollars raised and professional, collegiate satisfaction. Everyone will have to give and get a little, and look out for everyone else's interests as well as their own. Everyone will share in each other's "Wins!"

## 2. MEMBERS (currently 30)

- Chief Development Officer
- Director of Development, *PMC Chair*
- Prospect Coordination Manager, *PMC Vice-Chair*
- Associate Director, Faculty Fundraising
- Major Gifts Manager
- Planned Giving Manager
- Campaign Operations Manager
- Faculty Development Officers
- Major Gifts Officers
- International Unit, Development Officer
- Annual Fund Manager

## 3. MANDATE

- Share prospect knowledge to ensure *best* person makes the *best* ask at the *best* time!
- Share UBC knowledge, resources
- Discuss and improve one another's strategies
- Monitor overall moves management activity
- Monitor overall progress toward reaching financial objectives
- Review and comment on "Suspect Lists"
- Assign Suspects for 6 month lease to be researched (PMC consensus)
- Discuss and confirm prospect ratings (PMC consensus)
- Review and assign Prospects to PRIMARY Account Managers (PMC consensus)
- Approve (or withhold approval): Partner Assignments (PMC consensus)
- Review and reassign un-researched or "languishing" prospects (PMC consensus)
- Resolve conflicts (PMC consensus)

# ESSENTIAL INFORMATION CODES

If everyone commits him or herself to *rigorously maintaining* the database system, it will be extraordinarily *helpful* to all of us. If a few decide it's not worth the effort, the system will skew reports and subsequent planning, and become a *liability* to all of us.

It is essential that everyone learn the following procedures, and pay close attention to diligently entering and updating data as appropriate.

Every assigned major gift prospect on the system needs to have a few *essential pieces* of information attached to his/her/its file:

1. Status Code    Active:    Current, valid prospect under cultivation

                  Inactive:    No strategy in place; not qualified; not assigned

                  Note:    Only *active accounts* are included in prospect management reports.

| | |
|---|---|
| Location on Viking: | Solicitors and Contacts Screen |
| Updated by: | PAM's &/or Arno |

2. Stage of Cultivation Code    These codes are assigned in consultation with Arno and must be updated regularly to properly reflect the continuing evolution of each prospect's relationship with UBC.

- Identification
- Cultivation
- Solicitation
- Pending
- Committed
- Stewardship
- Declined
- Withdrawn

| | |
|---|---|
| Location on Viking: | Solicitors and Contacts Screen |
| Updated by: | Account Managers & Arno |

# PROSPECT TRACKING REPORTS

Currently there are *nine custom reports* that have been created on Viking for the purpose of prospect tracking. Others are still in the development stage, but should be available shortly.

Reports 1–6 listed below are run on a monthly basis by Arno, although they can be pulled at any time for periodic spot checks. Reports 7, 8 and 9 are run by Advancement Services. A sample of each report may be found in the appendices of the full version of the *UBC Prospect Management Handbook.*

1. *Active Count by Cultivation Stage*
   Total number of active, qualified prospects broken down by the cultivation stage codes in the preceding list, as well as by PRIMARY Account Manager. This is a good overall snapshot of the major gift "pipeline."

2. *Active Value by Cultivation Stage*
   Aggregate dollar value of the target ask associated with each active prospect. This report provides an indication of the total dollar potential of all prospects at each cultivation stage.

3. *Active Moves by Cultivation Stage*
   Total number of personalized (foreground) moves carried out over a one-month period, broken down by cultivation stage and PRIMARY Account Manager.

4. *Activity by Contact Type*
   Total number of personalized (foreground) moves carried out over a one-month period, classified by type of contact (i.e. phone call, meeting, correspondence) and PRIMARY Account Manager.

5. *Unassigned Active Prospects*
   Listing of prospects that have "fallen through the cracks." A useful tool for ongoing cleanup and maintenance of database integrity.

6. *Withdrawn from Pool*
   Listing of prospects that have been voluntarily removed by the PRIMARY Account Manager, due to a clear mismatch in donor interest and affiliation. These names are fed back into the overall pool and may be reassigned through the PMC.

# Appendix B i

UBPREP0040
3/17/99

## THE UNIVERSITY OF BRITISH COLUMBIA
## DEVELOPMENT OFFICE—PROSPECT MANAGEMENT
## COUNT OF ACTIVE PROSPECTS BY STAGE OF CULTIVATION
### AS AT MAR 17, 1999

| Development Officer | Identification | Cultivation | Solicitation | Pending | Committed | Stewardship | Declined | Withdrawn | TOTAL |
|---|---|---|---|---|---|---|---|---|---|
| Awards | 39 | | | | 1 | | | 9 | 49 |
| Director of Dvlpment | 12 | 2 | | | | | | | 14 |
| FDO—Agriculture | 13 | 23 | 1 | | 17 | 6 | 1 | 5 | 66 |
| FDO—Applied Science | 51 | 20 | | 1 | 1 | | | | 73 |
| FDO—Arts | 65 | 28 | 2 | | | 1 | | | 96 |
| FDO—Athletics | 34 | | 1 | 1 | 1 | 2 | | | 39 |
| FDO—Central Dvlpment | 5 | | | | | | | | 5 |
| FDO—Commerce | 69 | 2 | | 2 | 4 | 1 | | | 78 |
| FDO—Dentistry | 11 | 53 | 1 | | 1 | 1 | | | 67 |
| FDO—Education | 61 | 1 | | 1 | 1 | | | | 64 |
| FDO—Forestry | 30 | 13 | | | 1 | 4 | 6 | | 54 |
| FDO—Grad Studies | 38 | 21 | | | | | | | 59 |
| FDO—Law | 89 | 2 | | 2 | 1 | 1 | | | 95 |
| FDO—Libry./Frst Nation | 32 | 2 | | | | 1 | | | 35 |
| FDO—Medicine | 71 | 6 | | 1 | 3 | 17 | | | 98 |
| FDO—Pharm Sciences | 38 | | | | | | | | 38 |
| FDO—Science | 32 | 36 | 4 | 2 | 8 | 1 | | | 83 |
| FDO—Health Sciences | 1 | | | | | | | | 1 |
| FDO—Stdt/Acad Serv | 7 | | | | | | | | 7 |
| International Unit | 2 | 9 | | | 3 | 3 | | | 17 |
| Leadership | 28 | 106 | 2 | 2 | 4 | 8 | | | 150 |
| Leadership—West | | 1 | | | | | | | 1 |
| Mgr—UBC Fund | 114 | | | | | | | | 114 |

# Appendix B ii

UBPREP0041
3/17/99

## THE UNIVERSITY OF BRITISH COLUMBIA
## DEVELOPMENT OFFICE—PROSPECT MANAGEMENT
## VALUE OF ACTIVE PROSPECTS BY STAGE OF CULTIVATION
### AS AT MAR 17, 1999

| Development Officer | Identification | Cultivation | Solicitation | Pending | Committed | Stewardship | Declined | Withdrawn | TOTAL |
|---|---|---|---|---|---|---|---|---|---|
| Awards | | | | | 750,000 | | | | 750,000 |
| Director of Dvlpment | | 1,825,000 | | | | | | | 1,825,000 |
| FDO—Agriculture | 525,000 | 1,425,000 | 50,000 | | 1,200,000 | 50,000 | 25,000 | | 3,275,000 |
| FDO—Applied Science | 100,000 | 150,000 | | 2,000,000 | 1,000,000 | | | | 3,250,000 |
| FDO—Arts | 4,725,000 | 4,943,000 | 300,000 | | | 25,000 | | | 9,993,000 |
| FDO—Athletics | | | 110,000 | 230,000 | 140,000 | 92,043 | | | 572,043 |
| FDO—Central Dvlpment | 90,000 | | | | | | | | 90,000 |
| FDO—Commerce | 1,150,000 | 675,000 | | 50,188 | 1,278,000 | 25,000 | | | 3,178,188 |
| FDO—Dentistry | 75,000 | 5,155,000 | 25,000 | | 64,000 | | | | 5,319,000 |
| FDO—Education | 50,000 | 10,000 | | 26,665 | 14,000 | | | | 100,665 |
| FDO—Forestry | 575,000 | 1,175,000 | | | 50,000 | 3,000 | 450,000 | | 2,253,000 |
| FDO—Grad Studies | 2,000,000 | 1,775,000 | | | | | | | 3,775,000 |
| FDO—Law | 50,000 | 55,000 | | 55,000 | 50,000 | 1,000,000 | | | 1,210,000 |
| FDO—Libry./Frst Nation | 1,450,000 | 50,000 | | | | 1,000,000 | | | 2,500,000 |
| FDO—Medicine | 2,925,000 | 300,000 | | 681,000 | 1,112,000 | 950,000 | | | 5,968,000 |
| FDO—Pharm Sciences | | | | | | | | | |
| FDO—Science | 600,000 | 4,075,000 | 1,200,000 | 625,000 | 385,000 | 25,000 | | | 6,910,000 |
| FDO—Health Sciences | | | | | | | | | |
| FDO—Stdt/Acad Serv | | | | | | | | | |
| International Unit | | 11,025,000 | | | 7,000,000 | 2,000,000 | | | 20,025,000 |
| Leadership | 15,000,000 | 104,240,000 | 1,060,000 | 8,050,000 | 3,250,000 | 6,100,000 | | | 137,700,000 |
| Leadership—West | | 25,000 | | | | | | | 25,000 |

## Appendix B iii

UBPREP0042
3/17/99

### THE UNIVERSITY OF BRITISH COLUMBIA
### DEVELOPMENT OFFICE—PROSPECT MANAGEMENT
### MOVES BY STAGE OF CONTACT
### FOR THE MONTH OF FEB 99

| Development Officer | Identification | Cultivation | Solicitation | Pending | Committed | Stewardship | Declined | Withdrawn | TOTAL |
|---|---|---|---|---|---|---|---|---|---|
| Awards | | | | | 1 | | | | 1 |
| Director of Dvlpment | | 3 | | | | 4 | | | 7 |
| FDO—Agriculture | | 1 | | | 1 | 2 | | | 4 |
| FDO—Athletics | | | | 4 | | 1 | | | 5 |
| FDO—Dentistry | | 11 | | | | 1 | | | 12 |
| FDO—Forestry | | 1 | | | | | | | 1 |
| FDO—Law | | | 2 | | | | | | 2 |
| FDO—Medicine | | | | | | 1 | | | 1 |
| FDO—Science | | 1 | | | | | | | 1 |
| Leadership | | 14 | | 2 | 1 | 3 | | | 20 |
| Mgr-Planned Giving | | | | | | 3 | | | 3 |
| Total | | 31 | 2 | 6 | 3 | 15 | | | 57 |

# Appendix B v

## THE UNIVERSITY OF BRITISH COLUMBIA
## DEVELOPMENT OFFICE—PROSPECT MANAGEMENT
## UNASSIGNED ACTIVE PROSPECTS
## AS AT MAR 17, 1999

| Prospect ID | Prospect Name | Stage of Cultivation | Overall Cap/Inc | Overall Updated Date |
|---|---|---|---|---|
| 000049050 | | Withdrawn | 3E | 11/18/98 |
| 000054377 | | Committed | | 03/05/99 |
| 000065882 | | Stewardship | 2E | 02/26/99 |
| 000071627 | | Committed | 1E | 12/08/98 |
| 000077513 | | Identification | 3E | 11/18/98 |
| 000105185 | | Identification | 3E | 11/18/98 |
| 000115373 | | Withdrawn | 3E | 11/18/98 |
| 000138673 | | Stewardship | 2E | 01/22/96 |
| C00003957 | | Cultivation | 3D | 09/07/90 |
| C00005758 | | Identification | | 08/20/91 |

*Note:* Names have been deleted.

# Appendix B vii

03-MAR-99

## THE UNIVERSITY OF BRITISH COLUMBIA
## DEVELOPMENT OFFICE—PROSPECT MANAGEMENT
## ACCOUNT ACTIVITY BY ASSIGNMENT AS AT MARCH 3, 1999
## ASSIGNMENT: FDO—APPLIED SCIENCE

| Prospect ID | Prospect Name | Capacity/ Inclination | Stage of Cultivation | Last Closed Contact Date | Type | Next Open Contact Date | Type |
|---|---|---|---|---|---|---|---|
| 000000066 | | E 3 | Identification | 01-APR-98 | | 07-JAN-99 | |
| 000000123 | | E 3 | Identification | 01-APR-98 | | | |
| 000036921 | | A 2 | Cultivation | 04-DEC-98 | Correspondence | 26-FEB-99 | Background Move |
| 000047708 | | D 3 | Identification | 23-AUG-94 | | 21-DEC-95 | |
| 000058414 | | E 3 | Cultivation | 09-NOV-98 | | | |
| 000060209 | | E 3 | Cultivation | 18-MAY-98 | | | |
| 000089280 | | E 3 | Cultivation | 23-AUG-94 | | 03-SEP-97 | |
| 000092905 | | E 3 | Identification | 01-APR-98 | | | |
| 000099918 | | E 3 | Cultivation | 29-MAY-98 | | | |
| 000103714 | | C 1 | Committed | 29-MAY-98 | | | |
| 000136141 | | E 3 | Cultivation | 12-NOV-98 | | | |
| 000157739 | | E 3 | Cultivation | 08-JAN-99 | | | |
| 000166399 | | E 3 | Identification | 01-APR-98 | | | |
| 000173474 | | E 3 | Identification | 01-APR-98 | | 07-JAN-99 | |
| C00000126 | | E 3 | Identification | | | | |
| C00000557 | | E 3 | Identification | 01-APR-98 | | | |
| C00000596 | | E 3 | Identification | | | | |
| C00000600 | | E 3 | Cultivation | 01-APR-98 | | | |
| C00000608 | | E 3 | Identification | 01-APR-98 | | | |

Download: UBPREP0044    Access: PRSPMGMT    Report: Account Activity

*Note:* Names have been deleted.

## Appendix B ix

UBPREP0042
01/11/99

THE UNIVERSITY OF BRITISH COLUMBIA
DEVELOPMENT OFFICE—PROSPECT MANAGEMENT
OPEN MOVES BY STAGE OF CONTACT
FROM JAN 1 TO MAR 31 1999

| Development Officer | Identification | Cultivation | Solicitation | Pending | Committed | Stewardship | Declined | Withdrawn | TOTAL |
|---|---|---|---|---|---|---|---|---|---|
| FDO—Arts | | | | | | 3 | | | 3 |
| FDO—Athletics | | | | 1 | | | | | 1 |
| FDO—Grad Studies | | 1 | | | | | | | 1 |
| FDO—Science | | 1 | | | | | | | 1 |
| Leadership | | 1 | | | | | | | 1 |
| Total | | 3 | | 1 | | 3 | | | 7 |

**Resource 19**

# University of British Columbia Development Office

# Prospect Management Codes October 1998

1.  Prospect Status (Prospect Status Screen)

| Code | Description | Meaning |
| --- | --- | --- |
| AC | Active | Strategy & assignment established. |
| IN | Inactive | No strategy in place; on hold pending identification of appropriate partners/projects |

2.  Stage of Cultivation (Prospect Status Screen)

| Code | Description | Meaning |
| --- | --- | --- |
| ID | Identification | Prospect has been cleared by the PMC and has been assigned an initial LAI rating |
| CU | Cultivation | A program of regular, meaningful contact has been established with the prospect |
| SO | Solicitation | Prospect has been adequately engaged and is ready to be formally approached for a commitment. Ask is generally expected to be made within 3 months |
| PE | Pending | Approach has been made; waiting for response or in negotiation |
| CM | Committed | Prospect has agreed to support the university; documentation has been received |
| ST | Stewardship | Gift has been received and donor has been publicly recognized. Donor enters phase of ongoing relationship management and may be eligible for future re-solicitation |
| DE | Declined | Prospect has chosen not to support the university at this time; may be eligible for future re-solicitation |
| WI | Withdrawn | Prospect is no longer considered appropriate for the current approach/assignment; strategy & partners need to be re-evaluated |

"Inclination" is a composite code comprising measures of both "interest" and "linkage." This is a highly subjective assessment of donor motivation, and the definition attributed to each code should be regarded as a general guideline. As cultivation progresses these ratings will be adjusted (upward, hopefully!)

| *Capacity* | | *Inclination* | |
|------------|--------------|---------------|------------------------------------------|
| CODE  MEANING | | CODE  MEANING | |
| A | $5M+ | 1 | VERY STRONG |
| | | | • Strong volunteer history |
| | | | • Current or recent major donor |
| | | | • Interests/partners certain |
| B | $1M–$4.9M | 2 | STRONG |
| | | | • Active volunteer |
| | | | • Consistent donor |
| | | | • Interests/partners being identified |
| C | $500K–$999K | 3 | MODERATE |
| | | | • Moderate interest |
| | | | • Occasional donor |
| | | | • Partners unknown |
| D | $100K–$499K | 4 | MINIMAL |
| | | | • Minimal interest |
| | | | • Negligible donation history |
| | | | • Little or no previous contact |
| E | $25K–$99K | 5 | UNKNOWN |
| | | | • No known relationship |
| | | | • Possible hostility |

**Resource 19**

# UNIVERSITY OF FLORIDA OFFICE OF DEVELOPMENT
## 1ST QUARTER REVIEW
## 1998/1999 QUARTERLY REVIEW & STRATEGIC PLAN
### RUN DATE: OCTOBER 31, 1998

Development Officer: _____    College or Area Represented: _____

| | Year to Date Achieved | 1998/1999 Annual Goal | % Goal Achieved | 1st Qtr Goal | 1st Qtr Achieved | 2nd Qtr Goal |
|---|---|---|---|---|---|---|
| **A. GOALS** | | | | | | |
| 1. Amount Raised:[a] | | | | | | |
|   Gifts | | | | | | |
|   Pledges/Expectancies | | | | | | |
|   Total | | | | | | |
| 2. Proposals Submitted:[b] | | | | | | |
|   $1,000,000+ | | | | | | |
|   $500,000+ | | | | | | |
|   $100,000+ | | | | | | |
|   $10,000+ | | | | | | |
|   $2,000+ | | | | | | |
|   Total | 0 | 0 | 0% | 0 | | |
| 3. New Commitments Received:[c] | | | | | | |
|   $1,000,000+ | | | | | | |
|   $500,000+ | | | | | | |
|   $100,000+ | | | | | | |
|   $10,000+ | | | | | | |
|   $2,000+ | | | | | | |
|   Total | 0 | 0 | 0% | 0 | | |
| 4. Dollar Total of New Commitments Received: | | | 0% | | | |
| 5. Total Bonus Pay Percentage Points: | | | 0% | | | |
| 6. New Prospects Identified:[b] | | | | | | |
|   $1,000,000+ | | | | | | |
|   $500,000+ | | | | | | |
|   $100,000+ | | | | | | |
|   $10,000+ | | | | | | |
|   $2,000+ | | | | | | |
|   Total | 0 | 0 | | 0 | | |

7. Personal Contacts: / /

8. Bequest Society Proposals Submitted:[b]
   $100,000+ / /
   $10,000+ / /
                                                             / /

9. Annual Other Objectives 1998/1999:

10. Results of Annual Other Objectives During Last Quarter (not covered in 1–9 above):

    *Objectives*                                    *Results*

    a.

    b.

    c.

11. Next Quarter Other Objectives Planned:

    a .

    b .

    c .

[a]Gifts, pledges/expectancies as received by college/unit (including state match)
[b]From Prospect Tracking / Advance (excluding state match)
[c]From Prospect Tracking / Advance (including anticipated state match)

**Resource 19**

# UNIVERSITY OF FLORIDA OFFICE OF DEVELOPMENT
## 1ST QUARTER REVIEW, Cont'd.

B. TOP 10 GIFTS/PLEDGES RECEIVED DURING LAST QUARTER:

Commitments = gifts + documented pledges/expectancies.

Type = cash, securities, gift-in-kind, real estate, annuities and trusts, pledge, bequest, insurance.

C. PROPOSALS SUBMITTED FY TO DATE EXCLUDING STATE MATCH (details of #2 on page 1):

D. NEW COMMITMENTS RECEIVED FY TO DATE INCLUDING STATE MATCH (details of #3 on page 1):

E. NUMBER OF PERSONAL CONTACTS MADE BY TYPE OF VISIT DURING LAST QUARTER:

Recruitment/Volunteer      Identification      Cultivation

     Solicitation      Stewardship      TOTAL

F. MAJOR GIFTS FOR OTHER COLLEGES OR AREAS OR UNRESTRICTED TO THE UNIVERSITY IN WHICH YOU PARTICIPATED:
(applicable only to college or area development officers)

G. COMMENTS BY DEVELOPMENT OFFICER:

# UNIVERSITY OF FLORIDA OFFICE OF DEVELOPMENT
## 1ST QUARTER REVIEW, Cont'd.

H.  COMMENTS BY MANAGER:

Signatures:

_____   _____
Development Officer                (date)

_____   _____
Manager                            (date)

cc: Vice President, Dean or Director
Vice President for Development and Alumni Affairs

# UNIVERSITY OF FLORIDA FOUNDATION, INC.
## PROSPECT TRACKING/ADVANCE
## COUNTS AND MOVES REPORT FOR PRIOR MONTH

**Officer: Overall Officer Summary**

| | Status 1 Identification (Added) | Status 2 Cultivation (Moved) | Status 3 Solicitation (Moved) | Status C Committed (Moved) | Status D Declined (Moved) | Total |
|---|---|---|---|---|---|---|
| 1,000,000 and Up | 75 (5) 1.6% | 154 (3) 3.3% | 204 (12) 4.4% | 155 (8) 3.3% | 31 (1) .6% | 619 (29) 13.6% |
| 500,000–999,999 | 71 (5) 1.4% | 103 (12) 2.2% | 103 (8) 2.2% | 149 (5) 3.2% | 16 (1) .2% | 442 (31) 9.7% |
| 100,000–499,999 | 320 (8) 7.0% | 371 (17) 8.1% | 367 (26) 8.0% | 495 (15) 10.9% | 100 (3) 2.1% | 1,653 (69) 36.5% |
| 50,000–99,999 | 193 (9) 4.1% | 239 (10) 5.2% | 134 (8) 2.9% | 281 (17) 6.1% | 53 1.0% | 900 (44) 19.8% |
| 10,000–49,999 | 917 (12) 20.2% | 369 (8) 8.1% | 320 (19) 7.0% | 704 (19) 15.4% | 108 (7) 2.2% | 2,418 (65) 53.3% |
| TOTAL: | 1,576 (39) 34.8% | 1,236 (50) 27.2% | 1,128 (73) 24.9% | 1,784 (64) 39.3% | 308 (12) 6.8% | 6,032 (238) |

Number of Personal Contact Reports During Prior Month

| | |
|---|---|
| Recruitment/Volunteer: | 45 |
| Identification/Evaluation: | 60 |
| Cultivation: | 205 |
| Solicitation: | 156 |
| Stewardship: | 124 |
| Total: | 590 |

**Resource 19**

# RULES REGARDING CHARITABLE TAX DEDUCTIONS

PREPARED BY ALAN M. SPEARS, EXECUTIVE DIRECTOR,
OFFICE OF PLANNED AND MAJOR GIFTS,
INDIANA UNIVERSITY FOUNDATION,
ON THE BASIS OF
INTERNAL REVENUE SERVICE INFORMATION
(As of September 2000)

# Income Tax Charitable Deductions

   I. *Total amount of the charitable deduction*
     A. Cash: face amount
     B. Securities and real estate owned over one year: fair market value
     C. Securities and real estate owned one year or less: cost basis or fair market value, whichever is less
     D. Tangible personal property
        1. "Related use," owned over one year: fair market value
        2. "Related use," owned one year or less: cost basis or fair market value, whichever is less
        3. "Unrelated use," owned over one year: cost basis or fair market value, whichever is less
        4. "Unrelated use," owned one year or less: cost basis or fair market value, whichever is less
     E. Inventory (excluding inventory contributed for research and other special cases): cost basis or fair market value, whichever is less

*Note:* The above amounts apply to public charities, pass-through foundations, and private operating foundations. If the gift is made to a private, nonoperating foundation, the amount of the deduction is the face amount for cash and the fair market value for publicly traded securities, but for all other property the deduction is limited to cost basis (or fair market value if less than cost basis).

   II. *The amount of the charitable deduction that can be reported in any one year depends on the type of property contributed and the type of nonprofit organization to which the donor makes their gift.*
     A. Type of property contributed
        1. Cash and all ordinary income property: 50 percent of adjusted gross income (AGI)
        2. Appreciated long-term capital gain property: 30 percent of AGI
     B. Type of organization
        1. Public charities: educational institutions, churches, tax-exempt hospitals, governmental units, publicly supported organizations such as the American Red Cross or a symphony orchestra, broadly supported and private operating foundations—50 percent or 30 percent of AGI, depending on type of property.
        2. Private nonoperating foundations
           a. Cash and ordinary income property: 30 percent of AGI
           b. Long-term capital gain property: 20 percent of AGI

III. *Carryovers,* when the total allowable deduction cannot be reported in a single year. Donor has year of gift plus five carryover years in which to use it. (Carryovers apply to private nonoperating foundations as well as to public charities and operating foundations.)

IV. *Pledges.* The deduction is taken in the year the pledge is paid, not when it is made. The IRS takes the position that a written commitment or a promissory note is merely an intention to pay and not a payment. This is true even if the donor makes provision in his or her will to ensure that any outstanding balance on the pledge will be covered by bequest.

If all or a portion of the pledge is unfulfilled at the time of the donor's death, and the donor's promise is enforceable against his estate, the payment of the pledge qualifies for an estate tax deduction.

V. *When a gift is completed*

A. *Gift by check.* The effective date of the contribution is the day the check is mailed or hand-delivered, provided there are no restrictions on the cashing of the check. A check dated December 31, 1999, mailed and postmarked the same date, is deductible in 1999. It does not matter that the charity receives the check in the new year and that it is actually charged to the donor's account in January. However, a check dated in December but not mailed or handed to the charity until January cannot be deducted on the prior-year return. Neither can a check that is mailed in December but postdated so that it cannot be cashed until the next month.

B. *Gift of securities.* If the certificate is registered in the name of the donor and property endorsed or accompanied by a separate stock or bond power assignment, the date of the gift is the date on which the security is hand-delivered or mailed.

If the certificate is in "street name" and held by the donor's broker, the date of the gift is the day when, on proper instructions from the donor, the broker charges the donor's account and credits the charity's account with the particular shares or bonds donated.

If the donor has a certificate re-registered in the name of the charity, the date of the gift is the date on the certificate. This procedure is not advisable for year-end gifts, as re-registration by the transfer agent can take several weeks.

C. *Gift of real estate.* The gift is complete on the day when the signed deed is delivered or mailed to the charitable organization.

VI. *Valuation of securities.* For publicly traded securities, the deduction is the mean between the "high" and the "low" on the date of the gift. For unlisted securities (for example, those sold over the counter), it is the mean between the "bid" and "asked" prices. In short, the deduction is the average value of the securities on the day the donor relinquishes control. Value is not dependent on the net proceeds actually received by the charity when the securities are sold.

The valuation of some securities—such as certain municipal bonds and closely held stock—are not quoted and may not be readily ascertainable. A broker can usually ascertain market values of bonds. Closely held stock presents a different set of problems and must be valued by a qualified appraiser's accounting procedures that take into consideration a number of factors about the company.

VII. *Volunteers' expenses*

A. *Gifts of services.* The value of a volunteer's time is not deductible. For example, if an attorney who normally charges clients $150 per hour gives two hours of free legal service to the charity, the attorney may not deduct $300. Neither may volunteers who serve on committees and boards deduct the value of their time. Likewise, newspapers that grant free advertising space and radio and television stations that offer free broadcast time are not allowed a deduction. These are all treated as gifts of services and thus are not deductible.

B. *Out-of-pocket expenses.* Out-of-pocket expenses incurred by a volunteer while working for the charity are deductible. Examples of deductible items are telephone calls, stationery, postage stamps, and travel between home and the places where the volunteer renders services. A volunteer who uses a personal automobile may deduct the actual costs of gas, tolls, and parking (but not insurance or depreciation) or may calculate a flat 12 cents a mile. If the volunteer attends an out-of-town convention representing the charity in an official capacity, lodging, meals, and transportation are also deductible. These items are not deductible if the volunteer attends the convention merely to enhance knowledge and skills.

VIII. *Substantiation requirements (gift receipts)*

A. Gift of $250 or more—no goods or services provided to the donor
   1. Donor must obtain a receipt from the nonprofit to support the deduction. A canceled check is insufficient.
   2. Receipt must state that no goods or services were provided to the donor.
   3. The $250 requirement applies to each gift. The gifts to a single charity are not cumulative.

B. Gift of $75 or more—goods or services provided to the donor

1. Nonprofit is required to provide a receipt, informing the donor of the amount of the contribution that is deductible.
2. The receipt could contain either of two statements:
   a. If the value of the premium does not exceed $71 (adjusted for inflation each year) or 2 percent of the gift, whichever is less, the receipt could say something like "Under IRS guidelines, the value of the benefits is within the allowable limits; therefore, the full amount of your payment is a deductible contribution."
   b. If the benefits exceed these *de minimis* limits, the receipt must provide a good faith estimate of the value of those benefits and indicate the deductible amount.
3. Intangible benefits such as a name on a building or endowment are not counted.

C. Failure to provide the required information can subject the charity to penalties—$10 per contribution and up to $5,000 per fundraising event

IX. *Substantiation requirements*

A. Form 8283: Information About Donated Property
1. *Form 8283 is required* if the total value of all property contributed, other than cash, exceeds $500. Depending on the value and type of property contributed, the donor may need to complete Section A, Section B, or both.
2. Types of contributions reported in Section A
   a. Publicly traded securities
   b. Real estate and tangible property (paintings, boats, and other items) valued between $500 and $5,000
   c. Closely held securities (not traded publicly) valued between $500 and $10,000
3. Types of contributions reported in Section B
   a. Real estate and tangible property (paintings, boats, and other items) valued between $500 and $5,000. Section B must be completed if the aggregate claimed value of all similar items exceeds $5,000, even if the value of each single item is less than $5,000.
   b. Closely held securities (not traded publicly) valued in excess of $10,000.
4. *Qualified appraisal.* To receive a charitable deduction for gifts of property covered by the requirement, the donor must obtain a qualified appraisal and attach an appraisal summary to the tax return on which the deduction is first claimed.

   A qualified appraisal must meet the following criteria:

   a. It is completed not earlier than 60 days prior to the date of
      contribution.
   b. It is prepared by a qualified appraiser—a person who is profes-
      sionally qualified to appraise the type of property being valued.
      The appraiser should be independent of both donor and donee.
      The appraisal cannot be done by anyone affiliated with the charity.
   c. It does not involve a prohibited type of appraisal fee. The fee
      should not be based on a percentage of the appraised value of
      the property. It should rather be a flat fee based on the time and
      expenses of the appraiser.
5. *Appraisal summary.* The appraisal summary should be made on
   Section B of Form 8283 and include the following information as
   required.
   a. Donor's name and taxpayer identification number (social security
      number in the case of an individual)
   b. Description of the property
   c. Date of acquisition
   d. Donor's cost or other tax basis for the property
   e. Nonprofit's name, address, and tax identification number
   f. Date on which the nonprofit received the property
   g. Name, address, and tax identification number of the appraiser
      (Section B only)
   h. Fair market value of the property
   i. The appraiser's declaration that he or she is qualified and did not
      charge a fee under a prohibited method (Section B only)

*Note:* After completing the form but before filing it with the tax return, the donor
should have it signed by the nonprofit. The nonprofit should retain a copy.

B. Form 8282: Information About Sale of Donated Property
   1. *Form 8282 is required* if the nonprofit sells or otherwise disposes of
      the property (real estate valued in excess of $5,000, closely held stock
      valued over $10,000) within two years after receiving it.
   2. The nonprofit must file the form.
   3. Information reported on form
      a. Name and tax identification number of the donor
      b. Name, address, and tax identification number of the charity
      c. Description of the donated property
      d. Date of gift and date of disposition
      e. Appraised value
      f. Selling price or amount received from other type of disposition

    4. Donor is entitled to a copy. The nonprofit should send a copy of this information to the donor.

C. Form 1040: Income Tax Return

    1. Documents and information to be included for outright gifts

      a. For cash contributions of more than $3,000 to any one charity, state name of charity and amount given.

      b. For noncash gifts over $500, attach Form 8283.

    2. Documents and information to be included for irrevocable deferred gifts

      a. Name of charity, type of gift vehicle, and amount contributed

      b. Form 8283 for noncash gifts over $500, same as for outright gifts

      c. Computation form showing value of remainder interest

      d. Copy of the trust agreement, gift annuity agreement, or instrument of transfer

D. Form 709: Gift Tax Return

    1. *Form 709 is required* in the following circumstances:

      a. For gift annuities where gift value exceeds $10,000. Also if the annuitant is neither the donor nor the donor's spouse and the actuarial value exceeds $10,000.

      b. For bargain sales where gift value exceeds $10,000

      c. For charitable remainder trusts, pooled income fund gifts, and retained life estates where charity has a future interest, whatever the amount

      d. For charitable lead trusts in most instances

*Note:* The donor should file Form 709 even when no gift tax is due.

    2. Documents and information to be included: name of nonprofit, type of gift, amount contributed, and computation form showing value of remainder interest or other charitable interest

X. *Corporate contributions.* Same rules as for individual contributions, but with the following differences.

A. The maximum amount of charitable deductions the corporation can use in one year is 10 percent of taxable income.

B. Corporations may contribute inventory for research purposes or for the care of the ill and needy and deduct up to twice the manufacturing costs (see Section XI for details).

XI. *Corporate gifts of inventory.* Normally, if a corporation donates inventory to a charity, the deduction is limited to the cost basis (the actual manufacturing cost if the company produced the item). There are, however, two exceptions:

A. For a contribution of newly manufactured scientific equipment to colleges and universities for research and experimentation, including research training, the corporation is allowed a deduction of either cost basis plus 50 percent of the appreciation or twice the corporation's cost basis, whichever is less.

    The contribution must be to the physical and biological sciences—engineering, medicine, chemistry, physics, zoology, or the like. The increased deduction does not apply to gifts to the social sciences and humanities. Further, the following requirements must be met:

1. The corporation must have manufactured the equipment.
2. The contribution must be made no later than two years after the property was completed.
3. The original use of the property must be by the donee.
4. The donee cannot sell the property for money, services, or other equipment.
5. The donee must provide the corporation with a written statement that the use of the property will fulfill the requirements.

B. For a contribution of inventory to be applied for the care of the ill, the needy, or infants, corporations may also receive a deduction of either cost basis plus 50 percent of the appreciation or twice the corporation's cost basis, whichever is less.

# Gift and Estate Tax Charitable Deductions

1. *Gift tax* is levied on a person's right to transmit property during his or her lifetime. The amount of the tax depends on the size of the gift.
2. *Estate tax* is levied on the right to transmit property at death. The amount of the tax depends on the size of the estate the deceased leaves.
3. *Historical background.* The federal government adopted the estate tax first, followed by the gift tax. The purpose of the estate tax was to raise revenue and redistribute wealth. The purpose of the gift tax was to reinforce the estate tax by discouraging people from giving property during their lifetime in order to avoid the estate tax. Until 1976, the estate and gift taxes were largely independent of each other. If a person made a taxable gift during his or her lifetime, the tax was computed using the gift tax rate schedule. If the gift was made at death, the tax was imposed on the estate of the deceased and was computed using the estate tax rate schedule. It was generally advantageous for a wealthy person to give away as much as practical while living because the total tax would be less.

   The 1976 act eliminated the dual tax system and thereby removed most of the incentive for transferring property during one's lifetime. The two tables were replaced by a single progressive rate schedule that applies to the cumulative total of all transfers during life and at death. Thus if a person made $400,000 of taxable gifts during life and died with a taxable estate of $600,000, the transfer tax could be computed on a total taxable estate of $1,000,000.

   Another revision brought about by the 1976 act was the substitution of a single "unified" credit for the lifetime $30,000 gift tax exemption and the $60,000 estate tax exemption. Today, a person may transfer $675,000 of bequests to noncharitable beneficiaries without incurring tax. This will increase progressively to $1,000,000 by 2006.
4. *Annual gift tax exclusion.* An individual may give another individual up to $10,000 in cash or property each year without having to report the gift or incurring a gift tax. There is no limit to the number of individuals to which such gifts may be made. Husbands and wives may join together and give up to $20,000 (indexed for inflation under 1997 law) to any individual without tax (this is known as *gift-splitting*).

   To qualify for the annual exclusion, the gifts must be present-interest gifts. That is, the donee must have a right to benefit from the property now.
5. *Marital deductions.* Gifts of any size between spouses are not subject to gift tax. Likewise, the first spouse to die can now leave an unlimited amount to

the surviving spouse completely free of federal estate tax. The amount passing to the surviving spouse can qualify for this marital deduction if it is given outright or under certain approved trust agreements.

6. *Deductibility of lifetime gifts to charity.* A donor is allowed an unlimited charitable gift tax deduction for lifetime gifts to qualified charities. However, the donor is required to complete a gift tax return (Form 709) if making a future-interest gift such as a charitable remainder trust or a gift annuity.

7. *Deductibility of bequests to charity.* A donor is allowed an unlimited charitable estate tax deduction. If the bequest is in the form of a charitable remainder trust with survivor as income beneficiary, the deduction is for the present value of the remainder interest. If a surviving spouse is the only income beneficiary, the combination of the marital deduction and charitable deduction will eliminate estate tax on the property.

# IRS PUBLICATIONS AND FORMS

---

| Form **8233**<br>(Rev. October 1996)<br><br>Department of the Treasury<br>Internal Revenue Service | **Exemption From Withholding on Compensation<br>for Independent (and Certain Dependent) Personal<br>Services of a Nonresident Alien Individual**<br>▶ See separate instructions. | OMB No. 1545-0795 |
|---|---|---|

This exemption is applicable for compensation for calendar year 19 ......., or other tax year beginning ........................, 19......., and ending ............, 19 ...... .

**Part I    Nonresident Alien Individual Identification (See Specific Instructions)**

| Name | Taxpayer identification number .................................................... |
|---|---|
| U.S. address (number and street) (Include apt. or suite no. or P.O. box) | United States visa type and number ..................................... |
| City, state, and ZIP code | |

Citizens of Canada or Mexico complete either lines 1a and 1b or line 2 below; all other filers complete lines 1a, 1b, and 2.

| **1a** Country issuing passport ...................................<br>  **b** Passport number ........................................... | **2**  Permanent foreign address |
|---|---|

**3**    Compensation is for services performed by me as a:
☐ Self-employed person (independent personal services)    ☐ Foreign student    ☐ Foreign professor/teacher
☐ Foreign researcher    ☐ Business/vocational trainee

**Caution:** *If you are a foreign student, foreign professor/teacher, or foreign researcher, see the **line 3 instructions** for the required additional statement you must attach.*

**4**    Compensation for independent (and certain dependent) personal services:
  **a**  Description of personal services you are providing............................................................................................
........................................................................................................................................................................
........................................................................................................................................................................

  **b**  Total compensation you expect to be paid for these services in this calendar or tax year  $ ......................................

**5**    If compensation is exempt from withholding because of a U.S. tax treaty, provide:
  **a**  Tax treaty **and treaty article** under which you are claiming exemption from withholding ......................................
........................................................................................................................................................................

  **b**  Total compensation listed in 4b above that is exempt from tax under this treaty  $ .................................................
  **c**  Country of permanent residence .................................................................................................................

**6**    Additional facts to justify the exemption from withholding................................................................................
........................................................................................................................................................................
........................................................................................................................................................................
........................................................................................................................................................................

| **7**  Number of personal exemptions<br>      claimed ▶ | **8**  How many days will you perform services in<br>      the United States during this tax year? ▶ |
|---|---|

Under penalties of perjury, I declare that I have examined this form and any accompanying statements, and, to the best of my knowledge and belief, they are true, correct, and complete. I also declare, under penalties of perjury, that I am not a citizen or resident of the United States.

Signature of nonresident alien individual ▶                                        Date ▶

**Part II    Withholding Agent Certification**

| Name | Employer identification number |
|---|---|
| Address (number and street) (Include apt. or suite no. or P.O. box, if applicable.) | |
| City, state, and ZIP code | Telephone number<br>(      ) |

Under penalties of perjury, I certify that I have examined this form and any accompanying statements, that I am satisfied that an exemption from withholding is warranted, and that I do not know or have reason to know that the nonresident alien individual's compensation is not entitled to the exemption or that the eligibility of the nonresident alien's compensation for the exemption cannot be readily determined.

Signature of withholding agent ▶                                        Date ▶

**For Paperwork Reduction Act Notice, see separate instructions.**              Cat. No. 62292k              Form **8233** (Rev. 10-96)

Form **8282**

(Rev. September 1998)

Department of the Treasury
Internal Revenue Service

### Donee Information Return

(Sale, Exchange, or Other Disposition of Donated Property)

▶ See instructions on back.

OMB No. 1545-0908

**Give a Copy to Donor**

| Please Print or Type | Name of charitable organization (donee) | Employer identification number |
|---|---|---|
| | Address (number, street, and room or suite no.) | |
| | City or town, state, and ZIP code | |

**Part I**  Information on ORIGINAL DONOR and DONEE Receiving the Property

| 1a  Name(s) of the original donor of the property | 1b  Identifying number |
|---|---|

**Note:** *Complete lines 2a–2d only if you gave this property to another charitable organization (successor donee).*

| 2a  Name of charitable organization | 2b  Employer identification number |
|---|---|
| 2c  Address (number, street, and room or suite no.) | |
| 2d  City or town, state, and ZIP code | |

**Note:** *If you are the original donee, skip Part II and go to Part III now.*

**Part II**  Information on PREVIOUS DONEES—Complete this part only if you were not the first donee to receive the property. If you were the second donee, leave lines 4a–4d blank. If you were a third or later donee, complete lines 3a–4d. On lines 4a–4d, give information on the preceding donee (the one who gave you the property).

| 3a  Name of original donee | 3b  Employer identification number |
|---|---|
| 3c  Address (number, street, and room or suite no.) | |
| 3d  City or town, state, and ZIP code | |
| 4a  Name of preceding donee | 4b  Employer identification number |
| 4c  Address (number, street, and room or suite no.) | |
| 4d  City or town, state, and ZIP code | |

**Part III**  Information on DONATED PROPERTY—If you are the original donee, leave column (c) blank.

| (a) Description of donated property sold, exchanged, or otherwise disposed of (if you need more space, attach a separate statement) | (b) Date you received the item(s) | (c) Date the first donee received the item(s) | (d) Date item(s) sold, exchanged, or otherwise disposed of | (e) Amount received upon disposition |
|---|---|---|---|---|
| | | | | |
| | | | | |
| | | | | |
| | | | | |
| | | | | |
| | | | | |
| | | | | |

For Paperwork Reduction Act Notice, see back of form.                Cat. No. 62307Y                Form **8282** (Rev. 9-98)

| Form **8283** | **Noncash Charitable Contributions** | OMB No. 1545-0908 |
|---|---|---|
| (Rev. October 1998) | ▶ Attach to your tax return if you claimed a total deduction of over $500 for all contributed property. | Attachment Sequence No. **55** |
| Department of the Treasury Internal Revenue Service | ▶ See separate instructions. | |
| Name(s) shown on your income tax return | | Identifying number |

**Note:** *Figure the amount of your contribution deduction before completing this form. See your tax return instructions.*

**Section A**—List in this section **only** items (or groups of similar items) for which you claimed a deduction of $5,000 or less. Also, list certain publicly traded securities even if the deduction is over $5,000 (see instructions).

**Part I**   **Information on Donated Property**—If you need more space, attach a statement.

| 1 | (a) Name and address of the donee organization | (b) Description of donated property |
|---|---|---|
| A | | |
| B | | |
| C | | |
| D | | |
| E | | |

**Note:** *If the amount you claimed as a deduction for an item is $500 or less, you do not have to complete columns (d), (e), and (f).*

| | (c) Date of the contribution | (d) Date acquired by donor (mo., yr.) | (e) How acquired by donor | (f) Donor's cost or adjusted basis | (g) Fair market value | (h) Method used to determine the fair market value |
|---|---|---|---|---|---|---|
| A | | | | | | |
| B | | | | | | |
| C | | | | | | |
| D | | | | | | |
| E | | | | | | |

**Part II**   **Other Information**—Complete line 2 if you gave less than an entire interest in property listed in Part I. Complete line 3 if conditions were attached to a contribution listed in Part I.

2   If, during the year, you contributed less than the entire interest in the property, complete lines a–e.

a   Enter the letter from Part I that identifies the property ▶ _____. If Part II applies to more than one property, attach a separate statement.

b   Total amount claimed as a deduction for the property listed in Part I:   **(1)** For this tax year    ▶ _____ .
                         **(2)** For any prior tax years   ▶ _____ .

c   Name and address of each organization to which any such contribution was made in a prior year (complete only if different from the donee organization above):

Name of charitable organization (donee)

Address (number, street, and room or suite no.)

City or town, state, and ZIP code

d   For tangible property, enter the place where the property is located or kept ▶ _____

e   Name of any person, other than the donee organization, having actual possession of the property ▶ _____

3   If conditions were attached to any contribution listed in Part I, answer questions a – c and attach the required statement (see instructions).

| | | Yes | No |
|---|---|---|---|
| a | Is there a restriction, either temporary or permanent, on the donee's right to use or dispose of the donated property? . . . . . . . . . . . . . . . . . . . . . . . . . . . . . . | | |
| b | Did you give to anyone (other than the donee organization or another organization participating with the donee organization in cooperative fundraising) the right to the income from the donated property or to the possession of the property, including the right to vote donated securities, to acquire the property by purchase or otherwise, or to designate the person having such income, possession, or right to acquire? . . . . . . . | | |
| c | Is there a restriction limiting the donated property for a particular use? . . . . . . . . . . | | |

**For Paperwork Reduction Act Notice, see page 4 of separate instructions.**     Cat. No. 62299J     Form **8283** (Rev. 10-98)

Form 8283 (Rev. 10-98) Page **2**

| Name(s) shown on your income tax return | Identifying number |
| --- | --- |

**Section B—Appraisal Summary**—List in this section only items (or groups of similar items) for which you claimed a deduction of more than $5,000 per item or group. **Exception.** Report contributions of certain publicly traded securities only in Section A.

If you donated art, you may have to attach the complete appraisal. See the **Note** in Part I below.

**Part I** | Information on Donated Property—To be completed by the taxpayer and/or appraiser.

4 Check type of property:

☐ Art* (contribution of $20,000 or more) ☐ Real Estate ☐ Gems/Jewelry ☐ Stamp Collections

☐ Art* (contribution of less than $20,000) ☐ Coin Collections ☐ Books ☐ Other

*Art includes paintings, sculptures, watercolors, prints, drawings, ceramics, antique furniture, decorative arts, textiles, carpets, silver, rare manuscripts, historical memorabilia, and other similar objects.

**Note:** *If your total art contribution deduction was $20,000 or more, you must attach a complete copy of the signed appraisal. See instructions.*

| 5 | **(a)** Description of donated property (if you need more space, attach a separate statement) | **(b)** If tangible property was donated, give a brief summary of the overall physical condition at the time of the gift | **(c)** Appraised fair market value |
| --- | --- | --- | --- |
| A | | | |
| B | | | |
| C | | | |
| D | | | |

| | **(d)** Date acquired by donor (mo., yr.) | **(e)** How acquired by donor | **(f)** Donor's cost or adjusted basis | **(g)** For bargain sales, enter amount received | See instructions | |
| --- | --- | --- | --- | --- | --- | --- |
| | | | | | **(h)** Amount claimed as a deduction | **(i)** Average trading price of securities |
| A | | | | | | |
| B | | | | | | |
| C | | | | | | |
| D | | | | | | |

**Part II** | Taxpayer (Donor) Statement—List each item included in Part I above that the appraisal identifies as having a value of $500 or less. See instructions.

I declare that the following item(s) included in Part I above has to the best of my knowledge and belief an appraised value of not more than $500 (per item). Enter identifying letter from Part I and describe the specific item. See instructions. ▶ _____

Signature of taxpayer (donor) ▶ _____ Date ▶ _____

**Part III** | Declaration of Appraiser

I declare that I am not the donor, the donee, a party to the transaction in which the donor acquired the property, employed by, or related to any of the foregoing persons, or married to any person who is related to any of the foregoing persons. And, if regularly used by the donor, donee, or party to the transaction, I performed the majority of my appraisals during my tax year for other persons.

Also, I declare that I hold myself out to the public as an appraiser or perform appraisals on a regular basis; and that because of my qualifications as described in the appraisal, I am qualified to make appraisals of the type of property being valued. I certify that the appraisal fees were not based on a percentage of the appraised property value. Furthermore, I understand that a false or fraudulent overstatement of the property value as described in the qualified appraisal or this appraisal summary may subject me to the penalty under section 6701(a) (aiding and abetting the understatement of tax liability). I affirm that I have not been barred from presenting evidence or testimony by the Director of Practice.

**Sign Here**

| Signature ▶ | Title ▶ | Date of appraisal ▶ |
| --- | --- | --- |
| Business address (including room or suite no.) | | Identifying number |
| City or town, state, and ZIP code | | |

**Part IV** | Donee Acknowledgment—To be completed by the charitable organization.

This charitable organization acknowledges that it is a qualified organization under section 170(c) and that it received the donated property as described in Section B, Part I, above on ▶ _____ (Date)

Furthermore, this organization affirms that in the event it sells, exchanges, or otherwise disposes of the property described in Section B, Part I (or any portion thereof) within 2 years after the date of receipt, it will file **Form 8282,** Donee Information Return, with the IRS and give the donor a copy of that form. This acknowledgment does not represent agreement with the claimed fair market value.

Does the organization intend to use the property for an unrelated use? . . . . . . . . . . . . . . . ▶ ☐ Yes ☐ No

| Name of charitable organization (donee) | Employer identification number | |
| --- | --- | --- |
| Address (number, street, and room or suite no.) | City or town, state, and ZIP code | |
| Authorized signature | Title | Date |

Resource 21

| Form **1042** | **Annual Withholding Tax Return for U.S. Source Income of Foreign Persons** | OMB No. 1545-0096 |
|---|---|---|

Department of the Treasury
Internal Revenue Service

▶ See instructions.

**2000**

If this is an Amended Return, check here . . ▶ ☐    If completing only Part II as a transmittal document, check here . . ▶ ☐

| Name of withholding agent | Employer identification number | For IRS Use Only | |
|---|---|---|---|
| | | CC | FD |
| Number, street, and room or suite no. (if a P.O. box, see instructions) | | RD | FF |
| | | CAF | FP |
| City or town, state, and ZIP code | | CR | I |
| | | EDC | SIC |

If you will not be liable for returns in the future, check here ▶ ☐   Enter date final income paid ▶ ...............................
Check here if you made quarter-monthly deposits using the 90% rule (see **Deposit Requirements** in the instructions) . . . . . ▶ ☐

| **Part I** | | **Record of Federal Tax Liability (Do not show Federal tax deposits here.)** |
|---|---|---|

| Line No. | Period ending | Tax liability for period (including any taxes assumed on Form(s) 1000) | Line No. | Period ending | Tax liability for period (including any taxes assumed on Form(s) 1000) | Line No. | Period ending | Tax liability for period (including any taxes assumed on Form(s) 1000) |
|---|---|---|---|---|---|---|---|---|
| 1 | Jan. 7 | | 21 | May 7 | | 41 | Sept. 7 | |
| 2 | Jan. 15 | | 22 | May 15 | | 42 | Sept. 15 | |
| 3 | Jan. 22 | | 23 | May 22 | | 43 | Sept. 22 | |
| 4 | Jan. 31 | | 24 | May 31 | | 44 | Sept. 30 | |
| 5 | Jan. total | | 25 | May total | | 45 | Sept. total | |
| 6 | Feb. 7 | | 26 | June 7 | | 46 | Oct. 7 | |
| 7 | Feb. 15 | | 27 | June 15 | | 47 | Oct. 15 | |
| 8 | Feb. 22 | | 28 | June 22 | | 48 | Oct. 22 | |
| 9 | Feb. 28 | | 29 | June 30 | | 49 | Oct. 31 | |
| 10 | Feb. total | | 30 | June total | | 50 | Oct. total | |
| 11 | Mar. 7 | | 31 | July 7 | | 51 | Nov. 7 | |
| 12 | Mar. 15 | | 32 | July 15 | | 52 | Nov. 15 | |
| 13 | Mar. 22 | | 33 | July 22 | | 53 | Nov. 22 | |
| 14 | Mar. 31 | | 34 | July 31 | | 54 | Nov. 30 | |
| 15 | Mar. total | | 35 | July total | | 55 | Nov. total | |
| 16 | Apr. 7 | | 36 | Aug. 7 | | 56 | Dec. 7 | |
| 17 | Apr. 15 | | 37 | Aug. 15 | | 57 | Dec. 15 | |
| 18 | Apr. 22 | | 38 | Aug. 22 | | 58 | Dec. 22 | |
| 19 | Apr. 30 | | 39 | Aug. 31 | | 59 | Dec. 31 | |
| 20 | Apr. total | | 40 | Aug. total | | 60 | Dec. total | |

**61a** Total tax liability (add monthly total lines from above) . . . . | **61a** |

**b** Adjustments (see instructions) . . . . . . . . . . | **61b** |

**c** Total net tax liability (combine lines 61a and 61b) . . . . . . . . . . . . . ▶ | **61c** |

**62** No. of Forms 1042-S filed on **a** Magnetic tape ............. **b** Paper with this form............

**c** Paper with previously filed Form(s) 1042 (Parts I or II)...............................................

**63** For **all** Form(s) 1042-S and 1000:

**a** Gross income paid .............................. **b** Taxes withheld or assumed.....................

**64** Total paid by Federal tax deposit coupons or by electronic funds transfer (or with a request for an extension of time to file) for 2000 | **64** |

**65** Enter overpayment applied as a credit from 1999 Form 1042 . | **65** |

**66** **Total payments.** Add lines 64 and 65 . . . . . . . . . . ▶ | **66** |

**67** If line 61c is larger than line 66, enter **balance due** here . . . . . . . . . | **67** |

**68** If line 66 is larger than line 61c, enter **overpayment** here . . . . . . . . | **68** |

**69** Apply overpayment on line 68 to (check one): ☐ **Credit on 2001 Form 1042; or** ☐ **Refund**

**Sign Here**

Under penalties of perjury, I declare that I have examined this return, including accompanying schedules and statements, and to the best of my knowledge and belief, it is true, correct, and complete. Declaration of preparer (other than withholding agent) is based on all information of which preparer has any knowledge.

| ▶ Your signature | Date | ▶ Capacity in which acting |
|---|---|---|

| **Paid Preparer's Use Only** | Preparer's signature ▶ | Date | Check if self-employed ▶ ☐ | Preparer's SSN or PTIN |
|---|---|---|---|---|
| | Firm's name (or yours if self-employed), address, and ZIP code ▶ | | EIN ▶ | |
| | | | Phone no. ( ) | |

For Privacy Act and Paperwork Reduction Act Notice, see the instructions.    Cat. No. 11384V    Form **1042** (2000)

Form **1042-S**

Department of the Treasury
Internal Revenue Service

**Foreign Person's U.S. Source Income Subject to Withholding**

▶ For Paperwork Reduction Act Notice, see page 6 of the separate instructions.

2000

OMB No. 1545-0096

**Copy A** for
Internal Revenue Service

| Line | (a) Income code | (b) Gross income paid | (c) Withholding allowances (for Income code 15 or 16 only) | (d) Net income (column (b) minus column (c)) | (e) Tax rate (%) | (f) Exemption code | (g) U.S. Federal tax withheld (net of any tax released) | (h) Country code |
|------|------|------|------|------|------|------|------|------|
| 1 | | | | | | | | |
| 2 | | | | | | | | |
| 3 | Total | | | | | | | |

**4** Recipient code ▶

**5** Recipient's U.S. taxpayer identification number (TIN), if any ▶

**6** Account number (optional) ▶

**7** RECIPIENT'S name (first name, initial, and last name), street address, city or town, province or state, and country (including postal code)

**9** WITHHOLDING AGENT'S name and address (including ZIP code)

**10** Withholding agent's TIN

**11** PAYER'S name and TIN (if different from withholding agent's)

**12** State income tax withheld

**8** Recipient's country of residence for tax purposes

**13** Payer's state tax number

**14** Name of state

☐ **VOID** ☐ **CORRECTED**

Cat. No. 11386R

Form **1042-S** (2000)

---

9595 ☐ VOID ☐ CORRECTED

| PAYER'S name, street address, city, state, ZIP code, and telephone no. | | |
|---|---|---|

**1** Rents
$

**2** Royalties
$

**3** Other income
$

OMB No. 1545-0115

2000

Form **1099-MISC**

**Miscellaneous Income**

| PAYER'S Federal identification number | RECIPIENT'S identification number |
|---|---|

**4** Federal income tax withheld
$

**5** Fishing boat proceeds
$

**Copy A**
**For**
**Internal Revenue Service Center**

RECIPIENT'S name

**6** Medical and health care payments
$

**7** Nonemployee compensation
$

**File with Form 1096.**

Street address (including apt. no.)

**8** Substitute payments in lieu of dividends or interest
$

**9** Payer made direct sales of $5,000 or more of consumer products to a buyer (recipient) for resale ▶ ☐

For Privacy Act and Paperwork Reduction Act Notice, see the

City, state, and ZIP code

**10** Crop insurance proceeds
$

**11** State income tax withheld
$

**2000 General Instructions for Forms 1099, 1098, 5498, and W-2G.**

Account number (optional)

2nd TIN Not. ☐

**12** State/Payer's state number

**13**
$

Form **1099-MISC**

Cat. No. 14425J

Department of the Treasury - Internal Revenue Service

**Do NOT Cut or Separate Forms on This Page — Do NOT Cut or Separate Forms on This Page**

RESOURCE 22

---

## GIFT AGREEMENT TEMPLATES

---

# XYZ CHARITY
# ENDOWED GIFT AGREEMENT

◆

The _____ Scholarship

XYZ Charity's Name
Name of Account

DONOR(S): _____ ("Donor(s)")

AUTHORIZATION: *XYZ Charity* _____ *("Charity")*

WHEREAS the XYZ Charity ("Charity") receives, invests, administers, and manages private gifts for the benefit of XYZ Charity; and

WHEREAS the Donor(s) wishes (wish) to honor _____, and has (have) irrevocably given to the Charity the sum of $_____ for the purpose of establishing The _____ Scholarship/Fellowship ("Scholarship/Fellowship");

NOW, THEREFORE, IT IS AGREED:

*"scholarship/fellowship"* 1. It is the intent of the Donor(s) that income from this gift be used to support scholarships. *[criteria for selection of recipient can be spelled out here, i.e., "a student enrolled in the school who has an interest in the study of _____, and who has a record of academic excellence as demonstrated by a GPA of _____ on a 4-point scale, and that in selecting recipients, preference be given to (a woman, a graduate of _____ High School, an African American, etc.)."]* The number, amount, and recipient(s) of the scholarship will be determined by the Scholarship Committee of the School.

    -or-

*"professorship/chair"* 1. It is the intent of the Donor that *[criteria for selection of recipient can be spelled out here].* The use of income generated from this gift may include, but not be limited to, a salary or salary supplement for the designated holder of the professorship *[chair],* support for research, manuscript preparation, graduate research assistance, library and equipment acquisitions, and other requirements of an active scholar and teacher.

2. The use of this gift will be authorized by the Charity for the reasonable and customary requirements of authorized expenditures as indicated above in accordance with internal operating policies governing investments and administration as established by the Charity. An annual report on the status of the fund will be provided to the Donor(s).

3. The Charity acknowledges that the Donor(s) intend(s) that the original gift amount exist in perpetuity with the income being used to support the purposes of the gift. The Board of Directors of the Charity has established a spending policy which provides for the distribution of both income and a portion of the capital appreciation resulting from investment activity. This policy is consistent with the

Charity's investment philosophy to maintain the purchasing power of the original gift so that the endowments may keep pace with inflation.

4. The officers and directors of the Charity have the power, and final decision, to invest, to change investments, to accept property, to sell, to hold, or to reinvest all or any of the monies or property transferred to the Charity under the terms of this Agreement in such manner as they deem proper, and any additional gifts received in support of this purpose are subject to the terms of this Agreement.

5. In the event that the original purposes stated here can no longer be fulfilled, the Charity, through its Board of Directors, shall review the circumstances and shall modify this Agreement to the extent necessary to enable the gift to be used in a manner which coincides with the Donor's (s') original intent as closely as possible, and consistent with governing rules/regulations policies/procedures and the internal operating policies of the Charity.

6. The Agreement shall be governed by and interpreted in accordance with the laws of the State of _____.

Signed and dated this _____ day of _____, 200__.

DONOR

_____

[Name(s)]

XYZ Charity

By:_____
                , President

# INDIANA UNIVERSITY FOUNDATION
# ACCOUNT AGREEMENT

*For Foundation Use Only*

ACCOUNT NUMBER: _____

Indiana University Foundation
Name of Account

AUTHORIZATION: School of _____ ("School") *[Department of _____*
*("Department"); Indiana University _____ ("IU_____")]*

SOURCE OF FUNDS: *[add source of money coming into the account]*

WHEREAS the Indiana University Foundation ("Foundation") receives, invests, administers, and manages private funds for the benefit of Indiana University in an account designated for institutional funds (the "Account"); and

WHEREAS *[state any information on how the account was created if known].*

NOW, THEREFORE, IT IS AGREED:

1. This Account shall be used for . . . *(choose from descriptions below or modify as needed).* It is further agreed that funds in this Account will not be co-mingled with donor contributions.

Choose one of the following account descriptions or modify as needed:

*faculty and staff development*   Expenditures may include but are not limited to continuing education, research, departmental awards, travel expenses of faculty and staff, and faculty development.

> -or-

*capital and equipment needs*   Expenditures may include but are not limited to minor renovations to a building or rooms, improvements to the grounds, and purchase of equipment.

> -or-

*awards, fellowships, or scholarships*   The *[award, fellowship, or scholarship]* will be given out to *[spell out specific criteria here].* The number, amount, and recipient(s) of the Scholarship will be determined by the scholarship Committee of the School.

> -or-

*representation funds*   Expenditures from representation accounts shall meet four criteria: a direct benefit to the University, reasonable in amount, a necessary expenditure which may or may not be made from University funds, and have the appearance of proper use. Expenditures may include employee goodwill, membership dues, meals and entertainment (when the purpose is conducive to conducting university business), and memorabilia given in recognition of support of the institution.

-or-

*research*   Expenditures may include but are not limited to faculty and staff travel, lodging and travel of visiting scholars, lecturers and research collaborators, supplies and other items which may best serve the needs of the research program.

-or-

*general purposes*   Expenditures may include but are not limited to faculty and staff recruiting, faculty development, faculty travel, program promotion, and other expenses which may best serve the *[academic program or department]*.

2. The use of the funds in this account will be authorized by the *[School, Department, or Campus]* for the reasonable and customary requirements of authorized expenditures as indicated above in accordance with internal operating policies governing investments and administration as established by the Foundation, Indiana University, and the *[School, Department, or Campus]*.

3. The Foundation will annually make available the Account balance for the purpose(s) stated above. The Board of Directors of the Foundation established a spending policy which provides for the distribution of both income and a portion of the capital appreciation resulting from investment activity. This policy is consistent with the Foundation's investment philosophy to maintain the purchasing power of the original funds so that the account may keep pace with inflation. This Agreement is subject to the provisions of the Uniform Management of Institutional Funds Act (Indiana Code 30-2-12) ("UMIFA").

4. The officers and directors of the Foundation have the power, and final decision, to invest, to change investments, to accept property, to sell, to hold, or to reinvest all or any of the monies or property transferred to the Foundation under the terms of this agreement in such manner as they deem proper, and any additional funds received in support of this purpose are subject to the terms of this agreement.

5. In the event that the original purposes stated here can no longer be fulfilled, the *[Dean, Chairperson or Chancellor],* has the power and responsibility to review the circumstances and, if appropriate, modify the purpose of the Account to enable the funds to be used.

Resource 22

6. This Agreement will be terminated no later than one year after all funds received for this purpose have been expended according to the terms stated here.

7. The Agreement shall be governed by and interpreted in accordance with the laws of the State of Indiana.

Signed and dated this _____ day of _____, 200__.

INDIANA UNIVERSITY SCHOOL OF _____

By: _____
         [Name, Dean/Chairperson/Chancellor]

INDIANA UNIVERSITY FOUNDATION

By:_____
         [Name, Executive Director, Administration]

Resource 22

# INDIANA UNIVERSITY FOUNDATION GIFT AGREEMENT

*For Foundation Use Only*

ACCOUNT NUMBER: _____

Indiana University Foundation
Name of Account

DONOR(S):_____ ("Donor(s)")

AUTHORIZATION: School of _____ ("School") *[Department of _____ ("Department"); Indiana University _____ ("IU_____")]*

SOURCE OF FUNDS: *[add source of money coming into the account if funded by transfers]*

WHEREAS the Indiana University Foundation ("Foundation") receives, invests, administers, and manages private gifts for the benefit of Indiana University in an account designated for gifts (the "Account"); and

WHEREAS *[state any donor wishes (i.e. in honor or memory of someone) or information on how the account was created if known].*

NOW, THEREFORE, IT IS AGREED:

1. This Account shall be used for . . . *[choose from descriptions below or modify as needed].*

*faculty and staff development* Expenditures may include but are not limited to continuing education, research, departmental awards, travel expenses of faculty and staff, and faculty development.

-or-

*capital and equipment needs* Expenditures may include but are not limited to minor renovations to a building or rooms, improvements to the grounds, and purchase of equipment.

-or-

*awards, fellowships, or scholarships* The *[award, fellowship, or scholarship]* will be given out to *[spell out specific criteria here]*. The number, amount, and recipient(s) of the Scholarship(s) will be determined by the Scholarship Committee of the School.

-or-

*representation funds*   Expenditures from representation accounts shall meet four criteria: a direct benefit to the University, reasonable in amount, a necessary expenditure which may or may not be made from University funds, and have the appearance of proper use. Expenditures may include employee goodwill, membership dues, meals and entertainment (when the purpose is conducive to conducting university business), and memorabilia given in recognition of support of the institution.

-or-

*research*   Expenditures may include but are not limited to faculty and staff travel, lodging and travel of visiting scholars, lecturers and research collaborators, supplies and other items which may best serve the needs of the research program.

-or-

*general purposes*   Expenditures may include but are not limited to faculty and staff recruiting, faculty development, faculty travel, program promotion, and other expenses which may best serve the *[academic program or department]*.

2. The use of this gift will be authorized by the *[School, Department, or Campus]* for the reasonable and customary requirements of authorized expenditures as indicated above in accordance with internal operating policies governing investments and administration as established by the Foundation, Indiana University, and the *[School, Department, or Campus]*. An annual report on the status of the fund will be provided to the Donor(s).

3. The Foundation will annually make available the Account balance for the purpose(s) stated above. The Board of Directors of the Foundation established a spending policy which provides for the distribution of both income and a portion of the capital appreciation resulting from investment activity. This policy is consistent with the Foundation's investment philosophy to maintain the purchasing power of the original gift so that the account may keep pace with inflation. This Agreement is subject to the provisions of the Uniform Management of Institutional Funds Act (Indiana Code 30-2-12) ("UMIFA").

4. The officers and directors of the Foundation have the power, and final decision, to invest, to change investments, to accept property, to sell, to hold, or to reinvest all or any of the monies or property transferred to the Foundation under the terms of this agreement in such manner as they deem proper, and any additional gifts received in support of this purpose are subject to the terms of this Agreement.

5. In the event that the original purposes stated here can no longer be fulfilled, the Foundation, through its Board of Directors, and in consultation with the *[Dean, campus Chancellor],* shall review the circumstances and shall modify this Agreement to the extent necessary to enable the gift to be used in a manner which coincides with the Donor's(s') original intent as closely as possible, and consistent with the provisions of UMIFA and the internal operating policies of the Foundation.

6. This Agreement will be terminated no later than one year after all funds received for this purpose have been expended according to the terms stated here.

7. The Agreement shall be governed by and interpreted in accordance with the laws of the State of Indiana.

Signed and dated this _____ day of _____, 200__.

DONOR

By: _____
         [Name(s)]

INDIANA UNIVERSITY SCHOOL OF _____

By: _____
         [Name, Dean/Chairperson/Chancellor]

INDIANA UNIVERSITY FOUNDATION

By: _____
         Curtis R. Simic, President

# INDIANA UNIVERSITY FOUNDATION
# ENDOWED GIFT AGREEMENT

◆

The _____ Scholarship

---

*For Foundation Use Only*

ACCOUNT NUMBER: _____

---

Indiana University Foundation
Name of Account

DONOR(S): _____ ("Donor(s)")

AUTHORIZATION: School of _____ ("School") *[Department of _____*
*("Department"); Indiana University _____ ("IU__")]*

WHEREAS the Indiana University Foundation ("Foundation") receives, invests, administers, and manages private gifts for the benefit of Indiana University; and

WHEREAS the Donor(s) wishes (wish) to honor _____, and has (have) irrevocably given to the Foundation the sum of $_____ for the purpose of establishing The _____ Scholarship/Fellowship ("Scholarship/Fellowship");

NOW, THEREFORE, IT IS AGREED:

*"scholarship/fellowship"*   1. It is the intent of the Donor(s) that income from this gift be used to support a scholarship. *[criteria for selection of recipient can be spelled out here, i.e., "a student enrolled in the School who has an interest in the study of _____, and who has a record of academic excellence as demonstrated by a GPA of _____ on a 4-point scale, and that in selecting recipients, preference be given to (a woman, a graduate of _____ High School, an African American, etc.)."]* The number, amount, and recipient(s) of the Scholarship will be determined by the Scholarship Committee of the School.

-or-

*"professorship/chair"*   1. It is the intent of the Donor that *[criteria for selection of recipient can be spelled out here.]* The use of income generated from this gift may include, but not be limited to, a salary or salary supplement for the designated holder of the professorship *[chair],* support for research, manuscript preparation, graduate research assistance, library and equipment acquisitions, and other requirements of an active scholar and teacher.

2. The use of this gift will be authorized by the *[School, Department, Campus]* for the reasonable and customary requirements of authorized expenditures as indicated above in accordance with internal operating policies governing investments and administration as established by the Foundation, Indiana University, and the

*[School, Department, Campus].* An annual report on the status of the fund will be provided to the Donor(s).

3. The Foundation acknowledges that the Donor(s) intend(s) that the original gift amount exist in perpetuity with the income being used to support the purposes of the gift. The Board of Directors of the Foundation has established a spending policy which provides for the distribution of both income and a portion of the capital appreciation resulting from investment activity. This policy is consistent with the Foundation's investment philosophy to maintain the purchasing power of the original gift so that the endowments may keep pace with inflation. This Agreement is subject to the provisions of the Uniform Management of Institutional Funds Act (Indiana Code 30-2-12) ("UMIFA").

4. The officers and directors of the Foundation have the power, and final decision, to invest, to change investments, to accept property, to sell, to hold, or to reinvest all or any of the monies or property transferred to the Foundation under the terms of this Agreement in such manner as they deem proper, and any additional gifts received in support of this purpose are subject to the terms of this Agreement.

5. In the event that the original purposes stated here can no longer be fulfilled, the Foundation, through its Board of Directors, and in consultation with the *[Dean, campus Chancellor],* shall review the circumstances and shall modify this Agreement to the extent necessary to enable the gift to be used in a manner which coincides with the Donor's (s') original intent as closely as possible, and consistent with the provisions of UMIFA and the internal operating policies of the Foundation.

6. The Agreement shall be governed by and interpreted in accordance with the laws of the State of Indiana.

Signed and dated this _____ day of _____, 200__.

DONOR

By: _____
      [Name(s)]

INDIANA UNIVERSITY SCHOOL OF _____

By: _____
      [Name, Dean/Chairperson/Chancellor]

INDIANA UNIVERSITY FOUNDATION

By: _____
      Curtis R. Simic, President

Resource 22

# INDIANA UNIVERSITY FOUNDATION
# GIFT AGREEMENT

◆

**The _____ Scholarship**

> *For Foundation Use Only*
>
> ACCOUNT NUMBER: _____

Indiana University Foundation
Name of Account

DONOR(S): _____ ("Donor(s)")

AUTHORIZATION: School of _____ ("School") *[Department of _____ ("Department"); Indiana University _____ ("IU__")]*

WHEREAS the Indiana University Foundation ("Foundation") receives, invests, administers, and manages private gifts for the benefit of Indiana University; and

WHEREAS the Donor(s) wishes (wish) to honor _____, and has (have) irrevocably given to the Foundation the sum of $_____ for the purpose of establishing The _____ Scholarship/Fellowship ("Scholarship/Fellowship");

NOW, THEREFORE, IT IS AGREED:

*"scholarship/fellowship"* 1. It is the intent of the Donor(s) that this gift be used to support a scholarship. *[criteria for selection of recipient can be spelled out here, i.e., "a student enrolled in the School who has an interest in the study of _____, and who has a record of academic excellence as demonstrated by a GPA of _____ on a 4 point scale, and that in selecting the recipients, preference be given to (a woman, a graduate of _____ High School, an African American, etc.)."].* The number, amount, and recipient(s) of the Scholarship will be determined by the Scholarship Committee of the School.

    -or-

*"professorship/chair"* 1. It is the intent of the Donor that *[criteria for selection of recipient can be spelled out here].* The use of this gift may include, but not be limited to, a salary or salary supplement for the designated holder of the professorship *[chair],* support for research, manuscript preparation, graduate research assistance, library and equipment acquisitions, and other requirements of an active scholar and teacher.

2. The use of this gift will be authorized by the *[School, Department, Campus]* for the reasonable and customary requirements of authorized expenditures as indicated above in accordance with internal operating policies governing investments and administration as established by the Foundation, Indiana University, and the

*[School, Department, Campus].* An annual report on the status of the fund will be provided to the Donor(s).

3. The Foundation acknowledges that the Donor(s) intend(s) both income and principal, as required, may be used to support the purpose of the gift. The Board of Directors of the Foundation established a spending policy which provides for the distribution of both income and a portion of the capital appreciation resulting from investment activity. This policy is consistent with the Foundation's investment philosophy to maintain the purchasing power of the original gift so that the account may keep pace with inflation. This Agreement is subject to the provisions of the Uniform Management of Institutional Funds Act (Indiana Code 30-2-12) ("UMIFA").

4. The officers and directors of the Foundation have the power, and final decision, to invest, to change investments, to accept property, to sell, to hold, or to reinvest all or any of the monies or property transferred to the Foundation under the terms of this Agreement in such manner as they deem proper, and any additional gifts received in support of this purpose are subject to the terms of this Agreement.

5. In the event that the original purposes stated here can no longer be fulfilled, the Foundation, through its Board of Directors, and in consultation with the *[Dean, campus Chancellor],* shall review the circumstances and shall modify this Agreement to the extent necessary to enable the gift to be used in a manner which coincides with the Donor's (s') original intent as closely as possible, and consistent with the provisions of UMIFA and the internal operating policies of the Foundation.

6. The Agreement shall be governed by and interpreted in accordance with the laws of the State of Indiana.

Signed and dated this _____ day of _____, 200__.

DONOR

By: _____
[Name(s)]

INDIANA UNIVERSITY SCHOOL OF _____

By: _____
[Name, Dean/Chairperson/Chancellor]

INDIANA UNIVERSITY FOUNDATION

By: _____
Curtis R. Simic, President

# RESOURCE 23

## GIFT RECEIPT SAMPLES

# Backstreet Missions, Inc.

### BACKSTREET MISSIONS, INC.

215 Westplex Ave, Bloomington IN 47404
Phone: (812) 333-1905
http://www.backstreet.org

## Receipt

June 27, 2000

[Full Name]
[address]
[City State Zip]

Dear [Full Name],

Thank you for your support. We appreciate your compassion and concern for the homeless.

When Jesus was here on earth, He spent most of His time with people out on the streets. He was criticized for associating with them. He knew what it was like to be hungry, thirsty and tired.

He was familiar with hardship and He too had to look for a place to sleep at night.

He came to earth to express God's love for the oppressed. He touched them and changed their lives.

Thank you for helping continue God's work here on earth to this population within our reach.

May God Bless You,


Gene Kelley
Executive Director

This is to acknowledge the receipt of your tax deductible gift of [What Was given].


Note: No goods or services were provided by Backstreet in exchange for this donation.

# Children's Hospital Foundation, British Columbia

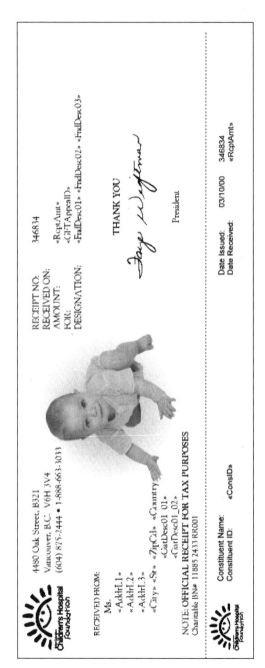

## American Red Cross—Monroe County Chapter

American Red Cross—Monroe County Chapter                    Sales Receipt
411 E. Seventh Street
Bloomington, IN 47408-3723

| DATE | SALE NO. |
|------|----------|
| 07/21/2000 | 6609 |

**SOLD TO**

JOHN Q. PUBLIC
1234 ANYWHERE STREET
BLOOMINGTON, IN 47401

| CHECK NO. | PAYMENT METHOD | PROJECT |
|-----------|----------------|---------|
| 9999 | CHECK | |

| DESCRIPTION | QUANITY | RATE | AMOUNT |
|-------------|---------|------|--------|
| GENERAL DONATION | 1 | 50.00 | 50.00 |

THANK YOU!

| | Total | $50.00 |
|--|-------|--------|

AMERICAN RED CROSS
MONROE COUNTY CHAPTER
411 E. SEVENTH STREET
BLOOMINGTON, IN 47408

Thank You for your donation of Books/In-Kind Items.
The items will be sold (books) or given (in-kind) to local victims of disaster.

Please retain this receipt for tax purposes.
Attach a list of your donated items.

Date: _____

Signature: _____

# FRONT

Indiana University Foundation
P.O. Box 500
Bloomington, IN 47402

January 1, 2000

Indiana University Foundation salutes:
Hubert T. Steerherder
P.O. Box 12345
Fort Somewhere, TX 12345-6789

### DONOR - INDIANA UNIVERSITY

999999-9999999
For your commitment and generosity to
Indiana University, the Officers and the
Board of Directors of the Indiana University
Foundation want to thank you for your gift
of $250.00 to IU Alumni Association.

Benefit Received by Donor:
IU Alumni Outing
Value of Benefit Received: $ 99.95
Deductible Amount of Gift: $150.05

---

Indiana University Foundation
P.O. Box 500
Bloomington, IN 47402

January 1, 2000

Indiana University Foundation salutes:
Hubert T. Steerherder
P.O. Box 12345
Fort Somewhere, TX 12345-6789

### DONOR - INDIANA UNIVERSITY

999999-9999999
For your commitment and generosity to
Indiana University, the Officers and the
Board of Directors of the Indiana University
Foundation want to thank you for your gift
of $250.00 to IU Alumni Association.

Benefit Received by Donor:
IU Alumni Outing
Value of Benefit Received: $ 99.95
Deductible Amount of Gift: $150.05

---

Indiana University Foundation
P.O. Box 500
Bloomington, IN 47402

January 1, 2000

Indiana University Foundation salutes:
Hubert T. Steerherder
P.O. Box 12345
Fort Somewhere, TX 12345-6789

### DONOR - INDIANA UNIVERSITY

999999-9999999
For your commitment and generosity to
Indiana University, the Officers and the
Board of Directors of the Indiana University
Foundation want to thank you for your gift
of $250.00 to IU Alumni Association.

Benefit Received by Donor:
IU Alumni Outing
Value of Benefit Received: $ 99.95
Deductible Amount of Gift: $150.05

Resource 23

# BACK

## INDIANA UNIVERSITY FOUNDATION

Showalter House, Bloomington
(812) 855-8311, fax: (812) 855-6956
50 South Meridian Street, Suite 400, Indianapolis
(317) 673-4438, fax: (317) 274-8818

"People who have been touched by Indiana University have developed a strong loyalty and have expressed that in faithful support and generous gifts. . . . They help to make a difference for the future, building the foundation of one of the great universities for the twenty-first century."

Herman B Wells
University Chancellor

Thank you for your generous gift to Indiana University.

The many dollars in private support contributed each year by people like you add up to a wealth of opportunities for Indiana University to serve the citizens of the state, the nation, and the world. Your gift enables the University to provide greater access to quality educational opportunities, enhance Indiana's tradition of excellence in higher education, contribute to economic development, and conduct research that will change the quality of human life for the better.

Your support is gratefully acknowledged.

*Curtis R. Simic*
Curtis R. Simic, President
Indiana University Foundation

---

## INDIANA UNIVERSITY FOUNDATION

Showalter House, Bloomington
(812) 855-8311, fax: (812) 855-6956
50 South Meridian Street, Suite 400, Indianapolis
(317) 673-4438, fax: (317) 274-8818

"People who have been touched by Indiana University have developed a strong loyalty and have expressed that in faithful support and generous gifts. . . . They help to make a difference for the future, building the foundation of one of the great universities for the twenty-first century."

Herman B Wells
University Chancellor

Thank you for your generous gift to Indiana University.

The many dollars in private support contributed each year by people like you add up to a wealth of opportunities for Indiana University to serve the citizens of the state, the nation, and the world. Your gift enables the University to provide greater access to quality educational opportunities, enhance Indiana's tradition of excellence in higher education, contribute to economic development, and conduct research that will change the quality of human life for the better.

Your support is gratefully acknowledged.

*Curtis R. Simic*
Curtis R. Simic, President
Indiana University Foundation

---

## INDIANA UNIVERSITY FOUNDATION

Showalter House, Bloomington
(812) 855-8311, fax: (812) 855-6956
50 South Meridian Street, Suite 400, Indianapolis
(317) 673-4438, fax: (317) 274-8818

"People who have been touched by Indiana University have developed a strong loyalty and have expressed that in faithful support and generous gifts. . . . They help to make a difference for the future, building the foundation of one of the great universities for the twenty-first century."

Herman B Wells
University Chancellor

Thank you for your generous gift to Indiana University.

The many dollars in private support contributed each year by people like you add up to a wealth of opportunities for Indiana University to serve the citizens of the state, the nation, and the world. Your gift enables the University to provide greater access to quality educational opportunities, enhance Indiana's tradition of excellence in higher education, contribute to economic development, and conduct research that will change the quality of human life for the better.

Your support is gratefully acknowledged.

*Curtis R. Simic*
Curtis R. Simic, President
Indiana University Foundation

Resource 23

# American Diabetes Association

Receipt #655     Date: _____

Received of _____

_____ Dollars $ _____

Donation to Peacetree Family Camp, Inc.      Tax Deductible

Check# _____          By _____

# CORPORATE MATCHING GIFT COMPANY LISTING

# A List of Companies with Matching Gift Programs

Abbott Laboratories
ABC, Inc
ACF Industries, Inc.
Acuson
Adams Harkness & Hill, Inc.
Addison Wesley Longman
Adobe Systems, Inc.
Advanced Micro Devices
AEGON USA Inc.
Aetna Inc.
AG Communication Systems
Air Products and Chemicals
Alabama Power Co.
Albany International Corp.
Albemarle Corp.
Alberta Energy Co., Ltd.
Albertson's Inc.
Alcan Aluminum Corp.
Alexander & Baldwin, Inc.
Alexander Hass Martin & Partners
Allegheny Ludlum Corp.
Allegiance Corp. and Baxter International
Allegro MicroSystems W.G. Inc.
Allendale Mutual Insurance Co.
Alliance Capital Management, LP
Alliant Techsystems
AlliedSignal Inc.
Allstate Corp.
Aluminum Co. of America
Amcast Industrial Corp.
Amerada Hess Corp.
American Electric Power
American Express Co.
American General Corp.
American Home Products
American Honda Motor Co. Inc.
American International Group Inc.

American Investment Advisory Service
American National Bank
American National Bank & Trust Co. of
   Chicago
American National Can Co.
American Optical Corp.
American Standard Inc.
American States Insurance Co.
American Stock Exchange
American United Life Insurance Co.
Ameritech Corp.
Amerus Group
Amgen Inc.
AMP Inc.
AmSouth BanCorp.
AMSTED Industries Inc.
Anadarko Petroleum Corp.
Analog Devices Inc.
Anchor/Russell Capital Advisors Inc.
Accenture
Andersons Inc.
Anheuser-Busch Cos. Inc.
Aon Corp.
Appleton Papers Inc.
Aqua Alliance Inc.
Aquarion Co.
ARAMARK Corp.
Archer Daniels Midland
ARCO
Argonaut Group Inc.
Aristech Chemical Corp.
Aristokraft Inc.
Arkwright Mutual Insurance Co.
Armco Inc.
Armstrong World Industries Inc.
Armtek Corp.
Arrow Electronics Inc.

Arthur Andersen, LLP
Ashland Inc.
Aspect Telecommunications
Associates Corp. of North America
Astra Merck Inc.
AT&T
Atlantic City Electric Co.
Augat Inc.
Autodesk Inc.
Automatic Data Processing Inc.
Avon Products Inc.
Axel Johnson Inc.
Ball Corp.
Baltimore Gas & Electric Co.
Bancroft-Whitney
Bank of America Corp.
Bank of California, NA
Bank of Montreal
Bank of New York
Bank One, NA
Bank South Corp.
BankBoston
Bankers Life and Casualty
Bankers Trust Co.
Banta Corp. Foundation Inc.
Barber-Colman Co.
Barclays Capital Inc.
C.R. Bard Inc.
Barnes Group Inc.
Barnett Associates Inc.
Barrett Technology Inc./
    Barrett Communications Inc.
BASF Corp.
Bass, Berry & Sims, PLC
Bay Networks
Bechtel Group Inc.
Becton Dickinson and Co.
Belden Wire and Cable Co.
Bell Atlantic Corp.
BellSouth

Bemis Co. Inc.
Bergen Record Corp.
L.M. Berry and Co.
Bestfoods
Bethlehem Steel Corp.
BF Goodrich Co.
BHP Minerals International Inc.
Binney & Smith Inc.
Bituminous Casualty Corp.
Black & Decker Corp.
Blount Foundation Inc.
Blue Bell Inc.
BMC Industries Inc.
BOC Group Inc.
Boeing Co.
Bonneville International Corp.
Borden Family of Cos.
Boston Edison Co.
Boston Gear
Boston Mutual Life Insurance Co.
Bowater Inc.
BP Amoco Corp.
Bridgestone/Firestone Inc.
Bristol-Myers Squibb Co.
Bronco Wine Co.
Brooklyn Union
Brown & Williamson Tobacco Corp.
Brown Group Inc.
Brown-Forman Corp.
BTR Sealing Systems Group
Buell Industries Inc.
Buffalo Color Corp.
Burlington Industries Inc.
Burlington Northern Santa Fe Corp.
Burlington Resources
Business & Legal Reports Inc.
Butler Manufacturing Co.
Cabot Corp.
Cadence Design Systems Inc.
Calex Manufacturing Co. Inc.

**Resource 24**

CambridgeSoft
Campbell Soup Foundation
Canadian Pacific Railway
Capital Group Inc.
Capital One Services Inc.
Carolina Power & Light Co.
Carpenter Technology Corp.
Carson Products Co.
Carter-Wallace Inc.
Castrol North America
Caterpillar Inc.
CBI
CBS Foundation Inc.
Central and South West Corp.
Central Illinois Light Co.
Certain Teed Corp.
Chamberlain Manufacturing Corp.
Champion International Corp.
Charles River Laboratories Inc.
Chase Manhattan Corp.
ChemFirst Inc.
Chesapeake Corp.
Chesebrough-Pond's USA
Chevron Corp.
Chicago Title and Trust Co.
Chicago Tribune Co.
Chrysler Corp.
Chubb and Son Inc.
Church & Dwight Co. Inc.
Church Mutual Insurance Co.
CIBA Specialty Chemicals Corp.
CIGNA Corp.
Cincinnati Bell Inc.
Circuit City Stores Inc.
Cisco Systems Inc.
CITGO Petroleum Corp.
Clariant Corp.
Clark Construction Group Inc.
Cleveland-Cliffs Inc. and Associated Cos.
Clopay Corp.

Clorox Co.
CNA
Coats North America
Coca-Cola Co.
Colgate-Palmolive Co.
Collins & Aikman Corp.
Colonial Management Association Inc.
Colonial Parking Inc.
Colonial Penn Group Inc.
Columbia Gas System Inc.
Columbus Life Insurance Co.
Comerica Inc.
Commercial Intertech Corp.
Commonwealth Edison Co.
Commonwealth Energy System
Commonwealth Fund
Community Bank System Inc.
Compaq Computer Corp.
Computer Associates International Inc.
Computer Network Technology Corp.
ComputerWorld
COMSAT Corp.
ConAgra Inc.
Congoleum Corp.
Connecticut Natural Gas Corp.
Conoco Inc.
CONRAIL Inc.
CONSOL Inc.
Consolidated Edison Co.
   of New York Inc.
Consolidated Natural Gas Co.
Consolidated Papers Inc.
Consumer Programs Inc.
Consumers Energy/CMS Energy
Co-Op Banking Group Cos.
Cooper Industries
Cooper Tire & Rubber Co.
Copley Press Inc.
Copolymer Rubber and Chemical Corp.
CoreStates Financial Corp.

Corning Inc.

Corporate Software and Technology

Covington & Burling

Crane Co.

Cranston Print Works Co.

Cray Research Inc.

Credit Agricole Indosuez

Crestar Financial Corp.

Crompton & Knowles Corp.

Crowe, Chizek, and Co.

Crown Central Petroleum Corp.

Crum & Forster Insurance

CSC Index

CSX Corp.

Cummins Engine Co. Inc.

CUNA Mutual Life Insurance Co.

Cyprus Amax Minerals Co.

Dain Rauscher

Dana Corp.

Danforth Foundation

Datatel Inc.

David L. Babson and Co. Inc.

Dean Witter Discover

DEKALB Genetics Corp.

Deloitte & Touche

Delta Air Lines Inc.

Delta Dental Plan of Massachusetts

Deluxe Corp.

Demont & Associates Inc.

Avery Dennison Corp.

Deposit Guaranty National Bank

Detroit Edison Co.

A.W.G. Dewar Inc.

Dexter Corp.

DFS Group Ltd.

Diebold Inc.

Difco Laboratories

Digital Sciences Corp.

Direct Marketing Technology

Dole Food Co. Inc.

Donaldson Co. Inc.

Donaldson, Lufkin & Jenrette

R.R. Donnelley & Sons Co.

Dow AgroSciences, LLC

Dow Chemical Co.

Dow Corning Corp.

Dow Jones and Co. Inc.

Dresser Industries Inc.

Dresser-Rand Co.

DSM Engineering Plastics Inc.

DTE Energy

Duff-Norton Co.

Duke Power Co.

Dun & Bradstreet Corp.

Duquesne Light Co.

Duracell International Inc.

Eastern Enterprises

Eastern Mountain Sports

Eaton Corp.

Eaton Vance Management

Eckerd Corp.

Ecolab Inc.

Eddie Bauer

Edison International

Educators Mutual Life Insurance Co.

El Paso Energy Corp.

Elf Aquitaine Inc.

ELF Atochem North America Inc.

Eli Lilly and Co.

Elizabethtown Water Co.

Emerson Electric Co

Engelhard Corp.

Enron Corp.

ENSERCH Corp.

Equifax Inc.

Equistar Chemicals, LP

Equitable Life Insurance Co. of Iowa

Equitable Resources Inc.

ERE Yarmouth

Erie Insurance Group

Ernst & Young, LLP
ESSTAR Inc.
Esterline Corp.
Ethyl Corp.
European American Bank
Exxon Corp.
Exxon Education Foundation
Fannie Mae
Federal Home Loan Mortgage Corp.
Federal-Mogul Corp.
Federated Department Stores Inc.
Feingold & Feingold Insurance
Ferro Corp.
Fidelity Investments
Fiduciary Trust Co., Boston
James and Marshall Field Foundation
Fifth Third Bancorp
FINA Inc.
Fingerhut Corp.
Fireman's Fund Insurance Co.
First Allmerica Financial Life
   Insurance Co.
First Data Corp.
First Energy Corp.
First Maryland Bancorp
First National Bank of Hudson
First Union Corp.
First Virginia Banks Inc.
Flavorite Laboratories Inc.
Fleet Financial Group
Fleming Cos. Inc.
Fluor Corp.
FMC Corp.
Follett Corp.
Ford Motor Co.
Ford Motor Co. of Canada, Ltd.
Fort James Corp. and Subsidiaries
Fortis Woodbury
Fortis Health
Fortune Brands Inc.

Foster Wheeler Corp.
Foundation for Educational Funding Inc.
Foxboro Co.
FPL Group Inc.
Freddie Mac Foundation
Frederic W. Cook & Co. Inc.
Freeport-McMoRan
Fuji Bank, Ltd.
H.B. Fuller Co.
Fulton Financial Corp.
Galileo Corp.
E. & J. Gallo Winery
Gannett Co. Inc.
Gap Inc.
Gartner Group
Gary-Williams Co./Piton Foundation
GATX Corp.
GenCorp Inc.
General Accident Insurance Co. of
   America
General Cable Co.
General Defense Corp.
General Electric Canada Inc.
General Electric Co.
General Mills Inc.
General Motors Corp.
General Re Corp.
M. Arthur Gensler Jr. and Associates Inc.
Geon Co.
Georgia-Pacific Co.
Georgia Power Co.
Gerber Products Co.
Gilbane Building Co.
Gillette Co.
Gilman Paper Co.
Glaxo Wellcome Inc.
Glenmede Corp.
Globe Newspaper Co. and Subsidiaries
Gnat Inc.
Golden Books Publishing Co. Inc.

Goldman, Sachs & Co.

Good Value Homes Inc.

Goodyear Tire & Rubber Co.

Gould Electronics Inc.

Goulds Pumps Inc.

Government Employees Insurance Co.

GPU Inc.

W.R. Grace & Co.

Graco Inc.

W.W. Grainger Inc.

Grant Thorton, LLP

Grantham, Mayo, Van Otterloo & Co., LLC

Graphics Controls Corp.

Graybar Electric Co. Inc.

Great West Casualty Co.

GreenPoint Bank

Greenwood Mills Inc.

Gregory Poole Equipment Co.

Grenzebach, Glier & Associates Inc.

Grinnell Mutual Reinsurance Co.

GTE Corp.

Guardian Life Insurance Co. of America

Guidant Corp.

Guide One Insurance

H & R Block Inc.

Haemonetics Corp.

Halliburton Co.

Hallmark Cards Inc.

Hambrecht & Quist, LLC

Hampton & Harper Inc.

M.A. Hanna Co.

Hanover Insurance Co.

Harcourt General Inc.

Harleysville Mutual Insurance Co.

Harrah's Entertainment Inc.

Harris Corp.

Harris Trust & Savings Bank

Hartford Insurance Group

Hartmarx Corp.

Hasbro Inc.

Hawaiian Electric Industries Inc.

Haworth Inc.

H.J. Heinz Co.

Heller Financial Inc.

Henry Luce Foundation

Hercules Inc.

Herold & Associates

Hershey Foods Corp.

Heublein Foundation Inc.

Hewitt Associates, LLC

Hewlett-Packard Co.

Hibernia National Bank

Higher Education Publications Inc.

Hillman Co.

Hoechst Marion Roussel Inc.

Hoffman-La Roche Inc.

Holmes & Narver Inc.

Holyoke Mutual Insurance Co. in Salem

Home Depot

Homestake Mining Co.

Honeywell Inc.

Hormel Foods Corp.

Houghton Chemical Corp.

Houghton Mifflin Co.

Household International Inc.

HRTek Corp.

HSB-Industrial Risk Insurers

Hubbard Milling Co.

Hubbell Inc.

J.M. Huber Corp.

Huffy Corp.

Hughes Electronics Corp.

Hunt Corp.

ICI Americas Inc.

IDEX Corp.

IES Industries Inc.

IKON Office Solutions

IKOS Systems

Illinois Tool Works Inc.

Inco United States Inc.

**Resource 24**

Independence Investment Associates Inc.

Industrial Bank of Japan, Ltd.

Information Technology Systems

Ingersoll-Rand Co.

Instron Corp.

Integon Corp.

Intel Corp.

Interlake Corp.

International Business Machines

International Flavors and Fragrances Inc.

International Multifoods Corp.

International Paper

International Student Exchange Cards Inc.

Intuit Inc.

IPALCO Enterprises Inc.

ITT Corp.

J. Walter Thompson Co.

Jefferies Group Inc.

Jefferson-Pilot Communications Co.

Jefferson Pilot Financial

John Brown Inc.

John Hancock Advisers Inc.

John Hancock Mutual Life Insurance Co.

John Wiley & Sons Inc.

Johns Manville Corp.

Johnson Controls Inc.

Johnson & Johnson Family of Cos.

S.C. Johnson & Son Inc.

Jones, JA Inc.

Jostens Inc.

JSJ Corp.

Kansas City Southern Industries Inc.

Karmazin Products Corp.

Kearney-National Inc.

Keefe, Bruyett & Woods Inc.

Kellogg Co.

W.K. Kellogg Foundation

M.W. Kellogg Co.

Kemper Insurance Cos.

Kennametal Inc.

Kerr-McGee Corp.

KeyCorp

Keystone Associates Inc.

Kimberly Clark Foundation

Kingsbury Corp.

Kiplinger Washington Editors

Kmart Corp.

KN Energy Inc.

Knight-Ridder Inc.

H. Kohnstamm & Co. Inc.

Korte Construction Co.

KPMG Peat Marwick, LLP

Laboratory Corp. Of America TM

Lam Research Corp.

Lamson & Sessions Co.

LandAmerica Financial Group Inc.

LaSalle National Bank

Law Co. Inc.

Law Cos. Group Inc.

Lehigh Portland Cement Co.

Leo Burnett Co. Inc.

Levi Strauss & Co.

LEXIS-NEXIS

Lexmark International Inc.

Libbey-Owens Ford Co.

Lincoln Financial Group

Link Engineering Co. Inc.

Thomas J. Lipton Co.

Litton Itek Optical Systems

Liz Claiborne Inc.

Lockheed Martin Corp.

Loews Corp.

Lone Star Industries Inc.

Lotus Development Corp.

Louisiana Power & Light Co.

Lubrizol Corp.

Lucent Technologies

Lucky Stores Inc.

Lukens Inc.

M/A/R/C Group

**Resource 24**

John D. and Catherine T. MacArthur
  Foundation
MacLean-Fogg Co.
Josiah Macy, Jr. Foundation
Madison Mutual Insurance Co. (NY)
Mallinckrodt Group Inc.
Marathon Oil Co.
Maritz Inc.
Marley Co.
Marsh & McLennan Cos. Inc.
Massachusetts Financial Services
  Investment Management
Massachusetts Port Authority
MassMutual-Blue Chip Co.
MasterCard International Inc.
Mattel Inc.
Maxus Energy Corp.
May Department Stores Co.
Maytag Corp.
Mazda (North America) Inc.
MBNA America Bank, NA
McCormick & Co. Inc.
McDonald's Corp.
McGraw-Hill Cos.
McKesson HBOC Inc.
McQuay Inc.
Mead Corp.
Mebane Packaging Corp.
Medical Consultants Network Inc.
Medtronic Inc.
Mellon Bank Corp.
Menasha Corp.
Merck & Co. Inc.
Meredith Corp.
Meridian Insurance Co.
Merit Oil Corp.
Meritor Savings Bank
Merrill Lynch & Co. Inc.
Metropolitan Life Insurance Co.
Mettler-Toledo Inc.

Michigan Mutual Insurance Co.
Micron Technology Inc.
Microsoft Corp.
Midland Life Insurance Co.
Miehle-Goss-Dexter Inc.
Milgard Matching Gift Program
Milliken & Co.
Millipore Corp.
Milton Bradley Co.
Milwaukee Electric Tool Corp.
Minerals Technologies Inc.
Minnesota Mutual Life Insurance Co.
Mississippi Power & Light Co.
Mitsubishi Electric America
Mitsubishi International Corp.
Mobil Oil Corp.
Moen Inc.
Monroe Auto Equipment Co.
Monsanto Co.
Montana Power Co.
MONY Life Insurance Co.
MOOG Inc.
Morgan Construction Co.
J.P. Morgan & Co. Inc.
Morgan Stanley Dean Witter & Co. Inc.
Morrison & Foerster, LLP
Morrison Knudsen Corp.
Mortgage Guaranty Insurance Corp.
Morton International Inc.
Motorola Inc.
Charles Stewart Mott Foundation
MSI Insurance
MTS Systems Corp.
Murphy Oil Corp.
Mutual of America
Mutual of Omaha Cos.
NACCO Industries Inc.
Nalco Chemical Co.
National City Bank of Pennsylvania
National City Corp.

**Resource 24**

National Computer System
National Gypsum Co.
National Semiconductor Corp.
National Starch and Chemical Co.
National Steel Corp.
NationsBank Corp.
NationsCredit Corp.
Nationwide Mutual Insurance Co.
NCR Corp.
NEES Cos.
Neles-Jamesbury
Nellie Mae
Network Associates
New Century Energies
New England Business Service Inc.
New England Electric System Cos.
New England Financial
New Jersey Bell Telephone Co.
New Jersey Natural Gas Co.
New York Life Insurance Co.
New York State Electric & Gas Corp.
New York Stock Exchange Inc.
New York Times Co.
Newmont Mining Corp.
Niagara Mohawk Power Corp.
Nicor Gas
Nielsen Media Research
NIKE Inc.
Nissan North America Inc.
Nordson Corp.
Norfolk & Dedham Group
Norfolk Southern Corp.
Northern States Power Co.
Northern Telecom Inc.
Northern Trust Co.
Northwestern Mutual Life Insurance Co.
Norton Co.
W.W. Norton & Co. Inc.
Norwest Corp.
Novartis Corp.

Novell Inc.
John Nuveen & Co. Inc.
NVEST Cos., LP
Occidental Petroleum Corp.
Ohio National Life Insurance Co.
Oklahoma Gas and Electric Co.
Olin Corp.
Ontario Corp.
Openaka Corp. Inc.
OppenheimerFunds Inc.
Oregon Portland Cement Co.
Orion Capital Corp.
Osmonics Inc.
OSRAM SYLVANIA
Otter Tail Power Co.
Outboard Marine Corp.
Owens Corning
Owens-Illinois Inc.
Oxford Industries Inc.
PACCAR Inc.
Pacific Enterprises
Pacific Life Insurance Co.
Pan-American Life Insurance Co.
PanEnergy Corp.
Parker Hannifin Corp.
Paul Revere Cos.
Pella Corp.
PCL Constructors Inc.
Penn Mutual Life Insurance Co.
J.C. Penney Co. Inc.
Pennsylvania Power & Light Co.
Pennzoil Co.
Pentair Inc.
People's Bank
Peoples Gas Corp.
PepsiCo Foundation
Perkin-Elmer Corp.
Peterson Consulting Ltd. Partnership
Pew Charitable Trusts
Pfizer Inc.

PG&E Corp.

P.H. Glatfelter Co.

Pharmacia & Upjohn Inc.

Phelps Dodge Corp.

PHH Corp.

Phillip Morris Cos. Inc.

Philips Electronics North America Corp.

Phillips Petroleum Co.

Phoenix Home Life Mutual Insurance Co.

Pioneer Hi-Bred International Inc.

Pioneer Group Inc.

Pitney Bowes Inc.

Pittston Co.

Pittway Corp.

PLATINUM technology inc.

Playboy Enterprises Inc.

Plum Creek Timber Co., LP

Plymouth Rock Foundation

Plymouth Bank

PNC Bank Corp.

Pogo Producing Co.

Polaroid Corp.

Pope & Talbot Inc.

Potlatch Corp.

PPG Industries Inc.

PQ Corp.

Preformed Line Products Co.

Premark International Inc.

Price & Pierce International Inc.

PricewaterhouseCoopers, LLP

Principal Financial Group

Procter & Gamble Co.

Proskauer Rose, LLP

Protection Mutual Insurance Co.

Provident Cos. Inc.

Provident Mutual Life Insurance Co.
   of Philadelphia

Providian Corp.

Providian Financial

Prudential Insurance Co. of America

Public Service Electric and Gas Co.

Purolator Products Inc.

Quaker Chemical Corp.

Quaker Oats Co.

Quaker State Corp.

Ralston Purina Co.

Rand McNally

Rayonier Foundation

Raytheon Co.

Reader's Digest Association Inc.

Reebok International Ltd.

Reliable Life Insurance Co.

Reliance Insurance Cos.

ReliaStar Financial Corp.

Republic National Bank of New York

Research Institute of America Inc.

Revlon Inc.

Rexam Inc.

Rexnord Corp.

Reynolds Metals Co.

Rhodia Inc.

Rhone-Poulenc Rorer Inc.

Riviana Foods Inc.

RJR Nabisco Inc.

RJR Nabisco Foundation Inc.

RLI Insurance Co.

Robert Wood Johnson Foundation

Rochester Midland Corp.

Rockefeller Brothers Fund Inc.

Rockefeller Family & Associates

Rockefeller Group

Rockwell

Rohm and Haas Co.

Rohr Inc.

RONIN Development Corp.

Ross, Johnston & Kersting Inc.

Royal & SunAlliance Insurance

Rubermaid Inc.

Ryco Division, Reilly-Whiteman Inc.

Ryder System Inc.

Safeco Corp.

St. Paul Cos.

Sallie Mae

Samuel Roberts Noble Foundation Inc.

Sanwa Bank California

Sara Lee Corp.

SBC Communications Inc.

Schering-Plough Corp.

Charles Schwab and Co. Inc.
and Subsidiaries

Scientific-Atlanta Inc.

Scientific Brake & Equipment Co.

Scott, Foresman and Co.

E.W. Scripps Co.

Joseph E. Seagram & Sons Inc.

Sealed Air Corp.

Sealright Co. Inc.

G.D. Searle & Co.

Sedgwick Inc.

Sentry Insurance Foundation Inc.

Service Merchandise Co. Inc.

Seton Co.

SGL Carbon Corp.

Shaklee Corp.

Shearson Lehman Brothers Inc.

Sheldahl Inc.

Shell Oil Co.

Shenandoah Life Insurance Co.

Sherwin-Williams Co.

Showa Denko Carbon Inc.

Siemens Corp.

Sierra Health Foundation

Sierra Pacific Resources

Sifco Industries Inc.

Signet Banking Corp.

Silicon Graphics Inc.

SKF USA Inc.

Smith International Inc.

SmithKline Beecham

SNET

Sonat Inc.

Sonoco Products Co.

Sony Corp. of America

Spiegel Inc.

Springs Industries Inc.

Sprint Corp.

SPS Technologies Inc.

SPX Corp.

Square D Co.

Sta-Rite Industries Inc.

A.E. Staley Manufacturing Co.

Staley, Robeson, Ryan, St. Lawrence Inc.

Standard Insurance Co.

Standard Products Co.

Stanhome Inc.

Stanley Works

Star Enterprise

State Farm Insurance Cos.

State Street Corp.

Stauffer Communications Inc.

Steel Heddle Manufacturing Co.

Steelcase Inc.

Stone & Webster Inc.

Stop & Shop Cos. Inc.

STREM Chemicals

Stride Rite Corp.

Subaru of America Inc.

Summit Bancorp

Sun Life Assurance Co. of Canada

Sun Microsystems Inc.

Suntrust Bank, Atlanta

SUPERVALUE Inc.

Susquehanna Investment Group

Swank Inc.

Swedish Match

Swiss American Securities Inc.

Swiss Bank Corp.

SYSCO Corp.

20th Century Insurance Co.

3Com Corp.

3M
Tandy Corp.
TCF Financial Corp.
Teagle Foundation Inc.
Technimetrics Inc.
Tektronix Inc.
Telcordia Technologies
Teledyne Inc.
Tellabs Inc.
Temple-Inland Inc.
Tenet Healthcare Corp.
TENNANT
Tenneco Inc.
Tesoro, Hawaii
Tesoro Petroleum Corp.
Tetley USA Inc.
Texaco Inc.
Texas Instruments Inc.
Texon International
Textron Inc.
THAT Corp.
Thomson Financial Services
Tietex International, LTD
Time Warner Inc.
Times Mirror Co.
Times Publishing Co.
Tomkins Corp. Foundation
Toro Co.
Torrington Co.
Towers, Perrin, Forster, & Crosby
Toyota Motor Manufacturing,
    Kentucky Inc.
Toyota Motor Sales, U.S.A. Inc.
Transamerica Corp.
Transtar Inc.
Travelers Express Co. Inc.
T. Rowe Price Associates Inc.
TRW Inc.
TTX Co.
Turner Corp.

Tyco International, Ltd.
UAM Charitable Foundation Inc.
UGI Corp.
Unibase Direct
Unilever United States Inc.
Union Central Life Insurance Co.
Union Electric Co.
Union Mutual Fire Insurance Co.
Union Pacific Corp.
Unisource Foundation
United Fire & Casualty Co.
United Parcel Service
United Services Automobile Association
United Technologies Corp.
Unitrin Inc.
Universal Foods Corp.
Universal Studios
Unocal Corp.
UNUM Corp.
U.S. Bancorp
U.S. Borax Inc.
U.S. Trust Corp and Affiliates
US West Inc.
USA GROUP Inc.
USG Corp.
USLIFE Corp.
UST Inc.
USX Corp.
Utica National Insurance Group
Valero Energy Corp.
Vanguard Group Inc.
Victaulic Co. of America
Virginia Power/North Carolina Power
Vulcan Materials Co.
Wachovia Corp.
Wal-Mart Stores Inc.
Wallace & Wallace, Ltd.
Warnaco
Warner-Lambert Co.
Washington Dental Service

Washington Mutual

Washington Post Co.

Waters Corp.

Watkins-Johnson Co.

Wausau Insurance Cos.

C.J. Webb Inc.

Welch Foods Inc., a Cooperative

Wells Fargo Bank, NA

Western Resources Foundation

Westvaco Corp.

Weyerhaeuser Co.

Whirlpool Corp.

White Consolidated Industries Inc.

Whitman Corp.

Whittaker Corp.

Willamette Industries Inc.

Williams

Williams Gas Pipeline/Transco Energy Co.

Winn-Dixie Stores Inc.

Winter Wyman & Co.

Wiremold Co.

Wisconsin Energy Corp.

Wisconsin Gas Co.

Wisconsin Power & Light Co.

Witco Corp.

Wolverine World Wide Inc.

Words At Work Inc.

WordsWorth Books

Wyman-Gordon Co.

Xerox Corp.

Xtra Corp. Charitable Foundation

Young & Rubicam Inc.

Zurich-American Insurance Group

Zurn Industries Inc.

*Source:* Adapted from Council for Advancement and Support of Education, Washington, D.C.

Resource 24

# CORPORATE MATCHING GIFT FORM

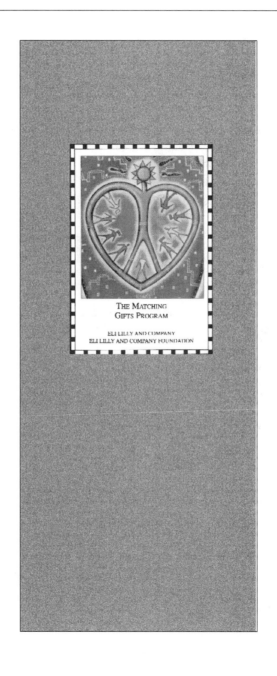

## THE MATCHING GIFTS PROGRAM

Eli Lilly and Company recognizes the importance of individual support for non-profit organizations. Through the Matching Gifts Program, the Lilly Foundation assists many nonprofit institutions by combining the generosity of employee giving with corporate resources.

The Eli Lilly and Company Foundation's Matching Gifts Program is designed to encourage your participation and promote your personal support of those qualifying institutions that are important to you.

While many nonprofit organizations are directly supported by the company and the foundation, the Matching Gifts Program allows you to help determine how to spend a portion of the company's philanthropic resources. This brochure describes the program and the procedures for obtaining matching funds for your donations. The attached form is for use in making a contribution. Additional forms may be obtained from receptionists in all plant lobbies, personnel areas at all plant sites, and the retirement area and credit union office at corporate headquarters or by contacting the Matching Gifts Program at (317) 276-2663.

## PROGRAM TERMS

The Eli Lilly and Company Foundation will match personal contributions of eligible contributors to qualified educational institutions, cultural organizations, and health care organizations subject to the guidelines of the program.

- Because of the voluntary nature of the program, matching gift requests must originate with the contributor.
- Gifts must be paid (not merely pledged) in cash, check, credit card, or in negotiable securities with an established market value determined by the average price on the day the gift is made.
- Original completed forms must be received within six months of the date of the donor's gift.
- Payments to a school or organization will be made quarterly, and the donor will be notified by the foundation at the time the gift is matched.
- An employee may give personal gifts of $25 or more but not exceeding $30,000 in each of the following qualified categories:
    EDUCATIONAL INSTITUTIONS: $25 MINIMUM, $30,000 MAXIMUM
    CULTURAL ORGANIZATIONS: $25 MINIMUM, $30,000 MAXIMUM
    HEALTH CARE ORGANIZATIONS: $25 MINIMUM, $30,000 MAXIMUM
- A retiree or retired board member may give personal gifts of $25 or more but not exceeding $2,500 in each of the following qualified categories:

EDUCATIONAL INSTITUTIONS: $25 MINIMUM, $2,500 MAXIMUM
CULTURAL ORGANIZATIONS: $25 MINIMUM, $2,500 MAXIMUM
HEALTH CARE ORGANIZATIONS: $25 MINIMUM, $2,500 MAXIMUM

All eligible gifts will be matched by the foundation $1 for $1.

- For your gift to an individual college or university to qualify for matching, you must have a personal affiliation with the institution: you or a member of your immediate family (spouse or child) must have received a degree from, attended, or currently be attending the institution or have been or currently be a member of its administration, faculty, or governing board (i.e., its board of trustees).

### Eligible Participants

- Current regular employees of Eli Lilly and Company working full-time or more than 20 hours part-time
- Retirees of Eli Lilly and Company
- Members of the board of directors of Eli Lilly and Company

### Not Eligible to Participate

- Spouses and surviving spouses of employees, retirees, or members of the board of directors

## ELIGIBLE INSTITUTIONS

### Educational Institutions

- Graduate and professional schools
- Four-year colleges and universities
- Two-year junior and community colleges and technical institutes
- Public and private, primary, and secondary schools offering a four-year program at least equivalent to a high school curriculum and granting a diploma upon satisfactory completion of such program
- All schools must be accredited by a nationally recognized nonsectarian, regional, or professional association or a state department of education
- Tax-exempt educational funds (e.g., United Negro College Fund, American Indian College Fund, Hispanic Association of Colleges and Universities, and Foundations for Independent Higher Education) if the sole purpose is to raise money for constituent member colleges that individually are eligible under the program

**Gifts made to support intercollegiate athletic programs, athletic scholarships, booster clubs, sororities, and fraternities do not qualify.**

### Cultural Organizations

- Museums
- Art councils
- Cultural centers
- Botanical or zoological societies
- Public broadcasting systems
- Libraries
- Symphony orchestras
- Historical associations
- Performing arts companies (dance, theater, orchestras, opera, etc.)

### Health Care Organizations

- Affirming the concerns of our employees, the Matching Gifts Program supports organizations that serve patients who are fighting diseases for which we offer or are searching for pharmaceutical treatments and positive outcomes.
- For a listing of eligible organizations, please see the reverse side of the Matching Gift Applications Form, Card A.
- For ease of processing, gifts must be made to the organization's national headquarters. Donors may designate that their gift be directed to a local chapter if desired.
- Ineligible gifts include payments for medical treatment or any gift not intended to further the general program of the organization.

**All eligible educational institutions, cultural organizations, and health care organizations must:**

- Be located within the United States, its possessions, or the commonwealth of Puerto Rico.
- Be recognized by the Internal Revenue Service of the United States Department of Treasury as a tax-exempt organization and listed in the Cumulative List of Organizations, IRS Publication 78, gifts to which are deductible under the United States Internal Revenue Code.
- Be able to make available audited financial statements upon request.

## INELIGIBLE ORGANIZATIONS AND GIFTS

The following are not eligible for a matching gift:

- Gifts made more than six months before receipt of the completed form
- Gifts made with funds given to the donor in whole or in part for donation purposes by other individuals, groups, or organizations
- Gifts entitling the donor to some personal benefit, e.g., payment for tickets, subscription fees, or fundraising dinners or events; tickets for athletic, cultural, or other events; auction items; publications
- Gifts intended to fulfill a person's pledge, tithe, or other church-related financial commitment
- Community foundations
- Private foundations
- Conservation, environmental, and ecological organizations
- Fraternities, sororities, honor societies, educational associations, and campus organizations
- Nonaccredited educational institutions
- Preschools and day care centers
- Pledges not paid
- Gifts made by surviving spouses of employees, retirees, or directors
- Volunteer hours
- Bequests, pledges, tuition payments, or payments in lieu of tuition or other student fees
- Athletic activities, scholarships, and facilities
- Scholarships or financial aid that benefits specific individuals
- Programs that operate under the sponsorship of a religious organization that are not separately incorporated as independent, nonreligious, tax-exempt organizations
- Life income plan gifts, trust funds, and insurance policies
- Bequests or in-kind (noncash) gifts of real estate or personal property (other than securities)
- Alumni foundations unless they support the primary academic objectives of the institution
- Health care organizations other than those listed as being eligible
- Political parties
- Political advocacy, lobbying, or action organizations
- Organizations engaging in illegal activities
- Community fundraisers, such as walk-a-thons, that raise money by soliciting sponsors

**Photocopies of forms are not eligible for consideration.**

## APPLICATION PROCEDURE

1. Contributor—Completely fills in Card A of the attached form and sends it with his/her gift to the organization. The donor must sign the form—typed signatures are not acceptable. (Incomplete forms cannot be processed and will be returned to the contributor.)
2. Gift Recipient—Upon receipt of the gift and form, the designated financial officer of the institution reviews the contributor's information, completes Card B of the form, and signs. Facsimile signatures are not acceptable. The entire form must be mailed to:

> Matching Gifts Program
> Eli Lilly and Company Foundation
> Drop Code 1618
> Lilly Corporate Center
> Indianapolis, IN 46285

3. Lilly Foundation—Upon verification of the eligibility of the donor, gift, and the organization, the foundation will issue a matching gift check and will send a receipt to the donor indicating that payment has been made. Processing will occur on a quarterly basis.
4. If you have indicated a specific department or purpose for your contribution, the matching gift will be designated for that same use.

The Eli Lilly and Company Foundation may suspend, change, revoke, or terminate this program at any time but only with respect to gifts made after such action.

The program will be administered by the contributions committee of the Eli Lilly and Company Foundation, and its interpretation of the program will be final.

It is the policy of the Eli Lilly and Company Foundation not to furnish names, addresses, or other employee information to any organization or solicitation agent.

Requests for additional forms or for information concerning the program should be sent to:

> Matching Gifts Program
> Eli Lilly and Company Foundation
> Drop Code 1618
> Lilly Corporate Center
> Indianapolis, Indiana 46285

*Attention: New Recipient Institutions*

If you have not previously received matching gifts from the Eli Lilly and Company Foundation, it will be necessary to attach the following to the Matching Gifts form:

- A brochure describing the organization's activities and programs offered to the public
- A copy of your IRS 501(c)(3) tax-exempt certification and foundation classification under Section 509(a)
- A statement signed by a financial officer of your institution that your operations are as stated in the determination letter and that there have been no changes in your purpose, character, or method of operation
- A list of the members of the current board of directors of your organization

# RESOURCE 26

## ACKNOWLEDGMENT LETTERS

# General Letter to Individual(s)

*Date*

*Donor Name*
*Address 1*
*Address 2*
*City, State Zip*

*Salutation:*

Thank you for your donation of *($ amount)* designated to the
*(allocation description)*.

Our mission at *(organization name)* is to *(mission statement)*.
Generous support from our loyal friends further strengthens our
commitment to *(subject matter – ie. children, the environment,
medical related causes)*. This year, we will be able to *(what? ie.
feed 10,000 children, develop a cure, provide scholarships)*.

We deeply appreciate your contribution.

Sincerely,


Development Officer

# General Letter to Corporation/Foundation

*Date*

*Corporation*
*Contact Name*
*Address 1*
*Address 2*
*City, State Zip*

*Salutation:*

On behalf of *(organization),* it is a pleasure to thank *(company name)* for its gift of *($ amount).* As requested, your generous support will benefit *(description).*

As your investment facilitates *(organization's name)* efforts, it also strengthens the *(mission).* We take pride in the work we do *(description of work),* and your generous donation helps further our efforts. Your support plays a vital role in accomplishing these goals.

Again, thank you.

Sincerely,

Development Officer

# General Letter for Gift-in-Kind

*Date*

*Donor Name*
*Address 1*
*Address 2*
*City, State Zip*

*Salutation:*

Thank you for your donation of *(donated item[s])* designated
to the *(allocation description)*.

Gifts-in-kind are a fundamental form of philanthropy at
*(organization name)*. Thoughtful gift(s) like yours represent
special and effective way(s) of supporting the organization.

We appreciate the careful consideration made when providing
this gift.

All the best,


Development Officer

## General Letter for Gifts of Securities

*Date*

*Donor Name*
*Address 1*
*Address 2*
*City, State Zip*

*Salutation:*

On behalf of *(organization)* I would like to acknowledge and thank you for your gift of *(numbers of shares and name of stock).* On *(date),* the high price of this security was *($ amount),* the low was *($ amount),* and the mean value was *($ amount),* making the value of your contribution *($ amount).* Your gift has been credited to the *(allocation description).*

I am enclosing Internal Revenue Service Form 8283, which is required for gifts of securities valued at more than $500.00. Section A of the form should be completed by you and filed with your *(year)* tax return, claiming the charitable deduction for your gift. Completion of Section B is not required for gifts of publicly traded securities. Should you have any questions concerning this procedure, please let me know.

Pursuant to Internal Revenue Service substantiation requirement, *(organization)* confirms that it has not provided you with goods or services in consideration of your making this gift.

Once again, thank you for your generosity and support of *(organization).*

Sincerely,


Chief Executive Officer

## General Letter to Donor of $10,000+

*Date*

*Donor Name*
*Address 1*
*Address 2*
*City, State Zip*

*Salutation:*

"No duty is more urgent than that of returning thanks."
On behalf of *(organization),* it is a pleasure to thank you
for your gift of *($ amount).*

*(Organization)*'s excellence is directly tied to the private
support it receives. This assistance makes it possible to
achieve outstanding results in our mission of *(mission).*

*(Personal note if donor is known by Chief Executive Officer.)*
We are most grateful to you for being an integral part of
our vision.

Sincerely,


Chief Executive Officer

# FORMS OF DONOR RECOGNITION

Resource 27

**Donor wall**

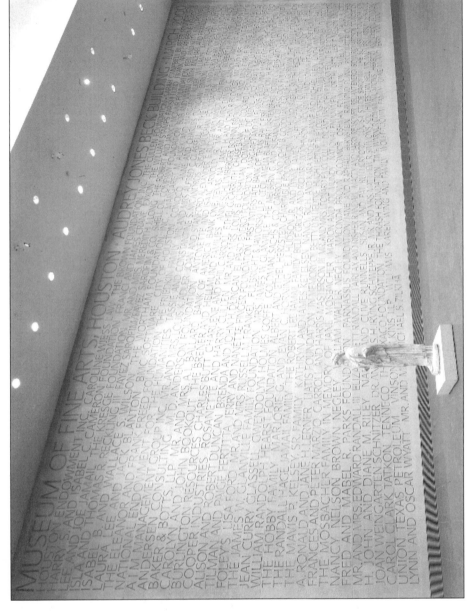

Courtesy of the Museum of Fine Arts, Houston, Texas. Photograph by Laura Wells.

## Donor bricks

Virgil T. De Vault Center Patio, Indiana University Alumni Association, Bloomington, Indiana. Courtesy of IU Foundation.

## Donor plaque

Courtesy of IU Foundation.

## Named facility

Donald C. (Danny) and Patricia P. Danielson Center in New Castle, Indiana. Courtesy of IU Foundation.

## Named natural space

Bronze leaf recognition. Tulip Trace Council of Girl Scouts, Inc., Bloomington, Indiana. Courtesy of IU Foundation.

## Donor and volunteer thank-you

Monroe County (Indiana) United Ministries donor and volunteer thank-you. Courtesy of IU Foundation.

## Recognition wall

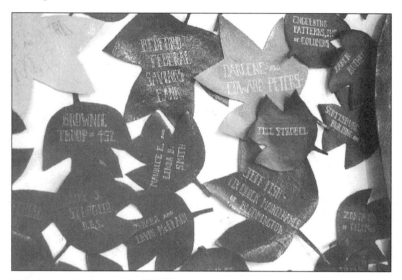

Tulip Trace Council of Girl Scouts, Inc. provides donor recognition using a distinctive recognition wall. Courtesy of IU Foundation.

## Donor tree

Bloomington (Indiana) Hospital
Foundation. Courtesy of IU Foundation.

## Close-up of donor tree

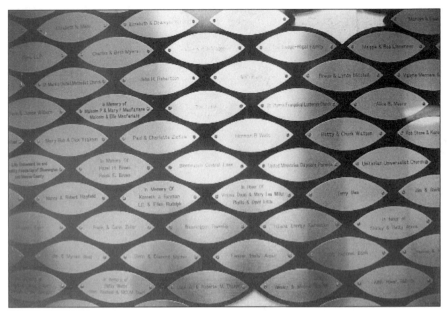

Bloomington (Indiana) Hospital Foundation. Courtesy of IU Foundation.

## Volunteer medallion

## Donor tile

Medallion was produced as a thank-you for volunteers by Hoosier Hills Food Bank, Bloomington, Indiana. Courtesy of United Way.

Pear tile was handmade for the Hoosier Hills Food Bank. It was given to donors as a thank-you. Courtesy of United Way.

## Creative annual report

A grocery bag with food is used as a creative annual report for the Hoosier Hills Food Bank. Courtesy of United Way.

## Donor paperweight

Courtesy of IU Foundation.

## Donor certificate

Certificate created by nationally syndicated cartoonist of *Speedbump* that was used throughout the campaign and then adopted by other United Ways across the country. Courtesy of United Way.

# RESOURCE 28

## NEWSLETTERS

# NEWSLETTER

## IN THIS ISSUE

- Second Century Fund Passes 60 Percent of Goal
- Parents Scholarship Fund Established
- Alumni Lead Local Efforts to Assist Campaign
- Small or Large — Every Gift Counts

### A Gift from the William Friedman Memorial Book Fund

### Established by Gifts from his family and friends

*In memory of William Friedman L'25, longtime trustee and former secretary of the Board of Trustees who died earlier this year, a book fund in the Law Library has been established by gifts from his family and friends as part of the Second Century Fund. Books purchased through the memorial book fund will be affixed with the book plate shown above.*

## Second Century Fund aided by gifts of all sizes and types

Every gift and pledge to the Second Century Fund, regardless of amount, brings the University closer to its $25 million fund raising goal and helps ensure a thriving future for Drake during the next 100 years.

Many donors are contributing a variety of gifts to the three-year capital campaign.

Some highlights include:

**Marlyn C. "Mike" Augustine** — A liberal arts graduate of 1944, Mr. Augustine deeded a five-acre parcel of land in Phoenix, Arizona, to Drake as a contribution to the Second Century Fund. Value of the land is estimated at $80,000.

**Jean A. Bandy** — Namesake for a new mineral discovered by her late husband Mark Chance Bandy, Mrs. Bandy Ed'21 Ed'56, an Arizona resident, pledged $10,000 to the Second Century Fund for earth sciences study.

**Bertram Holst** — A liberal arts graduate of 1913, Mr. Holst enjoys a long record of giving to Drake's annual fund. This year, in addition to his annual giving, Mr. Holst made a surprise outright gift of $50,000 to the Second Century Fund in support of the University's capital campaign efforts to assist the College of Liberal Arts.

**Yosh Inadomi** — A former alumni trustee and a 1945 business administration graduate, Mr. Inadomi pledged $25,000 to establish an endowed scholarship in his father's name. The John K. Inadomi Scholarship Fund will be used to assist students studying

business administration.

**Jeffry R. and Sharyn Kopriva Jontz** The Jontzes pledged $5,000 to Drake's annual scholarship fund as a Second Century Fund contribution. Now a Florida attorney, Mr. Jontz is a 1966 liberal arts graduate; Mrs. Jontz is a 1968 journalism graduate.

**R. Wayne Skidmore** A life member of the Board of Trustees and a 1933 business graduate, Mr. Skidmore, along with his wife Maxine, have established a named gift in Aliber Hall, the new College of Business Administration building. The seminar room in Aliber Hall will bear the Skidmore name because of their generosity.

The Second Century Fund offers donors a number of methods of giving, including outright gifts of cash, gifts of securities, gifts of real property, gifts of life insurance, planned gifts (which can take many forms) and gifts through a will.

One or a combination of these methods may have a particular appeal in planning a gift. Drake University provides donors with help and advice in planning their gifts.

For more information regarding these or other named or memorial gift opportunities, contact: Office of Institutional Development, Drake University, 319 Old Main, Des Moines, Iowa 50311, telephone 515/271-3154.

# UPDATE

VOLUME 3, NUMBER 1

THE ENDOWMENT CAMPAIGN
*for* INDIANA UNIVERSITY    JANUARY 1999
BLOOMINGTON

## ONGOING SUPPORT REINFORCES CAMPAIGN GAINS

The Endowment Campaign for IU Bloomington, despite its name, is not just about endowments. It's about everything to do with IU.

It a great university bases its reputation on the quality of faculty and students it attracts, that reputation must also be reinforced by every aspect of the campus itself. The Campaign's $200 million goal for Ongoing, Private Support aims to provide the resources for this reinforcement.

As IU grows in stature, thanks in large part to the continuing success of the Endowment Campaign, the need for annual gifts becomes even greater. "IU's horizons are widening all the time," explains Ken Beckley (BS '62), National Chair of IU's Annual Fund, "and the more that happens, the more opportunities arise unexpectedly. You have to act quickly to take advantage of those opportunities."

### SUPPORTING A DIVERSE UNIVERSITY

The very diversity of IU's programs and departments makes it hard to sum up in a few words the work of Ongoing Support. It

> "IU's horizons are widening all the time, and the more that happens, the more opportunities arise unexpectedly. You have to act quickly to take advantage of those opportunities."
>
> — KEN BECKLEY, NATIONAL CHAIR OF IU'S ANNUAL FUND

affects every unit, every building, every inch of the Bloomington campus. Kenneth Gros Louis, Vice President for Academic Affairs and Bloomington Chancellor, explains: "Deans and Chairs look to the annual fund for those essential extras that are not built into the annual budget." This can mean anything from scholarships and travel grants to cutting-edge technology and equipment, from teaching aids in the College of Arts and Sciences to the support of IU's network of libraries and museums. This flexible approach, says Gros

Louis, "often makes possible what otherwise would not have been dreamed possible."

"We need to close the gap between IU and the other Big Ten universities in terms of annual support," says Beckley, "and with higher alumni participation we will be able to do that."

With the Campaign now 72.2% through its timeline, Ongoing Support is 70.9% towards that $200 million goal; the gap is closing, but there is still some way to go. And when the Endowment Campaign is over, the work of Ongoing Support will continue.

Not everyone is able to make an endowed gift, but Ongoing Support enables donors to make a gift of any size to the school or program of their choice. Jack Kimberling (BA '57, JD '30) Co-Chair of the National Campaign Steering Committee, sees everyone having a role: "I don't care whether you can only give ten dollars or whether you can give a million dollars. I think every one of us who does anything to help the University, does something for society."

**on·go·ing sup·port**
(on'gō-ing sə-pôrt')
1. A shorthand term for the many varieties of non-endowed gifts made to the Endowment Campaign. 2. A source of flexible funds to be used at the discretion of the Deans in response to sudden needs or opportunities. 3. A wide ranging program of campus support, which will continue once the Campaign is over. 4. A vehicle for gifts of any size.

## The Next Generation

*Jack Kimberling with Kelley Scholar*

*Andrew Acito (left) and John H. Myers*

*Scholar Keith Zapp (right) at a reception*

*held in October, 1998 by IU Foundation*

*President Curt Simic. For more on*

*endowed scholarships, see page 3.*

see page 3

**en·dow·ment** (ĕn-dou'mənt) *n.*
1. Money invested for future growth, with only a portion of the return being used today. 2. One of the best vehicles a university can use to keep tuition costs affordable. 3. A good strategy to offset the effects of inflation and reduced state appropriations. 4. An important aid in attracting and retaining today's outstanding faculty as well as tomorrow's brightest scholars.

VOLUME 2, NUMBER 3

# UPDATE

THE ENDOWMENT CAMPAIGN
*for* INDIANA UNIVERSITY    SEPTEMBER 1998

BLOOMINGTON

*Additional $2 Million Investment Could Reap Large Returns*

## TRUSTEES EXPAND ENDOWMENT MATCHING PROGRAM

*A* $6 million investment that could well bring back $150 million?

It's no dream: Indiana University officials can expect such results, because this particular investment is via the University's innovative Faculty Endowment Income Matching Program.

On May 8, the IU Board of Trustees authorized adding another $2 million to the $4 million already allocated to the successful matching program, which encourages private donors to set up faculty endowments by dedicating University funds to match endowment earnings.

*"The loyalty and support of Indiana University's donors continues to impress me. They have taken advantage of the matching program at a much faster rate than anyone anticipated. Twice we've had to go back to the trustees to add more funds, just to keep pace with the demand."*

*— PRESIDENT MYLES BRAND*

The brainchild of IU president Myles Brand, the program began in 1995 when the trustees agreed to set aside $1 million to match the payout (the spendable income generated by the invested principal) of new endowment gifts of $500,000 or more. The program proved so popular with donors that they added $3 million in 1997. With the latest infusion, a total of $6 million has been set aside for the matching of endowment income. Half of the money comes from the president's budget, and the other half comes from the campuses.

Has it been worth it? Brand thinks the numbers speak for themselves. "It's really quite startling," he says. "In its entire 175-year history before the Bloomington Endowment Campaign, the University had received only 31 faculty endowments. I challenged the IU Foundation to increase that number by 100. There was some hard swallowing and a few ashen faces," he chuckles, "but I was optimistic." He convinced the Foundation board of directors and the University trustees that with the matching program as an incentive, donors would give at the high levels needed for endowment support: $500,000 for a professorship, $1 million for a chair. The strategy worked.

As a result of the first $4 million investment, the IU Foundation has already recorded $101 million in gifts. That translates to 105 new faculty endowments. "We've more than tripled our endowed positions in just two years," says Brand.

By that measure, the new $2 million will result in another $40 million in gifts: 50 more endowed positions. "I believe that's a conservative estimate," adds Foundation president Curt Simic. "When this is over, I think we will have leveraged over $150 million."

*"we've more than tripled our endowed positions in just two years."*

*— PRESIDENT MYLES BRAND*

The Foundation is so confident, in fact, that it has raised Brand's original challenge—with scarcely a gulp. The goal is now *150* new endowed faculty positions. "That is definitely feasible," says Simic. "Our donors have been remarkably enthusiastic about the idea. That shouldn't surprise us, really. These folks know a good deal when they see one."

As Brand points out, "It's a win-win situation for everyone. The University gets the financial stability and competitiveness the endowments provide, and the donors get the satisfaction of seeing the results of their gifts right away. Suppose a donor

*more on page 2*

**en•dow•ment** (ĕn-dou′mənt) *n.*

1. Money invested for future growth, with only a portion of the return being used today. 2. One of the best vehicles a university can use to keep tuition costs affordable. 3. A good strategy to offset the effects of inflation and reduced state appropriations. 4. An important aid in attracting and retaining today's outstanding faculty, as well as tomorrow's brightest scholars.

# RESOURCE 29

## MEDIA COVERAGE

**573**

## PENN STATE PRESS RELEASE

# News

PENN**S**TATE _____   Telephone: (814) 865-7517

1855            Department of            The Pennsylvania State University
                Public Information       312 Old Main
                                         University Park, PA 16802-1504

**EMBARGOED UNTIL 2 P.M. SEPTEMBER 12, 1997**

September 12, 1997

**$30 MILLION GIFT FROM SCHREYERS WILL CREATE HONORS COLLEGE—
LARGEST INDIVIDUAL GIFT IN PENN STATE HISTORY**

University Park, Pa.—"This extraordinary gift to Penn State will establish the
nation's premier honors college. It will profoundly enhance our ability to attract
the nation's best students and elevate our Scholars Program to new levels of
excellence while nurturing international perspectives among students."

With those words, Penn State President Graham Spanier today accepted a
$30 million gift from William A. Schreyer and his wife Joan to create an honors
college at the University. The gift is the largest ever received by the University
from an individual or couple.

The new honors college will enlarge and transform a highly successful,
nationally renowned scholars program into a multidisciplinary center of undergraduate academic excellence. Three hundred freshmen will enter the program
each year and will be supported by scholarships. With its own Dean and
selected faculty from the university at large, the college will provide study
abroad opportunities, professional internships, mentoring by alumni, thesis
research, special classes taught by top teachers and scholars, and a national
forum for new learning methods. One of the unique features of the new college
is its linkage with the Schreyer Institute for Innovation in Learning, a think tank
to develop and test new approaches to learning and to implement these
throughout the University. In essence, the honors college will become the test
laboratory for the innovative approaches to teaching and learning that emerge
from the Schreyer Institute.

Schreyer Gift—page 2

William Schreyer is chairman emeritus of Merrill Lynch & Co., Inc., the worldwide financial services firm, and former chairman of Penn State's Board of Trustees. He has long been involved in philanthropic activities on behalf of the University. A Williamsport native, he graduated from Penn State in 1948 with a degree in commerce and finance. "This is certainly one of the most exciting moments of our lives," said Schreyer. "Joan and I wanted to give something back to the University for all it has done for us, and President Spanier's vision of an honors college that would attract top students and give them an international perspective had tremendous appeal. It will create unique opportunities for gifted young people in Pennsylvania and, indeed, all over the world, while advancing Penn State's stature as a world class university.

"We are extremely proud of what Penn State has accomplished, and we want to see it continue its climb to the top among our nation's public universities. One of the best ways to do that is to attract highly motivated students from all walks of life. That's where we hope the honors college will play an extremely important role, particularly in nurturing and inspiring responsible citizenship and a global perspective among students for the 21st century."

The Penn State Board of Trustees voted today to name the new college The Schreyer Honors College, making it the first such college at a major public university in America to be named for its benefactors. The college builds on the success of the University Scholars Program, which annually enrolls about 1,500 academically gifted undergraduates. In the most recent survey of its kind, the program was ranked among the eight best at America's public universities. Students entering the program in recent years consistently post average SAT scores well above 1,400, placing them in the upper 1 to 2 percent of all American university students.

"Every time the University has needed Bill and Joan, they have been there for us," said Spanier. "Whether as Chairman of our Board of Trustees, Chairman of our first capital campaign, or now in providing this philanthropic leadership, Bill has always come through for Penn State. He and Joan have made an impact on this institution that will be felt by countless future generations of students.

Schreyer Gift—page 3

"Virtually all of our programs will benefit from interaction with the teachers and students in The Schreyer Honors College. It will have a tremendous ripple effect across the entire University and put a university-wide focus on academic excellence."

The Schreyers' gift will:

- Establish in perpetuity the honors college
- Help provide Academic Excellence Scholarships to 300 students each year
- Provide up to 100 international study awards annually to students who will be known as Schreyer Ambassadors
- Provide interaction with national figures who will inspire responsible citizenship
- Establish fellowships for Penn State faculty and distinguished visitors
- Provide funds for national conferences on teaching and learning

The college will also conduct special outreach to first generation college students, in keeping with the Land Grant tradition upon which Penn State was founded.

A professional advisory board consisting of distinguished members of the business, education, and public service communities will be formed to link the academic program of The Schreyer Honors College to the world outside the university.

"I am particularly excited about the opportunities this gift makes possible," said Professor Louis Geschwindner, Chair of the Faculty Senate. "The Schreyers' gift will allow Penn State to build on the success of the University Scholars Program, a program initiated by action of the University Faculty Senate in 1980. This will be very positive for the overall quality of undergraduate education at Penn State, which is an important priority. It builds on previous consultations with faculty committees and we look forward to doing all we can to help make The Schreyer Honors College the best in the nation."

Bill Schreyer pointed out that the gift reflected not only his own view of the importance of higher education, but that of Merrill Lynch as well.

Schreyer Gift—page 4

"Our company's founder, Charles E. Merrill, had a strong commitment to education," he said. "He saw it as a sound investment in the future of our society, and that philosophy made a lasting impression on me."

Prior to the most recent gift, the Schreyers had given several million dollars to various Penn State programs. Merrill Lynch provided matching gifts for many of those contributions.

In addition to being the largest gift in Penn State history, the Schreyers' gift is among the top 20 gifts to a public university in America.

In 1987, the Schreyers committed $1 million to endow the William A. Schreyer Chair in Global Management Policies and Planning in The Smeal College of Business Administration. In 1993, the couple pledged $1 million to help build the new Paterno Library, if Penn State faculty and staff collectively gave at least $2 million that year to University programs of their choice. Ultimately faculty and staff commitments totaled $2.4 million.

In 1995 the Schreyers gave $1 million to renovate "Lisnaward," an historic State College home, to make it the residence of the University President. The sale of the former President's house netted $700,000, which the Board of Trustees directed to support the Schreyer Institute for Innovation in Learning.

The Schreyers also have made gifts to help build the Bryce Jordan Center at University Park campus and the biomedical research building at Penn State's Hershey Medical Center, to establish the Schreyer Libraries Endowment in Global Management Policy and Planning, and to help fund a faculty chair in Jewish studies in the College of the Liberal Arts.

Bill Schreyer spent his entire business career with Merrill Lynch. He joined the firm as a trainee and in 1950 became an account executive in the firm's Buffalo, N.Y., office. He subsequently served as manager of Merrill Lynch offices in Trenton, N.J., and Buffalo. He also served two years (1955–56) on active duty as an Air Force lieutenant. He rose through a succession of sales, trading, and investment banking positions and was named a Merrill Lynch vice president in 1965. He then served in several top executive positions with the parent firm and its subsidiaries and became president of the parent company, Merrill Lynch & Co., in 1982. He was named chief executive officer in 1984 and chairman in 1985.

Schreyer Gift—page 5

Under his leadership, Merrill Lynch ascended to its position as the world's largest and most profitable securities underwriter and a leading strategic financial advisor to corporations, governments, institutions and individuals worldwide. Mr. Schreyer became chairman emeritus in 1993 and continues to serve as a director of a number of national and international companies.

He has been involved with Penn State for many years. He has been a University Trustee since 1986 and served as president of the board, 1993–96. He led the University's first comprehensive fund-raising campaign, The Campaign for Penn State, a six-year effort that concluded in 1990 and raised $352 million in private gifts for academic programs.

From 1990 to 1993 he headed the National Development Council, the University's top fund-raising advisory body. In that three-year span, Penn State received more than $195 million in gifts. Last fall President Spanier appointed him an honorary chair for the University's forthcoming capital campaign.

Penn State named him a Distinguished Alumnus in 1979, the highest distinction it can bestow on one of its graduates.

Joan Legg Schreyer is a native of Buffalo. A full partner in her husband's philanthropic efforts, she was named an Honorary Alumna of the University in 1991.

Contact:

| Bill Mahon | Alan Janesch |
|---|---|
| (814) 865-7517 (office) | (814) 865-7517 (office) |
| (814) 237-5625 (home) | (814) 867-3721 (home) |
| np3@psu.edu | axj12@psu.edu |

## EXCERPT FROM PRESIDENT SPANIER'S
## STATE OF THE UNIVERSITY ADDRESS, SEPTEMBER 1997

# The Schreyer Honors College

. . . I am very pleased to report that today the Board of Trustees approved the establishment of an honors college at Penn State. This new college will expand the number of University Scholars as well as the breadth of the scholars' educational experience.

We are able to take this important step as a result of an extraordinary gift from Bill and Joan Schreyer. I am delighted to announce that they have contributed $30 million—the largest personal gift in Penn State's history—to endow The Schreyer Honors College. In so doing, they are making possible a profound opportunity for generations of students. A substantial portion of the Schreyers' gift will create an additional 160 endowed scholarships in the honors college. The endowment will also establish Schreyer Ambassador Awards to support study abroad for 100 honors students each year. Other initiatives with The Schreyer Honors College will include community/internship experiences, alumni and professional mentoring, a leadership development program, visiting fellows, Penn State faculty fellows, a recurring national conference at Penn State on teaching and learning, and a link with the existing Schreyer Institute for Innovation in Learning.

# RESOURCE 30

## HONOR ROLL OF DONORS

# DEVELOPMENTS
## Spring 2000
## Giving Back

### Foundation Board President and Development Council Chair See Support of Bloomington Hospital Foundation as Way to Give Back to the Community

Their leadership in Bloomington Hospital Foundation isn't the only common bond between Pat Fell-Barker and Cary Curry.

Fell-Barker, president of Bloomington Hospital Foundation Board of Directors, and Curry, chair of the Development Council, also operate two thriving businesses in Monroe County—businesses that have been serving south central Indiana for more than 75 years each. Because of their deep-seated history with Bloomington and the surrounding areas, both feel it's important to support community-based services.

"As the fourth-generation Curry to operate this business, I think it's important for me to be actively supportive of important community resources such as Bloomington Hospital," said Curry, who is president of Curry Buick-Cadillac-Pontiac-GMC.

Curry's great-grandfather founded the dealership in 1915. Since that time, the company has supported various community services including Bloomington Hospital, the IU Auditorium, the Boys' and Girls' Club, Girls Inc., Wonderlab, the John Waldron Arts Center, the United Way, Big Brothers Big Sisters, and the Indiana Theater restoration project.

As CEO of B.G. Hoadley Quarries, Inc., which has operated in south central Indiana since the 1870s, Fell-Barker knows how important quality health care is to her employees and their families.

"From birth to life's end, our people have their medical needs met by Bloomington Hospital. We all benefit from the expanded services and the excellent quality that our community hospital provides," she said.

Both Fell-Barker and Curry view the Foundation as a productive way to support Bloomington Hospital, and in turn support the community and their employees. Since becoming involved with the Foundation in 1995, Fell-Barker says she has seen an increase in the Foundation's commitment to the hospital in both fund-raising and as an advocate for better and extended community health care.

"Through the purchase of the Healthmobile and with Susan Lyons' Development Council concept, there has been an increased awareness of the hospital, and the activities of the Foundation have been growing. More people have become involved," she said.

As chair of the Development Council, Curry sees firsthand the importance that the Foundation's events play in positioning Bloomington Hospital in the community as a provider and advocate of greater access to health care. One of the Development Council's major goals for this year was to obtain successful awareness of the new Alzheimer's Resource Center. (See related story.)

"The year-end appeal was very successful. It allowed us to tell our story and to garner support for a much-needed service here in Monroe County," explained Curry. "We hope that we can continue the success by increasing our Business Honor Roll membership."

Which, Curry says, can only be done through education. So, with assistance from Mark Bradford, chair of the Business Honor Roll, Curry has arranged a few luncheons that will involve inviting interested businesses to learn more about the Business Honor Roll and Bloomington Hospital Foundation.

"We'll be asking them to make a one-year financial commitment," Curry said. "And, this year's Business Honor Roll members will be supporting Hoosiers Outrun Cancer, an event that is going to need a tremendous amount of support but will assist Bloomington Hospital cancer patient services and Indiana University cancer research projects."

Additional Foundation-funded events will include the Children's Photo Clinic, which will offer physically challenged children an opportunity to have their picture taken at no charge, and the Youth and Middle School Football Coaches' Clinic, which is led by former IU football head coach Bill Mallory and is designed to teach youth football coaches how to teach players proper football techniques, including safety.

Fell-Barker and Curry have both made a commitment to give back to the community. They are helping to provide to others what has been given to them for years—quality, caring, accessible health care services.

## Why Local Businesses Support Bloomington Hospital

What makes a business feel it needs to support any community service, let alone a hospital? For some, it's a personal experience that ties them to the hospital; while for others, it's a desire to give something back to the community.

For example, Lee Carmichael, CEO and president of Weddle Brothers construction Co. Inc., has a unique tie to Bloomington Hospital.

"Weddle Bros. was the general contractor for Bloomington Hospital's addition between 1982 and 1984. On July 16, 1983, shortly after midnight, my daughter, Amanda, was born at Bloomington Hospital—the very same time we had coordinated a 12-hour shutdown of all water and several other services during the renovation of the maternity ward. I guess timing is everything," he said.

Mark Bradford, CEO and president of Monroe County Bank, shares an experience similar to Carmichael's.

"Shortly after we moved to Bloomington in 1990, my oldest son, Matt, broke his leg playing football," Bradford explained. "He was in traction at the hospital for 18 days. Katy [his wife] and I were new to the community and had two small children at home, so this was a particularly tough time for us. Matt received excellent care at the hospital, and we were very impressed with the people who provided the care. Everyone went out of their way to make the experience as positive as possible."

Like many residents of Bloomington, Lynn Dillon, area administrative officer at Rogers Group, was born at Bloomington Hospital. He has also had several family members receive care from Bloomington Hospital, including his mother. When she was diagnosed with pancreatic cancer, Dillon and his family turned to Hospice of Bloomington Hospital for support, which helped them care for his mother at her home until her death.

Still others have chosen to join the Business Honor Roll as a way for them to provide their communities with quality health care services and greater access to medical care.

Supporting Bloomington Hospital is a top priority for Owen County State Bank, says president and CEO Gordon Wells. Because of Bloomington Hospital's strong presence in Owen County and the fact that the residents appreciate and need its services, Owen County State Bank chose to join the Business Honor Roll when it was created in 1998.

"The residents of Owen County have a strong feeling about Bloomington Hospital's expansion into Owen County. The addition of the medical practices in Owen County has created a favorable attitude compared to what it was about five years ago. And, it's only getting better," said Wells.

According to Dr. Martin O'Neill, cardiovascular surgeon and partner with Shumacker Isch, joining the Business Honor Roll meant not only an excellent way to support Bloomington Hospital, but it also meant giving more support to the community, which helps maintain Bloomington as a good place to live.

"Obviously our community involvement helps build a better life for all of us," Dillon said. "As a board member of the Bloomington Economic Development Corporation, we are always recruiting new firms to locate within this area. One of the strong selling points is Indiana University, but I also feel that the hospital is a vital resource and often plays a major role in helping to recruit new businesses to the area."

Carmichael says that during a time when global competition for quality employees is expanding, promoting the high quality of life in Bloomington that includes a strong and growing hospital helps everyone continue to attract the highly skilled professional who will help set apart our businesses from other communities'.

Carmichael also believes that supporting the hospital "is the right thing to do."

Based on the various projects that the Business Honor Roll supports, it is clear that supporting Bloomington Hospital is a right thing to do. Plus, as Bradford, chair of the Business Honor Roll, points out, businesses can plan for their Business Honor Roll contribution in their budgets because it only requires an annual donation.

Pat Fell-Barker, chair of the Foundation board and president of B.G. Hoadley Quarries, Inc., agrees.

"The Business Honor Roll plays an extremely important role in providing the financial opportunity for the area businesses to contribute a single sum at an appropriate level for their business. Then, those contributions can be used for the expansion and improvement of our health care services," she said.

Business Honor Roll funds are used to support usually one or two fundraising events, which in turn will support several BHHS services. Last year, the Business Honor Roll raised $115,000. Those funds supported the Festival of Trees and Lights, which raised money to support various services, including childhood immunizations and the distribution of 500 coupons offering free mammography screenings to women who qualify. Also, funds provided additional support for the Olcott Center for Breast Health.

This year, according to Bradford, they are hoping to raise $200,000, which will support Hoosiers Outrun Cancer. In addition to providing monetary support to the race, the Business Honor Roll members will also offer volunteer support.

As Dr. O'Neill said, "If I'm not on call, I plan to run."

*To inquire about Business Honor Roll membership, call (812) 353-9528.*

## Heritage Society:
## The McDaniels—Taking Care of the Future

Although their typical days at work don't mirror each other, their common professional interests do. Mr. Terry and Dr. Deb McDaniel both spend their days taking care of the future.

Dr. McDaniel has been a pediatrician in the Bloomington area and has been on the Bloomington Hospital Medical Staff for the past 15 years, while Mr. McDaniel has been a school administrator at Spencer-Owen Community Schools for the past 23 years, where he now serves as superintendent. Helping to shape the future is what they do. Both play a vital role in the physical, mental and emotional development of children, and they carry this interest into their community involvement.

As members of the Heritage Society, the McDaniels support such programs as the Health-mobile, which visits area schools to provide children with immunizations and checkups. Their support also enables the Foundation to offer such programs as the youth football coaches' clinic, which teaches coaches how to properly teach football techniques in a manner that ensures the health and safety of the children.

"We joined the Heritage Society because it is important to support the organizations that support the health and well-being of the people of our community," explained Mr. McDaniel. "Without the type of financial support the Heritage Society and the Foundation offer, our communities can never be provided those items that offer extra assistance to the medically needy. These resources are about human relations and support, which are just as important as the medicines that help people become healthier."

The McDaniels' commitment to the Heritage Society is a significant one. Plus, it's one that they encourage others to consider.

"There is nothing better than seeing those in need receive assistance," said Mr. McDaniel. "The Heritage Society is one way to provide help for others' quality of life."

*Membership in the Heritage Society can be obtained by paying a lump sum of $10,000 or in 10 annual payments of $1000. Donors may also specify another payment plan. For more information about the Heritage Society, call (812) 353-9528.*

### Employee Award Gives Benefactor a Chance to Recognize Laboratory Professionals

For most of his life, Dr. Marvin Carmack has been surrounded by chemistry labs, research, students, and books. His lifetime interest in chemistry began in 1937 when he received the A.B. Honors in chemistry at the University of Illinois. Soon after, he earned his master's and doctoral degrees in chemistry from the University of Michigan. From 1941 to 1953, Carmack was a member of the faculty of chemistry at the University of Pennsylvania. During World War II, he directed research in military explosives at Penn. Later, he participated in research on antimalarial medicines. Beginning in 1953, Carmack was a professor of chemistry at Indiana University-Bloomington, where he continued to teach until 1978.

In the past, Carmack has had two separate opportunities to do research. During a sabbatical leave in 1949, under a Guggenheim Foundation Fellowship, he spent one year researching with Nobel Laureate Professor Vladimir Prelog at the Swiss Federal Institute of Technology in Zürich, Switzerland. In 1960, Carmack received a Fulbright Research Fellowship, and he spent a year in Melbourne, Australia, working in Sir Robert Price's laboratory, studying potential new medicines from the plants of tropical Australia and New Guinea.

Carmack knows first-hand the value that fellowships can add to a person's career. So, he and his wife, Joan, decided in 1987 to establish the Joan and Marvin Carmack Award for Exemplary Performance in Laboratory Services. This employee award is given to hospital lab technicians or level II phlebotomists who demonstrate outstanding technical performance, commitment to the laboratory profession, enthusiasm for the value of laboratory services in medical care and good interpersonal skills.

Marvin says he and his wife both wanted to recognize clinical lab employees, who do not often get much attention because they do so many behind-the-scenes jobs that are extremely important.

"So, we chose to give an award that will allow the employee to take an intensive course somewhere other than Bloomington which perhaps may also give the employee and their spouse a much-deserved break," Marvin explained.

Although he now lives in Green Valley, Ariz., Marvin, a former Foundation board member, tries to return to Bloomington once a year to visit. He also keeps up to date on the Bloomington Hospital and Healthcare System news.

"I'm very impressed by the regional growth that Bloomington Hospital has experienced in recent years. It's wonderful that they can now reach so many people who otherwise would have a difficult time accessing health care."

The Carmacks' award is one of 17 that are awarded annually to Bloomington Hospital and Healthcare System employees. The award winners are nominated and selected by their colleagues.

### Hoosiers Outrun Cancer Designed to Raise Awareness

"For our part, Bloomington Hospital is both thrilled to be the beneficiary on behalf of its cancer patients and honored to be asked to help make it happen," said Lyons.

Funds raised from Hoosiers Outrun Cancer will support Bloomington Hospital cancer services and cancer outreach and educational programs, along with cancer research conducted on Indiana University's Bloomington campus. In addition, Hoosiers Outrun Cancer will help provide financial assistance to qualifying patients and families. With a fundraising goal of $200,000, Hoosiers Outrun Cancer will feed funds into the Bloomington community and surrounding areas.

Scheduled for Saturday morning, October 14, Hoosiers Outrun Cancer will feature a 1-mile family walk, a 5K walk and a 5K run. All events will begin at IU's Assembly Hall. To boost public support and awareness of the event, Coach Bob Knight and his IU Hoosiers will make several public appearances, including a pre-race public practice session on Friday evening, October 13, and an autograph session following the races. Also on Saturday, an afternoon basketball clinic will be offered.

Plans for Hoosiers Outrun Cancer will be further developed throughout this spring under the leadership of Karen Knight, Ellis and Lyons. Numerous volunteers are needed to help plan, promote and carry out this event. Interested persons can call (812) 353-9528 for information.

### Bloomington Hospital Alzheimer's Resource Center Will Provide Continuing Support to Patients and Families

It is a frightening disease, masked by mystery, and it can affect anyone. Understanding Alzheimer's and knowing how to care for someone who suffers from it is difficult. Bloomington Hospital recognizes the difficulty. In an effort to help families facing Alzheimer's, Bloomington Hospital will soon offer the Alzheimer's Resource Center.

Located in the Medical Arts Building on 619 W. First St., the center will open in early summer. Jody Curley, former director of the Adult Day Center, with assistance from other health care professionals, will help families of Alzheimer's patients determine the best way to manage their physical and emotional needs. She will also provide patients and families with caregiver education and training and connect them to support and respite services, including BHHS services.

For example, if a family has elected to care for their loved one at home, the family may be encouraged to consider enrolling their loved one in the Adult Day

Center programs. By taking advantage of these programs, the Alzheimer's patient is engaging in daily activities and social interaction. The caregiver also receives a much-deserved break and a chance to run errands. When a family feels it can no longer care for their loved one at home, the Alzheimer's educator may discuss with the family their options for residential care, which might include 24-hour skilled nursing from the specially trained staff at Bloomington Hospitality House's Center for Alzheimer's and Dementia Care, or at another extended care facility in the community which meets the family's needs.

Funds from the 1999 year-end appeal, which equaled $35,000, will support the new center. That money will be used to pay for start-up costs, such as books and resource materials, computers, and office supplies. In addition, for this year Bloomington Hospital Foundation's Hopewell Circle has committed its fund-raising efforts to support the Alzheimer's Resource Center. (See page 15 for the Hopewell Circle recognition list or to learn more about becoming a Hopewell Circle member.)

By adding this third component, Bloomington Hospital and Healthcare System is providing the Bloomington community and surrounding areas with a continuum of care for Alzheimer's patients and their families. Together with the Adult Day Center and the Center for Alzheimer's and Dementia Care, the new Alzheimer's Resource Center will answer the community-wide call for additional support and services.

## Jody Curley Accepts Chance to Direct New Alzheimer's Center

Jody Curley, former director of Bloomington Hospital's Adult Day Center, has joined the new Alzheimer's education and resource center as director. Jody will spend the next couple of months setting up the new center and developing the new programs.

"Although I've loved working in adult day services, I have imaged myself moving in the direction of more consultation and teaching and less direct service and clinical supervision," she said.

With a master's in counseling psychology and 28 years of experience in working with older adults and their families, Jody brings a great deal of expertise to the table, especially in behavior management of people with dementia. In addition, she is a certified occupational therapy assistant, which has given her a solid affiliated health professional background and strong training in assisting people with activities of daily living.

As director, Jody will serve as a consultant giving caregivers advice, education and resources on how to care for their loved ones. She will maintain a referral network for in-home and extended care and will act as liaison for other dementia

**Resource 30**

services of BHHS. In addition, Jody will hold behavior management seminars for family caregivers and health professionals and will facilitate support groups.

Jody began her new position in April. And everyone's favorite Canine Companion for Independence, Peanut Butter, will still visit clients at the Adult Day Center as well as other BHHS departments and services.

### Retired Veterinarian Finds Enjoyment Working in Hospital

His mornings could be described as typical. He gets to the hospital around 6:15 A.M. and begins his shift promptly at 6:30. He answers phones and questions, checks the patient census, delivers messages, and since his desk is located in a busy area, often greets familiar faces. "Occasionally," he may help a visitor here and there.

In reality, Dr. Pat Riggins's day isn't typical. He doesn't *have* to be there at all. Yet, he wants to be there. Every Tuesday and Thursday from 6:30 to 9 A.M., Riggins, a retired veterinarian and 27-year resident of Bloomington, volunteers at the hospital's information desk. And, every Tuesday and Thursday he helps people—visitors, patients, and employees. He answers the phone with vigor and thrives on greeting people, answering questions, and just being there.

"I guess you could say I'm a frustrated maître d'" he said. "I had extra time on my hands and had previously been involved with the hospital [Riggins served on the hospital board of directors in the mid to late '80s], so it seemed like a good idea for me to volunteer."

Riggins isn't alone, though. Nearly 240 people volunteer on a weekly basis at Bloomington Hospital. Since May 1999, the volunteers have given 21,796 hours to the hospital. The volunteers form the Auxiliary, which is led by the Auxiliary board, of which Riggins is chair. The Auxiliary helps operate the hospital gift shop, and all profits earned from the gift shop support hospital-related services and programs. Last year, the Auxiliary pledged $410,000 to the Foundation payable over the next three years. The money will be deposited into the Foundation's capital fund to support various programs.

In addition to volunteering in various hospital departments, they also contribute money and time to produce or purchase layette kits for new mothers and stuffed animals for children.

"Volunteers do a number of things that are vital to the hospital," explained Riggins. "It would be a tremendous economic burden to employ people to do some of the jobs volunteers do, especially those that may only take a few hours a week."

Riggins also says that volunteers offer another vital component to a hospital.

"The volunteer program gives people a stake in the hospital. It adds nearly 240 representatives of the hospital to the community.

Riggins has volunteered at Bloomington Hospital since retiring in 1995 as director of Indiana University's Lab Animal Resources. Prior to working at IU, Riggins spent 14 years operating a veterinary office and 12 years in the pharmaceutical industry doing clinical research for animal medications. He and his wife, Dotti, have four sons and four grandchildren.

To find out more about volunteering at Bloomington Hospital, call (812) 353-9468.

# RESOURCE 31

## EVENT PLANNING CALENDAR

# EVENT PLANNING CALENDAR

## Eight weeks or more ahead

Develop event purpose/mission
Develop broad event agenda and timeline
Select designer for invitations and programs
Select site
Select caterer
Select musicians
Begin compiling guest list
Begin compiling event binder

## Six weeks ahead

Write copy for invitations and programs
Finalize invitation and program design
Purchase mailing supplies
Purchase nametag supplies
Print mailing labels for invitations
Refine agenda and timeline
Select menu and wines
Address transportation needs
Notify University offices as appropriate

## Five weeks ahead

Select florist and place preliminary flower order
Select photographer
Order gifts and favors
Receive invitations and envelopes from printer
Develop database to track invitation responses

## Four weeks ahead

Mail invitations; fax copy to international guests
Begin tracking invitation responses
Meet with florist on-site to confirm colors and flower arrangement style
Review fabric samples and select tablecloth/napkin fabrics with caterer
Confirm all vendor contracts as signed, returned and received

## Three weeks ahead

Print nametags for all guests
Print or send out guest list for placecards and escort cards. Order extra blank
  cards for last-minute changes

Track invitation responses
Refine agenda and timeline
Develop minute-by-minute event timeline

## Two weeks ahead

Begin calling "no responses" for confirmation
Meet with caterer to review minute-by-minute timeline; revise as needed
Confirm number of serving staff needed to meet timeline goal
Prepare resource materials for event staff

## One week ahead

Meet with event staff to review mission, agenda and timeline
Test audio-visual set up
Walk through entire event; time and review against timeline
Confirm final count and serving times with caterer
Confirm event time and location with photographer, musicians, valets and
 transportation provider
Confirm event time with site vendor, including access to site for setup and
 cleanup
Confirm number of arrangements and delivery time with florist
Develop seating arrangement for confirmed guests attending
Prepare alternate head table scenarios

## One day ahead

Alphabetize nametags
Pull nametags for confirmed guests attending; put in nametag sleeves;
 alphabetize.
Put remaining nametags in alphabetical order in an envelope marked "Guests
 not attending/no response"
Repeat with placecards and escort cards
Place table numbers on the back of nametags (if not using escort cards)
Compile box with pens, highlighters, pins and nametag chains, sewing kit, etc.
Deliver materials to site

## Event

Track guests attending for follow-up

## Week after event

Send thank-you notes to staff and others who supported or facilitated event

---

*Source:* Office of Development, University of Tennessee. Reprinted with permission.

# RESOURCE 32

## SPECIAL EVENT INVITATIONS

**9th annual**

## Steak & Steak Dinner

**Thursday • June 17 • 1999**
BLOOMINGTON CONVENTION CENTER

*featured speaker*

**Keith Smart**

**Steak & Steak Dinner**
*Boys & Girls Club of Bloomington*
P.O. Box 1716
Bloomington, IN 47402-1716

BULK RATE
U.S. POSTAGE
**PAID**
Bloomington, IN
Permit # 86

**Thanks** TO OUR EVENT **Sponsors!**

**GET YOUR Tickets AT:**

Boys & Girls Club of Bloomington or send in the attached *reservation form*

**ADMIT ONE**

Front

Back

## MAKE YOUR Reservations now!

9th Annual Steak & Steak Dinner

Company Name (if applicable)

Name of Person(s) Attending:

_____

_____

_____

Address: _____

City, State _____

Zip Code _____

Phone (day) _____

Phone (evening) _____

☐ Reserve _____ Steak & Steak Dinner(s) at $100 each.
☐ Reserve a corporate table for 5 at $500.
☐ Reserve a corporate table for 6 at $600.
☐ I am unable to attend; please accept my $100 donation.
    ☐ check enclosed    ☐ bill me later

### MAIL Reservations TO:
**Steak & Steak Dinner**
c/o Bloomington Boys & Girls Club
P.O. Box 1716 • Bloomington, IN 47402-1716
Ph: 812-332-5311 x 10 (or Fax: 332-6108)

Because we need adults at each table, please notify the Club if you are not planning to attend.

***Note:*** Seating Priority is determined by the ***date*** reservation is received, so reserve ***early!***

...................... PLEASE CUT ON DOTTED LINE ......................

## featured SPEAKER Keith Smart

Keith Smart is best known for striking the game-winning shot for Indiana University in the 1987 NCAA Championship game against Syracuse University. He scored 12 of IU's final 15 points in that game, and was named Most Outstanding Player in the 1987 NCAA Final Four. He was also a Junior College All American at Garden City (KS) Community College and a member of the U.S. basketball team in the 1987 Pan Am Games.

Keith was originally drafted by the Golden State Warriors in the second round (41st overall) of the 1988 NBA Draft. Over the course of his nine-year professional career, Smart played in two CBA Finals (1990, 1992) and helped his teams win four division titles.

Keith joined the Ft. Wayne Fury prior to the 1996-97 season and appeared in 49 games, averaging 10.3 points and 22.5 minutes per game, and after serving as a player assistant coach in 1997, he assumed the role of head coach. Keith Smart is now in his second season as head coach of the Fury, having led his team to a franchise record 31 wins and the American Conference Championship last season. He has been named American Conference Coach of the Month three times.

A native of Baton Rouge, Louisiana, Smart earned a degree in communications from IU. Keith and his wife, Carol, reside in Ft. Wayne with their two-year-old son, Andre.

## TONIGHT'S Program

5:00 pm-6:30 pm    Reception and Auction

6:30 pm-7:15 pm    Welcome and Dinner

7:15 pm    Featured Speaker, Keith Smart

## Auction ITEMS INCLUDE:

**Vacation condominiums**
*Autographed items*
**Golfing opportunities**
**Unique gifts... and much more in a variety of price ranges**

## BRING YOUR Appetite FOR Fun!

The **9th Annual** Steak & Steak Dinner is a wonderful opportunity for you to sponsor a steak dinner for a member of the Boys & Girls Club of Bloomington. The adults as well as the children will enjoy a wonderful meal including thick, juicy steaks!! So bring your friends, family, associates or clients to join Keith Smart and the boys and girls of Bloomington for an exciting **Steak & Steak Dinner!**

## THE Proceeds

from this event stay in Bloomington and will help support the local Boys & Girls Club. In addition, profits will help fund the outreach programs at Crestmont and Henderson Court, the social worker, an expanded tutorial service, arts programs, and the free after school transportation system.

## RESERVATION Information

Reservations are $100 per sponsor. Corporate tables of five or six may be reserved for $500/$600.

*The tax deductible contribution is limited to $100 per person, less the value of your meal.*

*Source:* Reprinted with the permission of Rubeck & Company, Bloomington, Indiana. Event coordinator Kathleen Rubeck. Brochure design Lianne Brummett, Fine Print, Bloomington, Indiana.

**Resource 32**

CALIFORNIA ALUMNI ASSOCIATION
AND
UNIVERSITY OF CALIFORNIA,
BERKELEY FOUNDATION

AWARDS
RECOGNITION
DINNER
1986

To make reservations, please make check payable to California Alumni Association and return with form in enclosed envelope by the reservations deadline, September 12, 1986. No refunds after September 16, 1986.

From San Francisco: Take Bay Bridge to Highway 24 East. Exit at Claremont Avenue, turn left on Claremont, then right on Ashby.

For additional information, please call Alumni House. (415) 642-1571

Resource 32

You are cordially invited
to attend the
1986
Awards Recognition Dinner
Friday, September 19, 1986

Gaslite Ballroom
Hotel Claremont
41 Tunnel Road
Oakland

Cocktails 6:00 p.m.
Dinner 7:00 p.m.
$50.00 per person

HONORING FOR 1986

CALIFORNIA ALUMNI CITATION

Robert E. Bates, 56
Richard L. Battelle, 57
John I. Gompertz, 25
Iona Rockwell Main, 49
William J. Milliken, 34
Thomas F. Whitesides, 32

ROSALIE M. STERN AWARD

Debra Brown, 74
Pamela A. McElvaine, 81

ROSALIE M. STERN AWARD
FOR CONTINUING EDUCATION

Katherine M. Griffin, 82
Angelica N. Kaner, 84

BRADFORD S. KING AWARD

Kent S. Imrie, 78

CHANCELLOR'S AWARD

Michael N. Chetkovich, 59

WHEELER OAK
MERITORIOUS AWARD

Joseph F. Perrelli, 65
Willis S. Slusser, 38
John F. Sparks, 57
Arleigh Williams, 35

TRUSTEES CITATION AWARD

Peggy McGuire Bannister, 35,
Norma T. Catalin, 35 and
Joseph Smith, 35
Faiga Fram Duncan, 54
Lee Emerson, 38
Preston B Hotchkiss, 51
Byron Nishkian, 40
T. Gary Rogers, 65
Debbie Cole Stoney, 72

OUTSTANDING ALUMNI CLUB AWARDS

Black Alumni Club
Contra Costa Alumni Club

AWARDS DINNER RESERVATIONS

California Alumni Association
Alumni House
Berkeley, California 94720

Enclosed please find check in the amount of
$ _____ for _____ reservations at $50.00
each for the Awards Recognition Dinner.

Name _____  Class _____

Name _____  Class _____

Name _____  Class _____

Address _____  Residence Phone

City _____ Zip _____ Business Phone _____

*Source:* Copyright 1986 UC Regents. Reprinted with the permission of Brooke J. Conner, Director of Research, UC Berkeley.

# DONOR SURVEY

# TULIP TRACE COUNCIL OF GIRL SCOUTS, INC.
## Information Survey

*The following survey is being conducted as one way to determine whether we at Tulip Trace Council of Girl Scouts, Inc. are doing a complete job of stewarding those of you who have given so generously to this worthy cause.*

*We ask that you complete this survey to the best of your ability and return it in the enclosed envelope within 30 days. To ensure accurate records about you, please answer all questions. Please know that all responses will remain confidential.*

*Thank you in advance for helping us do our very best.*

Name(s) _____

Address _____

City _____ State _____ Zip _____

Home Phone _____ Work Phone _____

E-Mail _____

*Please circle the number that best describes your opinion.*

| | | |
|---|---|---|
| *5 = Superior* | *3 = Average* | *1 = Needs Significant* |
| *4 = Above Average* | *2 = Needs Improvement* | *Improvement* |

After making a gift to Tulip Trace Council of Girl Scouts, did you receive a letter of appreciation and receipt that you considered meaningful and appropriate?

         5        4        3        2        1

Was the timing of that letter and receipt acceptable?

         5        4        3        2        1

Beyond written correspondence, has Tulip Trace Council of Girl Scouts personnel responded adequately in expressing appreciation?

         5        4        3        2        1

After your gift was made, did you have ample opportunity to learn more about how your investment was making a noticeable difference in the lives of those served by Tulip Trace Council of Girl Scouts?

         5        4        3        2        1

(Please turn page over)

Resource 33

Please answer YES or NO to the following questions:

Would you like to remain on our mailing list?　　Yes　　No

Are you interested in receiving information on Planned Giving?　　Yes　　No

Are you interested in being a Volunteer?　　Yes　　No

Are you aware that we serve girls in 12 counties?　　Yes　　No
(They are Bartholomew, Brown, Decatur, Jackson, Jennings, Johnson, Lawrence, Monroe, Morgan, Orange, Owen, and Scott Counties.)

What kind of events would you be interested in attending? (Please circle)

American Girl　　　Women of Distinction　　Planned Giving Luncheons

Alumni Gatherings　　Golf Outings　　　Other (explain) _____

Do you plan to continue to support Girl Scouts?　　Yes　　No

If so, how? (Explain) _____

If not, why? (Explain) _____

Below please share any other information you would like us to know.

*Thank you so much for taking time to answer this survey. Please use the enclosed envelope or mail to: Julie Dailey, Development Director, Tulip Trace Council of Girl Scouts, P.O. Box 5485, Bloomington, IN 47407. If you have any questions, call 1-800-467-6804.*

Resource 33

# REFERENCES

Armstrong, J. *Planning Special Events.* San Francisco: Jossey-Bass, 2001.

Barth, S. "Finding the Needle in the Haystack: Use Computer Screening and Database Analysts to Discover the Hidden Major-Gift Prospects Among Your Alumni." *CASE Currents,* June 1998, pp. 32–36.

Baxter, F. R. "Prospect Management." Unpublished paper, University of California-Berkeley, 1987.

Coulter, A. Personal communication, August 1999.

Council for Advancement and Support of Education. *CASE Campaign Standards: Management and Reporting Standards for Educational Fund-Raising Campaigns.* Washington, D.C.: Council for Advancement and Support of Education, 1996.

Dove, K. *Conducting a Successful Comprehensive Campaign.* (2nd ed.) San Francisco: Jossey-Bass, 2000.

Emlen, J. "The ABCs of Stewardship." Presentation made at CASE Advancement Series Conference, Charleston, South Carolina, May 2000.

Frost, J. "Nuts and Bolts of International Research." International Advancement Conference, Salt Lake City, Utah, April 2000.

Fund Raising School. *Principles and Techniques of Fund Raising.* Indianapolis: Indiana University Center on Philanthropy, 1995.

Fund Raising School. *Study Guide from Course 101: The Internet and Fundraising.* Indianapolis: Indiana University Center on Philanthropy, 2001.

Harris, A. L. *Special Events: Planning for Success.* (2nd. ed.) Washington, D.C.: Council for Advancement and Support of Education, 1998.

Harrison, B. J. "Art and Science of Donor Walls." *Fund Raising Management,* Feb. 1999, p. 26.

Hunsaker, C. *Information Systems: Managing the Database.* New Directions for Philanthropic Fundraising, no. 21. San Francisco: Jossey-Bass, 1998.

Iwata, E. "Tech Tyranny Provokes Revolt." *USA Today,* Aug. 21, 2000, p. 1A.

Johnston, M. *The Nonprofit Guide to the Internet.* (2nd ed.) New York: Wiley, 1999.

Kelly, K. *Effective Fund-Raising Management.* Mahwah, N.J.: Erlbaum, 1998.

Kimball, R. *The Data Warehouse Toolkit.* New York: Wiley, 1996.

Lawson, D. "Wall Street for Fund Raisers." APRA-Indiana Spring Conference, Indianapolis, April 3, 1998.

Millar, R. G. "How Much Is That Donor in Your Records? Step-by-Step Advice for Figuring Net Worth and Giving Ability." *CASE Currents,* July/Aug. 1995, pp. 38–42.

Miller, J. D., and Strauss, D. *Improving Fundraising with Technology.* San Francisco: Jossey-Bass, 1996.

Murphy, M. Personal communication, April 1996.

Rehder, K. V. "Managing and Improving Your Program: Writing for Stewardship." Presentation made at CASE Annual Meeting of Donor Relations Officers, Charleston, South Carolina, May 2000.

Ruderman, S. "Panning for Gold." *Contributions Magazine,* May/June 2000, pp. 9–12.

Taylor, J. H. *Advancement Services: Research and Technology Support for Fund Raising.* Washington, D.C.: CASE Books, 1999.

Warwick, M. *Technology and the Future of Fundraising.* Berkeley, Calif.: Swathmore Press, 1994.

West, W. V. "Technology in Fundraising." In K. E. Dove, *Conducting a Successful Capital Campaign.* (2nd ed.) San Francisco: Jossey-Bass, 1999.

# INDEX